DATE DUE

MY 29 '97			
AP 20 '00			

DEMCO 38-296

Presidential Leadership

Making a Difference

by
James L. Fisher and James V. Koch

AMERICAN COUNCIL ON EDUCATION ★
ORYX PRESS ★
Series on Higher Education
1996

The rare Arabian Oryx is believed to have inspired the myth of the unicorn. This desert antelope became virtually extinct in the early 1960s. At that time several groups of international conservationists arranged to have 9 animals sent to the Phoenix Zoo to be the nucleus of a captive breeding herd. Today the Oryx population is over 1000, and over 500 have been returned to the Middle East.

© 1996 by American Council on Education and The Oryx Press
Published by The Oryx Press
4041 North Central at Indian School Road
Phoenix, Arizona 85012-3397

Published simultaneously in Canada
Printed and Bound in the United States of America

∞ The paper used in this publication meets the minimum requirements of American National Standard for Information Science—Permanence of Paper for Printed Library Materials, ANSI Z39.48, 1984.

Library of Congress Cataloging-in-Publication Data

Fisher, James L.
    Presidential leadership: making a difference / by James L. Fisher and James V. Koch.
        p.   cm. — (American Council on Education/Oryx Press series on higher education)
    Includes bibliographical references and index.
    ISBN 1-57356-020-0
    1. College presidents—United States. 2. Universities and colleges—United States—Administration.   3. Educational leadership—United States. I. Koch, James V., 1942–. II. Title. III. Series.
LB2341.F497   1996
378.1'11—dc20   95-26661
                                                                       CIP

CONTENTS

• • • • • • • •

FOREWORD

• • • • • • • •

by Kenneth A. Shaw

Firmly based on both theory and evidence relating to effective leadership, *Presidential Leadership* strongly challenges much current mainstream writing and thinking about the college presidency. Contrary to the views of many, the authors assume that a college president is a transformational individual who can make a dramatic, positive difference in the life of his or her institution. They reject the notion that presidents are as "interchangeable as light bulbs" and argue that transactional (rather than transformational) leadership is a recipe for mediocrity and stagnation on American campuses.

Fisher and Koch contend that a successful president must be established as the final authority on campus; that the primary function of the governing board is to appoint, evaluate, and support the president, and to make policy; that the governing board should not be involved in the administration of the institution; that it is both naive and counterproductive to appoint faculty or currently enrolled students to governing boards; and that the primary functions of faculty are teaching, student advising, scholarship, service, and responsible and accountable participation in campus governance. All these positions are presented from the experience of the authors and others in the college presidency and from research done on the subject of the college presidency.

In the truest sense, the Fisher and Koch positions are not radical, for their views fall well within the guidelines of the 1940 and 1966 statements of the American Association of University Professors on academic freedom and shared governance. Nonetheless, perceptions of the college presidency have changed subtly over time, and some will find this book disturbingly transformational in both spirit and substance. The authors stake out strong positions when they discuss the dangers of seemingly beneficent management initiatives and the relative insignificance of race and gender as fundamental determinants of leadership success. In addition, they provide instructive chapters and exhibits on presidential searches, trustee responsibilities, and presidential compensation and evaluation, as well as insightful chapters on effective presidential relationships with faculty, students, administration, alumni, benefactors, politicians, and the media. These discussions will be extremely useful to any president (or any board), regardless of their approach to the presidency.

Of the several different conceptual approaches to the nature of the American college presidency, the two most prominent are occupied by the transactionalists (led by Cohen and March, Birnbaum, Chafee, Chait, Bensimon, Greene, Neumann, and Seymour) and the transformationalists (Fisher, Fisher and Koch, Bass, Kerr, and Gade).

Transactionalists emphasize collegial leadership based upon consensus and suggest that presidents should not attempt to make profound differences in their institutions and often do not do so anyway. Fisher and Koch believe that collegial leadership, as advocated by transactionalists, is ultimately an oxymoron that results in organized anarchy associated with lack of purpose, pedestrian leadership, and academic decay. They argue that many academic institutions are foundering today because of the public perception that colleges lack purpose, are inefficiently run, have reduced their standards, have failed to apply their resources to societal needs, and may even be subject to narrow and "politically correct" approaches to the issues of the day. These deficiencies, they contend, are substantially due to the increasing absence of visionary, transformational leadership in the college presidency.

The authors believe that presidents (and board members) should be cautious about taking seriously the views and offerings of various national higher education associations. They feel that these organizations are often controlled by career higher education bureaucrats whose survival depends upon a "to get along, go along" approach to the affairs of the day.

Fisher and Koch wish to "enable the president to be the president" and to effectively empower and hold accountable all who are part of this "grandest of enterprises," the American higher education system. Their views are challenging, even provocative, and the instructed reader need not argue with every position they take. But there is much to learn from this important book and much to think about. It is a "must read" for any current or aspiring president, student, or governing board member who seeks to better understand higher education.

Finally, the thoughtful reader should bear in mind that Fisher was, and Koch is, an outstanding college president.

Kenneth A. Shaw
Chancellor, Syracuse University
1995

INTRODUCTION

• • • • • • • •

It is not accidental that notable steps forward in higher education have been identified with the names of individuals.

Harold Dodds, 1962

The uncertain (leaders) always walk in a crowd.

Father Theodore Hesburgh, 1979

Lead, and I follow.

Alfred, Lord Tennyson

Do college presidents make a difference in the lives and prospects of their institutions? The answer is a resounding YES! We believe that nearly all college presidents are capable of having profound and positive impacts upon the institutions they lead—if only they understand the nature of the challenge before them. We conclude that both leadership theory and reliable empirical evidence demonstrate that college presidents are not "interchangeable as light bulbs," as Cohen and March (1986) have maintained. Quite the opposite. Presidents who are successful understand, perhaps instinctively, the principles that promote an effective college presidency.

Thus, college presidents can make a difference, and they are capable of transforming their institutions. As Harold Dodds (1962), president of Princeton University for a quarter century, put it, "Let no president assume that his office does not make a difference." Abundant evidence indicates that the office, and how it is used by a president, can inspire, motivate, invigorate, and transform the life of even the most stodgy or troubled colleges.

Many college presidents fail at their tasks or achieve little of note during their tenures. However, such failures are not inevitable. Presidents who conscientiously apply the principles and evidence that relate to effective presidential leadership vastly increase their chances of success. This book describes those principles and the available empirical evidence in order to help current and prospective college presidents master what can only be described as an extremely challenging and sometimes enigmatic position.

The stakes are tremendous. Colleges and universities carry with them the best hopes and prospects of a fearful, often confused society that cries out for focus, vision, and leadership. For generations, citizens have looked to the leaders of colleges and universities to supply generous portions of each of these qualities. Giants such as Eliot of Harvard, Hutchins of Chicago, Hannah of Michigan State, and Wells of Indiana changed the directions of their institutions and gave them a mighty push toward excellence. Other presidents, such as Harvard's Conant, had a major impact upon national science policy, while Notre Dame's Hesburgh profoundly influenced civil rights policy and, at the same time, changed the course of Catholic higher education.

Yet, it is generally agreed today that the college presidency, once the situs of many such powerful, effective, and inspirational leaders, has decayed and all too frequently now is a refuge for ambivalent, risk-averting individuals who seek to offend no one,[1] and as a consequence arouse and motivate no one. The result is a visible lack of academic purpose, declining institutional effectiveness, and (most lamentable) inferior education. The cost of such collegiate shortcomings to society grows ever more significant.

The United States in the 1990s finds itself in the midst of an increasingly competitive, nonmilitary struggle for survival. Astute observers such as M.I.T.'s Lester Thurow in *Head to Head* (1993) describe the accelerating economic and social competition between Japan, Europe, and the United States. No institution is more critical to American success in this competition than its colleges and universities. Indeed, the most respected authority on the sources of new jobs and local and regional economic growth in the United States, David Birch (1987, 1993), regards higher education as *the* factor that differentiates one city and region from another where economic growth and quality of life are concerned. But, colleges and universities cannot fulfill this vital role, and invigorate and lead society, if they themselves are not led by presidents of intelligence and vision who understand the sources of academic leadership and their fitting exercise.

Therein resides the challenge. If colleges and universities are capable of being decisive in improving economic welfare and enriching the human condition, then what kind of academic presidential leadership is most conducive to inspiring activities that will achieve these ends? That question will occupy us for 22 additional chapters.

---

[1]Many college presidents are in great danger of falling gradually into such a behavior pattern, for as Robert Maynard Hutchins (1956), the immensely effective president of the University of Chicago from 1929 to 1945 noted, a president "will seldom be seriously disliked if he does nothing."

THE LITERATURE ON PRESIDENTIAL LEADERSHIP: A FIRST LOOK

Unfortunately, most current work on presidential leadership in higher education is without substantive foundation and is therefore little better than a rationalization for the experience and opinions of the writer. With few exceptions, none of the literature today is grounded in the generic research on leadership, power, or management. Compounding this shortcoming is the apparent lack of awareness of most authors of the scientific method. Only a few empirical studies involving the college presidency are replicable in a scientific sense; instead, most studies represent the instinctive beliefs of the researcher, supplemented by stylized vignettes that appear to support these beliefs. Most studies make only the barest reference to the literature to support their conclusions. Further, other than case studies and interviews (both soft techniques), virtually no existing empirical study relies upon research designs of scientific sophistication to support its conclusions.

The Battleground: Transactional Versus Transformational Leadership

Virtually all modern discussions of presidential leadership are based eventually upon one of two competing concepts—transactional or transformational leadership. Briefly, the transactional position maintains that effective presidents are individuals who democratically meet the needs of their campuses and who emphasize inclusive, participative governance processes based upon consensus. A leading transactionalist, Robert Birnbaum (1988), suggests that the very nature of colleges and universities makes their management "difficult if not impossible" and therefore concludes that "Presidents may have relatively little influence over outcomes when compared to other forces. . . ." Indeed, as Walker (1979) has put it, "the view of the university as the shadow of a strong president is unrealistic. . .if indeed it was ever accurate."

The contemporary parent of the transactional position is *Leadership and Ambiguity* by M.D. Cohen and J.G. March, an oft-cited book first published in 1974. These influential authors liken decision making in a modern academic institution to a highly complex "garbage can" over which the president, in the last analysis, has little control. Stated succinctly, they argue that "It is a mistake for a president to imagine that what he (or she) does affects the institution significantly" (2nd ed., 1986). The earlier forbearers of Cohen and March included James Cattell and Thorstein Veblen, who championed faculty control and democratic governance processes within academe. Cohen and March observe that the most prestigious colleges and universities usually have highly involved, participative, consensual governance models that feature strong faculty control and relatively weaker presidents.

On the other side, the transformationalists believe that presidents with vision and energy can and should make a great deal of difference. Clark Kerr (1984) argues that "Strengthening presidential leadership is the most urgent concern on the agenda of higher education." Transformationalists generally believe in shared governance, but hold that within such a system individual accountability must be maintained and that the president is the final authority under the board in all matters. The transformational position dates back to the founding of Harvard and, with few exceptions, characterized presidential expectations until World War II. The position was reinforced without strong objection in 1940 and 1966 by statements by the American Association of University Professors (AAUP) on academic freedom and shared governance.

We unabashedly endorse the transformational model of presidential leadership. Our preference for the transformational model is a function both of theory and empirical evidence. Chapters 1 through 5 of this book, but especially chapters 2 and 3, review the literature on leadership, its constituent parts, and the empirical evidence that has been accumulated on these matters. These chapters provide the basis for subsequent chapters that apply the theory and evidence to particular aspects of a modern college presidency.

A spate of books and articles exists on the role of the college president. Virtually every one of these books eventually comes down on one side or the other of the transactional/transformational debate. On the transactional side, one can read works by Birnbaum, Bensimon, and Neumann, as well as by Balderson, Cohen and March, Epstein, Green, Millet, Parks, and Walker. On the transformational side, books by Bennis, Corson, Cowley, Fisher, Gilley, Kauffman, Kerr, Peck, Riesman, Sharp, and Vaughn are most notable. There are also books on the subject by Benezet, Blake, and Crowley, who might be called objectivists.

These authors are the major scholars in the field today. Most of these authors have also published in such national journals as *AGB Reports*, *Educational Record*, and *Change*. Only one of these authors deals seriously with generic research on leadership (the second step in the scientific method), and only two have applied rigorous statistical tests in analyzing their data. Even then, transactionalists Cohen and March applied these statistical tests to survey data gathered from a relatively small sample of only 42 institutions. On the transformational side, Fisher has drawn on both the generic research on leadership, and, with Tack and Wheeler in *The Effective College President* (1988), has used appropriate statistical tests to analyze the behavior of presidents acknowledged by the sample to be effective.

This difference in methodology is typically overlooked in higher education. The transformational conclusions of Fisher, buttressed by the generically authoritative Bass, are empirically rooted. *Fisher's conclusions can be generally verified by a disinterested or even adversarial third party. Fisher's work is based in quantitative research methodology and reinforced by qualitative study.* The conclusions of virtually all transactionalists, generic and in higher education, are based in soft and unverifiable methodology. Although case studies, interviews, inventories, and the like are often considered legitimate scholarship tools of the qualitative research school, qualitative research without quantitative predecessors is little better than the personal opinion of the investigator. If those who dispute the conclusions of the study cannot repeat the process and arrive at essentially the same results, the results remain eminently debatable and without foundation.

Studies of the American college presidency often assume the role of a presidential memoir and typically involve ubiquitous "story telling." Without a doubt, anecdotes and vignettes can sharpen, burnish, and illustrate a point. Nonetheless, such stories do not constitute replicable scientific evidence that another researcher might support or reject. "Stories" are best used to elucidate or illuminate a point that flows from theory or empirical evidence. Stories without a theoretical or empirical foundation are just that, stories, and do not advance our knowledge of the presidency.

Nonetheless, we acknowledge that certain circumstances appear to reflect the need for transactional leaders. If an institution's position is, or is believed by its trustees to be, comfortable and consistent with the needs of its constituents and mission, a more reactive than proactive president will appear acceptable, even appropriate. In effect, the president responds to the consensus reflections of constituents, particularly the faculty, rather than attempting to build consensus around a forward idea. In such institutions, the faculty shapes curriculum, promotion, tenure, and academic policies, and ultimately plays the major role in the appointment of academic officers, including the president. The president must therefore be transactional, and, if there are no serious problems, the transactional president will survive, and there will be no substantive changes in the institution.

The Sources of Presidential Leadership and Power: A Brief Look at Our Argument

For our purposes, leadership is the ability of A to get B to do something B might not otherwise have done. The most important forms of presidential leadership in a college or university are, in ascending order of importance,

- *Coercive*, which is the threat or use of punishment by the president;
- *Reward*, which involves the ability of the president to reward and provide incentives;
- *Legitimate*, which is the importance of presidential position and which must be provided by the institution's governing board;
- *Expert*, which is based on the real or perceived knowledge of the president; and
- *Referent, or charisma*, which is based either upon a feeling of trust and oneness with the president, or a desire for such a feeling, and which should result in the development of a significant public presence.

Charismatic leaders have an extraordinary ability to inspire trust, loyalty, confidence, and performance. This distinctly transformational characteristic is measurably the single most important dimension of leadership, and its position as such has been reinforced since Fisher's *Power of the Presidency* (1984) by the writings of Gardner, Bennis, Kotter, Burns, and Galbraith.

Many individuals in higher education are uncomfortable discussing these types of leadership, for they soon discover that each eventually reflects the exercise of *power*, a term that often carries negative connotations in the egalitarian atmosphere of higher education. Academics tend to be individualistic, independent souls who instinctively distrust the existence of campus power, particularly when they fear its application might impinge on their options. Many faculty are given to quoting Lord Acton on the ability of power to corrupt.

Of course, power can corrupt. However, all worthwhile and effective leadership is based upon the effective exercise of power, and it is fruitless to deny this unless one is interested in deliberately obfuscating how the world actually operates. As Arthur Goldberg, a former U.S. ambassador to the United Nations, opined in a different context, "Law not served by power is an illusion." Power exists in every arena; the relevant questions are: What arrangements and leadership characteristics generate power? For what ends is power used?

Academic institutions whose activities revolve around departments, senates, and the like are no exception to general principles of leadership and the exercise of power. Denying the principles of leadership and the power they generate does not somehow abolish them from human interaction and existence, even when the subject is undergraduate general education requirements or the distribution of research grants. Recognizing this, we seek to demonstrate where power comes from, and how it can be wielded judiciously, effectively, and appropriately by a college president to lead his or her institution to a brighter future.

The heroes of our stories are those sophisticated presidents who understand the various types of leadership and how they can most effectively exercise the power that these forms of leadership provide them. These heroes typically have been provided leadership legitimacy by their governing boards, and then rely primarily upon their own expert and charismatic leadership to inspire and move their institutions to greater heights. We readily acknowledge that some of the great villains of history (Adolf Hitler constituting a grand example) have excelled at some or all of the types of leadership that we explore here. Our heroes, however, exploit the power that leadership provides in a socially responsible fashion. They also subscribe to Disraeli's admonition that "All power is a trust (and) we are accountable for its exercise." Indeed, we condemn any contrary use of power as immoral and degrading.

Where Do Higher Education Organizations Stand?

Today the behavioral norms propagated and reinforced by most of the national higher education organizations militate against the kind of assertive leadership called for by the transformationalists during the past decade.[2] The American Council on Education (ACE) has had the wisdom to publish both transactional and transformational articles and books. Unfortunately, other national associations are all but exclusively transactional. Transformation implies change, and change is often painful. Further, it

---

[2]As one reviewer of this manuscript commented (with a tone of approval), "transactional, collegial theories of leadership. . .have been embraced by most of academe."

requires faculty, administrators, and trustees to act—and to allow each other to act—in ways that radically depart from the transactional beliefs that are increasingly ingrained in public notions about leadership and power. These attitudes have spilled over to many public and some private college trustees and now dominate the thinking of a majority of administrators and nearly all faculty about the proper relationship between administration and faculty.

National higher education organizations, such as the American Association of Colleges and Universities, the American Council on Education, and the Association of Governing Boards, evince a distinct preference for the transactional approach to higher education leadership, and this preference is readily in evidence at the sessions they sponsor for deans, presidents, and board members, and in the literature they distribute. Regrettably, we believe that these organizations, while admirably motivated, may be contributing to the current leadership malaise and confusion in higher education. The road to institutional hell can in reality be paved with good transactionalist intentions.[3]

The case of the American Association of University Professors (AAUP), traditionally the most important national faculty organization in higher education, requires special discussion insofar as presidential leadership is concerned. It is important to place the AAUP's views in context.

In Western Europe and most of the Pacific Rim countries, national systems of higher education exist and national governments dictate how institutions of higher education should be governed and what the role of their chief executive officers should be. The same enforced consensus does not exist in the United States, where institutional diversity is the rule, especially where governance is concerned. Consequently, the United States has no universally accepted standards for the governance of colleges and universities or the role of presidents.

Nonetheless, there do exist two documents that most knowledgeable observers and professional organizations such as the AAUP accept as rational and sensible standards on matters of general governance: *The Statement on Academic Freedom and Tenure* (1940),[4] and *The Joint Statement*

---

[3]As the Romans astutely observed, "*Facilis descensus averno,*" that is, "The descent to hell is easy." They could have been talking about the populist nature of the transactionalist approach to academic administration and its debilitating effects upon institutional leadership and effectiveness.

[4]The 1940 *Statement* is the joint product of the AAUP and the Association of American Colleges. The *Statement* has been endorsed by nearly all professional academic organizations.

on Governance of Colleges and Universities (1966).[5] Both statements are endorsed and circulated by the AAUP and describe the rights and responsibilities of faculty members, presidents, and governing boards.

Few faculty members and administrators, to say nothing of board members, have taken time to read the 1940 and 1966 statements. To the surprise of some, either type of presidential leadership (transformational or transactional) could fall within the limits of both statements. Indeed, clever transactionalists can use the 1966 *Statement* on "shared governance" to justify exclusive faculty power without accountability, and imaginative transformationalists can use the same *Statement* to justify their commitment to accountability.

This breadth of potential interpretation in the statements is important to note because some dialecticians on both sides have led readers to believe that their stylized interpretation of both statements is exclusive. For example, faculty members on some campuses are famed for their ability to cite the 1940 *Statement* (which most often is associated with the AAUP and the subject of academic freedom) as the "basis" for their rejection of any supervision of their efforts, such as attempts by administrators or colleagues to evaluate the effectiveness of their classroom teaching. Similarly, some administrators will (inappropriately) use the 1966 *Statement* as justification for their unwillingness to undertake meaningful discussion of certain topics with faculty members. A careful reading of the statements will not support either stance. Chapters 6, 8, 9, and 10 will examine these topics in detail.

THE CURIOUS CASE OF A NEW HYBRID: TOTAL QUALITY MANAGEMENT

A new approach to higher education management is worthy of additional mention, if for no other reason than it has become *de rigueur* for campuses to assert that they are following its precepts. This "new" approach, Total Quality Management, or TQM, may offer promise to colleges and universities, but is potentially as dangerous as it is promising. Generically stated, TQM is a design for increasing customer satisfaction by providing timely,

---

[5]The 1966 *Statement*, while endorsed by the American Association of University Professors and many professional organizations, has not been adopted by important national organizations such as the American Council on Education and the Association of Governing Boards. It is directed primarily at governing board members and presidents and describes and promotes the oft-cited notion of "shared governance" on campuses.

higher quality services and products through a process that includes three distinct subsystems: customer focus, continuous improvement, and employee involvement.

TQM has become the rage within higher education, not the least because few can quarrel with its goals. Stimulated by private industry and abetted by higher education associations, notably AAHE, AACC, ACE, and private foundations and government, many public colleges and universities (e.g., Oregon State, Wisconsin-Madison, Penn, Colorado State, Maryland, Minnesota, Clemson, Georgia Tech, and dozens of community colleges) and wealthier private institutions (e.g., Harvard, Carnegie Mellon, Lehigh, Chicago, Miami) have rushed to embrace TQM as the solution to their problems.

For many in academe, TQM represents a subtle and seductive way to forestall or avoid the conflict that comes from hard decision making. For that reason, TQM must be approached carefully and with tested principles of efficiency, accountability, and leadership in mind. To date, we fear that this necessary approach has not always been followed. As in the past with such "hot" concepts such as long-range and strategic planning, management by objectives, zero-base budgeting, and statewide coordination, colleges and universities may embrace costly panacea that revere process over results, and ultimately reduce their ability to make difficult decisions. We detail these concerns in Chapter 7.

THE ORGANIZATION OF THIS BOOK

This book is divided into five parts. Part 1, encompassing the first three chapters, focuses on the theory of presidential leadership and power, and the limited empirical evidence available on these subjects.

Part 2 (chapters 4 and 5) gives additional attention to critical presidential characteristics such as style and charisma and how they affect performance. Attention also is given in this part to the influences of gender and race upon presidential effectiveness.

Part 3, comprising chapters 6 through 15, deals with presidential constituencies and tasks. A modern college president interacts with a bewildering number of different constituencies, among them trustees, faculty, administrators, students, alumni, supporters of intercollegiate athletics, business vendors, entertainment organizations, regulators, politicians and public figures, media, and friends and donors (Davis, 1972; Clark and Clark, 1994). Each of these constituencies presents a president with challenging and distinct problems in terms of how they are best approached and used to further the legitimate interests of the institution. Each of the chapters in this part explores the relationships peculiar to a specific constituency, albeit while connecting these relationships to more universal principles of leadership and to the available empirical evidence.

Part 4 (chapters 16 through 21) examines the role of college governing boards and how they relate to the president. Legally, the trustees who comprise the governing boards are the most important constituency of any institution and its president. Trustees exercise a public trust by setting institutional policies the president is expected to administer. Experts agree that the trustees of an institution should not seek to administer an institution themselves, but rather see that it is administered effectively (Hesburgh, 1979). The critical questions, however, are these:

- Do boards of trustees actually understand their appropriate roles and responsibilities vis-á-vis the president and the campus?
- Do boards (and presidents) understand how poorly devised governance structures, rules, and regulations can reduce or eliminate "legitimate" leadership and thereby doom even the most charismatic and productive president?
- Do boards discern the crucial importance of having a well-done institutional evaluation in hand before they search for a new president?
- Do boards appreciate the complex nature of presidential searches, appropriate presidential compensation, and evaluations of the president's performance?

Unfortunately, many members of college and university governing boards have never addressed these questions systematically. Consequently, they fulfill their duties as board members blissfully unaware of how leadership theory and empirical evidence could inform their answers to these questions and vastly increase the probability that their president (and their institution) will be successful. Part 4 treats these topics in detail.

Part 5 consists of a single chapter (chapter 22) that summarizes the findings of the book and comments on their considerable relevancy to the current presidential milieu.

FINAL THOUGHTS

Centuries ago, Plutarch perceptively noted that "In times of crisis, nearly everything may depend on the regard and confidence placed in some man who possesses the experience and qualities of a leader." We agree. Nonetheless, this observation almost begs the question of what the "experience and qualities of a leader" are. We pursue that question, and its answers, in the remaining chapters of this book.

PART

1

The Model and
the Evidence

CHAPTER
one
• • • • • • •

In the Spirit of
Saint Simone

An institution is the lengthened shadow of one person.

Ralph Waldo Emerson

Power tends to corrupt, and absolute power corrupts absolutely.

Lord Acton

Absolute power is OK, if you're careful.

Julius Caesar
(loosely translated from the Latin)

Acomment attributed to a man named Simone relates to the college presidency. Simone, an early Christian ascetic, felt the need to demonstrate dramatically to others that the then popular and easy practice of Christianity was not the essence of faith. Simone erected a 60-foot tower topped by a platform. For 20 years, he stayed up there, preaching to the multitudes who came to observe the spectacle. Simone was so effective from that platform that the Roman Catholic Church made him a saint. After 20 years, Saint Simone said of his experience: "The most difficult part was getting on top of the platform."

Most college and university presidents would probably agree that the most difficult aspect of the presidency is not the climb up that tower—securing an appointment—but getting onto the platform and staying firmly put. The platform was Simone's way of creating an aura of distance and mystery about his person, a medium through which his message could be more powerfully delivered. The president also has to create a platform from which to lead his or her institution effectively. That platform or medium is a powerful presidential image.

NEED FOR MORE KNOWLEDGE ABOUT THE PRESIDENCY

Few college or university presidents have sufficient formal knowledge of the legitimate and tested techniques of leadership and power derived from research, and too few realize that these techniques are applicable to a more effective presidency.[1] Yes, few would have become presidents without a desire for power, but most do not know enough about its nature or use and are, therefore, less effective than they might be. Presidents often fail to understand the value of the presidential position—the platform atop the tower—to their ability to accomplish legitimate and essential institutional goals. As a result, many fall short of their purpose and do not understand why.

To many incumbents, the presidency resembles the greased pole at the annual Italian Fair in Baltimore; like the hearty spirits who try to climb that pole, presidents ascend with vigor and descend precipitously. Presidents know how important the office is, but are at first ignorant of its price, and later are unsure they are willing to pay it. The presidency offers a heady combination of confidence and uncertainty. This is why the job is such an enigma, such a delightfully bewildering mystery—and to a psychologist, such a classic approach/avoidance conflict.

Before their appointments, most presidents know little about the role. In 1978, David Riesman wrote that no career line prepares for the college or university presidency. Subsequently, in a preface to an examination of the current status of the presidency, Riesman observed that in contrast to most chief operating officers of large American corporations, "college presidents are almost universally amateurs" when they assume the job (Kerr and Gade, 1986).

Practically, the only person who approaches the office with any real knowledge is someone who has previously held a successful presidency, but one presidency is usually enough for most people. For most presidents, the first venture into that fascinating and lonely office is a situation worlds apart from anything they have experienced before.

---

[1]The word "power" has accrued ugly connotations and makes many people uncomfortable. Power refers to the human capacity to act effectively, to influence and lead other humans so as to realize a worthwhile action and its driving purpose. Power, in its purest sense, is as ethical a concept as action.

Many new presidents have served under other presidents, but only in lesser administrative posts. Former academic deans often find it difficult or impossible to break old patterns of behavior, even though they know that a pattern of close personal involvement with faculty members, for example, almost certainly reduced their own effectiveness as an academic dean and doubtless now has the same effect upon their presidency.

The problem is aggravated for the faculty member who is abruptly catapulted from a professorship into the presidency with virtually no experience in management or administration. Most observers readily understand that such an individual, no matter how intrepid, is severely disadvantaged by his or her lack of experience. Fewer also discern how difficult it is for the erstwhile professor to breach old habits and friendships and exercise meaningful authority over former colleagues.

Some university governing boards have opted to appoint former business or government executives to their presidencies. Such individuals may be better prepared for many of the managerial duties of the office; however, they, too, often find it impossible to gain the respect and appreciation of faculty members who style themselves as peers but are often reluctant to accept leadership from outsiders. The same problem exists, to a lesser degree, for a former vice president for development, public relations, business, or student services, or an assistant to a president. Previous academic appointments are valuable preparation, especially when these appointments have been on other campuses. Experience counts, particularly when it is acquired in one location and then transferred to another where the user's past friendships (and enmities) do not work against him or her. In general, the more diverse the past academic experiences of the new president, and the larger the number of presidents he/she has been able to observe closely, the more likely the new president is to have acquired an understanding of the peculiar nature and potential of the position. Academic administrative experience acquired at other institutions does not guarantee success, but it makes success more probable.

From that first day, the president is expected to perform as a master of everything—an effective combination of Abraham Lincoln, John F. Kennedy, Queen Elizabeth I, and Mother Theresa. He/she is expected to know and use effectively domains and persons heretofore foreign, from business affairs and fund raising to the care and feeding of boards of trustees and Rotary clubs. The president is expected to deal effectively with a sometimes arrogant faculty that demands results and—at the same time—demands to be equal; dissident students whose protests disregard reality; alumni who resent change, love football, and expect the good reputation of Old Siwash to be maintained at all costs; demanding, demeaning, and wasteful governments; and givers who are sometimes selfish, petty, or worse. Whatever befalls the institution, the president is expected to resolve the problem brilliantly.

Prior to their appointment, most presidents have worked in specific fields with defined tasks, where success was primarily the result of collegiality and scholarly expertise. To be suddenly thrust into a leadership role that demands additional and quite different qualities can be all but totally bewildering and at times overwhelming.

SOME PRESIDENTIAL MISSTEPS

Although committed and informed, many presidents are naturally reluctant to be presidential. Virtually all their pre-presidential experience is insufficient and most simply don't know enough about the nature and uses of tested power and leadership concepts and their value to an effective presidency. Not understanding how to use presidential power can create problems, as illustrated by the 10 examples given below.

Case 1: *A college president in Massachusetts called one day about a serious loyalty problem with his academic dean who, on a day of crisis for the institution, had telephoned to announce that he was taking a day's vacation. After we talked a while, the college president exploded, "Damn it, I'm going to drive right to his house and tell him what I think!" We advised him that it might be wiser to have his secretary call the dean and indicate that the president wanted to see him at a certain time, and then perhaps keep the dean cooling his heels for a while before seeing him. The president responded, "But, he lives almost an hour and a half from the campus." The president, a nice guy but dead wrong, later resigned and blamed the dean for most of his presidential problems.*

Case 2: *A dismissed state university president in New York bitterly denounced his academic vice president. "I had an uncertain feeling about the guy when I was appointed, and by my third year I knew he was working against me with the faculty. I talked to him and he assured me that I was mistaken; and, although I still had misgivings, I still couldn't bring myself to replace him. Today I know I should've fired the s.o.b." The academic vice president is still in place, and the president is looking for a job.*

Case 3: *A few years ago in Kentucky, the newly appointed president walked into the basketball arena to attend a game. He had a choice: to walk in front of the stands in full view of 15,000 fans, or to walk behind. He chose to walk behind the stands. As far as 15,000 people were concerned, the president hadn't even attended the game. He continued this kind of self-effacing behavior until he resigned three years later, declaring, "I had always thought I wanted to be a president until I became one. I just couldn't be a president."*

Case 4: *Two newly appointed presidents called in their alumni officers and summarily dismissed them. Each acted without assessing the dismissed officer's support among faculty and alumni. Although both acted within their authority, the first president resigned during his third year because of a recalcitrant constituency, and the second, after his first year in office, faced an alumni board unanimously opposed to his decision.*

Case 5: *The president of a large Middle Atlantic public university attended social functions reluctantly. Declining most invitations, she would attend no more than one each evening, usually a campus academic group. Most of her time at the event was spent engaged in serious discussion with the same people. Never considered an effective president even among those faculty members with whom she spent so much time, she simply never understood the importance of presidential presence. The same was true for the Midwestern community college president who spent $12,000 per year on faculty/staff entertainment and couldn't understand why his goals were not enthusiastically embraced by the faculty. The faculty may have liked and viewed him as a colleague, as he believed, but a faculty petition to the board indicated they certainly didn't respect him.*

Case 6: *A president of a public college in California and a small liberal arts college president in Texas couldn't understand why their faculties didn't follow their leadership. Both spent lots of time attending faculty functions and speaking on campus, taught at least one class a year, and attended departmental meetings in their disciplines. One is now teaching again and the other is barely hanging on, unwilling or afraid to maintain the distance necessary to provide the leadership the faculty wants.*

Case 7: *A president in Pennsylvania, who sat at the table as a colleague at campus governance meetings and stayed for the entire meeting, was perplexed because the group argued with him and didn't seem to respect his office. In his second year, the faculty already wished his more "presidential" predecessor would return.*

Case 8: *A college president in Pennsylvania complained of misgivings about the academic vice president's loyalty. He was confused by the vice president's lack of respect for him. "After all," he declared, "we decide everything together."*

Case 9: *A community college president in Maryland had problems with faculty meetings: "I have four faculty meetings a year, and I stand right in front and encourage them to get what's bothering them off their chests." After resigning, he accepted a presidency in Texas, where two formal faculty meetings are held each year. At the first, the president presents a "state of the college" address, and at the second, the academic dean makes a similar address, but in more specific terms. The president enjoys Texas much more than he did Maryland.*

Case 10: *The president of a prestigious, private university in the South had trouble with the board and asked for a consultant to come in and speak to the trustees. "I can't understand it. I've been in office three years, and I've involved them in virtually everything that goes on. Now they give more advice than money."*

There are countless other examples. One president was always on time at social functions and stayed late. Another wore a polyester suit and a double windsor knot in his tie and wondered why he felt uncomfortable with local bankers and corporate heads. Another declined to articulate an agenda when she was appointed and instead decided to "wait and see the lay of the land," only to find that when she finally did formulate a vision, no one wanted to hear it. A fourth boasted of cleaning house the first year and was asked to resign the third. Another appointed an executive vice president his third year "to run the institution on the inside" and had a revolution on his hands in the fifth year. Another, weighed down by tremendous demands on his time, didn't understand the need to get out on campus and even into the residence halls. (The story circulated about him is that "He came out of his office on February 2nd, saw his shadow, and went back in for another year.")

Another unfortunate president tried so hard to be friends with everyone that he was soon presented with the mandatory opportunity to return to the faculty with his friends. Lastly, consider the president who refused to allocate precious resources to his public relations, alumni, and development areas—convinced that support would come when word got around about the institution's excellence. It did, during the tenure of his successor.

Superficial indictments? Maybe somewhat. Obvious? Not to the presidents who committed these acts. Mistaken? All were, according to the research and literature on power and leadership.

POWER AND THE PRESIDENCY

Exercising presidential power well often appears a mysterious talent, and in some respects, it is. Some presidents just seem to do it right, almost invariably coming out on top. Quite naturally, other presidents rationalize their failures by saying that the successes don't have it as tough or are just luckier, but most will usually conclude that something about the person—attitude or knowledge or style—makes things go right. When perplexed and in difficulty, troubled presidents who can screw up the courage and swallow their pride often turn to these "winners" for advice. What is this special characteristic? Why do some succeed and others fail?

A closer look at the presidency in the light of the allegory of Saint Simone is in order. How does a president gain that platform and, more importantly, how can a president remain there in reasonable comfort?

How much the incumbent knows about leadership can be fundamentally valuable in the exercise of office. What the literature of power teaches can be accepted or rejected, but should at least be understood by all college or university presidents, for it reveals certain truths that can reduce the mystery of that lonely office and can put meaning and design into what was before largely vacuous behavior. Indeed, during the authors' almost two decades of experience as college presidents, we most seriously floundered when we ignored or forgot what was in the literature or when we thought we knew better.

Yes, some presidents seem intuitively to grasp the basic principles of leadership, but most do not. Most seem to blunder along being a combination of what they have seen, what they think they ought to be, and what they are. All can improve their insight and performance by knowing, appreciating, and making use of the established research on leadership and power. This is not to suggest that there is only one effective presidential style, but rather that any leadership role is enhanced by an awareness of related research and experience.

Talk of leadership and power pertains to something basic to the individual psyche and to society. Virtually all psychologists, sociologists, political scientists, and even historians would agree that the ability to influence or control is one of the most important aspects of human life. Indeed, leaders are simply people who are more consistently powerful than others—everyone attempts to be influential (Katz, 1973). No thoughtful observer of human behavior would deny that human life is a ceaseless search for identity, recognition, and importance, and that this process invariably leads to attempts to influence, lead, or exert power over others. Psychologists increasingly agree that power is a central concept for any attempt to understand social behavior (Kipnis, 1976). Somehow though, people are more comfortable with the socially acceptable term, "influence," which is simply a synonym for power.

Few human expressions are not designed to influence or to impress others. This is true on the job, in politics, with friends and loved ones, in a religious or social group, or during barroom conversation. In fact, the extent to which a person successfully influences another is directly related to his or her positive self-estimate. People feel better about themselves when they convey their particular message and become cynical and bitter if they fail. Indeed, psychoanalysts tell us that people of little power are more likely to become depressed and suffer from other mental problems. Rollo May, in *Power and Innocence* (1972), suggests that those who are unwilling to exercise power and influence may experience unhappiness throughout their lives. David Kipnis suggests that virtually all studies indicate that mental health and self-satisfaction are connected with position. In effect, the more resources you control, the better you feel (Kipnis, 1976). Because everyone is involved in the process of acquiring and using power, the real question boils down to the extent to which the power process is understood and used by "good" rather than "bad" persons.

Many people think acts of power are engaged in by dark and pernicious figures unlike anyone they know, least of all themselves (Kipnis, 1976). Meanwhile, virtually every one of their own subtle efforts to influence another is a power act that conveys many of the same psychological consequences for them as for those dark, pernicious figures so foreign to their understanding.

Of particular interest to those involved in or aspiring to positions of leadership is the research of the highly respected psychologist, David C. McClelland, who, along with his colleague David H. Burnham, concluded that "contrary to what one might think, a good manager [or leader] is not one who needs personal success or who is people oriented, but one who likes power" (Hawker and Hall, 1981). Power is a reality of organizational (and personal) life; the effective use of power is critical in all organizations that would possess authority and influence. McClelland and Burnham found that a strong power motivation was essential to good management; indeed, power was a more effective characteristic of effective leaders than either a need for personal achievement or a need to be liked by others. In fact, the latter two characteristics appear to act counter to effective leadership. They concluded that "the highly self centered nature of a strong need for achievement . . . leads people to behave in very special ways that do not necessarily lead to good management." The person with a strong need to be liked "is precisely the one who wants to stay on good terms with everybody and, therefore, is the one who is likely to make exceptions in terms of particular needs" (Hawker and Hall, 1981).

In summary, the effective leader must have a desire for impact, for being strong and influential. Moreover, this need must be stronger than either the need for personal achievement or the need to be liked by others.

POWER IN UNIVERSITIES

In spite of these facts, power is probably the most mysterious, abused, and misunderstood human capacity (Nisbet, 1970). Although it has fascinated humans through the ages, scientists have only recently begun to study the subject systematically (Kipnis, 1976; Bass, 1990).

Even the literature of organization theory neglects power. Stanford University Professor Jeffrey Pfeffer (1981) suggests that power is too uncomfortable a subject to be compatible with the philosophy implied in most writing on management and leadership. In their helpful book on academic leadership, *The Academic Administrator Grid*, Blake, Mouton, and Williams (1981) do not even discuss the subject; and, in almost 350 bibliographic citations, they list fewer than a dozen authors who have published significantly in the field. Like many observers of tranquil times, they seem more concerned with harmony than with results. While harmonious relationships in organizations are, of course, good, they do not necessarily spring from egalitarianism and do not guarantee results.

Because ideology and practice often conflict, it is understandable, if not theoretically sound, to ignore topics—such as power—that detract from the fundamental theory served by the writing. Although power is understood at American colleges and universities, few will discuss the subject candidly because it violates normative and comfortable beliefs about the nature of universities and academic life. A study at the University of Illinois, based on interviews with 29 department heads, asked each respondent to rate the power of all the university departments; only one department head needed to ask for clarification of the term "power" (Pfeffer, 1981). The ratings showed "enormous" consistency, with particular consensus on the most and least powerful departments. Many perceive the very asking of these questions as illegitimate and upsetting. During a study at two University of California campuses conducted by Pfeffer (1981), one humanities department chairperson, after reviewing a copy of the questionnaire in advance of the interview, refused to cooperate with the study: "If I saw the university in the terms implied in your questionnaire, I would be seeking, frankly, some other way of making a living, instead of practicing the profession I've been engaged in for the last three decades."

Yet, interest in power seems normal and even popular. In bookstores, one often notices two anxious coveys of people looking furtively over their shoulders to see if anyone is watching. They are huddled around the books on sex and pornography—how to be more attractive, lovable, and sexy— and the books on power and influence—how to be more important, assertive, and successful. Michael Korda's *Power: How to Get It, How to Use It* (1976) dramatized this when it became the nation's number one best-seller. Korda's book told us where to sit, what to wear, and what kind of briefcase to carry; although not well-documented, it wasn't far off the mark.

Power is a subject about which leaders—perhaps especially college presidents—are seldom candid. The current style is to apologize for using the authority of position and to speak of its terrible burdens. The secret seems to be to contrive a pose of refined disinterest and modesty behind which one wields all the power possible. As a president of a medium-sized independent university put it, "respectable people don't talk about using power, just like they never openly confess that they really are interested in being a candidate for another, more prestigious presidency."

A FIRST LOOK AT THE ROLE OF GOVERNING BOARDS

This book is also written for members of college governing boards and considers those fundamental governing board responsibilities that can ensure effective leadership. Although all board responsibilities are covered, emphasis is on five key areas: institutional evaluation, the presidential appointment process, governance structure and design at both the board and campus levels, presidential compensation, and presidential evaluation. Here again, the perspective is taken from the creditable research on effective leadership and, wherever possible, includes exhibits that illustrate appropriate practices.

Countless commissions, task forces, studies, and conferences have concluded that the current status of the college presidency is gloomy, and that the opportunity for a president to achieve success is increasingly precarious. The primary reasons are the impact of a generally democratized society and the diminution of quality in virtually all areas of higher education. The most significant result of this process, for purposes of this book, is the diminished status of the college president who, although reduced in station and authority, nonetheless remains accountable to the board for the conduct of the institution.

The president is often left teetering between the faculty on the one side and the board on the other. He/she is accountable *for* the faculty and *to* the board, but without sufficient wherewithal to satisfy either. So, presidents come, go, or stay amidst the growing lamentation of all, and too many governing boards continue to treat the symptoms rather than the problem. They hold the president responsible, but divide his or her authority with a variety of other power groups, especially faculty, students, and alumni. Then, compounding the error, boards too often permit these other groups to use this authority to make decisions even though these groups cannot be held responsible or accountable for the quality of the decisions they make (or, as is more often the case in recent years, the decisions they refuse to make).

Governing boards are ultimately responsible for the poor condition of the presidency. They have approved policies and practices that have unintentionally compromised the ability of the president to lead. Boards are urged to review their policies and, if need be, restore legitimacy (authority) to the presidency.

THE COLLEGE PRESIDENCY TODAY

This book is not about collegial leadership, although it does applaud collegial, friendly, interactive interpersonal relationships in every university community. Instead, it documents through research that the concept of collegial leadership is, to the informed, almost an oxymoron. One can be a colleague in teaching and research, but collegial *leadership* presents insurmountable contradictions. Collegial leadership is a proposition offered by the uninformed, by those who have never been presidents, have experienced a difficult presidency, or come from the few institutions that have little need for inspiring leadership (1 to 2 percent). For example, Harvard may not currently need a fully empowered president but, on its way up, Harvard was led by persons who are counted among the strongest presidents with the strongest prerogatives in the history of American higher education. Many institutions follow a familiar pattern: strong presidents established them and left them prospering, only to be succeeded by "collegial" presidents who in time brought them into difficulty, until they in turn were replaced by strong presidents.

On virtually every front, from the initial appointment process, to board policies and practices, to institutional governance, to presidential evaluation, limits are placed on the presidential office and the ability of the president to lead. The formerly legitimate conditions of presidential authority have been reduced or eliminated. Presidents are referred to as "mediators," "support mechanisms," tinkers," "chairs," "apostles of efficiency," "faceless," "managers," "clerks of the works," and "sweepers and dusters." At the same time, conferences and commissions conclude that *the* imperative of a good future for higher education is strong presidential leadership.

Contradictions abound. On the one hand, the president is expected to lead the institution to a better condition (indeed, is usually held accountable for doing so) and, on the other, he/she receives less support, both formal and psychological, to do the job. Wherever the president turns, he or she runs into a faculty or staff member, a student with a vote, or a trustee with a bent toward administration, with the interference of each made legitimate by board bylaws. Accordingly, the typical board, whose policies and practices have caused this condition, is totally unaware of what it has done. One of the authors experienced this when he participated in a retreat to review the governance documents of a distinguished liberal arts college where board members were astonished at what they had approved over the years. In countless instances, they had granted to the faculty as rights what the president should have been able to grant (or not) as privileges, yet the board continued to hold the president fully accountable for the conduct of the institution.

This lamentable situation has led national studies to conclude that "strengthening presidential leadership is the most urgent concern on the agenda of higher education in the United States" (Kerr, 1984). These groups invariably fall short of seriously addressing a solution. In most institutions today, a president would be foolhardy to "lead strongly" under the precarious governance conditions that exist. One president reported, "It would be professional suicide for me to candidly address the problems of the curriculum, tenure, teaching load, or intercollegiate athletics." For some presidents, this statement is prophetic.

These developments did not appear magically from the mist. A reformist movement in the early 1900s transformed much of higher education, waned during the Depression years, and was renewed with great energy in a variety of egalitarian movements in the early 1960s. Reformers, often sporting complex political and social agendas, sought to sweep out hypocrisy and install equal opportunity throughout society. Many of the products of this activity, such as the extension of civil rights to disenfranchised populations, addressed fundamental questions of justice and, after the fact, nearly all individuals of goodwill agreed these developments had a salutary influence on society.

However, the same vigorous egalitarianism that opened doors of opportunity to many also left in its ebb an increasingly institutionalized organizational parity that compromised traditional form and order and, in effect, made everyone a philosopher-king. Faculty and students were added to governance boards; administrators were often selected by majority votes of faculty and students; budgetary and strategic decisions frequently became subject to approval by faculty and student senates; and, less serious, but symbolic of the trend, some campuses abolished all reserved parking places. To many, these developments brought to mind Plato's pithy observation that at the height of the degenerate democracy "Even the dogs become arrogant."

As faculty members and students pressed for closer informal and normal ties to governing boards, the nature and condition of the institution began to change; in all things the process began to be more important than the outcome. Faculty/student committees reported directly to boards, joint faculty/student committees were appointed, campus governance bodies established normal relationships with boards of trustees and assumed full authority over academic matters. Increasingly, the president was left out of everything but final accountability. Thus, it was only as a result of a natural and logical progression that faculty and students began to serve on board committees and even on governing boards and, in increasing numbers, on presidential search and evaluation committees. The president was caught in a squeeze.

The only thing wrong with this new process was the original assumption, "Parity begets leadership." Like the classic paranoid personality, those who accepted this fallacious assumption perceived everything that followed as so logical that it defied rational objection. That this new form of participatory governance was antithetical to virtually all the objective research on effective management and leadership and even contrary to classic governance assumptions offered by the AAUP was scarcely given passing consideration. "The people" had gained the day, and most institutions soon became as politicized as the general society.

Indeed, many board and campus governance documents stopped mentioning the shared government statement offered by the AAUP because they had so far exceeded it—a situation analogous to the Magna Carta or the Bill of Rights being considered reactionary documents (see Chapter 8). Presidents were neutered, pensioned off, or forced out of office as governing boards blamed them for not being able to direct this fundamentally irrational process. The leader president became the exception. Yet, the basic assumption continued unexamined, primarily because a distorted notion of what constituted "shared governance" had, in this particular context, become "politically correct" and no longer subject to rational, analytical debate.

But, were "the people" happy? Were things better? According to surveys reported in higher education publications and the public media, the only group unhappier than college presidents were faculty.[2] According to a spate of reports from federal and state governments, the private sector, and higher education itself, this rudderless unhappy state was largely responsible for an undergraduate curriculum that had declined to an all-time low. Conditions were so bad by the late 1980s, states began mandating core academic requirements for public institutions (and the federal government offered *unequivocal* core recommendations). In intercollegiate athletics, decades of fiascos attracted congressional hearings and regulatory legislation. Today, the prospect of government control in higher education looms large.

THE SOLUTION: LEGITIMIZE THE PRESIDENCY

Most individuals in higher education are aware of our problems; indeed, these problems can no longer be concealed. But, those who have the power to change the circumstances causing the problems persist in treating only symptoms. Most boards are either reluctant or uninformed about the extent of the problems, and most presidents are bound to equivocate for the sake of their jobs. National associations are, by their nature, more or less obligated to take compromise positions, and so problems go unaddressed as institutions continue to drift.

Instead of looking hard at the presidential appointment process, institutional governance, the true condition of the institution, presidential evaluation and compensation, and other board responsibilities, committees (often including both faculty and board members) are involved with other matters. They study the curriculum and fiscal matters, engage in strategic planning, appoint administrators, review athletic programs, and work directly with governing boards—as if any real progress could be made without a rational operating design and a legitimate leader recognized by the university.

The restoration of presidential legitimacy is the major issue in higher education today, for without clear conditions of responsibility and authority, little can be accomplished. Research (discussed in detail in chapters 2 and 3) clearly establishes legitimacy as an essential condition for leadership in all but the most exceptional cases. Legitimacy of position enhances all

---

[2]However, this brings to attention the acerbic observation of the president of one of the most prominent national higher education organizations that "faculty morale is always at an all-time low."

leadership forms; it makes expertise more certain, rewards more meaningful, inspiration more likely, and the use of coercion less attractive. Legitimacy grants both informality and largess for the officeholder. Expressed thoughtfully, legitimacy can make a leader out of almost anyone of reasonable sophistication and high motivation. Only the board can grant presidential legitimacy; once the grant is made, leadership is up to the president.

FINAL THOUGHTS

During recent years, one of the authors of this book has spoken to several hundred college presidents and academic deans on the subject of power. Presidents are always attentive, although often uncomfortable and silent, and academic deans are sometimes downright hostile. But later, many presidents—and even deans—want to speak in private about the subject, and both continue to write and call.

Some hold that administration (leadership) is more art than science, and there is certainly much to support this position. This book is largely the result of having attempted to apply the results of research in the fields of leadership and power for almost 20 years in the presidency. This is not to suggest that research will always show a clear and certain path, but it can influence the course of action. At a minimum, knowledge of studies in these fields can provide confirming reassurance to the president who always behaved that way in the first place.

After attempting to establish further the need for strong presidential leadership, the research and discussion presented in the forthcoming chapters establishes the significant contribution that understanding of tested techniques of leadership and power can make to the strength and progress of any institution—company, country, or college.[3] If the mission is worth pursuing, so is this kind of knowledge. Of course, although examples of the use of power are presented, how presidential power is employed remains a personal matter that can be determined only by an incumbent president. The key is to make the most of that power, and to remember the following:

- Enjoy the presidency.
- Relax; after you are gone a year or two, you will not even be missed.
- You are the president, whether the office fits comfortably or not.
- *Never* get off that presidential platform.

---

[3]In succeeding chapters on the use of power by a college president (chapters 4 through 15), available research informs, but does not dictate, the presentation. The prescriptions and lessons of the research underpin the behavior of successful presidents, whether or not they are aware of it.

- Never act beneath your office or hide behind the office.
- Stand when you speak; if you do it right, only you will know your feet are in sand.
- At least once a week, show up where you are least expected.
- Try not to mix personal life and business.

CHAPTER
two
•••••••

Research on
Leadership and Power:
Principles and Evidence

*I see it said that leaders should keep their ears to the ground. All I can say
is that the British nation will find it very hard to look up to the leaders
who are detected in that somewhat ungainly posture.*

Winston Churchill, 1941

A leader is a dealer in hope.

Napoleon I, in *Maxims*

Are effective college presidents different from effective corporate, political, or military leaders? Increasingly, the answer appears to be "no"; if there are any differences, they exist in shades rather than clear contrasts. In general, a leader is a leader is a leader. All leaders, then, play off the same general themes even though their personal styles and mannerisms may differ.

Leadership has been defined in many different ways, probably because through the years the subject has fascinated so many scholars, all of whom approached it from countless different perspectives. Studies of leadership characteristics are legion and often conflicting. Further confusing the subject are those who maintain that leadership is related to the situation rather than to the person.

Through the years, author James L. Fisher, a psychologist, explored the subject of leadership in detail, but remained uncertain and equivocal about it until he discovered a power topology postulated by John R.P. French and Bertram Raven (1959) at the Institute for Social Research in Ann Arbor, Michigan. Subsequently, John Kenneth Galbraith, in *The Anatomy of Power* (1983), independently examined the nature of leadership and reached most of the same conclusions as French and Raven. These works clarified an otherwise murky and puzzling subject and led to Dr. Fisher's book, *Power of the Presidency* (1984), which associated the various and ostensibly disparate studies on leadership under one of the five French and Raven rubrics. In 1988, Dr. Fisher co-authored *The Effective College President*, which was based on an Exxon-funded study of the characteristics of effective college presidents (described in the following chapter). This study essentially corroborated the extrapolations set forth in *Power of the Presidency*.

During this same period, Dr. Fisher taught several seminars on leadership and power to classes composed of able and skeptical doctoral students. Author James V. Koch, meanwhile, became a university president and interacted daily with hundreds of students, faculty, staff, and citizens. Together, over a period of several years, this diverse group of individuals considered virtually all the published studies on leadership and found that, without exception, each study logically fell under one or more of the French and Raven power forms.

LEADERSHIP AND POWER

What meaning can we attach to the concept of "power?" Power has been defined as "the probability that one actor within a social relationship will be in a position to carry out his own will despite resistance, regardless of the basis on which this probability rests" (Weber, 1947). More simply, power may be "the possibility of imposing one's will upon the behavior of other persons" (Weber, 1947), or, it may be "the ability to employ force" (Bierstadt, 1950). Kanter (1983), who writes frequently about the corporate world, defines it more simply: "Power is the ability to get things done."

What meaning can we attach to the concept of "leadership"? "Leadership is the basic energy to initiate and sustain action that translates intention into reality" (Bennis and Nanus, 1985). Some define leadership as the ability to influence or induce. Others define leadership as "the process of control of social phenomena," as "the process by which an agent induces a subordinate to behave in a desired manner," or as "an act in which others respond in a shared direction." John Gardner (1986) defines leadership as "the process of persuasion and example by which an individual induces a group to take action that is in accord with the leader's purposes." This definition focuses upon what has become known as referent or charismatic power, which we shall consider later.

French and Raven define leadership in terms of differential power, "the ability of A to get B to do something that B might otherwise not have done." Twenty different but exhaustive reviews of leadership and power have focused upon this definition for both leadership and power. This is the definition we use in this book.

THE FRENCH AND RAVEN TOPOLOGY

Most researchers agree that the bases of influence and power are diverse, varying from one situation to another. They also agree that people use a combination of conscious and unconscious factors in attempting to lead others. For purposes of analysis, convenience, and discussion, these characteristics were elaborated in a topology by French and Raven (1959), which has been used by other researchers and adopted for this book. According to French and Raven, all forms of power or leadership fall under one or more of the following categories: coercion, reward, legitimate, expert, and referent ("charisma"). Some have questioned the French and Raven topology, but their objections appear unwarranted because of a lacking of acceptable alternatives and the increasing tendency in the field to use the French and Raven classifications either directly or by other names (Bass, 1990; Burns, 1978; Galbraith, 1983; and Patchen, 1974). In other words, all attempts to lead or influence use a combination of these power forms.

Before discussing these forms, we should describe the forms a leader's motives can take (although any motive—base or altruistic—applied intelligently yields results). According to McClelland (1969, 1975), a person's desire for impact, strength, or influence may take either of two forms: (1) an orientation toward achieving personal gain and aggrandizement, or (2) an orientation toward achieving gain for others or the common good.

In the first instance, the need for influence is essentially self-serving and, psychologists would argue, likely colored by unresolved achievement needs. This species of leadership drive is often criticized because on occasion it has led to disastrous outcomes in some economic, political, and military arenas. However, as Mandeville observed in his *The Fable of the Bees* ([1714] 1970), personal vice can result in public virtue. This theme was further developed by Adam Smith ([1776] 1917), who noted that the consistent pursuit of individual betterment simultaneously by many individuals may (somewhat ironically) produce socially desirable outcomes, especially in the economic domain. Consider the avaricious businessman who seemingly cares only about himself, but whose drive for personal wealth nonetheless results in the employment and prosperity of hundreds of workers. Casual observation suggests that variants of this behavior are exhibited by more than one ambitious (and often highly successful) college president (Demerath, Stephens, and Taylor, 1967; Kerr and Gade, 1986).

In the second instance, the person's motivation is often labeled "socialized," as opposed to "personalized." He or she values the power to lead as an instrument to use for the common good of the whole organization and its members. Today, standardized tests are available to determine a person's level and type of power motivation (Hall and Hawker, 1981), but either motivation would better enable a person to lead and is essential to any dynamic movement.

This book focuses on "socialized" leadership motivation for the common and corporate good, but recognizes that "personalized" leadership motivation, when properly channeled, has the potential to achieve significant results. While most leaders ritually deny it, their leadership styles reflect both strands of motivation.

This review assumes that leadership and power also embrace influence and authority, and the terms are used synonymously. Authority without power is nothing. The effective leader will learn how to use authority and recognize its value. Indeed, leadership, influence, and authority are all a function of the intelligent use of the various power forms. To lead, to influence, and to use authority is to be powerful.

TRANSACTIONAL AND TRANSFORMATIONAL LEADERSHIP

The study of leadership theory and practice typically begins with a book by Bernard M. Bass entitled *Bass and Stogdill's Handbook of Leadership* (3rd ed., 1990). This all-encompassing reference work is the empirical standard for the field; it includes the various acceptable definitions of leadership as well as an exclusive study of leadership theory and practice, including some 22,000 citations of worldwide research. Bass, along with other scholars, describes two competing theories on leadership: transformational and transactional (Bass, 1992). These two conflicting paradigms are not unique to higher education. The transformational and transactional leadership theories compete in all fields, always dividing scholarship and research between them. Both theories employ French and Raven's topology of power as well as Fisher's charismatic components; however, they do so in vitally different ways.

Before analyzing specific differences as well as those variances reflected in higher education, we must introduce James MacGregor Burns' Pulitzer Prize winning book *Leadership* (1978), for Burns is credited with originally defining the differences between transformational and transactional leadership. In his "Prologue: The Crisis of Leadership," Burns writes

> I will deal with leadership as distinct from mere power-holding and as the opposite of brute power. I will identify two basic types of leadership: the *transactional* and the *transforming*. The relations of most leaders and followers are *transactional*—leaders approach followers with an eye to exchanging one thing for another: jobs for votes, or subsidies for campaign contributions. Such transactions comprise the bulk of the relationships among leaders and followers, especially in groups, legislatures, and parties. *Transforming* leadership, while more complex, is more potent. The transforming leader recognizes and exploits an existing need or demand of a potential follower. But, beyond that, the transforming leader looks for potential motives in followers, seeks to satisfy higher needs, and engages the full person of the follower. The result of transforming leadership is a relationship of mutual stimulation and elevation that converts followers into leaders and may convert leaders into moral agents.

For Burns, the relationship of leader and follower in transactional theory is as "bargainers seeking to maximize their political psychic profits." Transformational power is altogether different as described by both Burns and Bass.

> According to Bass (1985), the items describing leaders that judges generally found to be transformational, in terms of Burns' (1978) definition of transformational leadership, emerged as four factors in surveys of subordinates' ratings of their military or industrial superiors: (1) charismatic leadership ("Share complete faith in him or her"), (2) inspirational leadership ("Communicates high performance expectations"), (3) intellectual stimulations ("Enables me to think about old problems in new ways"), and (4) individualized consideration ("Gives personal attention to members who seem neglected").[1]

The reader should bear in mind how closely Bass' transformational characteristics compare with the French and Raven topology used in this book. Distinguishing between transformational and transactional power is vital. Defining power and its components is crucial also. The college or university president's role is important to the nature of the institution. The transforming leader has a clear vision of a future in which others invest; this vision maximizes the mission of the institution and enables a capacity for

---

[1] Peter Drucker, *Managing the Non-Profit Organization* (1990), pp. 45–49.

innovation and boldness that transcends provincial outlooks. Virtually all members of the community are empowered as they help to shape the vision.

Transactional theory, with its "bargainers seeking to maximize their political and psychic profits," is egalitarian in outlook. Akin to an exchange, transactional leadership does not allow for transcendence. In maximized transactions, shared faith, intellectual stimulation or inspiration, and consideration of the individual are not crucial components. Transactional leadership does not possess the power of substantive improvement, change, or reform. Faith in the individual (belief in his or her worthiness, and confidence in his or her ability to reform impediments) is not a primary component.

Transformational leadership, on the other hand, asks for transcendence. Burns' transformer addresses Ralph Waldo Emerson's call to reform:

> Reform leadership by definition usually implies moral leadership, and this imposes a special burden. It means that reformers must not follow improper means in trying to achieve moral ends, on the ground that the means can taint and pervert the ends.

By transcending their own particular concerns and working for the communal good, transformational leaders in general, and those in higher education in particular, achieve shared faith, intellectual stimulation or inspiration, and consideration of the individual. In the end, the individual will be an effective leader.

Both the transactional and transformational types of leadership fall appropriately under one of the French and Raven power forms noted above. Transactional leaders attempt to tweak optimal performance out of an organization by participative, democratic leadership techniques that place strong emphasis upon process in order to overcome what Cohen and March (1986) label the "organized anarchy" of modern organizations such as universities. Transactional leaders typically do not advocate a strong agenda or vision and often implicitly adopt the views of Birnbaum and of Cohen and March, which hold that the president is unlikely to be able to make a significant difference in the history of his or her organization. Hence, the president tends to think in terms of "maintenance management" behaviors that are designed to meet the needs (sometimes emergencies) of the day that accumulate in Cohen and March's decision "garbage can." Surviving the day (or the year) and eventually being able to step down from leadership with appropriate huzzahs and long-term personal friendships intact often motivate the transactional leader's behavior. The prestige associated with being "in command" and ultimately being viewed as a successful, nondestructive leader who met the challenges of the day are sufficient rewards for the transactional leader.

To the surprise of some, many senior military officers turn out to be transactional leaders. Senior generals or admirals may occupy a particular post for only two (or a maximum three) years. During such a brief time period, they will find it difficult to break existing organizational molds and may instead opt to make friends, avoid problems, and position themselves for the next billet.

Transactionalists, whether or not generals and admirals, rarely intervene, tend to shift and delegate responsibilities, and sidestep difficult decisions by relying on committees or plugging a contentious issue into the bowels of the existing governance structure. They administer "by the book" and seemingly give validity to the Japanese aphorism that "the nail that sticks out gets pounded down." While this approach to leadership can soothe frayed nerves, and seldom results in the outright rejection of a leader, it is slow and rather directionless. It seldom results in major reforms, and is ill-suited for difficult times.[2] The transactional approach is a paradigm for why many military and academic organizations find it so difficult to reform themselves and change directions.

Because transactional leaders ordinarily do not carry with them a strong agenda or vision, and because they tend to administer "by the book," they often rely upon the less effective power forms—coercion and reward. This type of leadership is premised on an exchange—promise and reward for good performance, threat or discipline for poor performance. Transactional leadership is unlikely to stimulate extraordinary performance from large numbers of individuals for long periods of time.

Although a leader should know and exercise certain aspects of transactional leadership, literally countless studies in virtually all work arenas indicate that transformational leadership is the only kind of leadership that leads to superior performance (Bass, 1992). These studies contradict a flood of transactional articles and books in higher education that are not empirically based. Bass, the most highly regarded source on leadership, is based almost exclusively on empirical evidence.

The transformational leader relies primarily on legitimate, expert, and, especially, referent or charismatic power. To the surprise of some, charisma (or "public presence") can be learned by anyone of reasonable intelligence and high motivation. The transformational leader provides vision, instills

---

[2]A transactional leader who becomes activated tends to be oppressive, watching for deviations from rules and standards, ready to take correcting action.

pride, inspires confidence and trust, expresses important goals in simple ways, promotes intelligence, and treats everyone individually.

Transactional leaders are more likely to be seen by their colleagues and employees as satisfying and effective leaders than are transactional leaders. This, at least, is the conclusion Bass (1992) has drawn from colleagues', supervisors', and employees' responses on the Multifactor Leadership Questionnaire (MLQ). Similar results have been found in various organizational settings and in different cultures.

Let us now consider in more detail the five power/leadership forms, all of which are measurably effective ways of influencing the behavior of others.

COERCIVE POWER

Coercive power uses threats and punishments to gain compliance. Although usually the least effective kind of power for a leader, it is often the most used. Many would-be leaders believe it to be the key to authority. Studies indicate that the threat of punishment induces greater conformity than punishment itself (French and Raven, 1959). More recently, researchers have discovered that leaders' perceived legitimacy reduces resistance to conformity and makes punishment more acceptable to the punished. If a leader is generally admired, followers more readily accept the implied use of penalties.

But, once the leader actually uses punishment, he or she is likely to become less effective (French, Morrison, and Levinger, 1960; Iverson, 1964). Coercion, even in its more subtle forms, invites resistance and retaliation (Kotter, 1985). People will work harder for a leader they find attractive (charismatic) and legitimate than for one they perceive to be coercive (Zander and Curtis, 1962; Bass, 1990). This hypothesis is supported by laboratory experiments (Howell, 1985) and voluminous survey research spanning many countries and cultures (Smith, 1982; Bass, 1985; Waldman, Bass, and Einstein, 1986; Gibbons, 1986; Onnen, 1987; Seltzer and Bass, 1987; and Yokichi, 1989).[3]

Nonetheless, the threat of punishment, when buttressed on occasion by its visible use, does tend to induce compliance. It can serve as a deterrent to hostile behavior as long as the punishments are respected or feared (Kipnis, 1976). The relationship between state governors and public university presidents illustrates this point. In an eastern state, the governor reduced the budget of a university whose president and constituents had criticized

---

[3]Most studies find the simple correlation between numeric measures of charisma and measured leadership effectiveness to be in the range of .5 to .7. Correlations between other significant leadership characteristics and leadership effectiveness generally are significantly lower, or even negative.

and offended him. The message was not missed by the other presidents in the state, who became silent as church mice. Needless to say, this governor was not loved (at least by the universities), but he was feared, and perhaps respected as well. In a western state, the governor did not respond to escalating and often misdirected criticism from the university community and other constituencies, and gradually came to be perceived as weak and out of touch.

When the threat of punishment never leads to actual punishment, it usually loses its significance. The leader who threatens punishment, but does not deliver, will be ignored or even reviled. Witness the almost innumerable warnings directed by world leaders in the 1990s at warring factions in the former Yugoslavia. For a threat to be credible, it must occasionally be exercised, swiftly, judiciously, and in a context that delivers an unmistakeable message (Dixit and Nalebuff, 1991; Poundstone, 1992). Nonetheless, the most effective leader seeks to avoid situations where threats of punishment, or actual punishment, become necessary.

Some evidence suggests that less confident leaders tend to rely more heavily on coercive and legitimate power than on other forms of influence (Kipnis, 1976). In addition, the maturity of people and relationships tends to reduce the already questionable value of punishment as a motivating condition because more mature groups are usually more productive under less punitive conditions (Kipnis and Wagner, 1967). As two prominent former university leaders, Henry Rosovsky of Harvard (1990) and Clark Kerr of the University of California (Kerr and Gade, 1986) sometimes ruefully point out, university faculties, by inclination and tradition, provide a visible example of a mature, putatively self-regulating professional group. For centuries, university faculty members throughout the world have resisted leaders who have relied extensively on punishment and coercion to accomplish their goals (Weber, 1947; Demerath, Stephens, and Taylor, 1967). Punishments willingly accepted in one work situation (e.g., the military) may be entirely inappropriate in another (e.g., a university).[4] In either case, charismatic leadership that inspires rather than threatens is more likely to be successful.

When other forms of power are wanting, that is, when an administrator is not granted sufficient authority to exercise power (by a board or an administrative superior), he or she may be more inclined to use covert and coercive means to obtain ends (Kipnis and Vanderveer, 1971). This condition is obvious in universities and colleges where increased authority has

---

[4]However, even highly educated people are willing to administer punishment when commanded to do so by an established authority figure. The Milgram (1965) studies established this to an unsettling extent. When individuals were ordered by authority figures to administer "dangerous" degrees of electric shock to others, they almost invariably did so.

been given to faculty, staff, and students. Periods of tension are invariably laced with a level of suspicion and hostility that seems to justify extremes in behavior. Even during normal periods when authority is assumed by staff, the leader can no longer grant the privilege of participation because it is simply assumed as a right, resulting in a less effective leader and a less dynamic organization.

When excessive authority is assumed by those who report to a leader, the leader often develops diminished feelings of self-worth and visibly reduces his or her expectations of successful influence. This in turn leads to a greater reliance upon the use of coercion with less effective results. Under these conditions, most leaders are moved to use fear, arousal, and stealth as influence techniques (Kipnis, 1976). As the power holder's expectations of successful influence rise, the tendency to exert more pressure by the use of coercive influence increases (Goodstadt and Hjelle, 1973).

Raven (1974) concludes that if the "goal of the leader (power holder) is to produce long-lasting changes in behavior, then the leader would probably avoid coercive means of influence." The psychometric research of Posner and Kouzes (1993) involving 5,000 managers and 30,000 subordinates provides empirical support for this hypothesis. However, if long-lasting compliance is not an issue, then the power holder might decide to invoke strong coercive sanctions. In the short-run, coercion may yield short-term results. If coercion must be used, it is better for the leader if punishment or sanctions are meted out by delegates who can later be reinforced by the leader. A secure leader rarely resorts to coercive power to achieve the common good.

In summary, although the threat of punishment as penalty tends to induce compliance, an astute leader uses it seldom, if ever. On those rare occasions, research suggests that the individual punished should be isolated as much as possible from community support. Punishment should never be applied in anger or pique. The wise leader will supply individuals with the inspiration necessary to change their behavior and, as necessary, will supplement that vision with positive incentives for change. Such tactics are more likely to induce long-term changes in behavior than overt punishment.

REWARD POWER

Through reward power, a leader accomplishes desired outcomes by distributing favors, recognition, or rewards to group members. In our predominantly capitalist economy, rewards (especially financial ones) allocate resources, influence behavior, and send messages about what is deemed to be significant. Only a confirmed and astigmatic Utopian would deny the influence of financial rewards on human behavior. The demise of Soviet-style planned economies in recent years underlines this point.

Nonetheless, we are well advised to keep three things in mind: (1) many meaningful rewards exist other than those involving money; (2) the manner in which one distributes rewards can be the cause of numerous problems; and, (3) rewards (or their mirror image, penalties) seldom motivate as effectively as a captivating vision that unifies and invigorates the members of an organization. The leader who does not understand these limitations is destined for problems.

Although difficult to do, rewarding those we do not like or those with whom we feel little kinship is often an astute move. Rewarding and influencing those who are attractive or similar to us is easy; more effort is required with dissimilar personalities, or with those with whom we disagree. Yet, changing the behavior of those "outlier" individuals might benefit the organization most.

The effective leader rewards those who support the goals of the organization, regardless of his or her personal feelings. Rewards are also a way to bring personality opposites into the fold. Unfortunately, leaders too often use rewards to prevent rather than to eliminate existing resistance (Lawler, 1971). Anyone who relies heavily on reward power should reward contributing supporters, but positive attention must be given to potential converts also.

The leader should not expect too much from reward power, for while rewards may influence outward behavior, they are not likely to change attitudes permanently. As soon as rewards cease, the rewarded person will probably revert to former attitudes and behaviors (Raven and Kruglanski, 1970). Further, withholding rewards results in resentment. Do not expect dramatic results from bestowing recognition, favors, or money on members of the organization unless those items are clearly related to correcting a visible injustice. Other leadership conditions are far more inspiring.

Other observations support the position that reward power often is an uncertain instrument for long-term change (Foa and Foa, 1975). Thinking that money is an effective way to ensure support, admiration, or affection is easy but not attuned to human psychology. Long before there was any systematic research in the field, Machiavelli warned the prince that "liberality" (rewards) could not guarantee the prince would be held in high regard by his followers. In fact, Machiavelli concluded that it was better to be feared than to try to gain support with rewards (Machiavelli, 1952).

Thus, financial rewards (or their absence) can and do influence behavior, especially in the short run, but will not necessarily be accompanied by a sharing of vision and purpose, which is more likely to evoke exceptional performance. In 1940, when Nazi Germany threatened to conquer Great Britain, British workers responded by generating a truly stupendous and unanticipated increase in the production of airplanes and other war material (Keegan, 1989). Financial rewards were minimal. Instead, a charismatic leader, Winston Churchill, provided each British citizen with a common, inspiring vision that obliterated previous pacifistic tendencies in the population and stirred the British people to achievements that previous leaders desired, but could not elicit.

In the mid-1960s, the concept of equality over equity gained even greater acceptance. More and more people, including those in higher education, found "share and share alike" to be more acceptable than the traditional notion that rewards follow personal effort and contribution. Salary schedules and "across the board" salary increments became much more common inside academe, government, and corporate America. This is one among many reasons why quality and production in corporate America (profit and nonprofit) dropped to all-time lows and, according to countless reports and commissions, education, including higher education, reached its nadir. *Among equals, there are no strong leaders.*

A subtle, but not generally recognized argument in favor of merit pay mechanisms is that they reduce the perception that all individuals in an organization are somehow "equal" and therefore are equally qualified to exercise (or reject) leadership.

Rewards work for the leader, but in a highly democratic society individuals involved in reward-yielding situations develop feelings of responsibility for one another. Thus, subtle informal agreements and coalitions develop (Weber, 1947; Thibaut and Gruder, 1969) that result in greater acceptance of parity and equity rather than a sharply differentiating system of reward distribution. This situation does not bode well for the leader who tries to reconcile the differences between merit and acquiescence (Murdoch, 1967).

For instance, in terms of merit pay (which, in the last analysis, is the only effective way to pay), the astute executive, while reserving final authority, should delegate considerable responsibility for salaries and promotions to others, directing controversy elsewhere. Controversy will always attend such matters. (In the case of collective bargaining, financial reward power usually is so diffused that it is virtually nonexistent, at least at the presidential level.)

Excepting vice presidents and others in a direct reporting line, college presidents should use rewards more subtly. For example, one can use selective words or notes of praise or make appointments to key committees. Thoughtful, deliberate, and sincere acknowledgement and support from the leader has no substitute. Positive reinforcement regarding salary and promotion is the wisest choice; its absence may transmit confusing messages and cause severe morale problems. Use merit pay, but let others do it wherever possible. Most importantly, bear in mind always that there are limits to the secure and effective use of rewards. Worthwhile long-term support cannot be bought.

LEGITIMATE POWER

To be most effective, the leader needs structure, form, station, authority, and protocol (a position from which to be inspiring, compassionate, giving, and charming). Legitimate power is the leader's platform. The effective leader should get on that platform and stay there. Once there, the leader can negotiate the platform with warmth, sincerity, and benevolence. The leader must accept the prerequisites of authority and position and, from the first day, appear to live comfortably with them. The leader should never apologize for or downplay a position. To do so is simply a way of telling others that you do not deserve the office, and a way to certify a less effective performance.

Legitimacy is based on a group's acceptance of common beliefs and practices, which include the distribution of influence within the particular setting. This acceptance binds the group members together through their common perspective. The group adheres to leaders who fit certain roles consistent with their expectations, endowing those leaders with certain power. For instance, the titles of general, chairperson, mother, judge, president, manager, doctor, dean, priest, and senator all grant legitimate power to the individual within a given context.

Certain activities and actions come to be expected and accepted from those leaders and are considered legitimate. "In all cases, the notion of legitimate involves some sort of code or standard accepted by the individual by virtue of which the external agent can exercise his or her power" (French and Raven, 1959). Some consider this condition authority rather than power (Burns, 1978; Pfeffer, 1981), while others style it leadership. For our purposes, the acceptance of common forms and traditions enables a leader to exercise power that otherwise might not be accepted by the group. *By so legitimizing power, its exercise is transformed in a remarkable way, for it makes*

the use of all other leadership forms (coercive, reward, expert, and charismatic)
more acceptable to the group.

In most social situations, the exercise of power involves costs. We pay the cost of resources, make commitments, and have a greater need to rely on the other power forms. In effect, the leader uses up potential for influencing the group because in most situations parity of opinion prevails. Without legitimate authority, all players are expected to take turns on center stage.

The possession of legitimacy or authority will be, if used effectively, a significant enhancement in the effectiveness of the leader, for it will not cost him or her other power forms. People in legitimate authority positions are expected to use their authority and at times are even punished for not doing so (Dornbusch and Scott, 1975). Most newly appointed executives are afraid to exercise the limited authority they have. Their anxiety and uncertainty make them say, "Wait awhile until I get the lay of the land." They fail to articulate an attractive vision accompanied by action, and by the time they realize their mistake, it is too late (Bensimon, 1993). This initial uncertainty has long-lasting effects on the executive's ability to become a leader.

Conversely, too little legitimacy is often given to those who are expected to lead. Bosses and boards limit the authority of a legitimized figure and then wonder why the person cannot produce up to expectation (Burns, 1978; Kanter, 1983; Bennis and Nanus, 1985; Kotter, 1985; Bennis, 1989a,b). During recent years, countless executives in industry, education, and government have experienced this situation, so much so that Bennis (1989b) labels it "an unconscious conspiracy." Benezet, Katz, and Magnusson (1981) bemoan the existence of university governance structures that virtually dictate a passive, managerial role for university presidents rather than a transformational, inspirational role. As Weber (1947) predicted many years ago, even skilled university presidents find it impossible to lead when stripped of legitimate authority.

People generally follow legitimate leaders with whom they agree. Those with whom they disagree are likely to be ignored, subverted, and, finally, sent packing. That is the reason expert and charismatic power (which will be discussed below) are so important to the leader. While legitimacy is a significant element of influence and control, like coercive and reward power, it is not universally effective and must be supplemented (House, 1984). The leader needs more than legitimacy. People who do not at least reluctantly agree with their leader often disobey or ignore him or her. In emergency cases, they even try to overthrow the leader. Legitimate leaders who noticeably overstep the bounds of their roles invite resistance. This is particularly true in academe, where traditions of democracy, diffusion of authority, and a certain disrespect for central administrative authority are deep-seated (Weber, 1947).

A delegate leader who does not discharge his or her office causes a "power vacuum," the antithesis of a competent application of leadership principles. This common and troublesome situation is often characteristic of university administrators. It occurs when the appointed leader, usually through collegiality, does not assume the responsibilities of the office. This condition, coupled with other compromised standards, makes for apathy, frustration, and resentment.

Assignment to a legitimate leadership role does not confer any leadership abilities, only the potential for leadership. Legitimatized leadership opportunities must be grasped and exploited. Unfortunately, as the University of Chicago's redoubtable Robert Hutchins often noted, many individuals who are placed in decision-making roles become paralyzed. They allow others to assume, diffuse, and diminish their authority until there is none. Inevitably, both production and morale drop.

Nonetheless, within formal organizations such as universities and corporations, norms and expectations invariably develop that make the exercise of power expected and accepted. Thus, reasonable (and sometimes even unreasonable) control of behavior becomes an expected part of corporate life. *Legitimate power is of fundamental importance to all would-be leaders because it will not be resisted unless it is abused or ineffectively used.*

Once power becomes legitimate, it no longer depends on the resources, arguments, or power that produced it in the first place. It can stand alone. Indeed, the more legitimate the leader becomes, the more the group accepts the leader and rates his or her competence. The more legitimate the leader, the more the leader is endowed with superior personal qualities (Clark, 1956; Hollander, 1961; Pepitone, 1958; Sherif and Sherif, 1953; Sherif, White, and Harvey, 1955). Thus, the more legitimate the leader, the more effectively he or she can exercise the wonderful "incremental" forms of leadership that follow expertise and charisma.

Holding a position of high status does not automatically make a leader; it simply provides a great advantage to the effort (Smith, 1982). The higher the leader advances, the more care he or she should take in resisting the tendency toward detail, inflexible procedure, and a custodial mentality (Gardner, 1986). The unsuccessful hide behind these kinds of things.

Legitimacy is maintained, then, not so much by its originating sanctions but rather by the degree to which the group continues to adhere to the common and unifying bonds that produced the legitimate leader in the first place. If a holder of legitimate power—such as a corporate officer, a judge, a store manager, or a college president—conducts the office poorly, then power again becomes diffused. The group spends more time in conflict than in growth. Legitimate power adds stability to the group and can be used most effectively after the leader thoroughly understands and appreciates the other forms of power (leadership).

Research has also established that group members perceive an organization's status structure and production potential to be most effective when high-status members consult widely and enjoy the reputation of being good listeners, but clearly retain final authority. However, the effective leader is not the "good buddy" type. Rather, the leader moves around the organization frequently, being warm and friendly, but not overly involved or intimate, and always remaining on the platform. The president is always the president.

Indeed, legitimate power largely depends on the extent to which group members perceive the leader's role in the first place, and they cannot perceive someone who is overly involved with them as an inspiring leader (Scott, 1956). People are less inclined to be resentful and hostile when they are operating under common and understood norms with fully legitimized leaders.

Despite conflicting research, appointed leaders are generally considered more legitimate and effective than elected leaders (Bass, 1981; Julian, Hollander, and Regula, 1969). Rather than making an academic leader more secure and effective, election may result in anxiety, insecurity, and vulnerability. In European and Asian universities, the faculty customarily elects the rector (president). Candidates campaign for the post and promises are made as in any political contest. All too often, the result is a noncontroversial leader who offends no one, but does little. Indeed, that is why he or she was elected. Many elected rectors of European or Asian universities have found their election by the faculty to be a millstone about their necks when circumstances arise that call for action. Indeed, German university rectors often are derisively referred to as "the Rektor Impotenz" (the impotent rector) because of their fundamental lack of legitimate authority (Kerr and Gade, 1986).

Upon occasion, leaders may diminish criticism of difficult decisions by carefully pointing out that their authority to act came from those who elected them. However, the "you elected me, and this is what you get" approach to leadership becomes tiresome in a hurry and a wise elected leader will rely upon it only sparingly. If the quality of one's leadership and decisions are poor, no measure of appeals to legislated authority will suffice to produce a desirable outcome.

The recent documentation of the loss of public confidence in most contemporary institutions has consequences for decision making in all corporate life. The acceptance of some form of authority is critical to all forms of organizations, from the family group to the most "collegial" university. Without authority, the organization proves ineffective in times of difficulty and either disintegrates or is replaced. Burns makes a compelling case for increasing the legitimate authority of the U.S. president to overcome the government's inefficient and obsolescent system of checks and balances (Burns, 1978).

Exercising control of general direction by relying solely upon rewards and punishments is difficult, although both are legitimizing power agents. Using only expert or even charismatic influence is also inconsistently effective. Having a legitimate power base with sufficient authority to back it up is essential. Thrones may be out of fashion, but authority still requires a cultural frame in which to define itself and advance its claims (Geertz, 1983).

Legitimacy allows the leader to make choices in a fashion that approximates the rational model (Pfeffer, 1981). When authority erodes through the loss of confidence and legitimacy, followers are less likely to accept decisions without question. What was once a rational process for decision making becomes a political struggle that can undo the organization itself.

Only a masterful, legitimate leader can overcome the currents of the general society. This is the case with corporate leaders under conditions of extreme unionism, religious leaders during periods of demysticism, and political and educational leaders during periods of egalitarianism. Because everyone has a piece of the action (power), little or nothing gets done. The tyranny of the many is every bit as debilitating as the tyranny of the few.

In sum, legitimate power is essential for the effective leader. People accept a legitimate leader when they agree with his or her policies and actions. The legitimate leader will be effective to the extent that he or she appreciates and uses the various other forms of leadership. Most reasonably intelligent and educated people can be effective legitimate leaders. Although election to a leadership role is preferred by some as the way to become a leader, being appointed seems to be the best way to ensure effectiveness for a college president. Leaders who present themselves as legitimate tend to be more effective. They are generally better liked and their attempts to influence are better accepted.

The discussions of expert and charismatic power that follow represent a kind of "incremental power" characteristic of an individual. Legitimate, reward, and coercive power tend to be organizationally derived from a legitimizing agent (governing board, corporation, country, religious organization, society itself) that enables the leader to hold position and to reward or punish. Only the extraordinary person weaves the expert and charismatic forms of power into his or her exercise of leadership. Most people of reasonable ability and motivation can exercise the first three forms of power, but those who adroitly use expert and charismatic power will be the most effective leaders.

EXPERT POWER

Expert power, which reflects the deference accorded a perceived authority, tends to further legitimatize leaders and make them more effective. Expert power, in most circumstances, is the most consistently effective power discussed so far. There are two ways to wield the influence of an expert: to be introduced to a group as an expert (unless you make a monumental mistake, you will be the controlling influence in the group); or, to actually become an expert, a person who is knowledgeable and informed about the subject at hand. The difference between the two may be obscure to observers who are inclined to accept expert power uncritically. For instance, Lowe and Shaw found that even though authoritative attempts to predict the future were sometimes inaccurate, the forecasts were accepted and influential in decision making because of the confidence and perceived expertise of the forecaster (in Pfeffer, 1981).

Appearing to withhold information or expertise is a measurably significant power form (Pettigrew, 1972, in Pfeffer, 1981), but one that must be used with care. Modern technological advances no longer allow leaders to withhold information from their constituents as they might have done in the past. Computer networking, e-mail, software such as Lotus "Notes," and information banks now provide faculty members with a wealth of data (on topics ranging from university budgets to enrollments) that enable them to become potential inquisitors of the administration. In most situations, leaders now find they are better served by making information generally available than by attempting to restrict access to it. Most college presidents understand that nothing is ever "off the record" with the media; they also should understand that virtually no information of consequence can be held as a secret on a campus for long.

A leader attempting to garner support for a particular cause can benefit from being perceived as an expert. This perception both inspires support for a common cause and reduces unproductive conflict. People frequently accept expert pronouncements because it takes time and effort for an opponent to gather information for an alternative position. Most are not willing to risk the loss of popularity involved in going against the confident leader. Charles Eliot, the transformational president of Harvard University at the turn of the century, once observed that he simply wore down his opponents with expert knowledge (Kerr and Gade, 1986).

There is another side to this coin. Leaders who demonstrate that they are not expert, or misinformed, court disaster. Consider the case of the president of a large public university who, when appearing before a state legislative appropriations committee, was asked what it cost an undergraduate student to attend his university, that is, how much were his institution's tuition and fees? Unfortunately, he could not answer, and he promptly lost the attention of the appropriations committee. In all but a few situations, conspicuous lack of expert knowledge imparts a range of negative images that diminishes leadership effectiveness.

Research further demonstrates the value of perceived expertise. People introduced as prestigious feel better accepted and more at ease than people assigned low-prestige roles. They are measurably more effective and influential. (People introducing speakers should get this message.)

Groups with more than one expert are less certain of their judgment, and even the experts are less effective (Collaros and Anderson, 1969). This echoes the Marine Corps adage, "It's better to have one idiot in charge than two geniuses." The more acknowledged experts in a group, the less effective their expert powers. Even the experts become inhibited. In groups with many experts, high status legitimate power rather than expertise can be a more significant determinant of behavior (Torrance, 1955). Combining expertise with high position is a most effective posture, providing the leader demonstrates expertise consistently. Therefore, key executives should rarely speak in groups unless they are certain of their subject material. The effective leader no longer enjoys the luxury of spontaneous brilliance or foolishness.

As Sir Francis Bacon observed in the sixteenth century, knowledge is power. Knowing more about a subject than others, combined with the legitimacy of position, gives an incumbent a decided advantage in any situation. The leader should always try to be perceived as knowledgeable, which means that he or she rarely participates in groups of other experts, delegates as many details as possible, always strives for greater expertise, and often refrains from speaking. The main job of the leader is to inspire, occasionally offering a trace of detail merely to imply greater knowledge. But, if wrong or mistaken, he or she should admit the error at once, without dwelling on it. The leader who bullishly refuses to acknowledge mistakes or overlooks them loses all the most effective leadership forms.

Finally, as Cleveland (1985) and others have noted, the role of expert knowledge in buttressing power has become more fluid because knowledge is so easily accessed, analyzed, and transported. The geometric expansion of knowledge threatens overload and makes expertise more valuable; however, technological advances have made it possible for more individuals to acquire expertise if they wish to do so.

CHARISMATIC (REFERENT) LEADERSHIP

Charismatic leadership, the single most effective form of leadership, is based on the admiration and liking that people feel toward an individual. The charismatic leader has an extraordinary ability to inspire trust and confidence. Some researchers have used the term "referent power" for this category, and others have used the terms "heroic," "charismatic," or "possessing a public presence." We prefer the term charismatic, in spite of its sometimes uncomfortable connotations. This is not the charisma of divine inspiration, a special gift, grace, or talent that some have and most have not, but rather a quality of trust and confidence that almost anyone can honestly cultivate.

For centuries, philosophers have viewed gaining the affection, trust, and respect of others as the most effective form of leadership. Throughout history and literature, we find people who have become heroes by winning the adulation of others. People feel secure with these heroes; some go so far as to become worshipful (Geertz, 1983). People like Eisenhower and MacArthur became heroes and then charismatic leaders. Today, researchers are increasingly able to document that those characteristics referred to as "charismatic" constitute the behavior that is most effective in inspiring others to follow and support a leader (Foa and Foa, 1975; Galbraith, 1983; Geertz, 1983; House, 1977; Machiavelli, 1952; Mott, 1970). Clearly, someone who is respected and trusted by others is most able to exert influence over them (Tedeschi, Lindskold, Horai, and Gahagan, 1969).

The way to lead people beyond the limited capacity of more conventional leadership forms, and even beyond themselves, is to study charismatic leadership and then learn to use it ethically. One need not feel uncomfortable at the thought of wanting to be respected and admired, for, increasingly, researchers are concluding that this urge relates more to the need to accomplish high goals than to ego gratification (McClelland, 1975).

People want to agree with and to follow charismatic leaders who establish a public presence, and they may twist their own logic to agree with the charismatic leader's position. Followers defend a charismatic leader when he or she is not present and take strong exception to those who unfairly criticize the leader. (Some "friends" won't do that.) People who follow charismatic leaders are convinced that things will get better, whatever the present condition, and they always feel better about themselves (French and Snyder, 1959).

The most effective leader combines charismatic power with expert power from a legitimate power base, adding carefully measured portions of reward power and little or no coercive power. For their part, the followers subordinate their own interests to those expressed by the charismatic leader. This creates a symbiotic relationship in which followers work to bring the visions of the leader into existence. The personal influence coming from charismatic power both complements and exceeds the impression made by position, rewards, penalties, and expertise.

Indeed, charisma can often produce results without calling upon other more common methods of power. Most people want to cooperate and to be part of an exciting and potentially significant activity. They seek a mission in life beyond their personal dreams. The leader who takes advantage of all the dimensions of rational charisma provides this mission. The duration of effective leadership depends almost exclusively upon the leader's ability to use charismatic power (Falbo, 1957).

Effective leadership is always rooted in charismatic qualities rather than in other leadership forms or in more traditional factors. For example, Smith (1982) identified a group of 30 leaders regarded as "charismatic" and a control group of 30 leaders who were not regarded as such. The charismatic leaders generated greater worker productivity from subordinates who worked longer hours. Particularly interesting, however, is the controlled laboratory experiment undertaken by Howell (1985), who compared the effects of three different types of leadership (charismatic, structuring, considerate) on worker productivity. Charismatic leaders generated the most productivity among their workers, both when coworkers encouraged and discouraged each other. In general, empirical research reveals that top performing managers in any occupation are more frequently viewed as charismatic. These results are consistent with Bass' (1990) observation that "Charismatic leaders inspire and excite their employees with the idea that they may be able to accomplish great things with extra effort."

A superficial examination of charisma has led some to conclude that charisma can be effective only when a more intelligent leader interacts with a less intelligent group of followers. Not so. Charisma is a vital constituent part of leadership, both among highly educated groups and peers, as well as among the less educated. Although groups of people with complex personalities change leaders more often, sophisticated people are just as prone to succumb to the appeal of power figures as others (Schroder, Streuferet, and Welden, 1964). In fact, they will often go to ridiculous lengths to gain the acceptance of such leaders (Hurwitz, Zander, and Hymovitch, 1953; Jones and Jones, 1964) and sometimes behave like school children when in the presence of charismatic athletes and politicians. Further, even other high-status figures cooperate with, and become followers of, the charismatic leader (Slusher, Rose, and Roering, 1978).

The leader can dramatically increase his or her influence by recognizing and responding to the fact that people are attracted to those with power. Followers are especially loyal if association with a perceived authority figure seems to offer a chance to enhance their own reputation or status. A wise leader provides opportunities for reputation building and the empowerment of others (Kanter, 1983).

The leader is more easily perceived as charismatic when viewed from a more distant vantage point (Hollander, 1978), such as a podium, stage, or movie screen. Charismatic influence and a developed public presence are more effective in structured than in unstructured situations (Cohen, 1953,1959). In unstructured settings, attractive personal qualities are less likely to influence behavior (Godfrey, Fiedler, and Hall, 1959). Structure firmly sets limits and priorities and establishes positions, thus further reinforcing the importance of legitimate power to the leader. These are optimum conditions for the leader, within which he or she can act familiarly with followers without compromising the position of authority. Structures, however, should come before familiarity, and even then familiarity should be limited. Power is structurally determined, but also affected by the leader's capacity to convince followers of his or her value and importance. The charismatic leader who inspires trust and confidence makes other people feel valuable as well (Pfeffer, 1981).

An imprecise mission gives a leader a comparatively high degree of influence and control over group behavior (Smith, 1982). Under these conditions, even if the leader fails to achieve specific goals, people become more accepting, display higher satisfaction, and maintain support for the leader. Vague but lofty goals are good insurance for the leader.

The application of these general principles to the college presidency is interesting and direct. A president of a well-established institution with a clearly identified mission has more difficulty becoming a transforming, charismatic leader than a president of a less prestigious, amorphous institution with a less well-defined identity. The presidencies of institutions such as Yale University, Oberlin College, and Stanford University are highly prestigious positions and provide their incumbents with a bully pulpit. But, prestigious institutions with enviable past histories also carry with them a great inertia that presents profound difficulties to a leader who wishes to change directions. As Henry Rosovsky (1990) put it, "Harvard's past can be a burden or an inspiration." Individuals who aspire to be transformational presidents and leave their marks on their institutions are well advised to consider colleges and universities without well-established missions; these more flexible and ambiguous situations allow a charismatic leader to exercise the most influence.

In any situation, outstanding leaders are considered persons of great vision. People are more likely to feel comfortable and rewarded, and be supportive if they perceive the leader as both important and somewhat mysterious. Measurable goals and specific objectives should be subordinate to the quest to be effective and to articulate an achievable and empowering vision (Kotter, 1982, 1988). The effective leader approaches the job with overall ideas and high goals, rather than concrete plans.

These, then, are the five power forms of the effective leader: coercive, reward, legitimate, expert, and referent or charismatic. Effective leadership is totally dependent on the extent to which the leader understands, develops, and astutely uses a sensitive combination of these power forms. The greatest of these is charisma, the ability to develop a public presence that inspires trust and confidence. A charismatic presence can best be developed from a strong base of legitimate and expert power. The charismatic leader always makes the most of position and never stops learning the trade.

THE DEVELOPMENT OF CHARISMA

Despite popular opinion, charisma and public presence are neither genetic nor intuitive, but simply the ability to inspire trust and confidence. Bass, in his authoritative *Bass and Stogdill's Handbook of Leadership* (1990), concludes that charismatic behavior can be taught and learned and public presence developed. Anyone of reasonable intelligence and high motivation can develop charismatic characteristics. Age, gender, race, height, weight, and other obvious personal characteristics have little or nothing to do with the ability to develop and use charismatic influence. Virtually anyone of reasonable intelligence and strong motivation can accomplish it.

Many factors contribute to charisma: sincerity, appearance, focus, confidence, wisdom, courage, sensitivity, discipline, vision, reliability, and strength. After reviewing almost every published study on the subject, we conclude that these traits fall under three principal categories: distance, personal style, and perceived self-confidence. The most clearly documentable of the categories is distance, specifically social distance.

THE IMPORTANCE OF SOCIAL DISTANCE

Although distance[5] may seem an uncomfortable concept at first, this most certain requirement for charisma becomes more acceptable as it is better understood. Day-to-day intimacy destroys illusions and makes charisma more difficult to establish at the lower level of most organizations. The man or woman immediately above, with whom you work and talk every day, may have many strengths, but frequent contact obscures strengths, emphasizes weaknesses, and obliterates charismatic impressions. That is why a leader's closest associates offer the greatest test of leadership.

The leader tries to appear on important occasions and to be present often, but briefly, in the workplace. The leader shows up for celebrations and, in times of sadness, knows where the coffeepots are, but doesn't stay too long anyplace. The leader always remains sufficiently remote and doesn't let modesty, fear of embarrassment, or naiveté get in the way of accomplishing the mission.

Some would-be leaders, particularly those in large and complex organizations, may allow the bureaucracy (or whatever the "system" is called) to overwhelm them. If they are unwilling to rise above those structures, they become little more than coordinators who dare to work only at the fringes of their organizations. Indeed, some in higher education (Cohen and March, 1986; Birnbaum, 1992) believe that this is all a college president can really do. March (1980), one of the strongest exponents of this view, suggests that college presidents are "interchangeable," somewhat "like light bulbs." Presidents who view themselves in this fashion may survive, but they rarely succeed, for their activities evince a self-fulfilling prophecy—they feel that real leadership is impossible in large universities. Exactly the opposite is true. Effective leadership is both easier and of longer duration in large organizations than in small ones.

Arthur Schlesinger (1959) and Richard Neustadt (1960) have discussed this problem in their analyses of the U.S. presidency. Both used Franklin Roosevelt as an example of a president who would not allow himself to become captive to the complexity of the office. Roosevelt was close enough to the group to permit personal identification but sufficiently removed to be perceived as mystical. He perceived himself as a superior and inspiring figure. This mystical quality encourages those being led to attach to the leader.

---

[5]Distance, taken to the extreme as a personal lifestyle, can lead to serious problems. But no research concludes that too much distance is a problem for people who want to be leaders. While many effective leaders are considered overly remote and distant, this condition almost invariably helps the leader, who can then demonstrate unusual humanness by occasional forays into the open. Too many exposures, however, make the leader overly familiar to those he or she would lead.

Some find the concept of distance distasteful. Anyone deliberately using such a stance for personal advantage might seem calculating, even dishonest. How can it be right to be less than open, less than completely honest? Aren't trust and confidence rooted in complete revelation and the exchange of intimate feelings? The answer to these questions is no, not if you want to lead and inspire others. Think of the good relationship between parent and child, teacher and student, religious leader and congregation, or even between intimate friends. Think of the priest who is warm and friendly, but always remains the priest. Think of those countless relationships that bind human beings together and that involve and even depend on "distance."

Leaders who admit full personal parity with those they are to lead invite uncertainty, anxiety, confusion, and often chaos. Families, nations, congregations, companies, and classrooms have been devastated for want of respect. Respect must be earned, but is also a product of values and tradition, and is best sustained through distance. A parent, teacher, or any leader must maintain enough closeness to promote understanding, but enough distance to be respected. Psychological distance on the part of a college president may result in a certain degree of necessary loneliness (Kerr and Gade, 1986).

Familiarity often breeds unproductive controversy. Distance is essential, for it allows those at the various levels in an organization to maintain reasonable order and ensure progress. The effective charismatic leader maintains optimal psychological distance from subordinates. The leader is neither close enough to be hampered by undue emotional ties nor so distant that emotional contact is lost. The leader must find the proper balance. Most leaders are more likely to be overly familiar rather than too distant. The leader should initiate the drive for familiarity, always keeping in mind that familiarity breeds debate, questions, doubts, and reservations. Leaders are essentially no different from followers, and they should never think otherwise. A good example of this point is a religious leader. One minor lapse in conduct can jeopardize such a person's image as a moral, thoughtful, and controlled leader. Successful leaders will not allow an office to be devalued, either by themselves or by others. If anyone else exceeds the bounds of propriety in the presence of such a person, the demeanor of the effective leader abruptly negates this depreciation.

High-status people in close association with others in their organization tend to compromise the stated goals of their organization more readily than others: the higher the office, the more likely the leader is to compromise (Mills, 1953). Authority figures who yield too readily to their group are more likely to be exploited by the group (Swingle, 1970). The leader should maintain psychological distance from the members of the group. Nice guys, at least to the degree that they compromise their office, do finish last. The idea of consensus or collegial leadership in this light is ludicrous, particularly during times of conflict and tension.

Distance has been a characteristic of effective leaders throughout history; such distancing need not be dishonest or unethical. Unless the leader is absolutely, unimpeachably wonderful (and who is?), he or she should not establish intimate relationships with members of the affected organization. Of course, some leaders will always be tempted to test this precept, and they will be exceedingly fortunate if those relationships don't come back to haunt them.

Distance means being open, but always remote. Distance is having a close associate, who has known you for ten years and would say, "Yes, he's my best friend and I would do virtually anything for him, but I can't say that I completely know him."

Distance is recognizing that a leader is no longer "one of the boys or girls." It is being a friendly presence: warm and genuine, concerned and interested, but rarely around too long and rarely getting too involved. Distance recognizes and uses the trappings of office, adjusting them only to suit the personality and sophistication of the audience or constituency. Distance balances remoteness with familiarity. The effective leader appears both exceedingly mysterious and utterly known. Distance involves being warm and attentive, open and casual, but never, never getting off the leadership platform with anyone the leader expects to influence.

Pulitzer Prize-winning historian Barbara Tuchman (1971) aptly illustrated the essence of distance and mystique in her description of General "Vinegar Joe" Stilwell of World War II fame. General Stilwell found time to eat periodic meals in the enlisted men's mess, talk for a few moments with the soldiers, and then, with a flourish, leave. This gave him instant credibility with enlisted men, but in no way compromised his authority or presence. Indeed, it contributed to the sense of mystery about Stilwell and enhanced his charisma. College presidents who occasionally play basketball with the undergraduates (perhaps having strategically leaked this event ahead of time), or who every now and then join their employees in raking the leaves or checking out books in the library, have mastered the lesson that Stilwell understood instinctively.

As long as the leader realizes that he or she is not really any different, except in perspective, from anyone else, distance will not become arrogance. From time to time, aware leaders laugh at the reassuring thought that they are personally insignificant. There is also a practical reason for this: The leader who takes the image too seriously or becomes self-serving will soon be found out and become less effective. In time, this leader will lose the most vital element in charismatic influence: the trust and confidence of followers. A lack of sincerity or commitment invariably shows itself to others.

If the leader loses interest in the job, then he or she should leave. The greater the effort to conceal the truth, the more transparent the lie. The greater the need to fabricate, the less attention given to nonverbal clues that are the first sign of the faltering leader.

The connecting force between the leader and the followers is an emotionally charged relationship. Leaders are idealized as those whose strength enables them to assume the responsibility for their followers. Who else can better devise solutions and direction? Even the most sophisticated followers may deny that leaders experience doubts, insecurities, or weaknesses. Followers react to their leaders' human foibles with disbelief, astonishment, dismay, and even anger. It is as if they were saying, "If you are not totally dependable, then you may not be dependable at all." Effective leaders may safely drop their reserve only with intimates who accept their humanness and who have no motive for placing them in idealized positions or roles of omnipotence.

The empirical evidence in favor of the concept of appropriate distance is not extensive, but has gradually accumulated over the past four decades. Shepherd and Weschler (1955) found psychological distance to be positively correlated with the ability of individuals to communicate. Seeman (1960) examined the effectiveness of school principals and found that teachers viewed more distant principals to be more effective. A degree of social distance increases worker productivity because it reduces extraneous interactions.

Vision is also a key characteristic of the effective leader and a valuable dimension of social distance. Vision is having and holding a goal, a commitment, even a dream that is greater than the organization itself, and possessing certain ideas about how the dream can be achieved. Several years ago, Father Theodore Hesburgh, president emeritus of the University of Notre Dame, was named the most effective college president in the U.S. When a USA Today reporter asked him "Why?," Father Hesburgh (after first asking for a recount) paused and answered simply, "The vision." Indeed, no single characteristic is so common in outstanding leaders.

The effective leader sustains the vision and does not allow it to be swallowed up by time and specific plans. When associates begin to lose sight of the vision and get caught in the corporate maze, the leader must raise their sights. The dream must always be there first; specifics will evolve, but they only serve to accomplish the dream.

RESEARCH SUPPORTS SOCIAL DISTANCE

Numerous studies and reports demonstrate the value of both social and psychological distance in effective leadership (Fiedler, 1967; Fiedler, O'Brien, and Ilgen, 1969; Hill, 1969; Hunt, 1967; Julian, 1964; Pfeffer, 1981; and Burns, 1978). All support the hypothesis that social distance relates positively to productivity when distance is defined as above and is not synonymous with leadership withdrawal.

Blau and Scott (1962) and others have concluded that distance between leader and followers strengthens group ties. Burke's 1965 research found that high-need achievement followers with low social-distance leaders rate their situations as more tense, regardless of the nature of the task. Stogdill then presents 21 studies demonstrating that psychological distance between leader and followers increases group productivity (Rubin and Goldman, 1968). Later, Bass (1981) further confirmed Stogdill's (1974) conclusions. Productivity is higher under leaders who maintain social and psychological distance between themselves and their followers.

As early as 1955, Shepherd and Weschler found that distance between the leader and followers resulted in fewer communication difficulties. When leaders worked side by side with subordinates, particularly in formal organizations, there were greater communication problems. Even authoritarian leaders who are relatively distant are more influential than others. Thiagarajan and Deep (1970) studied three types of leaders—authoritarian, persuasive, and participative—and found authoritarians were most powerful and participative leaders least powerful. Groups follow leaders who have a combination of a sense of office and a persuasive style. Followers gain security when they are associated with a strong leader. Individuals are conditioned to respond to clearly defined roles.

Despite this evidence, there are still skeptics. A distinguished college president described an earlier book on this subject by Dr. Fisher (1984) as "fascinating, and instructive but somewhat perverse." She did not seem to acknowledge the research premise for the assumption, an understandable misconception. The notion of distance may constitute an uncomfortable premise, but it should not be abandoned easily. Others mistakenly generalize about charisma in its most extreme forms (e.g., Rev. Jim Jones, the

Ayatollah Khomeini). They bring the entire concept into question and dramatically reduce the acceptability of this power form.

People perform more effectively when they like and esteem their leaders. Esteem for the leader is more likely to produce high performance among followers than the followers' esteem for each other. Followers like to be liked by high-status figures and will use subtle ingratiation techniques (Jones, Gergen, Gumpert, and Thibaut, 1965).

The higher the perceived status (legitimate power) of the leader, the more likely the group is to revere and accept him or her. Thus, status differences lead to psychological and social distance (Bass, 1981). A little self-disclosure by a leader will likely do more harm than good. For example, researchers have found that when people of presumed high status offer personal anecdotes, they compromise their status and reduce their leadership effectiveness. We expect our leaders to be superhuman, to be far superior to the rest of us. All would-be leaders should remember this, but not take it personally.

Seeman (1960) found that when public school teachers rate their principals high in status and perceive wide differences between their own status and that of the principal, they tend to like the principals and to rate them high in leader effectiveness. Scott's (1956) research suggests that effective leadership and achievement of distance are best accomplished when leaders operate less extensively throughout the organization, yet retain final authority. The leader should be everywhere and nowhere.

PERSONAL STYLE AND CHARISMA

Style distinguishes a leader from the pack, but without making the leader unique. Because its effectiveness is less well documented than the effectiveness of distance, style is a more debatable characteristic. Style can combine many things: energy, visibility, decision making, humor, trust, integrity, dress, appearance, speech patterns, and personal habits. Style is that fortifying inner sense that allows the leader to be individualistic. Above all else, it does not pander to every popular appetite and fancy, or attempt to be all things to all people.

Pliny the Elder, in talking about his fellow Romans, observed that there were "no two. . .who cannot be distinguished from each other" (Kerr and Gade, 1986). The same applies to effective managers and leaders. Management styles differ between and among effective managers even while their success invariably (and sometimes unknowingly) hinges upon the five sources of power that we have outlined above. Evidence suggests that many women and African-American managers may pursue management styles that differ somewhat from those of many Caucasian men (Cheng, 1988; Bensimon, 1989; Uhlir, 1989; Morrison and Von Glinow, 1990; Astin and Leland, 1991; Hackman, Furniss, Hills, and Peterson, 1992; Lipman-Blumen, 1992; Offerman and Beil, 1992; Posner and Kouzes, 1993). We will explore these differences in a later chapter. However, these differences in style reflect nothing more than alternate routes to the establishment of charisma, expertise, and other sources of power. They represent variations on the basic model, not contradictions of it.

With great legitimate power, a person can convincingly affect almost any style, regardless of how singular. For instance, very wealthy or high-status people can often get away with peculiarities in behavior or dress; distinguished professional/author/artist types may do the same. But, these peculiarities apply less often to successful college presidents or corporate and political leaders. Exceptions may include leaders of long tenure and exceptional accomplishment and leaders who operate in geographically unique locales. For example, were the President of the University of Hawaii to appear in a dark Brooks Brothers suit at many events, he or she soon would be regarded as strange by some and out of touch by nearly all.

Dress is an important component of style. When in doubt, the college president should dress at least as well and as formally as the regional business leaders do. While American business dress has become less formal and regimented in recent years, the college president who dresses down risks forfeiture of some authority.

Effective leaders comport themselves as if they have high energy. Boundless energy, limitless enthusiasm, and persistent dedication enable others to embrace the dream. Unfortunately, most effective leaders marry their vision and thus spend inordinate amounts of time either working or thinking about their responsibilities. Herman Wells (1980), former president of Indiana University, wrote, "My whole being was concentrated on this work; yet. . .it was so challenging that extraordinary effort was not only possible but exhilarating. The refreshment received in turning from project to project dispelled the tedium." Wells was a bachelor, and it is worth noting that other presidents have jeopardized their health and their marriages with such a commitment.

The effective leader usually adopts a visible style. On occasion, this style is refreshingly distinctive. An example is Benjamin Wheeler, president of the University of California at the turn of the century, who often rode his white horse around the campus to see what was going on and to talk with students and faculty. In a more modern context, Peters and Waterman

(1982) refer to visibility as "management by walking around." Mortimer and McConnell (1978) write that in colleges and universities "Unseen administrators will only become targets of anger and hostility in crises, because unfamiliarity (of this kind) breeds contempt." Cox (1985) goes even further, saying that would-be leaders who stay in their offices are "making a work style decision that is personally stultifying and harmful to the enterprise." While written communications can often be effective, the effective president must not allow paper communication to substitute for personal contact.

Conversely, numerous writers, including psychologists, have cautioned the leader to keep in check the desire for personal recognition (Astin and Scherrei, 1980; Birnbaum, 1988; Dressel, 1981; McClelland and Burnham, 1976). Birnbaum advises the "cybernetic" leader to be modest (p. 200). The visibility of the leader must serve the best interests of the mission and not the individual. The leader will know when the line is crossed. The visible leader not only shares the credit, granting the greater portion to others, but shares visibility as well.

Effective leaders recognize that visibility enhances their effectiveness and engenders confidence in both their institutions and themselves as leaders. They sense when to be seen and when to maintain a low profile. They also know that in acknowledging others, they enhance their own images, develop constituent loyalty, and, most importantly, more nearly accomplish the mission.

As the research on social distance indicates, the leader has warm, but not intimate, relationships with a large number of people. He or she is concerned about the worth and dignity of each individual. In higher education, the effective president is "people oriented, caring, supportive, and nurturing" (Gilley et al., 1986). Cox (1985) writes that "warmth is not only the province of the do-gooders and the naive, but also of top executives who are [successful]." The successful leader "sees the best in his people not the worst; he's not a scapegoat hunter" (Walker, 1979).

The effective leader has superb communication skills. In his pioneering piece on the college presidency, Thwing (1926) writes extensively about good interpersonal and communication skills: "The president should be free from cantankerousness, have tact, and should emphasize the merit of associates." A number of writers in higher education emphasize accessibility and listening as key elements in leadership style (Birnbaum, 1988; Dressel, 1981; Green, 1988; Townsend, 1985; Vaughn, 1989).

The charismatic leader acts out of informed insight. While not quick to make decisions, the leader is a bold decision-maker. Although recognizing the need for long-range planning, the charismatic leader does not allow the vision to get bogged down in planning for the future. This leader is more interested in inspiring consensus than in measuring—a very different approach from that of the uncertain leader[6] (Bennis, 1989a and b; Bennis and Nanus, 1985; Kotter, 1982; Peters and Austin, 1985; Peters and Waterman, 1982; Townsend, 1985). Bennis and Nanus (1985) say it well: "Effective leadership takes risks—it innovates, challenging and changing the basic metabolism of the organizational culture." Peters and Austin (1985) note that the leader is characterized by "hanging on after others have gotten bored or given up." Whetton (1984) calls risk taking "aggressive opportunism." At some point, the leader must be ready to "jump-start the future" (Nanus, 1992), especially when others grow timid.

Bass (1985) speaks of the transformational leader who "is less willing to be satisfied with partial solutions or to accept the status quo." The inspirational leader will press for what is right or good, not necessarily what is popular, or acceptable according to the established wisdom of the time.

The charismatic leader is both trusting and trustworthy. Gardner (1986) emphatically calls for leaders to build trust within their organizations. Fairness is perhaps the most important condition of trust and must be considered with every decision. Leaders use a kind of "ethical" integrity and honesty to build trust throughout the organization (Wenrich, 1985). They couple all this with a healthy and spontaneous sense of humor. They do not take themselves too seriously, at least not for long. When they do, they are able to laugh at themselves.

Effective leaders in business, industry, or higher education believe in and use shared decision making. They believe that things are better when those affected by decisions have a voice in their making. While retaining final authority, they use this authority gently.

Effective leaders give specific orders and tell people precisely what to do less often than many would believe (Kotter, 1987). Leaders set overall goals and inspire, delegate, and truly listen to the people in their organization, often counting subordinates' opinions more important than their own (Peters and Austin, 1985). They are politically astute, pragmatic, and skillful bargainers (Whetton and Cameron, 1985). Shared decision making is not necessarily collegial or consensus decision making, for in any effective

---

[6]Notwithstanding this general truth, effective leaders may find that a certain amount of precise measurement, perhaps performed by others, usually is a prerequisite for expert knowledge and power.

organization, lines of responsibility, authority, and accountability must be maintained.

Dress and appearance enhance style. In most corporate settings, including higher education institutions, conservative dress appropriate to the occasion is important. In the usual business situation, men should wear three-button navy blue or black sack suits with cuffs, accompanied by black shoes, white cotton shirts, and refined ties that do not detract from their leadership aura. Except in more relaxed social situations and unusual geographic locations, male leaders should avoid sport coats. Women should wear business suits and tasteful dresses, and generally avoid leather, exceptionally bright colors, large collars, and gaudy jewelry.

Such prescriptions concerning clothing strike some as the essence of superficiality. Perhaps. However, why jeopardize something as important as accomplishing the mission for something as easily corrected as clothing? The key is to dress for the situation. Clothing appropriate for attending basketball games and student art shows, or for competing on the tennis court, is not suitable for business leadership situations because it becomes the subject of conversation and thereby detracts from the president's message. The president who dresses conservatively and with impeccable taste will be accepted in any boardroom or country or university club, as well as at any social or professional function. As Demerath, Stephens, and Taylor (1967) succinctly put it, a president is expected to "look like a president."

PERCEIVED SELF-CONFIDENCE AND CHARISMA

Perceived self-confidence, another quality of the charismatic leader (Bass, 1981; McClelland, 1970), is conveyed through comportment, speech, and personal mannerisms, as well as through the decisions the leader makes. While self-confidence implies respect for others, it also conveys an unequivocal strength of purpose and conviction.

Effective leaders are so self-confident that they are willing to appoint as close associates those who are superior to them. One of the notable failings of unsuccessful presidents is their tendency to appoint to key positions sycophants or individuals much less talented than the president—individuals who have little ability to mold, enhance, question, or challenge presidential views. However, leaders can benefit mightily from astute associates who (in private) help the leader refine, test, and buttress his or her grand

and confident generalizations. Like the little boy in the fable, these colleagues must be accorded the ability to say to the president, "The Emperor has no clothes." Such candor must be cultivated in associates, and no doubt on occasion can be counterproductive, but also can save a president from egregious and embarrassing errors.

However, wise leaders always remember that they hold the ultimate responsibility. The leader is in charge and should never permit the clarifying discussions he or she has with advisors to become excuses for the leader's own inadequacies and unwise decisions. Scapegoating of associates has a durable history and can be traced back at least to Leviticus in the Old Testament; however, it brings no honor to a president who relies upon it to avoid responsibility.

Charismatic leaders have a positive self-image that grants greater self-confidence. This sense of self-worth engenders respect for others and allows leaders to care deeply about others because they care for themselves. Father Hesburgh (1979) noted that "self-confidence enables college presidents to stand alone rather than being drawn into the group." Self-confidence also allows the leader to maintain social distance and to tolerate the "real loneliness of high position" (Greenleaf, 1977).

Few leaders achieve the image of self-confidence by chance. Bass (1985) points out that effective leaders "engage in impression management to bolster their image of confidence, increasing competence, and faith in them" (p. 40). He also notes that effective leaders are wonderful actors who know that they are always on stage and perform accordingly.

Bennis and Nanus (1985) report that effective leaders "don't think about failure, don't even use the word" (p. 70). Whetton and Cameron (1985) agree that leaders concentrate on winning, that they have an "inoculation theory" against failure and are less threatened by its prospect.

Great leaders typically are not the most modest people, and their actions may reinforce their own self-interests more often than they readily admit. However, their self-confidence is not based on self-worship, arrogance, or coldness. Indeed, the leader will constantly behave in terms of the best interest of the overarching mission of the institution.

OTHER CHARISMATIC INFLUENCES

Other psychological factors may affect charisma. Katz (1973) discusses leaders who are charismatic because they become magical symbols of the solutions that followers want to solve internal conflicts. Followers can perceive a leader as having attributes that can advance their own particular interests. A defensive charisma not only depends on lofty goals, but continues (or replicates) dependence on a parent. The two conditions necessary for this identification are the parent figure's overwhelming power and the inability of the follower to escape the exercise of that power.

Each of these psychological factors, especially the first two (being perceived as a magical symbol or seeming to advance the interests of the followers), are products of the leader's effective use of distance, style, and perceived self-confidence. They enable the leader to symbolize hope and advance the interests of the people.

DIMINISHING CHARISMA

Charismatic qualities diminish with time. The leadership role becomes increasingly difficult for many reasons. Familiarity with colleagues almost inevitably increases as time passes. Most leaders, even those who know better, cannot maintain indefinitely the distance necessary for maximum leadership effectiveness. Time and experience reduce the mystique. As people come to know their leader, they find a reflection of their own doubts, uncertainties, and limitations. Although they like the person more, they admire the leader less and are likely to be less supportive.

A leader appointed from outside the organization develops charismatic qualities more easily than one appointed from within. Outsiders have a better chance of becoming long-tenured leaders. This is not to say that organizations should always go outside for leadership, but unless someone from within is truly exceptional, it is not a bad idea.

While there are a few exceptions, 7 to 10 years in a particular office is about the maximum term for effectively exerting charismatic power. Contrary to popular belief, the smaller and less complex the organization, the more difficult it is to maintain charisma. People come to know their leader more easily in these situations. While there are noteworthy exceptions to the 10-year rule, the wise leader rarely gambles on the odds. Typically, after 7 to 10 years, the charismatic leader must rely increasingly on expertise, which is not taken as seriously as earlier in his or her tenure.

Many leaders who have passed their peak effectiveness rely on legitimate or coercive power instead. They merely give orders that may be increasingly disobeyed. As a result, they often resign or are forced out of office. This is unfortunate because it compromises their earlier charismatic record. Once charisma is lost or on the wane in a particular setting, regaining it in that setting is almost impossible. The wise leader makes plans to move on before the glow is gone. A charismatic leader can move to another setting and start over again, following one success with another. When the leader has a genuine interest in the next position, he or she can be even more effective.

Charisma is the most significant form of leadership. What the astute leader does, to the extent possible, is gain each of the other leadership forms (expertise, legitimacy, reward, and coercive) and from that base apply the characteristics of charisma. Charisma is developed in the same way a virtuoso plays an instrument—thoughtfully, gently, intelligently, yet enthusiastically.

IMPLICATIONS FOR TRANSACTIONAL VERSUS TRANSFORMATIONAL LEADERSHIP

We believe that the literature on leadership developed by others supports our view that charismatic leaders—who also evince expert power and have been granted legitimacy—are the most effective leaders. We grant that the notion of transactional leadership holds sway in many minds as the "best" kind of leadership because it conforms with many individuals' ideas of proper democratic, participative organizational behavior. Transactional leadership is entirely appropriate for many situations in life. An aspiring transformational leader may ruin the local Lions Club or neighborhood civic league if he or she strays far from the traditional role of chairperson and vote taker.

Yet, challenging times are not surmounted by transactional leaders who, as Birnbaum puts it, emphasize the means rather than the ends—the process rather than the results. The literature tells us that change and visible progress require charismatic leadership that is dynamic and risk-taking in approach. Yes, Franklin Delano Roosevelt and Winston Churchill (both charismatic, successful leaders) were elected, but only the most naive among us would contend that they were as interchangeable as light bulbs and that other transactional, "follow the public" substitute leaders would have done as well.

FINAL THOUGHTS

In the next chapter, we will survey the best empirical evidence on the nature of effective presidents. The reader will note that the characteristics reported there (taken from the first systematic empirical study of the effective college president) are remarkably similar to the research discussed in this chapter.

CHAPTER
three
· · · · · · · ·

Systematic Evidence
on the Effective
College President

The President's hardest task is not to do what is right, but to know what is right.

Lyndon B. Johnson, 1964

The word "now" is like a bomb through the window, and it ticks.

Arthur Miller, in *After the Fall*

Bennis and Nanus noted in 1985 that there is relatively little agreement on what distinguishes effective leaders from ineffective leaders. That judgment rings especially true for college presidents. Only two significant studies of the behavior of college presidents exist. The first, by Cohen and March (1986), is based upon their analysis of the characteristics, attitudes, and work habits of 42 college presidents in the 1970s and early 1980s. Although their sample was small, Cohen and March were seeking the "average" president. Their work on how presidents allocate their time, even inside a given day or week, continues to have relevance today, for they apply rigorous statistical techniques, including multidimensional scaling, to their sample in order to draw inferences.

Our interest is focused much less upon the characteristics of college presidents in general (for example, how long they serve), and much more upon the behavior of effective presidents. We want to compare that behavior with a control group of presidents who are perceived to be ineffective. The only comprehensive, published, replicable study to do this was performed by Fisher, Tack, and Wheeler (1988). Some may quibble with our reliance upon this study as a major empirical plank to support our argument for the transformational president. After all, might not another study alter these findings? Perhaps. The Fisher, Tack, and Wheeler study is, however, the current state of the science insofar as empirical evidence concerning effective presidencies is concerned. Although anecdotes can be helpful in illustrating a point, this study is not anecdotal, but replicable; it uses appropriate statistical methodology and yields results consistent with the leadership principles developed in the previous chapter. Hence, we will devote this chapter to reporting the results of this study, which to some are startling, even counterintuitive.

We invite, even challenge, others to make rigorous, replicable, statistically sound contributions in the future to this relatively sparse empirical literature. Fisher, Tack, and Wheeler's study represents the first step, not the last step, in our march to learn more about what it takes to be an effective college president.

THE FISHER, TACK, AND WHEELER STUDY

In conducting the largest systematic, replicable, scientific study of the effective college presidency, James Fisher, Martha Tack, and Karen Wheeler (1988) were greatly helped by a previous study conducted by George Pruitt (1974). Although countless observers and researchers had previously reported on the model or typical college president, and others had written about presidential styles, Fisher, Tack, and Wheeler were unconvinced that those efforts gave a helpful representation of the effective president. Indeed, the contrary might be the case if the average became the standard. Armed with a grant from the Exxon Education Foundation, they directed their three-year study toward *effective* presidents rather than typical presidents. Precisely what, they asked, was *different* about effective presidents?

Fisher, Tack and Wheeler found that the effective president was different from the kind of person normally appointed by a governing board to a college presidency. The effective president holds a different kind of leadership philosophy. *The effective president is a strong, caring, action-oriented visionary who acts out of educated intuition. He or she is transformational rather than transactional and less collegial and more willing to take risks than the usual president.*

The Methodology

Initially, Fisher, Tack, and Wheeler identified a cadre of effective college presidents by asking 485 individuals familiar with higher education which presidents they believed to be most effective. Four hundred of these randomly selected "experts" were themselves college presidents. This process identified about 15 percent of the 2,800 presidents in the U.S. as effective. These effective presidents, along with a control group of other presidents not perceived to be especially effective, completed a questionnaire designed to ascertain their attitudes and behaviors concerning the college presidency and their campuses. The differences between the two groups (the effective presidents and the control group) were statistically significant.[1]

The Findings: A Summary

Fisher, Tack, and Wheeler's challenging findings can be summarized. Effective college presidents, relative to others, were

- less collegial and more distant.
- more inclined to rely upon respect than affiliation.
- more inclined to take risks.
- more committed to an ideal or a vision than to an institution.
- more inclined to support merit pay.
- more thoughtful, shrewd, and calculating than spontaneous.
- more likely to work long hours.
- more supportive of organizational flexibility.
- more experienced.
- more frequently published.

---

[1]Fisher, Tack, and Wheeler used a variety of statistical tests including ANOVA, t-tests, and Chi-square tests to examine the differences and relationships between and among variables. Only differences that were statistically significant at the 5 percent level were considered pivotal in terms of their analysis.

Why So Few? A Short Digression

Why are there so few effective presidents in higher education today? The primary reason seems to be that a number of forces currently at play make it easier to be a "headman," as Cowley (1980) termed it, than to be a leader. In other words, it is easier and safer to keep the lid on things than to stir them up.

These forces include the popular position that truly effective leadership is in effect when consensus consistently reigns (Parks, 1986), when everyone in the organization is happily involved, and when decisions invariably reflect the views of the majority. When consensus reigns, there are no serious problems. Under a consensus condition, how could a generally poor situation be improved? This question addresses the generally lamentable condition of general education today.

During the course of more than 200 consultations, Fisher, Tack, and Wheeler found that over-reliance by governing boards and presidents on popular rule and well-meaning, but misguided notions about collegiality had led to a dramatic reduction in the ability of the appointed president to lead. Additionally, they found a significant decline in both institutional morale and effectiveness.

As noted above, a number of writers maintain that the solution to the problems in higher education lies in decision making based on a consensus born of collegiality (Birnbaum, 1988, 1992; Epstein, 1974; Green, 1988; Parks, 1986; Walker, 1979). We agree that collegial leaders are readily accepted during periods of relative prosperity,[2] and that the collegial model more closely comports with usual notions of how affairs should be conducted on a college campus. However, during difficult times, collegial presidents tend to be ineffective. As one president put it, "When things get tough, the first one to go is the good collegial president."

Additional Discussion

Fisher, Tack, and Wheeler found that effective college presidents not only retain final authority and make hard decisions, but also support, praise, challenge, and encourage creativity (even contrary opinion), and are committed to participatory (shared) governance. To a much greater extent than the typical president, the effective president attempts to empower others. Based on these premises, the argument that an effective president

---

[2]Even then, however, it helps if the institution enjoys financial stability, which usually implies a sizable endowment.

cannot empower others *and* support shared governance is simply not true. Being an effective president is not "an either/or situation." During challenging times, others can rarely be empowered without strong leadership.

The history of higher education proves the point. At the fledgling University of Paris, unrestrained faculty power resulted in such chaos that the government finally assumed control. Later, at Oxford and Cambridge, only royal courts could sway these institutions dominated by senior faculty. Today, you need only review a few issues of the *Chronicle of Higher Education* to find features about inviolate faculty interests and an unresponsive curriculum.

Drucker (1954) concludes that, in the broader corporate world, every attempt at worker ownership of business over the past 150 years has failed. In higher education, the New School for Social Research tried to operate without a president for several years and eventually gave it up the plan as unworkable. And, the New School faculty was more united than most by their past experiences and common ideals.

Fisher, Tack, and Wheeler also found that effective presidents are greater risk-takers than their representative counterparts. They are not reckless; rather, they act out of informed insight rather than rigidly from documented strategic plans. They identify opportunities, analyze the information at hand, consult others, and then make a decision. They are willing to take prudent or calculated risks again and again in order to retain momentum.

However, as the people interviewed commented, in taking risks and making decisions, these presidents are not trying to play God. Effective presidents recognize that other people's lives and professions are at stake. They do not want to appear callous or to make decisions without careful consideration. They review all the variables before deciding which direction they will take. Once the decision is made, they use carefully selected language to convey it to others enthusiastically.

Effective presidents are strategists who think carefully about what they say and do. They do not speak extemporaneously as frequently as do their representative counterparts. They do not often engage in verbal exchanges and brainstorming sessions with members of their community. However, they encourage controversy and broad discussion.

Time and again, the 18 presidents actually interviewed in the study emphasized their belief that the effective president must have control over his or her emotions, actions, and words. They seemed to feel that someone was always observing, or even analyzing, their performance as president. Although no differences emerged from the study in the way presidents approach the management of their "image," effective presidents tend to be more concerned than other presidents about the messages they send to others. In essence, effective presidents believe an "aura" and a public presence are essential to effective leadership.

Effective presidents respect administrative structure, but do not feel as bound by it as others. They believe in a hierarchy and a chain of command to facilitate the smooth operation of the institution, but they refuse to be boxed in by organizational constraints. Those who work with such leaders soon learn that these presidents are likely to appear anywhere at any time.

How do these presidents feel about their institutions? In addition to being committed to their work (in fact, it is often difficult to distinguish the presidency from the person), effective presidents believe more strongly in the mission than in the institution itself. They candidly define the institution in terms of the mission.

Effective presidents value strategic and long-range planning, but they clearly believe more strongly in the power of ideas and vision. While they work hard to see that their colleges and universities succeed, both in terms of a high-quality academic reputation and responsiveness to societal needs, effective presidents see their institutions as part of a larger society with broader goals. For these individuals, the dream of what might be is always alive; their institutions are vehicles for achieving this dream. In fact, in this context, they sometimes make decisions that are not in the immediate best interest of their institutions.

The Effective College President and Social Relationships

When Fisher, Tack, and Wheeler looked at the human relations aspect of leadership, they found no overt differences in presidential behaviors—most presidents possess finely honed human relations skills. However, in social situations, effective college presidents relate to, and think about, others in dramatically differing ways from representative presidents.

As noted previously, self-confidence and risk taking seem essential to successful leadership. *Effective presidents confirm this, being more likely than their representative counterparts to believe that respect is more important than collegiality or popularity.* This is consistent with McClellan and Burnham's (1976) research in the broader leadership arena, in which they conclude that effective leaders are more concerned with results than with either affiliation or personal recognition.

This critical attitudinal difference exists because of the interactive nature of these important attributes: commitment to a lofty goal, an overwhelmingly clear vision for the future, competence, and the leader's confidence in his or her ability to lead. Father Theodore Hesburgh (1988), former president of Notre Dame and the most frequently named effective president, says, "Leadership is . . . not for one requiring praise and moral support. The leader gives these; he or she cannot count on getting them. The leader's task is to realize the vision in its totality; his or her reward is to see that happen."

While both effective and representative presidents respect the rights and opinions of others, effective presidents are more inclined to encourage staff and faculty to take risks, to think differently, to be creative, and to share their thoughts, no matter how diverse. Effective presidents seem willing to meet almost any test in the conviction that their vision will be enhanced. Moreover, these presidents try to surround themselves with exceedingly able people who are futurists and often unconventional. Effective presidents actively solicit input from constituents.

The interviewed presidents were more prone to support and encourage creative and reflective thought, even though they knew these ideas might be in conflict with their own views. They were willing to take a more tortuous course and to make controversial decisions because they believed that broad community respect and support could be achieved through this process.

Although completely contrary to conventional wisdom in higher education, effective presidents are not as constrained by consensus when making decisions as are representative presidents. Indeed, the effective presidents interviewed believed less in the importance of trying to achieve consensus than did all the other chief executive officers studied. In no way does this finding suggest that effective presidents exist in isolation; rather, they actively seek input from those who will be directly affected by the decision. They encourage the creation of mechanisms to provide this input. Effective presidents will make the hard decisions and, if need be, move against the winds of consensus, always trying to regain support.

A good example of the willingness of effective presidents to move against the mainstream is their support for the controversial idea of merit pay. Effective presidents believe more strongly in this concept than do those in the representative group. While effective presidents agree that money is not really a primary motivator, they recognize the importance of communicating to those who are the most productive that their efforts are appreciated. Although most believe merit pay to be subjective and controversial, effective presidents are more willing to take a stand on measuring an elusive excellence. They often campaign actively for the recognition of meritorious service.

These presidents are willing to make hard decisions, risk momentary disfavor, and move forward because of one key attitude: as presidents, they do not believe in close collegial relationships to the extent that representative presidents do. Most effective presidents believe intimate friendships with those they would lead are virtually impossible. We speculate that this is because of the constraints such friendships can place on the leader's ability to make, or to be perceived as making, unbiased decisions.

Presidents need to maintain social and psychological distance in order to enhance respect and appreciation. While honest debate is essential, familiarity breeds unproductive discussions. Effective leaders balance distance and privacy with closeness and familiarity. They lead warmly, with care and respect, but always from their presidential positions. As long as they are presidents, they do not try to pretend they are not.

Effective presidents use their positions with finesse. They are not always driven by the desire for personal recognition or popularity, nor are they bent on being kings or queens. Rather, they have their sights set on greater goals and work as intelligently as they can in order to achieve them. Although their leadership behaviors and attitudes may sometimes be misunderstood, they are almost invariably respected, though not necessarily regarded as friends.

The interviewed presidents said they were genuinely concerned about the welfare of those with whom they work, but they believed they must be willing to say "no" to serve the greater goals. Nonetheless, effective presidents also believe that when they have to use their presidential power to compel people to do something, they often lose a part of their ability to lead effectively. Therefore, they make every effort to achieve support and to depersonalize decisions.

Especially effective chief executive officers also believed strongly that they should often be out front and visible and that, in all but a few institutions, presidential visibility is necessary to advance the cause. These same presidents believe fervently in sharing the credit for success with others, including staff and faculty.

In summary, particularly effective, high-profile college presidents appear to be more confident and more willing to take risks, even when their personal welfare is involved. They are distant rather than collegial; they speak spontaneously less often than other presidents; and, they make hard, often controversial, decisions. Yet, they have a profound respect for, and appreciation of, the role of others (including faculty) in decision making. They have a greater sense of where higher education fits in the scheme of things, and they are able to represent their goals and values effectively (and they repeat them frequently before all constituencies). Their lofty aspirations for the enterprise and for their institutions push them to accomplish their goals. They feel that they are competent managers, intuitive decision-makers when necessary (though they respect data), and entrepreneurs.

FINAL THOUGHTS

In 1988, Davis concluded, "Where the president once was accorded a modicum of differential respect, he/she is now a public figure and fair game for [all]." We believe that the position of the college president must be strengthened and restored to some sense of legitimacy if we really expect any positive and lasting advances to be made in postsecondary education (Fisher, 1984; Kerr, 1984; Kerr and Gade, 1986). We feel that this view of the presidency in no way requires compromising the historic and important concept of shared governance (see Chapter 8).

The findings of the Fisher-Tack-Wheeler study are critical to such a development in several ways. First, the presidents thought to be effective usually are transformational, not transactional in their approach—these individuals are no mere vote takers and interchangeable light bulbs.

Second, those who aspire to become a president, or those boards who wish to select a successful president, would be well advised to heed this evidence. As Kerr's (1984) study concluded, too often the person selected to serve as the college president is the one to whom no one strongly objects. In view of Fisher, Tack, and Wheeler's findings, this is a revealing and sad commentary about the way we select the individuals who are to lead our institutions. The president to whom no one objects is less likely to be regarded as effective. Fisher, Tack, and Wheeler observe that "potential candidates for presidencies will be able to assess their own leadership behaviors to decide whether they approximate the newly established profile of the effective college president."

Third, effective presidents are more inclined to be risk-takers, tend to be less collegial and more socially distant, and seem more willing to swim against the stream than other presidents. They are highly visible and have cultivated a public presence, but usually are not social intimates with many, if any, individuals on their campuses. They give strong support and feedback to their administrative colleagues, and demand accountability.

Fourth, Fisher, Tack, and Wheeler find that effective presidents focus more upon higher education issues in general than upon parochial single campus issues. This does not imply that effective presidents are out of touch with their home campuses; rather, it means they are more likely to discern longer term trends, are less likely to be caught unawares by emerging national issues and needs, and are more likely to walk slightly ahead of the curve. Their campuses benefit as a result.

Fifth, Fisher, Tack, and Wheeler assert that many of the leadership behaviors associated with effective presidents can be learned. Even charisma, in the form of established public presence and power, can be increased by learned behaviors. This is not to say that all effective presidential behaviors can be learned, or all ineffective behaviors unlearned. It does suggest, however, that an astute president is capable of improving his or her performance. That is good news for all.

PART
2

Presidential
Characteristics:
Further Reflections

CHAPTER
four
•••••••

Charisma, Public Presence, and the Transformational President

The power which erring men call chance.

John Milton

Charisma is that wonderful quality of being taken more seriously than you deserve.

Kenneth Shaw

Because of the requisites of leadership and the limits that boards, bureaucrats, laws, and academic tradition have placed on presidential power, a president is well advised to consider various means of increasing his or her charismatic influence and public presence. Indeed, in many settings, these are literally all the president has. The president is expected to lead thousands with little but an ability to inspire confidence, trust, and hope.

Commitment, sincerity, goodness, and caring are at the core of any effort to increase charismatic influence. Unsuccessful presidents fail mainly from an inability to get outside themselves. Without these human qualities, a quest for charisma can become a transparent exercise in vanity.

THE PRESIDENT'S VISION

Unless the president articulates a special vision, mission, or cause for the institution, he or she will not be viewed as a true leader. A mission is grand and all-embracing, and includes lofty, humanistic concepts like peace, progress, freedom, and the welfare of the community and greater public, as well as the special mission for the institution. Do not be afraid to dream and to share that dream—it will even inspire you. Lofty and sometimes vague goals promote morale and leadership effectiveness, so long as the goals are legitimate and progress toward their achievement is made. George Gallup observed that "People tend to judge a man by his goals, by what he's trying to do, and not necessarily by what he accomplished or how well he succeeds" (Edelman, 1964). Pruitt's (1974) important study comparing effective with typical college and university presidents concluded that the former had a "mission" or "vision" that seemed to radiate from them.

Although important for all, a special presidential vision is especially important for small, liberal arts colleges and regional public institutions (two- and four-year). Within such situations, people need a more significant collective identity and a sense of pride that inspires both new heights and sacrifices for a greater common cause.

The president who appears to have achieved a personal integration with a higher purpose and can articulate it for others will become a charismatic figure (Katz, 1973). Father Hesburgh has written about the mission of an institution as follows (Fisher, 1980):

> The most important contribution a president can make to institutional advancement is to articulate his vision of the institution so persistently and persuasively that it becomes shared by all constituencies, internal and external, who adopt it as their own. Whatever else he is clear and enthusiastic about, the president must most of all elaborate his specific vision, rethink it as times change, perfect it as he learns from experience, and make his contribution to an evolving sense of institutional purpose.

Your vision should consider the desires and the nature of both external and internal constituents.

> We will become the finest institution of our kind in America, an institution whose faculty members truly care about students and their dreams, an institution that will nurture and provide opportunities for free and full expression . . . that will significantly contribute to enabling our society to realize its ultimate potential.

Remember, this is the time to dream.

Not infrequently, the presidential vision is confused with a more prosaic long-range plan and specific goals involving faculty, administrative staff, and students. No one becomes excited about a detailed 120-page strategic plan. It is fine to put together a planning group as a follow-up activity, but its precursor and inspiration should be the president's concise, exciting mission statement, stating his or her personal vision for the institution and its people. Initially, an informal refinement of these aspirations for close and valued associates is appropriate, but the public announcement should not be the product of a committee or any other campus group—it should be the president's.

The dream should be repeated on every possible occasion, to remind both the president and the campus. And, once the mission is determined, it should not change dramatically. People can absorb only so many dreams and so much inspiration. Although the president may tire of repeating the vision, the campus and the greater community will not tire of hearing it so long as its presentation is reasonable, sincere, and accomplished.

DON'T TAKE YOUR MYTH SERIOUSLY

Assuming that these things are done well, a legend or myth soon begins to grow around the president. The myth is the license to continue providing the inspiration needed to fulfill the president's high expectations for everyone on campus, including him or herself. By becoming hostage to extraordinary goals, everyone will achieve more than they—or the president—ever expected. People outside the institution will begin to expect exceptional, even impossible, things, but the president will often accomplish them. The myth, of course, will be bigger than the real people or institution; the myth can grow so long as the president does not take it seriously or accept it as fact.

The words of Dag Hammarskjold (1965) seem appropriate at this point:

> Around a man who has been pushed into the limelight, a legend begins to grow as it does around a dead man. But a dead man is in no danger of yielding to the temptation to accept his legend as reality. I pity the man who falls in love with his image as it is drawn by public opinion.

The fabric of the myth will be the impressions of the people the president would lead and influence, reflecting their dreams, hopes, and aspirations also. They provide the moral rationale for continued strength and progress.

ACT LIKE THE PRESIDENT

The charismatic president acts like a president. This is difficult, for most of us are never sure that we are worthy of the office, and sometimes convinced that we are not. In earlier days, before social mobility in the United States, many presidents were literally born to office and could be more comfortably impervious to their own limitations. As we have seen, effective leaders are self-confident, have an evident sense of identity and personal style, and understand that organizational structure contributes to effective leadership. The president carries the office and its trappings with assurance, neither apologetically nor with condescension. A matter-of-fact attitude and unspoken confidence toward personal accomplishments and attributes, and a forgiving spirit toward petty criticisms should characterize the president. The little things that are often uncomfortable to do, matter; for example, it is often a good idea to move about with an assistant who handles details and to allow your news and publications personnel to put your best foot forward with the media by means of well-devised advance materials.

The modest response to those who address the president by title, "Just call me Bob or Jane," is not always appropriate. A modest "Aw shucks" attitude should not be carried too far. The key is to be warm, kind, beneficent, and even a bit folksy while firmly situated on the presidential platform; remember, never get off that platform.

SPEAKING ENGAGEMENTS AND CEREMONIES

Take advantage of, and plan for, speaking engagements and ceremonies. To do otherwise is amateur theater. While the purpose is to impress the audience, the greater goal is to enhance the presidency and the special mission of the institution. Ceremonies provide occasions to mobilize support and quiet opposition (Pfeffer, 1981). Even the physical settings for appearances are important (Peters, 1978). The size, location, and configuration of the physical space provide the backdrop against which the president makes the presentation and thereby influence its interpretation and effects. Whether the occasion is a faculty meeting or a commencement, reverberations from any ceremony should be positive; as long as any president is in office, he or she is the institution, in spite of personal modesty or collegial inclinations. Remember that a leader's influence is significantly based on the group's acceptance of some kind of code or standard (French and Raven, 1959). Few things reinforce academic traditions more effectively than ceremonies and sensitively planned presentations on campus.

Do not accept all speaking engagements on campus. This insures that the president will stay in demand for years, and that the extent of his or her off-campus activities will be recognized. What most students and faculty really mean when they say, "We wish we could see more of the president," is that they really need a president and that they appreciate the president's off-campus activities on their behalf (Benezet, Katz, and Magnussen, 1981). Overexposure can be killing.

A brief but impressive introduction prepared by the president's assistant or public-relations officer can be helpful, especially to those who must introduce you at a Rotary or Kiwanis Club. (Pomposity is also out; Mr. or Madam President is not appropriate.) But, however well the audience knows the president, an introduction is important. According to recent studies in forensics, an impressive talk should begin behind an elevated rostrum located several yards from the audience. Later, to move from behind the rostrum is a gesture of warmth and informality. Some professors are absolute masters of this technique. Presentations in halls that can barely contain the crowd traditionally have worked for politicians, and they also generally work for presidents.

Any speech should begin with brief remarks about the state of the college or university and how that relates to the president's (and their) special mission or vision; the president is always the president, even if the subject is ornithology, and both the speaker and the audience need to be reminded of that fact. The special mission of the president's administration should, whenever appropriate, be kept before the community.

Question-and-answer periods after such formal presentations as a "State of the University" address are usually a bad idea. A preferable alternative is to adjourn the meeting, mingle with the crowd, and answer individual questions in individual conversations. This practice permits the speaker to be open and interested in reactions, but avoids the possibility of contrary and distracting speeches from the audience. The president can no longer enjoy the luxury of spontaneous brilliance or foolishness.

In other, less formal arenas, especially talented presidents can use question-and-answer sessions after speeches as an opportunity to demonstrate their expertise. The traditional question-and-answer session after a speech to a Rotary Club provides such an opportunity. Another example, especially important to a college presidency, is when the president meets with representative campus organizations, such as the faculty, student, and staff senates. These groups expect to ask the president questions, and the president who fails to entertain at least some questions will soon attain (and deserve) the reputation of being unapproachable. (This reputation is especially damning on campuses where financial retrenchment is occurring.)

Carefully orchestrated question-and-answer sessions can be particularly useful when they are preceded by the presentation of information or data that effectively answers or even quashes what might otherwise be antagonistic questions. But, beware! When you venture into an unstructured format, you risk being ambushed and misinterpreted. Only an exceptionally skilled and well-informed president can survive repeated free-for-all encounters. This is yet another reason why the president should not attend, and speak at, every meeting of the faculty senate.

In any case, good presidential speeches are interesting, informative, and, most of all, inspiring. Speeches to be delivered to large audiences or important groups should be written out. This shows seriousness about the occasion, prevents misstatements, and makes it easy to distribute copies to faculty, staff, students, and the media. If the president is a poor speaker, lessons are in order.

Although most campus appearances are relatively informal, more traditional, formal ceremonies can lend much to the presidential aura. The president should always deliver a brief and inspiring message at any ceremonial function on campus. The president's legitimate power can be augmented by traditional academic ceremonies and should be used. The trappings of office—a presidential chain and medal, distinctive though not gaudy presidential cap and gown, a mace carried by an associate—are important elements in formal ceremonies and should not be ignored.

Ceremonies like inaugurals, commencements, installations, orientations, and even banquets should be professionally and carefully arranged to enhance the presidency; the more medieval pageantry, the better. Ward off pressures to simplify or democratize these programs excessively; all kinds of unselfish reasons can be cited, such as authorities who indicate that ceremonies and tradition build morale and increase alumni loyalty and support for the institution. The distance that diffident yet dramatic flair can give is crucial.

In retrospect, most presidents wish that they had given more thoughtful attention to their inauguration. Inaugurals are excellent occasions to solidify and institutionalize presidential power. The inauguration can include an investiture ritual that further ratifies the importance of the office. These occasions almost automatically attract media attention and are an important way to broadcast the president's vision. Wide attendance at the inauguration, if it can be arranged without the appearance of authoritarianism, is valuable. Take pains to attract as many students, faculty members, trustees, legislators, and influential community leaders as possible.

For commencements, usually only flagship schools are able to arrange a "name" commencement speaker. This is all the better; the president can be the speaker. If you have an outside speaker, always send informational materials about the institution and, most particularly, your last state-of-the-institution address. The discerning speaker will always want to include local color (and perhaps even compliments) in an address and should be encouraged to do so. In any case, the commencement program should always include a brief president's charge to the graduates. If the president is not especially creative, an assistant or public relations officer can come up with a helpful draft for use at campus ceremonies. The chief academic officer or another vice president or staff member, never the president, should preside; the president should be introduced for a brief inspiring message.

THE LEGITIMATE ADVERSARY

Identifying a legitimate off-campus adversary or issue around which to rally the campus can give the president's standing a special boost. We must emphasize that the key word is *legitimate*. A legitimate controversy unites the campus and lessens the natural inclination to throw rocks at the president when local problems inevitably occur. The external issue must relate to achieving the objectives of members of the campus community (Katz, 1973). When an issue begins to wear thin, find another. If the issue is legitimate, do not be overly concerned about offending off-campus power forces. In the final analysis, the most important constituency for a college president is the campus—faculty, students, and staff.

In the process of meeting an issue, an inspiring rationale for the president's action and plans is essential. A ringing call for continued support and commitment as well as a candid, honest confirmation of legitimate and formidable off-campus opposition should issue from the president's office. Neither indictments nor criticism of individuals are wise; they insure permanent enemies and color the president's image with pettiness. When you take issue, take issue with questionable ideas, practices, concepts, and institutions—not with individuals. Never attack individuals, even when they attack you.

Katz (1973) provides an interesting discussion on the value of an inspiring rationale and the use of an external adversary in his comparison of two American presidents, Franklin D. Roosevelt and Harry S. Truman. Both espoused the cause of the common people vigorously and built effective links with them. Truman did not take the process far beyond simply creating the links. The common man believed that Truman genuinely represented the people's interests, but was himself a common man. "In Roosevelt, however, we had a leader whose power in the eyes of the people to achieve great things was almost unlimited" (Katz, 1973). Why? For one thing, he understood how to disseminate his vision for the country; for another, he understood organizations. He granted federal agencies sufficiently overlapping responsibility and appointed strong personalities as agency heads. This allowed him to be the natural arbiter and ultimate decision maker. Also, the events of the Great Depression and World War II further encouraged the people to regard him as a charismatic figure.

OTHER ADVERSARIES

There are always those who are waiting for the president to fail. This is only natural; front runners are watched and criticized as well as admired and envied (MacEoin, 1976). Some in the wings would like to replace the actor on center stage, or, at the very least, to see the actor displaced. Any advocate of change, at least initially, loses the support of representatives of the established order; in time, detractors will literally have no choice in the matter, and many will become enthusiastic supporters.

Open adversaries will be far easier to handle than more subtle denigrators—"friends" such as less successful college presidents, a few trustees, most politicians, some staff, and any others competing for attention in the same arena. They envy success and anyone who appears to do things more quickly or more effectively than themselves. Not infrequently, they are individuals who aspired to the presidency, a vice presidency, or a deanship, but were not selected. These are the people, usually quintessential long-term insiders, who will say, "It takes a while," or, "Be very careful before you act," or, "It's best not to rock the boat," or, "If you take the king's gold, you are the king's man." They will always counsel moderation and inaction and will invariably recommend a "cooperative" style as the best way to change and improve conditions. They will extol more "effective communication" as the key to better times. (Not that anyone really knows for sure what "more effective communication" is, or how people who achieve such a grand condition actually feel.) Of course, better communication is important, both on- and off-campus, but be wary of those who speak of it constantly.

In time, an effective president who does not overly personalize conflict will find most enemies deciding to become allies; some may even become fast and staunch supporters. In one instance, a state budget analyst for higher education who had initially turned livid at the very mention of the name of an assertive state university president, later became so enthusiastic that he taught part time on the university faculty and donated his entire salary to the university foundation—and urged the president to run for governor. Patience usually will win them over eventually, and on your terms.

DEMAGOGUES, ZEALOTS, AND MARTYRS

Beware of demagogues, zealots, and martyrs. Such people invariably inflict as much harm on their friends as on their opponents. Unless they are completely in violation of institutional policy or laws, grant them their missionary activities. They will gain some temporary support, but, unless there is absolutely no acceptable alternative, provoking or engaging them in debate is a mistake, for they usually have nothing to lose. With neither respect for authority nor appreciation for charisma, true zealots are beyond rational discussion. Issues are often only pretexts for recognition. They will seek to take everything anyone has to offer and demand more, and, in the end, can completely undermine the president's authority.

Ignore zealots if possible; if not, shunt them off on an associate whom you can later protect. If all else fails and their popular support is gaining, an insignificant issue can be granted to them, allowing the president to earn the support of the greater public so long as the move does not appear to be made out of weakness. However, if it is not possible to disarm zealots, ignore them, even when their demagoguery sorely tries your patience. The public will react negatively to a president who brutally squashes a zealous gadfly, even an uninformed one.

Certain overly zealous and parochial trustees are also best given a wide berth, particularly when they become energetic proponents of a single issue, for example, establishing a football team, eliminating all courses that might suggest global warming is occurring, or prohibiting speakers who argue the question of whether or not there is a large genetic basis to intelligence. (Each of these examples represents a real life campus occurrence.) Such individuals must be handled with patience and tact, provoking such a trustee openly is usually a mistake. But it is not a mistake to talk with the trustee quietly about the nature of a university and the role of trustees. The most effective work in this regard can be accomplished by other trustees. We discuss these possibilities in greater detail in Chapters 16 and 17.

Threatening to resign when trustees are vexatious and provoking runs the risk of appearing foolish and having your resignation accepted. The president who leaves should do so on his or her own terms. The best way to handle unreachable trustees is, to the extent possible, with polite avoidance; never give up on the prospect of conversation. Behind-the-scenes machinations against them with other trustees will only reduce the president's perceived self-confidence in the eyes of trustees who are supportive. Do not engage in gossip about trustees for any reason.

CONFLICT

Conflict, however, has its value (Katz, 1973; Stogdill, 1974). The very organization of a college or university invites conflict. Contained conflict can inspire healthy competition and produce more impressive results. It allows the president occasionally to redefine the limits of his or her delegates' authority, in the process elevating the presidential office. Perfect harmony is among the first signs of an unhealthy, dying organization, or one so structured that important work cannot be done. With no overlap, there is no tension, and without tension, there is neither movement nor constructive activity—and little need for a president. If the tension is present but in check, and a spirit of cooperation along with a sense of grand mission is instilled, the institution will neither "blow up" nor go to sleep.

OVEREXPOSURE AND COMMITTEE MEETINGS

How the president spends time has an important bearing on his or her charisma. Overexposure can be extremely disadvantageous to a leader's effectiveness. Because of their backgrounds or personal anxiety or both, some presidents seem bent on attending all meetings and representing themselves in virtually all important negotiations. Presidential membership on official committees, whether on- or off-campus, is almost always counterproductive or a waste of time. With precious few exceptions, spending two or three hours in a meeting waiting for a turn to talk cannot be justified. Most damaging, however, is the tendency of participation to turn the president into one of the people he or she is trying to lead, and to reduce the leader's effectiveness and ability to communicate (Shepherd and Weschler, 1955; Carp, Vitola, and McLanathan, 1963).

Excessive participation in meetings and committees also unnecessarily risks the possibility of making unwise statements. Instead, the president should send a trusted and able delegate and stay in touch with the delegate. This practice produces much better results. Although in the beginning people will earnestly press you to be a member of an "important" committee, if you equivocate and later assign a delegate, they will soon desist. Finally, people come to like this system better because it gives everyone on campus someone to petition—you.

THE FUNDAMENTAL IMPORTANCE OF THE PEOPLE

Of course, the foundation of campus charisma is the extent to which the president stays in touch with the people, the campus constituency—students, faculty, and lower-level support staff like housekeepers, cooks, and maintenance workers. These people must know that the president sincerely cares about them and their welfare. Many of these people will continue to support the president enthusiastically, even in the midst of exceedingly controversial activities or mistakes. Weber (1947) wrote of the "magic aura" that people attribute to such leaders, willingly overlooking their personal weaknesses. The leader is one of them, but apart from them, a visible and friendly phantom. Occasionally, the president stops for coffee and personal words about family and friends, but does not dwell upon work or campus politics.

This sense of identification of people with the president can be more important than the actual distribution of rewards and privileges. They know that the president cares and realizes that they are contributing to the institutional mission. The faculty will work harder, their teaching will be of the highest quality, the campus will look better, and the food will be tastier—all delivered with a smile and a sense of purpose. The campus is simply a great place to be, and "the president is the epitome of what a leader should be—"Our President."

Visit every building on campus regularly and know where the departmental coffee pots are. The president should be seen walking around the campus during class breaks, joining students for drinks at the campus social center. (Walk up and ask to join them.) Set aside a time each week for student drop-in office hours, or for taking a continually changing set of students to lunch. Whether enrollment is 500 or 50,000, the president still needs to see students and vice-versa; no business is more pressing. Similarly, it is wise to invite randomly selected groups of faculty to the office occasionally for discussion. The object is to stay in touch.

An ideal way to maintain close constituent relations is to be present during periods of exceptional difficulty or great joy in the lives of faculty, students, or staff. People will always remember that the president attended the wedding of a student. To visit a custodian in the hospital is not only thoughtful and cheering, but will do more to offset ill feelings during periods of contract negotiations than the highest-paid negotiator. These things should be done regularly, not just when your leadership is shaky. To share in the delicious joy of an athletic championship or the birth of a child is a feeling that binds leader and followers together in a way that will insure people's loyalty through minor difficulties and great catastrophes, and will contribute immensely to their confidence. If the president has done his or her job, it will be students and workers—the so-called "little people"— whose support will persist, even when the president has made a mistake, and it is they who will really make the job worthwhile.

Although a community of intellectuals is rarely demonstrative, when the president is in danger or trouble, they will come through in ways that are both reassuring and touching. Students will say, as they did of Robert G. Bone at Illinois State, "If the president knew about that leaky shower, it would be fixed." Faculty will say, as they did of Herman Wells at Indiana, "The president is our voice." Trustees, benefactors, politicians, public figures, bureaucrats, alumni, and parents will respect and admire the president. The media will write and talk about the president. In the process of straining to be what the campus and community think they see, you will become so much more than you thought you could be.

Faculty and staff salaries and benefits warrant a word here. When off-campus or in cloistered board rooms, the temptation to compromise the interests of those on campus is great. It would be easy to give in to the pressures of political expediency voiced by some trustees, public figures, alumni, and, in public institutions, system-wide officers, politicians, and state bureaucrats. But, within reason, the president's job is to take care of the people; if the president says one thing off-campus, and another thing on-campus, then he or she will soon be found out. The president's interests, as well as those of the sponsoring body, are better served if the prime denominator of the institution's health and vitality is specific and measurable (salaries and benefits) as well as the less tangible rewards paid to faculty and staff. The leader who takes care of people will be taken care of, and gladly granted executive privilege.

THE VALUE OF UNIFYING CAMPUSWIDE ACTIVITIES

Honest diversions for faculty and students—sports events, lectures, plays, competitions—are important and healthy and should be fostered by the president. These activities can unify an otherwise divisive campus and defuse pent-up emotion, anger, and threats—the president's, as well as everyone else's. If the number of outlets available is maximized, everyone should have sufficient opportunity to engage in attractive and worthwhile activities. These activities also give people a chance to excel and share the trappings of prestige in constructive ways.

Finally, campuswide activities such as lecture series and concerts can stimulate intellectual life and promote campus pride. Although no president should confuse the appearance of a well-paid nationally prominent lecture on campus with the institution's academic prominence, or the success of its football team with the number of Rhodes Scholarships awarded to its students, campuswide intellectual and athletic activities often provide the president with opportunities to *act as the president*. A discerning president will capitalize upon such events as a means to promote the institution to outside constituencies and to itself.

FINAL THOUGHTS

The most important points to remember from this chapter are the following:

- Have a vision. Stand for something.
- Think, talk, and walk like a president; smile and laugh and be especially nice to the "little" people even though you are harried.
- Get to know the cooks, the custodial force, and the maintenance people. They are the least complicated and most open people on the campus and, in times of difficulty, the most supportive.
- Do not give too many speeches on campus, especially to representative groups such as the faculty senate.
- Accept most reasonable off-campus speaking opportunities, if you have not already addressed the group.
- Be wary of talk shows and talk show hosts. Nonetheless, recognize that these shows generally have many watchers and listeners and their influence has grown tremendously in recent years.
- Zealots are irrational and unafraid; either assign them to someone else or let them run their course.
- Remember that even the most self-righteous are motivated by self-interest.
- Take regular walks around campus.
- Direct your thoughts and control your emotions, but use both.
- Get a personal assistant with whom you can blow off steam.
- Believe in yourself—otherwise no one else can or will.
- Your people rightfully expect you to be strong; never discuss your problems with them.
- Keep your distance.
- A test of whether you are any good is not how you treat the mighty but how you treat those who work for you, especially the most humble.

- If you have to remind people who you are, you are not who you think you are.
- Do not make excuses, and do not make the same mistake twice.
- If possible, take the center seat.
- The president who takes a strong and irrevocably certain position is usually wrong.
- Never admit you are tired except to your secretary, your assistant, and your spouse.

CHAPTER
five
· · · · · · · ·

Gender, Race, and the College Presidency

The best man for the job may be a woman.

Taken from a popular T-shirt

Aunt Jemima and Uncle Tom are dead, their places taken by a group of amazingly well-adjusted young men and women. . .ferociously literate . . .who are never laughed at.

James Baldwin, in *Notes of a Native Son*

One of the most overblown issues in discussions of presidential leadership in American colleges and universities is the influence of gender and race upon presidential performance. Rhetorical flourishes and strongly held biases have substituted for sound, dispassionate analysis of what makes a successful leader.

The truth, however, is that the characteristics of effective leadership are androgynous. Neither men nor women, nor Caucasians, African Americans, Asian Americans, or Hispanics consistently exhibit innate leadership qualities that excel all or any other groups. The major lesson of this review is that the principles of power and leadership can be learned, as can the means for exercising those principles.

Few topics in higher education are more sensitive and explosive than those relating to gender and race. On a typical campus, the mere mention of gender and race (or, the failure to mention them) is sufficient to stimulate emotion-laden hortatory responses that often diminish rather than enhance communication. Thus, it is difficult to discuss gender and race, and how they impact the college presidency, without causing the participants in the discussion to flee to previously held and passionately advocated positions, even when a rational analysis of theory and empirical evidence would suggest a contrary position.

Gender and race sometimes do affect the college presidency, though not necessarily in the preconceived fashion that some individuals believe. Unfortunately, most of those who write and speak on the effects of gender and race on the college presidency miss the point because they are not sufficiently familiar with the theory and empirical evidence that we review in this and previous chapters. Consequently, comparatively few reliable generalizations can be drawn from existing literature. Nonetheless, we can summarize those that are not contradicted by theory or empirical evidence (and preview this chapter) as follows.

First, in most periods and in many situations, it has been unusually challenging for either a sitting president or a presidential aspirant to be female, African American, Asian American, Hispanic, or a member of any other minority group.[1] While this general situation has changed somewhat over time, and many situations are highly idiosyncratic, the popular image of a college president is still usually a Caucasian male. This image, however, reflects in significant part the overwhelmingly high number of Caucasian males in the faculty ranks that eventually feed the presidency, as well as the membership of the governing boards that appoint presidents. As the demographics of these groups change, so will the demographics of the presidency.

Most governing boards, at least ostensibly, seek to appoint and retain a president with a distinctive and captivating vision—someone who is not "run of the mill." In its last review, a board is looking for someone who is both solid and exciting; many would add that they are also seeking someone who is safe. An astute and well-prepared member of a minority group, or a woman, can actually turn such a situation to personal advantage.

Second, sufficient empirical evidence has accumulated for us to conclude that women managers and presidents often have different operating styles than comparable men, and that, with some exceptions, African-American and other minority managers and presidents typically have operating styles comparable to Caucasians.

Third, regardless of any stylistic differences, the qualities that make for effective presidents, whether men or women, are surprisingly invariant. Power, vision, legitimacy, expertise, charisma, distance, public presence,

---

[1]The major exception to this general rule is, of course, the historically black colleges and universities (HBCUs). Today, the appointment of an individual who is not an African American to an HBCU presidency would be highly unusual, so unusual that it has been labeled "mutinous" (Gaither, 1992).

and other essentially transformational qualities do not depend on gender or race, or, for that matter, upon personal beauty. How a particular president develops charisma, cultivates appropriate distance, or articulates a transforming vision mirrors distinctive personalities and styles. To the extent that personality and style subtly reflect gender and race, they will determine the singular way in which each president pursues presidential responsibilities. There is, after all, more than one way to skin a cat. Nonetheless, the fundamental dynamics of leadership do not change because of gender or race. Effective presidents, regardless of style, gender, or race, either understand (or instinctively act as if they understand) the leadership principles that we have developed in previous chapters. Regardless of gender or race, those who understand these principles have a distinct advantage over those who do not.

HISTORIC DISADVANTAGES, OCCASIONAL ADVANTAGES?

For almost 300 years after Harvard College was founded in 1636, few members of a minority group were given serious consideration for a college presidency, much less appointed. Exceptions to this general rule were typically confined to Roman Catholic women's colleges and historically black colleges and universities (HBCUs).

Opposition to the appointment of a member of a minority group (and here we include women in this category even though they now constitute a majority of all students in higher education) has sometimes been open, other times muted and elusive. Yet, few minority presidents won appointment at prestigious, coeducational, racially integrated institutions until the 1970s. Three major arguments surfaced to explain these practices. Some governing boards exhibited reluctance to appoint as president a member of a minority group because they believed that these individuals were generally less talented and perhaps less experienced as well. Others argued that the managerial styles of minority group members are different (and less suitable) than those of Caucasian men. Still others rejected the notion that minority administrators are in any way inferior to Caucasian males in talent, style, or performance, but probably should not be appointed to most presidencies because they would start at a disadvantage.

These circumstances have changed, albeit gradually and unevenly, in recent years. Because the status of each minority group is differentiated, each requires further separate development.

Women

In 1970, only about 6 percent of all college presidents were women and 90 percent of this group consisted of the presidents of Roman Catholic women's colleges. By 1993, however, the percentage had doubled and 12 percent of all American college presidents were women. In the early 1990s, women occupied the presidencies of such prestigious institutions as Chicago, Duke, and Pennsylvania. The percentage continues to increase; of 218 new presidential appointments reported in the *Chronicle of Higher Education* in 1993, 40 (18.4 percent) were women.[2]

Further, the number of women occupying such traditional stepping-stone positions as academic vice president or provost has increased dramatically, indicating that many highly qualified women are in the pipeline. For example, in 1994, both Stanford and California-Berkeley appointed women to their provost position, the second ranking administrative officer in each institution. These women will undoubtedly have the future opportunity to assume the presidency of a prestigious institution, should they so desire.

Women now contend for most presidencies that they deem attractive, although the authors' own experiences suggest that some governing boards are still reluctant to appoint a woman president. Taken collectively, the developments of the last two decades do not constitute a revolution, but do indicate a gradually increasing likelihood that women will be considered on their own merits as presidents or presidential aspirants.

African Americans

The presidential progress of African Americans has been much more limited than that of women. In 1993, less than 5 percent of all American college presidents were African American, a slight increase since 1983. Apart from a few "marquee" exceptions such as Clifton Wharton at Michigan State and SUNY, and John Slaughter at Maryland and Occidental, African-Americans have typically succeeded to the presidencies of the nation's more than 90 HBCUs, plus a few "majority" public institutions located in metropolitan areas with large African American populations (for example, Blenda Wilson at Cal State-Northridge).

---

[2]This number stands in striking comparison to the lack of success of women in attaining presidential-equivalent appointments outside higher education. *Forbes* Magazine's 1994 listing of the largest 800 public corporations revealed that only one of these corporate giants had a woman CEO.

The governing boards of many "majority" colleges and universities remain hesitant to appoint African Americans to presidencies. The "he/she won't be accepted" rationale is paramount here, although racism no doubt continues to rear its ugly head. The political, fund-raising, and alumni responsibilities of a president are most often cited as specific areas where an African-American president might be disadvantaged—an argument that is still raised against some women presidential candidates, regardless of race. Only about 2 percent of "majority" institutions were headed by African-American presidents in 1991. One reason given, among many, for this low percentage is the historically small number of African-American faculty at "majority" institutions; the potential pool of future African-American administrators and presidents is small.[3]

Of course, until the 1960s, a significant segment of American higher education was racially segregated. Flagship state universities and many independent institutions throughout the Old South did not admit African-American students, employed no African-American faculty, and perforce did not have African-American presidents. Indeed, many HBCUs in these states were led by Caucasian men. For African-American women, however, the story was even more confining. Not only were "majority" institutions unwilling to appoint African Americans as presidents, but most HBCUs were unwilling to appoint African-American women as well (Alexander and Scott, 1983; Harvard, 1986). Spelman College, a current pacemaker among "women only" HBCUs, only appointed its first African-American woman president, Johnnetta Cole, in 1987. HBCUs arguably have been more male-dominated than other segments of higher education, although the recent appointments of African-American women at institutions such as Morris Brown, Benedict, and South Carolina State may signal the end of that tradition.

Asian Americans

Few Asian Americans have been appointed to American college presidencies. Among the more visible examples have been the linguist S.I. Hayakawa at San Francisco State (who was appointed in unusual circumstances as an

---

[3]Of course, thousands of African-American faculty members at HBCUs could constitute presidential candidate pools. However, it is extremely difficult for an individual to move from an HBCU to a "majority" institution. One current African-American president of a "majority" institution has noted that she had sought a presidency for many years, unsuccessfully. Finally, after one year's service in a "majority" institution, she suddenly was sought after by search committees.

outgrowth of Vietnam-era campus protests), Bob Suzuki at Cal Poly-Pomona, and Chang-Lin Tien at California-Berkeley. In 1993, none of the 218 presidential appointments reported in the *Chronicle of Higher Education* involved an Asian American, and only 17 colleges had an Asian-American president in 1991 (about .5 percent).

Until recently, few Asian Americans openly aspired to college presidencies. While some impute complex Asian-American cultural characteristics to this deficit of candidates, discrimination against Asian Americans traditionally has been present in American society. In addition, Asian Americans never developed the equivalent of the HBCUs that provided ready germination opportunities for African Americans. The rising number of Asian Americans in the United States, plus their striking success in many professional venues, bodes well for a future upsurge in Asian-American presidents if Asian-American candidates conscientiously pursue the leadership principles outlined in previous chapters. Proportionately, Asian Americans occupy about 10 times as many faculty positions as presidencies, suggesting a large potential pool of presidential aspirants.

Hispanics

Like Asian Americans, Hispanics have seen few of their number appointed to prestigious college presidencies. Tomás Rivera of California-Riverside was a path breaker and perhaps the best known Hispanic president. Lauro Cavazos was president of Texas Tech and became secretary of education under President Reagan. Hispanic presidencies ordinarily have been confined to institutions in the West and Southwest, and to urban areas with large Hispanic populations, such as New York City and Miami. Despite these limitations, the number of Hispanics appointed as presidents rose from 3.3 percent in 1983 to 4.6 percent in 1993. These presidencies are concentrated in California, Florida, Texas, and New York City.

Hispanics, like Asians Americans, have suffered from discrimination and the absence of incubating institutions such as HBCUs. In addition, the supply of Hispanic doctoral recipients traditionally has lagged behind most other minority groups, especially Asian Americans. Consequently, only about 2 percent of all college faculty members were Hispanic in 1991, indicative of a quantitative problem in identifying and developing attractive presidential candidates in the immediate future. Thus, fewer presidential aspirants than one would expect are coming from an ethnic group that now approaches 15 percent of the American population.

Gender and Race as Advantages?

The data cited above show clearly that minority status typically has been disadvantageous for an individual who aspires to be a college president. Nonetheless, some individuals (typically Caucasian males) argue passionately (though usually in private) that they were not appointed to a particular presidency because the governing board preferred to appoint a less qualified member of a minority group. Governing boards, on the other hand, retrospectively justify minority appointments both on the basis of outstanding competence and "good fit" with the institution.

Only the naive among us would deny that many governing boards give consideration to the precise characteristics that they believe will be most effective in the presidents they appoint. While it may be illegal to do so, it seems likely that many governing boards take gender and race into account when they make appointments. The notion of "fit," as well as the composition of the individuals in the selection pool, no doubt have resulted in the preponderance of minority candidates being appointed in metropolitan areas and in distinctive institutions such as Roman Catholic women's colleges and HBCUs.

On occasion, governing boards may wish to "make a statement" and deliberately seek to appoint a member of a minority group as president of a "majority" institution. Or, less dramatically, they may proceed under the assumption that "other things being equal," they would prefer to appoint a member of a minority group as their president. But things are rarely equal; candidates nearly always differentiate themselves during the search and screen process.

Thus, minority status can in some instances actually constitute a telling advantage in a search process in a "majority" institution. Almost 9 out of 10 sitting American college presidents are men, and slightly more than 9 out of 10 are Caucasian. More than 8 out of 10 newly appointed presidents are men, and more than 9 out of 10 fresh appointees are Caucasian. Hence, whatever advantage minority status occasionally confers within a presidential search can be empirically demonstrated to be small.[4] It is one thing to be invited to an interview, and quite another thing to be appointed.

---

[4]Distinguished African Americans such as retired General Colin Powell, former chairman of the Joint Chiefs of Staff, could command many different presidencies throughout the United States. In the eyes of some, however, such individuals can only be appointed because they are "safe" in the eyes of the majority community, having successfully crossed over in their careers.

This means that minority presidential candidates must focus on the search and screen process and how it works. Two things count in a typical search. The first is the credentials and experience of the candidates. Without appropriate credentials and experience, candidates will usually be eliminated well before having the opportunity to impress a search and screen committee. On occasion, a lack of experience may comprise a "Catch 22" circumstance for some minority candidates. Without experience, they cannot be appointed. However, to be appointed, they must have some experience. Many governing boards insist (not without reason) on presidents who have "paid their dues" by serving in a series of increasingly responsible administrative positions. Governing boards that are seeking to fill more attractive presidencies may virtually confine their search to sitting presidents because they wish to appoint an experienced hand with an established, more easily evaluated record. Such preferences work against minority candidates.

The second element of importance in a presidential search is a captivating vision, which must be imparted by the candidate with verve and charisma. This vision must simultaneously speak to the existing circumstances of the institution, but also appear to stretch the institution and stimulate excitement. A candidate must "fit" the situation well, but not too well, for if he/she gives the appearance of being nothing more than a custodian of the status quo, the candidate is unlikely to capture the imagination of the governing board.

Some institutions may be looking for a "break the mold" visionary president who is capable of navigating the increasingly roiled and unpredictable waters of academe. Such a circumstance may favor a minority candidate. The minority candidate who succeeds in convincing the governing board that he or she represents the future (and not the past) is bound to be attractive, perhaps more attractive, than a Caucasian male whose vision lacks sparkle and whose notion of the future involves a continuation of present conditions.

STYLE DIFFERENCES ACROSS RACE AND GENDER

One of the grounds quietly put forward to justify not appointing members of minority groups to college presidencies is that minority administrators in general, and women and African Americans in particular, have managerial styles that differ from those of Caucasian males. The direct implication is that these differing styles, broadly considered, are less productive and less conducive to good management than the styles associated with Caucasian males. Thus, unless minority administrators are willing to acquire and utilize Caucasian male managerial styles, they are more likely to fail.

At least two questions of considerable consequence flow from the above assertions.

- Do the styles of women and minority administrators differ from those of Caucasian males?
- What are the consequences of these findings for presidential effectiveness?

We will address each of these questions in turn.

Differences in Managerial Styles—Women

The preponderance of available evidence suggests that the managerial styles of men and women differ to some degree (Bass, 1990; Eagly, Makjijani, and Klonsky, 1992). The strongest assertions flowing from these studies (Cheng, 1988; Bensimon, 1989; Lipman-Blumen, 1992) suggest that the stereotypic woman administrator is "sensitive," "caring," "compassionate," "responsive," "democratic and participative," "nurturing," and values "commitment and affiliation." Women administrators are said to listen well, have fewer ego problems, be less inclined to protect turf, and have different ways of knowing than men administrators. Most of those studies are not replicable and their conclusions are highly debatable.

The stereotypic male administrator is said to be more "assertive," "dominant," "independent," "competitive," "task-oriented," and "hierarchical" than female managers. Those who speak approvingly of male administrative behavior also note that the stereotypic male manager exudes self-confidence and is particularly well suited to handle financial and construction matters. Male managers are also thought to be more politically astute and convey a greater understanding of the tough decisions and trade-offs that must be made by modern managers.

The problem with these straw women and men is that they bear little relation to reality. They represent exaggerated, charged, and ideologically motivated incantations that are designed to buttress preexisting parochial views of the world. If one's desire is to provide a justification for male managerial dominance, or the necessary vindication for a feminine managerial revolution, then one of these two straw administrators will accomplish that task admirably. But, the sources of managerial (and presidential) effectiveness are in fact essentially androgynous and the effective leader uses (and avoids) several of the styles and characteristics from both managerial stereotypes, although seldom to the exaggerated extent insinuated by the straw women and men.

These stereotypes skirt and even ignore the fundamental sources of leadership and transformational ability: legitimacy, expertise, charisma, distance, and the like. The problem with such caricatures is that the stereotypes divert leaders and college presidents from discussing and understanding the basic sources of power and leadership effectiveness. They cause us to talk around the basic issues, just as much of the received literature on presidential leadership fails to come to grips with fundamental, empirical notions of power, legitimacy, expertise, and charisma. The dominant literature simply ignores these things or dismisses them with easy disdain (Green, 1988).

Bem (1974) first challenged the notion of male versus female leadership characteristics and developed a Sex Role Inventory to determine stereotypic traits. Using Bem's work as a model, researchers have found that effective, transformational leaders exhibit androgynous characteristics that reflect a combination of so-called male and female behaviors. Studies in this genre include Bartol (1974), Bartol and Butterfield (1976), Friesen (1983), Noble (1987), Kapalka and Lachenmeyer (1988), and Hackman, et. al. (1992). These and other studies demonstrate that labelling some behavior "feminine" and other behavior "male" is not useful. Instead, some behaviors contribute to leadership effectiveness and other behaviors do not.

Hence, when Statham (1987) concludes that women administrators (more often than men) attempt to personalize their relationship with those they manage (thus reducing or eliminating "distance"), the lesson is not that women cannot manage. Instead, the lesson is that this behavior is not conducive to long-run managerial effectiveness, whether the manager is male or female.

Leaders, male and female, have a tendency to fall into bad habits. They may become too assertive, critical, or competitive (stereotypic male managerial attributes), or they may avoid decisions or become emotionally involved with those they manage (stereotypic female managerial attributes). The solution is to eliminate or moderate these bad habits and to substitute habits that contribute to greater leadership effectiveness.

Throughout chapters 1 through 4, we have suggested habits, techniques, structures, and styles that enhance leadership effectiveness. These suggestions are based upon leadership theory and replicable empirical evidence rather than a normative rendition of what an ideologue would like to be true. Taken in this light, the differences in style that may exist between men and women administrators are of less importance than whether or not these differences in style contribute to managerial effectiveness. The sources of power and leadership are androgynous and can be used by either men or women. More than one style can be effective, but only if the styles contribute to, rather than debilitate, the basic sources of power and leadership that we have outlined in previous chapters.

Differences in Managerial Styles—African Americans

We cannot say as much as we would prefer about the managerial styles of African-American leaders and college presidents, for little reliable and replicable scientific research has been done on managerial styles. Most discussion of the managerial styles of African-American managers and college presidents is impressionistic and anecdotal (Scott, 1982; Cole, 1984; Hughes, 1988; Bradley, Carey, and Whitaker, 1989; Holmes, 1989; Waters, 1992).[5]

The credible research that is available includes the study by Posner and Kouzes (1993) of more than 35,000 employees and managers, which indicates no substantive differences in the fundamental leadership *practices* of Caucasian and African-American managers. Their methods (styles) of achieving a particular end, however, may differ, as Morrison and Von Glinow (1990) point out.

The majority of African-American college presidents serve at HBCUs. Those African Americans who have served as presidents of "majority" institutions have done so under difficult conditions. From the outset, individuals such as Clifton Wharton and John Slaughter had to deal with the perception that they were "Affirmative Action" appointees, and that absent their race, they would not have been appointed. (Stephen Carter, in his *Reflections of an Affirmative Action Baby*, 1992, aptly describes this phenomenon and its impact upon African Americans.) This perception dogs African-American administrators and faculty members at all levels— are they here because they are good, or simply because of the color of their skin? (Of course, the same question might have been addressed historically to Caucasian members of the academic community who gained positions because of a variety of connections, including race.)

---

[5]There is virtually no evidence dealing with other ethnic minority groups such as Hispanics.

The upshot is that African-American presidents of "majority" institutions constantly toil in the spotlight and arguably must perform above average for a longer period of time in order to avoid the subtle stigma that is associated with "affirmative action" appointees. Some have suggested that, because such presidents are viewed as exemplars and do not wish to fail, they may have a tendency to avoid major risk-taking activities and to moderate or downplay their race in many situations. One of their major tasks is to make the Caucasian power structure comfortable with them. Therefore, they must consider carefully the public messages that they send and the symbolic gestures that they make. The African-American president on a "majority" campus who succeeds at this task is in an enviable position. He or she can develop respect and unite a variety of otherwise divisive communities in ways few others can. Thus, the African-American president of a "majority" institution is especially well advised to take to heart the lessons of leadership and style that we have drawn in the preceding chapters.

Frequently, it is easier for a Caucasian president than an African-American president to develop and pursue campus admissions and employment policies that stress ethnic diversity. The African-American president who does so may well be accused of favoritism and one-sidedness. One is reminded of the long-time foe of the communists, President Richard Nixon, going to the People's Republic of China and supping with Chairman Mao. It would have been difficult and controversial for a political Democrat such as George McGovern, or any Kennedy, to have done so. African-American presidents of "majority" institutions who pursue diversity goals may be wise on occasion to find indirect means to stimulate the accomplishment of these goals, for example, by kindling external mandates from their governing boards, state governments, or (best of all) from a local business community that needs a diverse, well educated labor force.

By contrast, the roles and styles of African Americans who occupy the presidencies of HBCUs are usually quite different. African-American HBCU presidents often are viewed by their campuses as their mediator with, and protector from, the Caucasian power structure. However, many HBCUs have traditionally had many Caucasians on their governing boards and, whether public or independent, have been forced to garner a lion's share of their resources from the Caucasian community. In addition, until recently, most HBCUs have been treated as second- or even third-rate institutions by legislatures, foundations, and monied citizens.

Most HBCUs have been sympathetically regarded by the power structure as socially redeeming enterprises, but usually not as significant institutions capable of producing high-quality graduates, excellent research, and quality advanced professional degrees. And, not infrequently, they have been viewed as being incapable of managing their own affairs, especially financial matters. Therefore, the president of an HBCU must frequently begin with a campaign to change public perception of the contributions of his or her institution.

The HBCU president operating in this milieu walks a thin and fluctuating line, and sometimes exhibits bimodal behavior. The Caucasian power structure (businesses, government, foundations) controls most of the resources and the HBCU president must accommodate the leaders of these groups sufficiently to garner needed resources for the institution. This accommodation requires cultivation of a moderate image, development of the perception of being tightly and efficiently managed, and respect for the traditional academic verities.[6] Among the most successful HBCU presidents to follow this model are Hampton University's William Harvey, under whose tutelage Hampton has flourished in nearly every respect, and Florida A&M's Frederick Humphries, who has been especially successful in enticing national corporations to invest in A&M's highly regarded business school.

On campus, however, and inside the African-American community, the expectations of an HBCU president may be radically different. The Caucasian power structure may be viewed as invasive and oppressive, particularly by some students and faculty, who may relish the sight of the HBCU president "going to war" with the power structure. In this context, the HBCU president is the defender of the campus, its knight in shining armor. Not infrequently, this group of constituents expects the president to chide the power brokers and call them to account, assert institutional and racial independence, and strongly support the development and recognition of African-American culture. Clearly, this more militant role can conflict with the more moderate role of the resource-gatherer who must cultivate the power structure, Caucasian or otherwise. For this reason, some presidents of HBCUs are occasionally seen as speaking with two disparate

---

[6]One HBCU president observed that a much larger proportion of his HBCU presidential colleagues are political Republicans than is true for the African-American population as a whole. Such political identification soothes and reassures the Caucasian power structure, and in certain time periods has led to significant federal largess for selected institutions, even while distressing many on the home campus.

voices—one for their external public and the other for their internal public. To the extent that this perception is real, it highlights one reason why functioning as the president of an HBCU is different—one's life tends to become bifurcated.

The modern HBCU president has much in common with the clergy of African-American churches, not the least because many HBCUs are religiously affiliated. The "pastor" of many African-American churches is a charismatic, strong, and sometimes authoritarian individual who usually inspires great loyalty. His or her words and view of the world are accepted by the congregation, which follows the pastor's lead. This description often doubles for HBCU presidents.

The constituents (including alumni and citizens) of an HBCU president frequently become personally invested in the president. They respect, defend, and advocate him or her to a degree seldom matched for Caucasian presidents. This loyalty, which often extends throughout the entire African-American community, can be used by the HBCU president as a powerful tool for change, if it is mobilized effectively. Thus, HBCU presidents may have fewer resources to work with than Caucasian presidents, but they often have a greater ability to mold those resources and transform their institutions. This ability, whether used for good or for ill, underlines the exciting nature of many HBCU presidencies in the 1990s. If there is any place in academe where a president can make a difference today, it is in an HBCU.

How Different Styles
Influence Presidential Effectiveness

Given that men and women presidents may have different operational styles, what difference does this make? The answer, ultimately, is "not much," unless on a consistent basis those styles are allowed to diminish a president's access to the sources of power and leadership. The analysis of the sources of power and leadership is unaffected by gender and race because those sources are androgynous.

Some writers go so far as to say the female/male dichotomy in managerial styles represents radically different versions of what is important in society. Men and women administrators are not identical in the ways they perform their jobs. Yet, these differences do not change the fundamental sources of power and leadership. Successful presidents continue to be individuals (female or male) who operate from a legitimate base of power, have considerable expertise, and have developed a public presence that enables them to radiate charisma. Whereas a female president may emphasize qualities such as sincerity and sensitivity to generate charisma, a male president may emphasize discipline and reliability to achieve the same. Both Jacqueline Kennedy and George Patton were charismatic.

The key, then, to the question of charisma, is less one of what particular style enables one to be charismatic (for many different styles will do so), and more one of do we understand and appreciate the critical role that charisma plays in leadership. Thus, presidents of either sex must realize that some behaviors tend to diminish charisma. For example, extensive empirical evidence indicates that social distance is perhaps the most important determinant of charisma and transformational qualities. When distance disappears, effectiveness declines. Whether male or female, a president should take this into account in cultivating a style that is both effective and comfortable.

Similarly, an African-American president of an HBCU knows the traditional importance of African-American churches in formulating public opinion and generating support in the African-American community. Thus, an HBCU president may make well-chosen appearances in the pulpits of African-American churches. Analogous behavior by the Caucasian president of a "majority" public institution would more likely spark allegations from faculty and others that the president may be inappropriately mixing church and state.

Another reason to reject the notion that styles are crucial is the tremendous variability in styles inside the ranks of both male and female presidents. The same statement may be said for other minority groups. Consider three charismatic, but stylistically different minority presidents. A charismatic African-American president such as George Pruitt of Thomas Edison State (NJ) does not exhibit the same style as another successful African-American president, Harrison Wilson of Norfolk State, who heads an HBCU. Both of these presidents differ in style from another successful president, Joseph McDonald of Salish-Kootenai Community College, a tribally controlled institution in Montana.

The definitive point is that the gender and race stereotypes that some writers view as significant and profound generally are of marginal importance. A variety of styles are capable of using the fundamental sources of leadership and power. Not all leaders use the same strategies. The detailed strategies that are appropriate in one higher education community may wither like seeds falling on rocks in another situation. For the foreseeable future, however, the cardinal sources of power and leadership will not change, and we must focus upon these as we take the actions necessary to restore the college presidency.

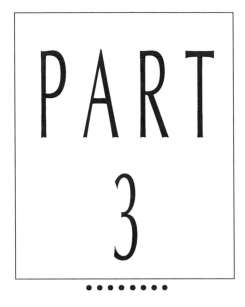

PART
3

Presidential
Constituencies
and Tasks

CHAPTER
six
•••••••

The President,
the Administration,
and the Spouse

The highest proof of virtue is to possess boundless power without abusing it.

Thomas Babington, Lord Macaulay, 1843

Power is pleasure; pleasure sweetens pain.

William Hazlitt, 1826

If you are the wife of the president, you better not have an ego, because you usually are going to be ignored, except when there's a party to be planned. Other than that, you're a fifth wheel.

(Bitter Presidential Wife)

It is not important that my (spouse) be remembered as having served as president, but, rather that the person who led this institution and those who worked here at this time in its history were persons of great faith and courage. I know that I am included in that group of people.

Carolyn Thyreen, Presidential Spouse

The following examination of college and university administration focuses on the research in leadership and power and on the authors' personal experience in the presidency. There are unquestionably other effective organizational, administrative, and presidential styles than those assumed in this chapter, as well as other appropriate applications of the research.

What is unique about this discussion, however, is the deliberate association of research, which has been tested in our personal experience and the experience of others and is presented in that light. This chapter argues that an institution's systems and management structures, no matter how well designed, will not operate as effectively as they should—and may operate disastrously—unless the president knows and appreciates the characteristics and techniques of leadership and power developed in previous chapters.

The leadership vacuum in higher education today may be, as some have suggested, all that can be expected of a society in transition where traditional leadership models are questioned and research on the subject is largely ignored. However, a thesis of this book is that leadership and the attempt to influence are immutable factors in human social behavior, virtually the same in all times and all societies. While the style and superficial characteristics of effective leadership and power wielding may change because cultures and situations vary, the bedrock sources of leadership and power remain essentially the same.

POWER AND THE ADMINISTRATION

Inside the university, substantial legitimate power is usually available to the president with regard to administrative staff, probably the only campus relationship for which this is the case. As we already have seen, reward power and coercive power with administrators are best used infrequently and with surgical precision by the president, and ordinarily should be confined to those who report directly to the president.

The administration should be viewed as mission oriented, dynamic, and enlightened. More than any other segment of the academic community, the administration—under its president's inspired direction—should seem unified. The president's job is always to appear inspired, despite any personal feelings to the contrary—and contrary feelings will emerge at times.

All administrators should be the president's and should be seen that way, for it is through the administration that the president's legitimate authority can be most obviously and effectively conveyed to others outside the administration. Administrators must understand that they work at the pleasure of the president. Administrators should not hold tenure (as administrators), and astute boards do not include them on presidential search committees.

Administrators should be systematically evaluated every two to four years by the president's office, but this process must not convey the message that the administrator is accountable to the evaluators. This mistake can lead to demagogues competing with the president, disloyal or autonomous administrators, and a frustrated president.

Administrators work for, and report to, the president; lines of authority should be clearly defined, with sufficiently overlapping responsibilities to insure that important areas are not overlooked (Burke, 1966; Katz, 1973; Caplow, 1968). Some overlapping in administrative responsibilities also contributes to a productive state of dynamic tension and an occasional opportunity for the president to arbitrate disputes, thus reinforcing the importance of the presidential office. Under optimal conditions, administrators have but three choices: to support the president, change the president's mind, or resign. The president should openly and candidly convey this concept of administration to all administrative officers and the entire campus community, preferably during the first weeks after appointment. While it is more uncomfortable for presidents of some tenure to announce this condition, it nonetheless should be done, but only after giving careful thought to methodology. If a comfortable strategy fails to emerge, announce the policy anyway, and stick to it without slipping back into old patterns of collegiality.

THE HOUSE-APPOINTED OR "INSIDE" PRESIDENT

Vigorously exercising presidential authority, difficult for many presidents, is even more so—and more essential—for persons appointed to the presidency from within an institution. The "inside" presidency is bound to be more challenging because it is so difficult to achieve the distance necessary to exercise charismatic leadership; people know you too well. Many ineffective "house-appointed" presidents would probably have been effective someplace else. Some people can make the transition from faculty or administrative post to the presidency of the same institution, but not many.

The successful emergent, "inside" president is often found in the small private college where a single individual occasionally emerges as an effective leader, a figure around whom virtually all forces of the institution converge and who therefore is uniquely qualified to assume the presidency. If you are this type of president, fine; if not, go back and reread Chapter 2 carefully. Some institutions have consistently pursued a policy of appointing the academic vice president or provost to their presidency. Although there are benefits associated with appointing a "known" quantity and having identified a presidential successor, both the theory and the empirical evidence described in previous chapters question this policy. The new appointee must be exceptionally talented and knowledgeable in order to overcome the lack of distance an insider brings to the position. In such circumstances, being a transformational president is difficult, even though the same individual might easily be transformational at another institution. Most presidents have a better chance if they are appointed from the outside. Although not born to the presidency, at least they do not carry the burden of past intimacies into the president's office.

PRESIDENTIAL ASSOCIATES

No president, even one with a totally captivating vision, can run an institution alone. Every president requires a team of close associates (often with the title of vice president, dean, or assistant to the president) who will implement that vision, assist the president in modifying it as necessary, and provide energy, ideas, moral support, and feedback to the president. The identity, ability, and skills of these team members are critical to the president. They must support the president, complement his or her skills and abilities, and ensure that diverse constituencies are represented and heard. These crucial individuals can ruin an otherwise promising and productive presidency. As Herman Wells of Indiana (1980) once observed, a policy of appointing second- and third-rate people to these vital positions is terribly expensive.

The crucial factor to consider is the president's working relationship with these individuals, whose talent and intelligence often are, at least latently, superior to his or her own. Indeed, presidents should strive to appoint individuals more talented than themselves. To be surrounded by persons of lesser ability or potential is to invite the burden of incompetence and, ultimately, of failure. The temptation is great to play king or queen with people of less ability, but such reigns are usually unsuccessful and short. The president must share the credit for successes, the lion's part, with subordinates, faculty, students, and trustees, and, at the same time, be willing to take virtually all the responsibility for failures. This may not be fair, but it is a must.

During periods of difficulty, associates should be so able that the president seeks their counsel, not out of courtesy but out of respect for their judgment. Indeed, Berkowitz and Daniels (1963) found that if a leader both shares credit for success and conveys his or her dependence on staff, people will admire the leader more and be more productive. Staff produce less and dislike a leader more to the extent to which they are made to feel responsible for failures.

ADMINISTRATIVE ORGANIZATION

A high degree of administrative organization and structure is implicit in nearly every effective presidential style (Burke, 1966; Caplow, 1968). This is especially true for charismatic leaders, since they must maintain a sensitive distance from those they would lead and manage. Ordinarily, a college or university will have three to five line divisions,[1] with the exception of some large and complex multiversities, and the president will have from one to three staff assistants. Only under unusual circumstances should other vice presidents report to an executive vice president (more on this later).

CLOSE ASSOCIATES AND PRESIDENTIAL DISTANCE

To preserve presidential influence and authority, the distance between the president and his or her closest associates should be kept clear. However, not all presidents will follow this advice in all cases, as we have not. Intimacy with close associates invites unproductive tension and can reduce productivity, morale, and admiration for the leader. As already suggested, the president's greatest test is to maintain the leadership role with these associates. They know the president best and so are most likely to exploit that relationship and challenge presidential authority, usually in the name of friendship and support. Associates should feel respectful anxiety toward the president. Neither they nor anyone else on campus should ever know, or even think they know, the president's innermost thoughts.

The day a president starts telling his or her real problems to vice presidents is the day he or she should begin planning to move on. Do not be hesitant to dismiss or reassign someone who persists in closing the distance. If you do not, your presidential territory will soon be completely occupied by your closest confederates—and it will be too late to act.

---

[1]Line officers have other professionals reporting to them; the academic vice president is an example. Staff officers report to line officers and have few or no professionals reporting to them; an example is the president's executive assistant.

SOCIALIZING WITH STAFF

Warmth and consideration should characterize the president's relations with the staff. Rarely is it wise to throw around presidential weight, but when you do, mean it.

Socializing with staff should be restricted to rare occasions. It is not wrong to socialize with staff, but studies clearly demonstrate that too much informal behavior on the part of leaders reduces both their legitimacy and their effectiveness. Where to draw the line is a personal matter, but the natural tendency is to err on the side of the familiar. By rarely extending or accepting purely social invitations, the president will gently discourage overtures. People will not like you less, but respect you more.

Frequently entertaining vice presidents and spouses is a waste both of time and institutional money and will automatically reduce the president's charismatic qualities. Since vice president talk about presidents anyway, why give them more to talk about?

Socializing more with outsiders will increase your effectiveness. This dictum, however, should not discourage cordial relationships with one's immediate staff, but one should always cultivate and maintain appropriate distance.

THE ROLE OF THE SPOUSE

Voltaire, in *Candide*, spoke of the "best of all possible worlds." In such a world, it should not be necessary to broach and discuss the matter of presidential spouses to the extent that we now will do. However, a realistic appraisal of the modern college presidency reveals the following important facts:

1. Most presidents are male and married.
2. On many campuses, a female presidential spouse is expected to support, and even work for, her husband, particularly in making ceremonial appearances and in planning and executing social events.
3. More than one-half of all women presidents do not have a spouse and therefore must answer the potentially delicate question of whether to use a male escort at social events.
4. Male presidential spouses will seldom be expected to plan and execute social events.
5. A woman president, whether or not she has a spouse, must still find a way to plan and execute social events.

There still exists a double standard in much of higher education with respect to presidential spouses. On many campuses, particularly those of smaller size, it continues to be assumed that the president's spouse (when a woman!) will organize and undertake significant social activities on behalf of the institution. When the female spouse is not interested in undertaking these tasks, is not skilled at these tasks, or has her own career that eliminates that possibility, misunderstandings can result. Any new (male) president is well advised to reach an understanding with his governing board about the role of his wife before he assumes office. Otherwise, traditional presumptions may be made by board members, local citizens, and the campus community, and his wife may be expected to "be a part of the team" and actively contribute to the planning and organization of social events in addition to making ceremonial, cameo appearances.

Some presidential wives enjoy the support role they play for their husbands. Many gain a tangible sense of partnership and accomplishment from their collegiate activities. In addition, these spousal activities on behalf of the institution provide common experiential ground for the president and his wife. They have a greater sense of being a "couple," and have a greater ability to converse on familiar topics than many presidential pairs whose professional lives go separate ways. This is important because sometimes only the president's wife has the knowledge and position to act as a confessor, advisor, and dispenser of deserved tributes and brickbats. Few, if any, members of the president's staff can function similarly.

However, many presidential wives bridle at undertaking a support role for the president, not the least because they have their own careers and ambitions, and they see no intrinsic reason why they should assume the role of chattel when their husband is appointed president. While understandable, such a view can result in problems on some campuses if a clear understanding has not been reached beforehand on the role of the spouse.

Should the work a presidential spouse performs, however willingly, be compensated? Some campuses have formally codified such a relationship and have identified the spouse as a paid employee of the institution. In such cases, the spouse cannot gracefully decline to be involved in a social event. And, inevitably, some of the institution's employees will resent the spouse's "interference" and perhaps criticize the spouse's efforts. Some spouses are reluctant to accept a "salary" and would rather see their contribution reflected in the husband's compensation package.

Spouses who are not compensated for their activities (and most are not) sometimes feel exploited and unappreciated. They work hard, but recognition typically focuses only on the president. The presidential spouse who agrees to undertake such activities should understand ahead of time that the rewards are likely to be small, and received vicariously through the president.

Our discussion has thus far assumed the president is a man. However, almost 20 percent of new presidents being appointed today are women, and more than one-half of these do not bring a husband with them to their job. Even when a spouse accompanies the woman president, he is often absorbed in his own career, which he considers to be logically separate from his wife's career. (Some women presidential spouses have had difficulty asserting the independence of their careers, especially in smaller institutions.)

When a spouse (woman or man) declines to undertake social activities with the president, or there is no spouse, who will fill that role? The ideal is for the institution to have funding and courage sufficient to employ an individual who will plan the president's social events. It should not be (but often is) assumed that the presidential spouse will undertake that responsibility. One new woman president in the mountain states employed an individual "to do what presidential wives often do." This staff appointment was greeted with animosity by some members of the public.

Another potentially awkward corner relates to the question of who, if anyone, will accompany a single woman president to college and university events. Nothing requires a single woman president to have an escort to social events. However, some campuses and cities will expect a single woman president to have a consort at certain social events. We can only note there exists an enduring asymmetry with respect to the expected social behavior by men and women college presidents. As a consequence, a woman president may develop a consistent companion who will appear with her at major events, or, she may designate various other male members of the college community to serve periodically in that role. Whatever the solution, it is best arrived at, and understood, by all concerned (especially governing board members) before the woman president assumes office. The degree of inspection accorded the social activities and style of a woman president exceeds that for a comparable man, and the discerning woman president acknowledges this (however unjust) and plans and behaves accordingly. The millennium has not yet arrived.

Taking a more catholic view, however, how much should a spouse be involved in the affairs of the college? Our advice, based upon many experiences and observations, is not to involve him or her in the daily routine of the institution. No matter how talented and intelligent the spouse, excessive entanglement by the spouse can create significant problems. Undue involvement by spouses can, and often does, lead to unspoken and unidentifiable problems between you and your staff, and between you and your spouse, who does not "report" to you in the usual sense and therefore is not accountable in the usual context.[2] Such circumstances can deteriorate to the point that you cannot honestly hold your delegates accountable for their areas of responsibility because of spousal interference. Ultimately, who is going to tell the president that his or her spouse is a pain? And, if they do, how will this change your relationship with them in the future, and, more importantly, how are you going to inform your spouse?

Several national presidential associations (the Council of Independent Colleges, The National Association of Land Grant Colleges and Universities, and the American Association of State Colleges and Universities, for example) have helpful material and even conferences on the role of the spouse. Experience is a great teacher for a spouse, and these organizations help individuals share their experiences. Perhaps more than anything else, such sessions enable spouses to avoid mistakes.

A final aspect of presidential spousal circumstances is the career or employment of the spouse. While no reliable statistics exist, casual empiricism indicates that a significant proportion of married college presidents divorce during their term. The reasons for such divorces are legion, but certainly include a perceived lack of appreciation and personal fulfillment on the part of the spouse. Being in the president's shadow, he or she has great difficulty establishing an independent identity. Further, many presidential spouses cannot find suitable employment in the area where the college is located; they are thus underemployed or unemployed, and often feel their life has deteriorated into a series of meaningless college social functions at which they are a fifth wheel. The end result may be unhappiness, separation or divorce, and a visible reduction in presidential effectiveness.

Governing boards, in appointing a president, should understand the spousal phenomenon and give due consideration to ensuring that the role of the spouse is mutually understood and that, wherever possible, the spouse has meaningful employment if he or she so desires. Unfortunately, many governing boards ignore this issue, perhaps even believing that they are in step with modern trends when they do not take the spouse into

---

[2] This problem has bedeviled the activities of Hillary Rodham Clinton, the wife of U.S. President Bill Clinton. Mrs. Clinton is universally viewed as a person of extraordinary intelligence and ability. Nonetheless, to whom does Mrs. Clinton report, and can she be fired? How can presidential associates critique or argue with such an individual?

consideration. Governing boards should not assume social activity and participation by a presidential spouse, but more presidencies will be productive and fulfilling, and endure longer, if the president's spouse is fittingly employed in a position that is well removed from the campus. A shrewd governing board will recognize this and act accordingly.

CLOSE FRIENDS AND INTIMACY

Employing close friends who report directly to you is usually a mistake, except for brief periods of time, when specific tasks must be completed by loyal or particularly gifted individuals. With rare exceptions, intimate friends usually make better confidantes than subordinates. Genuine friendships with close advisors are fine; to put up with a strong president, they will have to like the president. But, to retain the leadership role, the president must insure that those friendships retain a measure of mystique and objectivity, a task often impossible, but always advisable. Adolph Berle (1967) puts it this way: "One of the first impacts (upon assuming office) is realization that the obligations of power take precedence over other obligations formerly held nearest and dearest. A man in power can have no friends in the sense that he must refuse to the friend considerations, that power aside, he would have accorded." In reality, some advisors will be closer than others. Avoid any favoritism, for these relationships are known or suspected by all. Indeed, the close associate usually pays the price of friendship; the president should be careful that the associate earns fewer rewards and more pressure because of the relationship.

President Charles William Eliot of Harvard said that a college president is like the captain of a ship at sea; figuratively, he or she must eat alone. "He must not be tempted by friendship to falter in the service of the institution" (in James, 1930).

Similarly, do not establish intimate friendships with people whose influence you seek. You will need your mystique with them also. Nonetheless, you will probably make some exceptions, and with luck, those friendships will not jeopardize the accomplishment of your vision. Close friends want to debate decisions, even after the time for debate is over, when what the leader needs is to gain the support of important people.

The presidency is, by nature, a lonely position, and its incumbent needs someone to turn to. The temptation is to turn to close associates, family, and friends. To become overly familiar with close associates can compromise the leader's effectiveness with them as well as with others. Taking problems home can make the office an impossible full-time job that yields no respite and often leads to a troubled marriage. Although close friends off campus can be sympathetic, they seldom know enough to be helpful. A presidential assistant can help but is rarely able to be completely objective.

Many presidents find national meetings and special conferences sources of rejuvenation and settings for complete candor. Other presidents, regardless of their personal style, understand the problems of the office, and talking to one who is not in direct competition with you can provide consolation and even advice. It is helpful just to talk to someone who understands. Perhaps the most consistently valuable places for presidential catharsis and inspiration are the increasing number of special conferences and meetings offered for presidents by national professional associations: e.g., American Association of State Colleges and Universities (AASCU); American Council on Education (ACE); Association of Governing Boards (AGB); Council of Independent Colleges (CIC); Council for Advancement and Support of Education (CASE). Such conferences offer reasonable assurance of objectivity, understanding, advice, and enlightened honest company. However, be aware that these same meetings sometimes develop into crying towel sessions that result in demoralization rather than therapy.

THE KEY ROLE OF TOP ASSOCIATES

If the president appoints superior persons to top positions, they are the prime agents in accomplishing institutional goals. Their task is to implement effectively the president's plans and dreams, which they have helped to shape. A good president will always demand and continually press for more from top associates and advisors. The degree to which they remain committed depends almost entirely on the president's relationship with them. That relationship should maximize their contributions and minimize their incursions into the presidential domain. Support them, comfort them, inspire them, and, at the same time, keep them a bit anxious and wary. The president provides legitimate favors, opportunities to cultivate their own leadership styles and mystique, and rewards for good performance in the form of salary and perquisites. Although at least tacit support can often be bought from potential or real campus adversaries, taking care of associates is primary. Never take them for granted.

LOYALTY

As far as the administrative staff as a whole is concerned, loyalty is as important as competence. The only way to deal with disloyalty is to discharge the person. To tolerate even the slightest disloyalty from an administrative subordinate is to set a shorter time limit on an effective presidency.

Vice presidents, as well as other administrative staff, serve only at the pleasure of the president. Loyalty is as important as competence, and repeated erosion of presidential territory is a form of disloyalty, albeit unconscious.

This obligation of loyalty does not hold for faculty and students; the opposite is true. For a president to have maximum charismatic influence within a college or university community, faculty and students should be relatively unfettered to insure that their representations are relatively uninhibited and candid, and in the process, test the administration. And, of course, in an academic community, it is neither acceptable nor realistic to expect such compliance from nonadministrative staff.

COALITIONS

Watch out for coalitions. To attempt to gain support from others at the president's expense is a more serious act of disloyalty than a direct challenge to authority. When subordinates form a coalition against the president, they must go—and in a way that discourages anyone else from even thinking of the same tactics. If a person cannot be dismissed, then a way should be found to treat him or her openly as an adversary, which after a while will bring his or her resignation, assuming that other subordinates are loyal.

THOSE WHO DENIGRATE YOUR PREDECESSOR

An administrator who denigrates your predecessor is untrustworthy; you will be his or her next object. By discharging or returning that person to the faculty, the president will have made an example—probably the only one necessary—of an adversary. The president who is lucky and enters office stating strongly and candidly that loyalty is expected may not have to use any examples at all.

NEW ADMINISTRATORS

From time to time, the president will need new administrative staff. Bear in mind the possible need for new associates whenever meeting new people. Although bright, well-educated, enthusiastic, outgoing, and assertive people are usually harder to handle, they do a magnificent job if they are inspired. If experience is not too costly, look for it too. (Here again, be wary of the person who speaks critically of a former employer.)

When you appoint a new administrator who reports to you, you assume a professional obligation to mentor that individual as appropriate and necessary. This mentor/mentee relationship extends not only to providing instructive orientation and nonintrusive "how to do it" discussions, but also to helping that individual advance professionally. This help should include provision for their professional development at conferences and meetings, but ultimately may mean nominating or recommending the individual for positions at other institutions. A good president requires loyalty, but does not frustrate the legitimate career development of his or her administrative colleagues. It is a compliment for another institution to seek to employ someone whom you have trained and counseled. Ordinarily, a president suffers when he or she appoints someone no one else wants.

AN EXECUTIVE VICE PRESIDENT

Having a clearly designated second in command is a defensible, but potentially dangerous practice; the presidential platform only has room for one. Much depends upon the individuals involved and the nature of the "second in command" commission that the president gives. Let us consider the pluses and minuses of such a practice.

In most presidencies today, the president will spend a considerable segment of his or her time away from campus. While the prudent president will never be unreachable by the campus, situations arise where action must be taken and the president is not available, or simply has more important tasks to complete. In such a circumstance, the president should designate (perhaps by means of a well-defined and finite letter of delegation) who is the responsible person on campus, and what the chain of command is. This letter must clearly define the president's power, the circumstances under which the second in command can exercise some of that power, the limitation of the authority of the second in command, the need for the second in command to consult the president whenever possible, and the president's ability to reverse any decision.

Operating under such a rubric, the president might delegate to the second in command the authority to close the campus during an exceptionally heavy snowfall, or perhaps designate the second in command as the individual who chairs certain all-institution committees that deal with topics ranging from space utilization to amending the strategic plan. It should be firmly understood, however, that such committees will generate recommendations for the approval of the president. When the designated second in command is the academic vice president, or provost, this role generally will meet with the warm approval of the faculty, who interpret this as a strong statement in support of the primacy of the academic function of the institution. The provostian appellation typically formalizes such a second in command relationship, where the provost is the *primus inter pares*. Such a limited (and somewhat honorific) delegation may reduce vice presidential in-fighting and competition for presidential favor, which can be destructive and reduce productivity.

The danger with appointing such a second in command does not arise from such a well-defined and limited delegation of authority. Rather, it arises from delegating too much authority and from appointing a true executive vice president to whom other vice presidents report. Except in the largest institutions, the president must have all the major administrative officers representing the significant areas of the institution reporting directly to him or her. The president who establishes an executive vice president is courting trouble. At the very least, the president will soon be out of touch with many parts of the institution. At the worst, the executive vice president can develop a power base that can be used to frustrate the president's vision and even force the president from office. Only the most benevolent executive vice president can resist using his or her vast authority to further his or her own agenda, which may be qualitatively different from that of the president. By the time the president finds out whether his or her executive vice president is that rare benevolent and magnanimous individual, it will be too late.

The only time to consider appointing an executive vice president to whom other vice presidents report is when you feel your internal effectiveness is exhausted, but you have some external mileage left and are not inclined to look for another position. Then, an appropriate second in command would be a trusted and able associate of long standing. Even so, any contrary forces that develop on the campus may use this person as a rallying point against you. This is one reason why ancient emperors frequently waited until they were on their deathbeds to name their successors. The preferable plan is to delegate responsibility and authority clearly to several individuals, but always ensuring that all the players report to you and that their responsibility and authority are finite.

ADMINISTRATIVE SALARIES

Administrators should be paid competitive salaries based upon their individual credentials, experience, and (especially) performance. Both external market conditions and local traditions must be taken into account. Every president should realize that administrative salaries will be closely inspected by faculty and that the mavens of the media often dote on reporting administrative salaries. Further, virtually every survey reported in outlets such as the *Chronicle of Higher Education* has revealed that most faculty members believe that the typical administrator is overpaid. Thus, the wise president will keep his or her eye on regional and national salary data provided by organizations such as the National Association of College and University Business Officers (NACUBO) in order to ascertain that administrative personnel are neither grossly underpaid (which can lead to morale problems and sudden departures) nor obviously overpaid (which can also lead to morale problems). Of course, differences in campus fringe benefit programs, local living costs, and local geography and amenities will always mean that what is a competitive salary on one campus will not be competitive on another.

The president's goal must be to offer compensation packages (of which salary is only one part) that are sufficient to attract and retain talented individuals. Salaries should be based on merit as much as possible, and all administrators should know that this is the policy. Where feasible, one should fashion the compensation package to suit individual administrators. Items such as deferred compensation, faculty rank and tenure, the provision of an automobile, and paid leaves often can be more important in attracting and retaining a key administrator than salary.

In former years, it often was possible, even in public institutions, to keep private the amount each administrator was paid, and some continue to believe that is the wisest policy, where it is legal (Pfeffer, 1981). Many organizations outside higher education have adopted a policy of being selective about releasing salary information—a good model for college and university presidents, if they can follow it, for it reduces counterproductive bickering and contention.

However, in most public institutions today, "sunshine" laws and open records laws result in all salaries (administrative and faculty) being considered part of the public domain. Enterprising reporters will ask for salary information and publish it if they believe it to be interesting (which they surely will if a particular salary appears out of line with regional or national means, or a particularly large raise has been bestowed). Further, even on independent college campuses, industrious faculty and reporters typically find ways to discover any administrative salary they wish to know. As is the case with budget information, the astute president understands that there are few salary secrets on any college campus and that he or she is ill-advised to support any compensation decision that will later prove difficult or embarrassing to explain.

THE PRESIDENTIAL ASSISTANT

A loyal and able assistant can be the president's most important staff member. He or she belongs to you, for the assistant's role is defined exclusively in terms of your best interests. Without the president, the assistant has no professional existence. A good assistant performs everything from the menial to the magnificent: running errands, opening doors, driving to off-campus meetings, representing the president, and, at times, acting as vice president without portfolio. The assistant must be extremeley sensitive to even the slightest threat to the president or vice presidents. Because not everyone can subordinate their egos, the choice of an assistant requires great care. The president who runs through too many too fast becomes known as the "smiling facade" and the "in-office monster." Choosing to live with an ineffective assistant, on the other hand, will significantly compromise your presidency. The assistant is the professional confidante, the only person on campus with whom the president does not have to dust things off before saying them. Assuming the assistant has no significant line responsibility, freed of specific administrative duties, he or she will have a gestalt view of the institution, and be able to respond more in keeping with the president's interests. The loyal, intelligent, and broadly educated assistant who works 15 hours a day and has enough sense to keep quiet, translates into an exceedingly fortunate president.

With a good assistant, the president can relax, blow off steam without fear of harsh judgment, discuss plans and strategies without obligation— even raise hell and still be considered a nice person. The assistant and the president's secretary, if they are good, are the only persons on campus who really know you, and must truly like and respect you just to put up with you.

The number of presidential assistants should depend on the size of the institution, the nature of the president, and the winds of the day. Often, it is wise to designate a temporary special assistant for certain campus priorities like diversity and affirmative action, retooling, budget/planning, and so forth. This practice can assist you in meeting specific goals and deadlines and, coincidently, can function as a valuable "tryout" for prospective administrators. But "temporary" should mean temporary; when the assignment is finished, previous titles and assignments should be restored.

DELEGATION

The conventional divisions are usually academic affairs, advancement (often called development or college/university relations), business affairs, and student services. Larger universities will often establish semi-autonomous professional schools such as medicine and law. In addition, other areas such as alumni or government relations may be structured as line divisions reporting directly to the president. Of these various divisions, academic affairs is the most important, reflecting the fundamental purpose of an academic institution. Because of the growing importance to a successful presidency of generating additional extramural support and resources, the advancement/development vice president may be next in importance.

Some private colleges and universities are placing increased emphasis on the cultivation of consumers and potential benefactors, even going so far as to create vice presidents for marketing. Regardless of the office to which this function is specifically assigned, a strong consumer orientation should be an important consideration within each line division of the institution.

An increasing number of colleges and universities now are appointing vice presidents who embody the increasingly technological nature of modern academic institutions. The complex, but ill-defined interfaces between information science, computer science, and telecommunications claim rapidly escalating attention and resources, and few institutions today are not configured to permit students and faculty alike to access the Internet and utilize E-Mail. Consequently, many institutions have chosen to appoint a vice president for information or technology, whose standing and visibility on the campus frequently exceeds all others except the chief academic officer.

Similarly, some institutions have begun to appoint vice presidents for economic development. He or she is charged with mobilizing the resources of the institution to support local and regional economic development initiatives. The critical role of academic institutions (even liberal arts colleges) in promoting economic development is both recognized and documented (Birch, 1994). Today's "entrepreneurial hot spots" (the current jargon) invariably are located next to academic institutions. This vice president, then, interprets the campus to the business and entrepreneurial communities, and vice-versa. This role, unheard of even a decade ago, makes many academics uneasy because of the implicit statement it makes about the institution's *raison d'etre*.

More common is a vice president who deals with research issues. On many larger campuses today, the annual volume of contract research exceeds $100 million. It is big business, and operates largely on the basis of external, federally mandated rules and regulations. This vice president frequently is responsible for economic development issues as well. The prudent president will place someone in this position whom he or she trusts implicitly, because the number of ways in which these activities can result in financial, legal, ethical, and public relations problems are legion. Only intercollegiate athletics (which almost never is represented by a vice president, but which often reports directly to the president) can boast of such similar destructive potential.

However the institution is organized, the administrative structure should be lean and functional. Both the institution's mission and the president's vision should be enhanced by the administrative structure. Both the structure and the particular responsibilities of administrators ultimately should evince the special skills, interests, and weaknesses of these administrators. To some extent, one molds structure and responsibilities to fit particular individuals and personalities, particularly if a key individual is found to have outstanding strengths or weaknesses in specific areas.

Assuming the extraordinary competence of the top line officers, virtually all responsibilities for operating the institution should be delegated to them. While there can occasionally be overlapping responsibilities, there should be no dual responsibilities. Under these conditions, the president can hold prime delegates accountable and still keep a finger in each area. Rarely should the president be visibly involved in the direct operation of an office or department assigned to an officer of vice presidential rank except in a convivial or observational manner. Less visibly, and always in private, the president should mentor or counsel his or her chief administrators as necessary ("Let's think about the alternatives," or "Have you thought about this approach?" or, "Here is someone you might talk with about this problem.")

A president should touch base—visibly though briefly—with such offices as admissions, security, alumni, physical plant, and the academic departments. Such appearances are good for quality control and morale, and help keep vice presidents honest. Deeper involvement would compromise the line of delegated vice presidential authority and accountability. If a president chooses to become directly involved in an office (such as admissions) that ordinarily reports to a vice president, it is preferable to reorganize the office to report directly to the president rather than to risk the entire organization for a presidential preoccupation.

Some college presidents have reported that during periods of campus difficulty, their strongest, most unquestioning backers were support staff: secretarial, housekeeping, and maintenance people. This demonstrates how valuable those informal campus visits are.

THE PRESIDENT'S EXECUTIVE COUNCIL

With thought and care, the necessary weekly meetings of the key officers of the institution can become a strong plus for the president. A fancy title—Executive Committee, President's Council, or Administrative Committee—helps. The members of this group will be the only people on campus who really know the president, besides a presidential assistant and secretary, but even here familiarity is to be avoided. Katz (1973) concluded that "intimacy destroys illusions," and literally dozens of other studies support the concept of maintaining distance between a leader and staff (Stogdill, 1974). Vice presidents are the ultimate challenge because when mystery is gone, the president is open and vulnerable. Keeping vice presidents in line and inspired is probably the greatest single presidential test. Good ones are like colonels wanting to be generals; when the general's stars are tarnished by familiarity, the distance does not seem so far.

Meetings of the executive group should be chaired by the president and include only the top line officers of the institution. There is no rational justification for regularly including in these meetings people who report to the top line officers, with the exception of a presidential assistant who takes notes and does not participate in the discussions unless invited to do so by the president. On some campuses, presidents include in their advisory group persons like the director of admissions or deans who report to vice presidents. Such officers should only make reports to the president's group, leave the meeting after their report is finished, and never be full-fledged members. To do otherwise clouds lines of responsibility and reduces the president's right to hold prime delegates accountable. The same is true for faculty and student representatives. Because they simply cannot be held accountable, they should not be included on a regular basis, regardless of pressure.

On some campuses, for purposes of communication and trust, the minutes of these meetings may be made public or at least available in a public place on campus, such as the library. This practice seldom is more than cosmetic in nature and can be highly detrimental. If the minutes are candid and complete, then they surely will discourage meeting participants from speaking their minds and the result will be administrative paralysis and rump "meetings before the meetings." If they are not candid and complete, then the minutes serve only to titillate and mislead, neither of which is useful for a campus. In any case, if the minutes must be published, let sufficient time pass before publication for any controversial content to dissipate.

Notwithstanding this advice, it is always good policy to notify the campus regularly of actions that will affect its operation. Publishing the minutes of executive group meetings seldom is the best way to fulfill this need.

A frequent problem in presidential meetings is the "we" syndrome. Vice presidents, especially good ones, are at least subconsciously inclined to diminish or erode, through increased intimacy, the authority and the charisma of the president. Here, out of sight of the community, this tendency can be nipped in the bud. If it is not, the offending vice president will continue the behavior outside presidential meetings with faculty, other staff, students, and even trustees, and it will not be the fault of the vice president but of the president who allowed the behavior to pass in the first place. Although uncomfortable to say, each time a vice president refers to something "we" decided, he or she should be reminded decisively that "we" don't decide anything. This usually inhibits further attempts, unconscious or otherwise. This need not imply any lack of respect for your chief aides; rather, it serves as a healthy reminder to all, including the president, that the institution has only one ultimately responsible officer—the president.

Obviously, under these conditions, the vice presidents and the president have to be bound together by affection and respect as well as professional commitment. Nor does this suggest an imperial presidency; on the contrary, implemented early in one's administration, it insures against having to resort to imperiousness later when things may get out of hand.

THE CHIEF ACADEMIC OFFICER

The president's single most important professional associate is the chief academic officer, the prime conduit to the faculty and the president's de facto number two officer. No associate is more important, so despite the impact of democratization on the selection process, the president must have the most significant role in the appointment. Extraordinary competence and complete loyalty are of fundamental importance, and a search committee process must not compromise either of these conditions. A mistake here can mean the president's undoing, for either his or her leadership will be eroded by an overly self-serving number two, or an inordinate amount of time will be spent in the academic area because the chief academic officer is incompetent.

If complete rapport with the president is a given, the prime personal ability of the chief academic officer is leadership through consensus building, a remarkable and rare skill. The academic chief should understand and support the president's vision and goals and be able to resolve issues effectively in a way that supports these. In most instances, this should happen without the president's involvement. Academic disagreements should never be personalized or they will remain barriers long after the issues have been resolved. The dean—or provost or vice president of academic affairs—who can be these things is rare; the president should look carefully into the background of all candidates to be sure of their modes of problem solving before making a final selection.

To find the academic officer, institutional policy usually calls for a broad-based search and screen committee (clearly labeled "advisory"). A committee member appointed by the president, usually the most valued assistant, should serve as administrator and handle correspondence and other details. The president must be certain that the committee considers at least some candidates whom he or she generally endorses, and that after deliberations, they recommend, unranked, from three to five acceptable candidates. If, after carefully evaluating each of these candidates, the president does not feel right about any, the committee should start over. Get a chief academic officer who has both your support and the support of the faculty representatives. The president who, to satisfy the immediate desire to get on with business, appoints a vice president for academic affairs about whom he or she has even the slightest reservations will regret it later. For although the faculty understandably want an important role in selection and will take all the authority granted them, they will still hold the president absolutely responsible for the officer's effective performance.

If you inherit a chief academic officer, assess the incumbent carefully and confer candidly with him or her about expectations. Because an incumbent seems to enjoy the respect of the faculty and a reputation for integrity does not mean that he or she will be a comfortable and loyal officer for a new president. Academic deans serve at the pleasure of the president and should never hold tenure as administrators. If everything seems satisfactory about the incumbent, continuation in office should be confirmed, but keep a watchful eye. Even the slightest variation from mutually understood expectations should be noted. A better sense of things should develop within a few months. Because of the importance of this vice president, do not let a nagging doubt go undiscussed because of embarrassment or uncertainty.

If the incumbent must go, the new president's predecessor should, if possible, ease the person out before the change in administration and appoint an acting chief academic officer until the new president can make a permanent selection. In this instance, a distinguished professorship with appropriate perks may be worth many times the price when weighed against a questionable chief academic officer or a popular one discharged by a new "axe-wielding" president. A board of trustees can be helpful in this process, as long as it does not directly involve itself in the administration of the institution.

The wise and fortunate president has no closer relationship on campus than with the chief academic officer, sustaining, to the extent possible, the appropriate distance. The high degree of mutual respect between the two should be widely known by everyone, including other top administrators. With the right academic officer, the chances for a significant administration increase markedly.

In sum, administrators are the president's prime instruments, and should join with their leader in achieving the institutional vision as he or she has defined it. If they are superior, loyal, and enthusiastic, the president is well on the way to a successful tenure in office. And, if you are able to inspire the trust and confidence of such superior persons, yours will be a grand experience and a good and perhaps distinguished presidency. Always remember that the president is expected to be the leader. Know that this is especially difficult to do during times of difficulty when there is temptation to blame faculty, students, trustees, and even your administrative colleagues. If you can survive the stress of hard times without faulting others, then you will be "their president."

FINAL THOUGHTS

- Without truth and beauty, there is no university.
- Academic institutions do not exist for the purpose of making the lives of administrators more comfortable. Few presidents have failed because they placed the interests of their students above the selfish interests of a few administrators.
- Administrative subordinates either agree with the president, change the president's mind, or resign.
- Seldom violate the chain of command, but let associates know that you can.
- Surround yourself with superior persons, or you are dead.
- Middle level administrators who neither are hired by the president nor immediately visible to him or her, can frustrate and even derail the president's agenda. Find ways to maintain contact with these individuals and give them a sense of being a part of the team.
- Loyalty is as important as ability; hire both.
- Rarely entertain vice presidents and their spouses.

- Be sure that you and your associates respect one another. If not, they will not stand you for long.
- Leadership often is 5 percent position and 95 percent mystique.
- The more committee meetings you attend, the less effective you are.
- On campus, let somebody else do it.
- Delegate everything but final authority.
- Develop a clear delegation of authority for situations that occur when you are off-campus or unavailable. This will avoid bickering and vice presidential in-fighting.
- Do not retain or appoint an executive vice president to whom other vice presidents report unless you are on your last legs and still want to stay a few more years.
- You will never solve the parking problem. Delegate it to a committee, and let it take the heat.
- Unless invited, stay out of the personal lives of staff.
- Of course you are great, exceptional, and often persecuted, but you are also lucky to have your job.

CHAPTER
seven
•••••••

The President and TQM

Good ideas are often oversold, and then the world settles down to reality

Main, 1994

All decisions...are inherently qualitative

White, 1974

Who can argue with a management system that promises increased customer satisfaction through higher quality services achieved through customer focus, continuous improvement, and employee involvement? Total Quality Management (TQM) has, by making those promises, become somewhat the rage in higher education. Its advocates typically issue strong promises, largely undocumented, that TQM will involve and unite the entire campus, increase employee satisfaction, and improve nearly any process that it touches.

Nonetheless, the empirical evidence in favor of TQM is essentially anecdotal and surprisingly sparse, particularly in view of TQM's vogue in higher education today. The problem with TQM is not the goal—increased efficiency and greater employee and customer satisfaction—but the process, which is already being abandoned by some of its earliest advocates in industry. Any president who aspires to real change or who has serious concerns about costs should approach TQM cautiously. Few institutions have successfully implemented TQM in any meaningful way, and the relatively small gains generated in these institutions usually have been overshadowed by the time and effort expended to generate them.

TQM and such close relatives as Continuous Quality Improvement (CQI) are well worth study by a college president, if for no other reason than they are so frequently cited as solutions to many of higher education's problems. Undeniably, TQM is a concept with momentum: private industry has been outspoken in urging campuses to adopt TQM; TQM is viewed by many as a solution to campus conflicts and financial problems; national higher education associations have endorsed its application; and foundation, endowment, tax, and student fee dollars have funded its use. All this despite the fact that colleges and universities adopting TQM frequently spend more money on its implementation than they save.

Unquestioning disciples of such noted TQM gurus as Deming, Juran, Crosby, and Iami are featured speakers and writers for the conventional mainstream in higher education. National higher education organizations such as the American Association for Higher Education distribute TQM materials free and sponsor societies such as the Academic Quality Consortium. Expressions such as "culture of quality," "quality is everybody's job," and "teamwork" have become bywords of higher education conversations. The implication is that TQM, conscientiously applied, can solve nearly any campus problem.

Already endorsed and adopted in whole or in part by tax-supported institutions and wealthier private institutions, TQM is today being implemented or considered in some form by hundreds of institutions.[1] Although TQM is not without its achievements, we fear that the piper is playing and others will blindly follow.

TQM'S BACKGROUND

The theoretical constructs of TQM have been developed primarily by W. Edwards Deming, a statistician who devoted his life to quality control and related topics, and Joseph J. Juran, an expert on group problem solving who operates the Juran Institute, a consulting firm that specializes in quality-oriented tasks. Both individuals worked extensively with Japanese firms after World War II, and for many decades were prophets without honor in their home country, as American industry largely ignored their jeremiads about the consequences of quality deterioration upon ultimate profitability.

---

[1] The former include Oregon State, Wisconsin-Madison, Colorado State, Maryland, Minnesota, Clemson, Georgia Tech, and many community colleges, and the latter include Harvard, Penn, Carnegie Mellon, Lehigh, Chicago, and Miami.

When, in the 1970s and 1980s, many American firms experienced economic difficulties and found themselves becoming less competitive with a variety of foreign competitors (most visibly, automobile and consumer electronics producers from Japan), many of them turned for advice to Deming, Juran, and other trailblazers of what has become known as the "quality movement." Undeniably, many American firms had lost the international competitive edge they enjoyed in the 1950s, and all too frequently their operations were characterized by bloated costs, slothful product development, a certain insensitivity to (and even disdain for) the desires of customers, nonsensical labor contracts and rules, declining product quality, administrative proliferation, and sclerotic leadership that exhibited a striking lack of vigor and vision. The almost inevitable result was declining market shares, sustained losses, unemployment, and massive soul-searching by firms that ranged from General Motors and Harley Davidson to Xerox and Motorola. The "deindustrialization of America" was said to be imminent.

These and many other firms turned to TQM (or some variant) as a means to make themselves more competitive. Then, and now, TQM campaigns typically incorporate one or more of the following principles:

- *Continuous Quality Improvement (CQI)*: A core concept of TQM, it relies on the Japanese notion of *kaizen*, or continuous quality improvement. The old notion of "If it ain't broke, don't fix it" goes out the window, replaced by an emphasis on working continuously to improve even those things that already are successful or function well.

- *Benchmarking*: Organizations are urged to audit what others are doing and, wherever possible, acquire comparative data that will allow judgments to be made concerning efficiency.

- *Employee Empowerment*: As Goldberg (1993) has put it, "TQM assumes that workers want to do their best, but that institutional structures get in their way." The solution is to provide employees with the means to change their work situations and, as necessary, fix things on the spot.

- *Reliance upon Data*: One TQM expert puts it this way, "If you can't measure it, you can't manage it." Thus, organizations are urged to generate data that permit quantitative measurement, for example, accounts serviced per hour, product defects per 10,000 units, or even credit hours generated per full-time equivalent faculty member.

- *Partnerships and Cross-Functional Teams*: The essence of TQM is group activity and the "democratic" sharing of responsibility among managers and workers alike, including those who work in different aspects of production. As Lackey and Pugh (1994) have expressed it, "Today, the 60's generation's 'power to the people' mantra is realized through TQM; more power for the employees means more value for the customer."

TQM, then, is a process-oriented, egalitarian approach to increasing productivity, decreasing costs, and improving quality. It stresses teamwork, finding better ways to do things, sharing responsibility, and changing institutional cultures so that dramatic improvements can be made.

Corporations ranging from Toyota and Allied Signal to General Electric and DuPont have adopted some variant of TQM, and all report at least some success. However, the most often cited example of the apparently successful implementation of TQM is Motorola, the electronics manufacturing firm whose sales have been doubling every five years, and whose goal is "six sigma quality"—fewer than 3.4 errors per million units of output. Each year, thousands of "wannabes" flock to Motorola for seminars on TQM. Motorola, in fact, copes with this demand by running its own continuing education operation (and satisfies much of its own higher education needs) via its own, highly regarded "Motorola University."

Some or all of the precepts of TQM are, and have been, attractive to higher education. Even anti-authority figures among the faculty who ordinarily bridle at notions such as "measurement," which are central to TQM, find its egalitarian, democratic assumptions attractive. As a consequence, TQM never has spawned the instinctive opposition from most academics that once greeted other management panaceas such as strategic planning and management by objective.

Yet, it is precisely this broad acceptability and lack of opposition to TQM that should cause alarm bells to ring. Any organizational system that does not acknowledge painful choice making, disguises or denies opportunity costs, and fails to recognize the loss of alternatives that flow from decisions, is, in the last analysis, not a "real" system. Yet, the perception that gains can be realized without sacrifice is at the heart of TQM. Participants are led to believe that if they simply "do things differently," that is, reform their procedures and processes, significant improvements will follow. No one need give up anything (except perhaps a bit of authority and ego involvement) in order for the promised land to be attained. Thus, TQM threatens few in higher education and is, understandably, popular.

TQM IN HIGHER EDUCATION

As noted above, many institutions of higher education have committed themselves to TQM programs. Thus far, however, the results are somewhat pedestrian, and include reformation of campus copy centers, better bill collection and check writing, more efficient handling of admissions and financial aid applications, and more productive scheduling of physical plant jobs. (See American Association for Higher Education, 1993 and 1994, for reviews of how TQM has been implemented in higher education.)

Of course, one should not sneer at such nonacademic improvements, for they have the potential to release badly needed resources for other important tasks within the institution, and probably result in increased student satisfaction. Nonetheless, there are three important observations to make about these TQM improvements. First, the magnitude of resources (especially employee time, which some campuses ignore) required to generate these advances typically has been large. Second, these advances might well have been obtained by other methods, which we discuss below. Third, there is a noticeable absence of things *academic* in these beneficent developments. As we will argue below, the most significant long-term internal problems facing American higher education today relate to academic philosophy and practices, not to the operation of copy centers and the collection of bills.

Very few TQM-oriented campuses have used the process to change the fundamental nature of their academic life or curriculum. An exception to that rule is Babson College, which in 1993 invited a wide range of its constituents, including members of the business community, to a three-day session designed to result in an overhaul of its curriculum. Student and business sector feedback has been used extensively to guide this process. Other campuses, public and private, have attempted to implement the "one minute paper" notion of K. Patricia Cross; at the end of each class, students write a one-minute paper describing the core ideas they derived from that day's classroom lecture or activities. Still other campuses have used TQM-type methods to develop improved assessment processes, or to benchmark (compare) certain of their academic practices with those of "outstanding" institutions.

Notwithstanding these and other useful examples, the impact of TQM on higher education has been concentrated upon the nonacademic side of institutions. Fundamental issues such as the curriculum and the allocation of faculty time have been extremely resistant to TQM campaigns, not the least because faculty usually cast a jaundiced eye on any development that threatens to loosen their grip over course and degree requirements, or their ability to allocate their own time. American industry generally has cast an approving eye on the advent of TQM in higher education. IBM, for example, has developed the "IBM-TQM Partnership with Colleges and Universities," which involves eight diverse institutions of higher education. The object is to instill TQM in every aspect of the lives of these institutions.

IBM's sponsorship of TQM initiatives in higher education is ironic. IBM has lost massive amounts of money in recent years and its market shares for most of its products have deteriorated significantly. Birch (1994), the leading national authority on how and where new jobs are generated in the American economy, has labeled IBM one of America's "dinosaurs." Whatever lessons IBM has drawn from TQM either have not been heeded, or have been faulty. IBM's experience underscores an important point: TQM has tended to operate around the margins of organizations that adopt it. By itself, it cannot reverse fundamentally adverse market conditions or the effects of mediocre, visionless leadership.

Higher education institutions have excelled at announcing TQM campaigns, but typically have been incapable of implementing them fully or reaping significant benefits. Entin (1994) surveyed 10 Boston-area institutions of higher education that committed themselves to TQM, often with great fanfare, early in the 1990s. By 1994, 5 of the 10 had stopped, delayed, or were not implementing their TQM projects. Four more were carrying out TQM to a limited extent. Only Babson was systematically continuing to implement TQM; only Babson appeared to be using TQM-based concepts to engineer fundamental changes in its curriculum and academic life. Entin concluded that "This report raises serious questions about the future of TQM (or CQI) in higher education."

The evidence from outside academe is substantially the same. An estimated 80 percent of *Fortune* Magazine's largest 500 industrial firms at one time or another have announced that they were initiating some type of TQM campaign. However, as Graves (1994) has noted, a study performed by the consulting firm Bain and Company found no correlation between the popularity of a management tool and a firm's financial performance. Main, the author of *Quality Wars: The Triumphs and Defeats of American Business* (1994), observes astutely that "good ideas are often oversold, and then the world settles down to reality." Hence, there is growing recognition, both inside and outside higher education, that TQM is a nostrum that requires a major commitment of time and resources by an organization, but is likely to produce only modest results. Indeed, one perceptive college president recently suggested to one of the authors that TQM is a game that can be played only by those institutions than can afford to lose.

WHY DOESN'T TQM WORK AS ADVERTISED?

Experience suggests that any concept, such as TQM, that is embraced so suddenly by the status quo must be questioned. TQM is popular because it does not threaten any major academic power blocs, including presidents, deans, and conscientious bureaucrats. TQM seldom addresses the really pressing issues facing higher education today, including the nature of the curriculum, academic standards, the access of students (especially "nontraditional") to higher education, how to increase learning "efficiency," the appropriate role of research and scholarly activity, the uses of faculty time, the validity of economic development activities, and, indeed, the very purpose of a university in the twenty-first century.

To read the gurus of the field, the problems of higher education center upon faulty processes, not upon values and people. Therefore, little emphasis is put on individual performance, accountability, costs, or leadership. The notion is that if the process is continually refined, then the organization will prosper, and it will be a relatively painless process. W. Edwards Deming, the grand TQM champion, unabashedly declared that any kind of competition in an organization was bad; he even refused to grade students in his classes!

TQM is attractive in many areas, but its potential for disappointment is as great as its promise. For too many, this new approach represents a quick fix, a universally acceptable solution; in reality, it may only be the most recent attractive way to forestall the conflict that inevitably comes from difficult decision making, individual accountability, and change.

THE REAL CHALLENGE

Consider the following illustration. Today, few would debate the assumption that the undergraduate curriculum is in worse condition than it was 30 years ago. Core requirements today are further away from meeting the needs of our students and society than they were in 1965, the approximate beginning of the egalitarian movement. Degrees at many colleges have become more watered down with each passing year, and, increasingly, we have made substantive academic experiences optional for bright, but largely uneducated and unchallenged students. Recently, it was reported that a top-ranked university had no specific course requirements for graduation. A disillusioned dean at an Ivy League institution said words to this effect: Of course our core requirements need serious attention, but to ask this faculty to consider revision would only dilute them further.

If your institution already requires, for all who graduate, fluency in at least one foreign language, computer literacy, demonstrated writing profi-ciency, a hard science, and coursework in international, interracial, and gender studies, then you escape our slings and arrows. If not, then your campus organization and leadership are not doing the job, and your gradu-ates are not being prepared for the year 2000. TQM would appear to have little to do with resolving this terribly important discussion about the purpose of higher education.

Think on this. Throughout this period typified by decline in academic discipline and quality on many campuses, our leading institutions (followed by most of the rest of academe) have adopted dozens of promising designs, virtually none of which has improved the quality of education, and all of which have served to distract us from our primary mission. We go to countless meetings, write articles and books, and pontificate piously, all the while treating symptoms instead of primary problems. To note a few that are no older than our professional lifetimes: zero-base budgeting, long-range and strategic planning, management by objectives, participatory governance, statewide coordination, and (we hardly need mention) trans-actional leadership.

If not because of, then surely in spite of these time-consuming and costly managerial innovations, educational quality has declined at many institu-tions, costs have risen, and the supporting public has become increasingly disillusioned. The only people who are not concerned about such a scenario are those who are deceived, or who are unseeing apologists. They, like many faculty, are constitutionally unable to address effectively the declining condition of higher education.

Many sacred cows will need to be sacrificed. Any changes of conse-quence in higher education must include consideration of the following: increased teaching loads for many faculty; a redefinition of "scholarly productivity" to include legitimate pedagogical research within specific disciplines and applied research directed at real world problems and issues; more careful monitoring of time devoted to unfunded scholarly research; required student advisees and posted office hours for every faculty member; increasing the learning efficiency of students by removing artificial barriers from their progress so that they can learn as rapidly as they are capable via a variety of methods and technologies that go beyond the traditional classroom lecture; dramatically reduced administrative staffs, especially in student services and academic affairs; the elimination of costly advanced graduate programs at hundreds of institutions; wrenching major revisions of general education requirements; the elimination or major modification of bureaucratic, resource-gobbling state higher education administrative systems; and, above all, the adoption of truly accountable college and university governance practices.

THE ROLE OF TQM

What can TQM do about these propositions? Based on our reading, not nearly as much as its proponents would have us believe. TQM can improve administrative service areas (registration, mail service, maintenance, billing, etc.), and it has been used to enhance certain quasi-academic areas such as library services. But TQM offers little that smacks of amputation, risk-taking, or dramatic change. Inspirational leadership is only rarely mentioned by its pundits, and then only in the most general terms. TQM emphasizes teamwork and getting along, making process and consensus more important than results—especially when dramatic change is in order. TQM makes minor changes in process a virtual certainty, but subtly erects roadblocks in front of major change.

Nonetheless, the reality is that if there is no demand for widgets, regardless of how well you make them, how elegant your processes, and how empowering your quality circles, then in time you will be out of business. This is one of the hard lessons that IBM, a TQM devotee, has learned with respect to its mainframe computers. Higher education must focus on the larger, core issues of its existence (and not on marginal changes) if it is going to survive and prosper.

TQM encourages colleges and universities to collect data that enable them to measure their progress in key areas—against themselves and against others. As a consequence, TQM campuses sometimes collect data describing miscellaneous phenomena such as the number of books checked out per student, square feet cleaned per day by janitorial staff, financial aid transactions completed per staff member, and credit hours generated per faculty member. To be sure, accurate, timely, and relevant data can be of great assistance in informing decision making. More data ordinarily are preferable to less data. The administrator who does not use appropriate, accurate data to inform decision making is partially blind and his or her management will suffer.

However, a data set is neither a value system nor a vision. Given adequate data, one must still decide what the data mean and what to do with them. In the last analysis, TQM can do little to improve an administrator who lacks values, purpose, and a compelling vision. Of what long-term value to society is, say, more efficient campus bill collection if academic standards are deficient, faculty contact with students minimal, and administrative ranks bloated?

Realistically, TQM in higher education appears to be a process for doing what we do better, but what we often need is to do something different. Real change has no constituency. For understandable but usually unfortunate reasons, people like the status quo. Only inspirational leadership provided with legitimacy and appropriate governance conditions can bring real change.

HAS TQM WORKED?

At this point, industry is the only place one can go to assess the long-term value of TQM because its impact upon higher education is still largely unknown. Is it working? A growing number of reports show that TQM is failing in Japan, and many American companies are discouraged by what they once saw as a cure-all. Douglas Aircraft, Florida Power and Light, Alcoa, and even The Wallace Company, a winner of the Malcolm Baldridge National Quality Award, have abandoned TQM. A survey conducted by Roth and Strong of Lexington, Massachusetts, graded TQM effort to improve market share, reduce costs, and make customers happy; most TQM companies received "D" and "F" grades. In an Arthur Little survey of 500 TQM companies, only 36 percent reported that TQM was having a significant impact on their ability to outdistance competitors. A recent empirical analysis of the best (and worst) managed American corporations found no impact for TQM among CEOs and financial analysts (Koch and Cebula, 1994).

In many TQM companies, executives now complain of excessive paperwork, time-consuming meetings, and a lack of accountability. While workers often find the egalitarian "we're all equal" approach of TQM attractive, they often complain that the TQM emphasis on charts, graphs, and reports takes too much time away from production and service. TQM's adoption by government agencies and by paralyzed and bureaucratized universities and colleges is scarcely reassuring.

TQM also tends to reduce the social distance necessary for managers to become empowering leaders. Social distance is the single most important condition for inspirational leadership for all leaders and in all areas of an organization, yet TQM encourages self-expression and reduces the perceived knowledge and status of the person expected to lead. Not only do TQM organizations talk, study, and work together, but TQM's participants are often expected to take personality tests and to share the results so they will know one another better. Nothing could make leadership more difficult. If true change is necessary, then inspirational leadership is necessary, and few have the capacity to lead after personal revelation.

During periods of economic decline, budget reduction, and staff and program cutbacks in industry, TQM environments often fail and result in conflict with management and within teams. Team values are replaced by feelings of betrayal, political and coercive strategies, and sabotaging behavior. Because TQM traditionally places no emphasis on competition or individual accountability, no one takes responsibility when an organization flounders; in such a system, no one is accountable (except, of course, the CEO, who initiated the program in the first place). The direct analog of this situation is the parlous status of the curriculum on most campuses today; because the faculty in a corporate sense holds the authority, no one individual is accountable, and therefore little of curricular consequence is accomplished. Under TQM, such inertia and easy thinking can generalize to the entire institution.

Finally, what does TQM do to costs? In industry, even TQM's most enthusiastic advocates do not suggest that it will maintain or reduce costs; in fact, TQM is known for increasing costs. As Entin (1994) noted in his survey of 10 institutions that have attempted to implement TQM, "TQM is not a tool or approach designed to lower budget deficits." One of the authors recently has acted as a "restructuring" consultant to several business firms and academic institutions. Those involved in TQM invariably reported to him that "if we only had some additional funds, we could really improve performance and quality." All too often, TQM turns out to be an elaborate, time-consuming technique for justifying additional expenditures and budget increases.

Higher education TQM enthusiasts say it will reduce costs, but invariably qualify this by saying that one should not expect such results for at least five years. Yet, in five years, an institution can easily be bankrupt! Does anyone who has responsibility for a payroll really think that TQM will seriously influence the major sources of cost increases in higher education (where approximately three-quarters of all expenditures are on personnel)?

In any case, by our reading, most TQM programs in industry today are a far cry from the original pre-depression idea of Walter Shewhart, who proposed statistical controls to ensure quality in telephone manufacturing, or of Deming himself as he first sold the concept in Japan in the 1950s. Today, these extraordinarily original ideas seem to have degenerated into a rather dreamy listing of Peters- and Waterman-like promises. Today, TQM may just need TQM!

A TELLING ILLUSTRATION

Recently, the authors were part of an evaluation team of four persons at a western institution wracked by dissension and problems. The faculty at the institution was one of the most mean-spirited, unprofessional groups any of us had ever encountered. They had forced out the president, and, because of some peculiar local political circumstances, effectively controlled their board of trustees. A significant number of these faculty blatantly used their classrooms for political purposes, intimidated the administration and faculty opponents, and in general had taken control of the institution. One trustee who disagreed with the position of the faculty organization had the tires of his car punctured by students. When anyone—administrator, trustee, or even faculty member—suggested something that was not in keeping with the perceived interests of the faculty organization, the person was either neutralized or effectively eliminated.

In addition, the institution was bloated with faculty and administrative positions, and every senior faculty member seemed to have his or her own special courses. "General education" consisted of a wide range of options, with few absolute requirements. The last dean who lost her job had been forced from office after trying to eliminate a department that had virtually no students. Today, everyone, even the faculty organization, admits that the institution is in chaos. Guess what the faculty organization proposed as a solution? TQM.

As we write this, nearly everyone at the college believes that it is in the "healing" throes of the meetings, focus groups, confessionals, and frequency polygrams that characterize TQM. One wonders what will happen to the department with no students. Further, how will TQM handle the patently obvious faculty and administrative bloat? What if someone decides they really need specific general education requirements?

AN ALTERNATIVE APPROACH

The authors have served as presidents of four organizations that are acknowledged to have reduced costs, changed dramatically, increased quality, and extended both their effectiveness and reach. We are convinced that if we had employed the full spirit of TQM, these four organizations would have remained essentially as they had been, but with much higher costs. The organizations might have done some of the same things better, but probably with higher costs.

How do successful institutions do it? First and foremost, the campus must adopt a unifying vision of its purpose and goals. The president, with the strong support of the governing board, must present and "sell" this vision, which is absolutely critical to campus tone, motivation, and direction. Second, it is essential to delineate the distinctive features of the campus—its focused points of excellence and its specialties—literally, its trademarks.[2] These features become points of pride that increase self-esteem and boost esprit de corps. Third, effective communication of goals and facts must occur by means of letters to the faculty, a finite number of well-chosen meetings, and speeches. The president must always be optimistic, but at the same time an open communicator and a teller of truth. Fourth, all activities must be directed toward the best interests of campus constituents (the most important of whom are individual students) rather than individual faculty and administrators. This implies a degree of consumer orientation that is foreign to many campuses. Fifth, the president and major administrators must demonstrate that they are involved and concerned by appearing where they are least expected: in the motor pool, the security office, department meetings, the corridors of classroom buildings, faculty/staff offices, gatherings for prospective students, and meetings and performances of student organizations ranging from the Black Student Alliance to the field hockey team. The president must be seen as knowledgeable and involved, yet not be viewed as an interfering micromanager.

In addition, the president and major administrators must do things that at first may seem silly—like asking all registration staff to wear smile buttons, or, at the beginning of each academic term, help students move into the residence halls. There is a salutary effect associated with the president putting on blue jeans to clear debris from a campus neighborhood street, serving food in a residence hall food line, or participating in a well-organized promotional bus tour of the institution's major service area. After several of these episodes, such activities will become stylish on campus.

More than a symbolic gesture, reallocating funds from administrative activities to instruction sends a message about what is most important, as does the example of the president and major administrators teaching classes. Raising funds from unexpected donors and sources similarly boosts morale and can help counteract harsh fiscal climates.

The point is this: Motivated, enthusiastic individuals can accomplish wonders if they buy into the institution's mission and are confident in its

---

[2]The importance of this point should not be lost. No institution in higher education today can afford to be all things to all people. Institutions must read their environment accurately and find their niche. This implies focus and specialization. TQM, while useful in some contexts, is about making processes more efficient, not about the crucial choice-making that produces the focus and specialization that ultimately will determine which institutions prosper in the future.

leadership. Nurturing this environment is the primary task of the president. TQM may assist some campuses in cultivating such an atmosphere; however, as we have seen, TQM is better at generating answers about *how* things should be done rather than *what* should be done. TQM focuses upon process improvements, not upon the gut-wrenching major challenges that confront American higher education today. And, TQM is often an expensive way to obtain these process improvements.

FINAL THOUGHTS

Higher education today finds itself in a whirlpool of fiscal stress, enrollment problems, disturbing academic flaccidity, tremulous leadership, and frequently declining public confidence. Only a few institutions have resisted this tide; nearly always, this success is due to an outstanding president who has been willing to swim against the tide.

Along comes TQM, and a frequently directionless and semi-paralyzed higher education establishment rushes out to buy. Are we making a mistake? Perhaps, because we fear that TQM has been oversold.

TQM can assist some institutions of higher education in improving their nonacademic processes. However, if TQM ultimately is to have a significant impact in higher education, it will be because TQM has been adapted to an environment specifically emphasizing inspirational leadership, a long-range vision emphasizing where the institution wants to go (and how soon), individual accountability, and cost reduction. If these conditions are not clearly and measurably present, no president will see an institution transformed or even significantly changed through TQM.

CHAPTER
eight
••••••
The President and Institutional Governance

Speak softly and carry a big stick. You will go far.

Theodore Roosevelt

If you empower dummies, you get bad decisions faster.

Rich Teerlink

Effective leadership means getting the best people you can find to share the vision and to help in achieving it.

Father Theodore Hesburgh

Over the past 20 years, faculty members, students, and administrative staff have assumed increasingly larger roles in campus governance. The concept of shared governance, born at our leading institutions, has become well established at many colleges and universities and, properly exercised, can greatly facilitate presidential power, particularly legitimate, expert, and charismatic power. Improperly exercised, however, shared governance can do just the opposite by promoting adversarial relationships, diluting presidential authority, and diminishing charismatic distance. In this chapter, we discuss principles that can make institutional governance both productive and rewarding.

RETAINING FINAL AUTHORITY

Although faculties, staff, and students should participate in governance, none of these constituencies should have or believe they have final authority over any dimension of the institution. Such arrangements lessen the ability of the president to lead and of the institution to act, and defeat the very purpose of participation in the governance process. These nebulous arrangements serve no one, neither faculty, president, students, trustees, or alumni. Divided authority simply does not meet the tests of troubled times.

During the Cold War, the Soviet Union proposed a *troika* form of leadership in which the agreement of three different parties (the Soviet Union, the United States, and a third power) would be required for any significant international action to be taken. The Soviets promoted this scheme as a means to increase trust and stability. The United States correctly viewed it as a recipe for inaction, which, of course, is what the Soviet Union had in mind. The astute governing board and president must realize that many faculty, staff, and student governance groups implicitly endorse the same sentiment. Their object is to reduce presidential power and discretion, thus enabling them to carry out or continue their own agendas under the guise of "shared" or "collegial" governance.

In virtually all dimensions of power, *troika*-type power-diffusing arrangements lessen the possibility of effective leadership. The wise new president of an institution with such a system will immediately create an appointed or elected commission to study governance. Better yet, the in-coming president will convince his or her governing board to reform the governance system before the new president arrives on campus. Scores of presidents have floundered or failed, not because of their own inability, but because their campus governance system effectively prevented meaningful leadership.

None of the above sentiments mean that a president can or should ignore the major internal governance constituencies on campus. An effective president is in constant touch with the campus, and values the interactions, information, and recommendations that flow from faculty, staff, and students. In some areas (for example, faculty curricular recommendations), these campus voices should be accorded great weight. In other areas (for example, student opinions of a foreign language requirement), these views should be assigned less weight. All legitimate constituencies on the campus must have avenues available to them to express their opinions, and the president must be available to hear those opinions. Such availability is not synonymous with agreement or automatic acceptance of the opinions expressed.

Ideally, a campus governance body has recommending authority over all matters that relate directly to the academic program and staff. Except for tradition and presidential uncertainty, nothing justifies giving binding authority over any area or concern of the university, including the curriculum, to any campus governance body. In all matters, the president should be the authority who is ultimately accountable to both the trustees and the concerned public. Handled sensitively, this design greatly facilitates the opportunity for charismatic leadership as well as for leadership using each of the other forms of power.

The literature of leadership and power indicates that the best form of campus governance has three main ingredients. First, those affected by decisions—faculty, staff, and students—should have a voice in their making. Second, administrators should be ex-officio nonvoting members. (Administrative staff are, in effect, agents of the president.) Third, the president must have final authority.

MODELS OF INTERNAL GOVERNANCE

Three major models of internal campus governance exist: a unicameral university senate composed of faculty, staff, and students; a combination of senates, each representing a separate constituency, such as faculty or students; and collective bargaining, which is consistent with, but sharply modifies, the two previous models.

An effective president can prosper with any of these three campus governance models, and there is no a priori reason to prefer one to another, with the possible exception of collective bargaining, which may be accompanied by other less attractive features that are unrelated to internal campus governance.

The theory behind a university senate—one that includes faculty, staff, and students—is that it represents the entire campus, and thus encourages unity and reduces internecine warfare. This is the experience of many campuses. Nonetheless, most university senates are dominated by faculty, and staff and students complain that their concerns go unaddressed. Therefore, these groups typically maintain their own representative bodies, and the president finds that he or she must contend with a proliferation of governance bodies, each of which purports to represent a particular constituency. Such a situation requires especially sensitive faculty leaders if a campus is to avoid divisiveness.

Separate assemblies allow each constituency to feel that its point of view is better represented, although a clever president can more easily play one assembly's interests against another, and internal dissension on priorities relating to pay raises and budget reductions can easily arise.

Where collective bargaining exists, the collective bargaining agreement typically defines and limits the scope of a faculty senate. If the bargaining agent wishes to weaken or neutralize the faculty senate, it will usually do so by means of the collective bargaining agreement. In such a circumstance, the faculty senate is often viewed as a powerless society. This perception can be dangerous for a president and disruptive for a campus, for it deflects the attention of enterprising faculty members toward matters not traditionally within the scope of faculty senates. For example, the faculty senate may become preoccupied with the evaluation of senior administrators (which is the duty of the president), or focus excessive attention on "democratizing" a range of campus processes, including promotion and tenure, granting of leaves, and nonsalary budget determination.

Collective bargaining does have a positive side for a president: It systematizes many governance processes and provides faculty with a ready means to express their views. It also allows a president to avoid criticism by simply pointing to a provision in the collective bargaining agreement and saying, "This is the way it is; the agreement says so."

Frequently, the actual negotiating and administering of a collective bargaining agreement for a public campus is done at a state-wide or system-wide level. Once again, this can be comforting to a president who wishes to hide behind the agreement; the president can legitimately point out that he or she "didn't do it." However, collective bargaining also limits the president's freedom and makes being a transformational president more difficult.[1]

Some argue that collective bargaining would never arise if administrators were more skillful and efficient; however, without discounting this explanation, it appears that collective bargaining more often emanates from adverse economic conditions that impinge on faculty salaries, pre-

---

[1] The assembled wisdom of presidents who have served on collective bargaining campuses is that collective bargaining makes improving the performance and quality of existing faculty more difficult. The tendency of campus bargaining units is to defend all the members of the unit, regardless of how deficient their performance might be. Further, bargaining units exhibit a strong preference for "across the board" salary systems in which current performance has little direct role. As a consequence, a president has few tools in his or her bag to influence the behavior of senior, tenured faculty members whose performance is inferior.

rogatives, and security. Whether or not collective bargaining exists, the president must deal with one or more internal senates or assemblies on nonbargaining, internal governance matters. The most powerful of those assemblies is the faculty senate, or a university senate dominated by faculty.

THE PRESIDENT AND FACULTY ASSEMBLIES

The relationship of the president to a faculty-dominated assembly is vitally important and primarily dependent on the extent to which the president is perceived on campus as having the status and authority to grant the privilege of participation in decision making. Faculty, like other human beings, respect power. If the president is seen as the source of internal governance power, then he or she is firmly seated on Saint Simone's platform.

On campuses where internal governance participation is a privilege granted by trustees, state legislators, or, as is increasingly the case today, off-campus chancellors, the effectiveness of the president is significantly undermined. The president can clamber up on to the platform, but the pole is greased.

To maximize presidential effectiveness, all formal access to a governing board should be through the president. Particularly in the public sector, statewide and multi-institution systems, coupled with the inhibitions of sunshine laws and required public meetings, often result in direct communication between presidential constituents (faculty, students, and administrative staff) and trustees and system officers, significantly reducing presidential power. Well-meaning boards create faculty or student liaison groups, or, even worse, provide faculty and students with membership on the governing board itself. This situation is ripe for disaster. Faculty and student board members have open conflicts of interest, are constantly importuned by their campus friends for the latest information, and seriously compromise the president's legitimacy, charisma, and distance. Faculty and student board membership should be avoided despite its populist appeal to campus constituencies and the public.

Many governance systems become impersonal unless the administration, led by the president, does its utmost to communicate effectively with faculty. Particularly if economic conditions are bad, faculty members are attracted to collective bargaining and dichotomies develop that make effective leadership less possible. The extent to which authority is vested in the office of the president and then delegated or granted by the president is closely related to presidential effectiveness.

One of the authors has served as a board member of six private colleges. Invariably, those institutions with the most problems and the highest presidential turnover have board members working together with members of the college community (faculty, students, and most staff)—members who normally fall under the authority of the board's appointed president. Those campuses whose trustees establish faculty or student membership on board committees or directly invite faculty or student input, or who assign trustees to interrogate members of the community (all in the name of effective communication and a concerned board), are almost always in a state of nonproductive tension. The president's job is to stay in touch with the campus constituency; if he or she isn't in touch, the board will find out soon enough.

THE PRESIDENTIAL VETO AND INFLUENCING CAMPUS GOVERNANCE

If the elected campus governance body only recommends, an effective relationship requires that the president rarely veto a recommendation from the assembly. Rather than veto faulty legislation, the president should call in the assembly leadership, persuasively outline his objections, and challenge them to return with an amended version more congenial to the institution's needs. The president who feels bound to use the veto often should probably make plans to move on; such a president is obviously not in harmony with the campus.[2] If such a poor relationship continues over an extended period, the president's charismatic power will diminish or disappear.

If the president and administrators play their roles effectively, vetoes will rarely be necessary. If high-ranking administrators are ex-officio assembly members, even without a veto, they can legitimately and ethically attempt to influence the assembly's consideration of issues, whether in or out of session, but particularly the latter. Studies have found that people expect their leaders to influence them and are disappointed when they do not (Torrance, 1959, 1961; Torrance and Mason, 1956). Faculty, staff members, and students will find an administration united together in good spirit a legitimate and admirable force. Most internal governance negotiations should be conducted by the president's agents (administrators), and it is always preferable to have the votes going into a meeting.

---

[2]A well-chosen veto, based upon sound academic or fiscal principles, can, of course, be good for the campus and for the president. Nonetheless, repetitive vetoes clearly suggest both communication and leadership problems.

Generally, faculty members (and students, when there is a student senate) like this system—except perhaps when it is explained this way—because their opinion is presented in an undiluted state to the president (often through an appropriate dean or vice president). Because presidential vetoes are rare, the process is accurately viewed by the campus community as the optimum in faculty-student participation in decision making. They not only participate but, in most instances, have the prime voice in academic decision making, yet the president both influences the voting process and remains in charge. This arrangement productively harnesses the talents of faculty and students, and, to most, is an acceptable form of shared governance.

A prudent president—in the spirit of Alexander Hamilton and the Whiskey Rebellion—may exercise the veto early in his or her term on a legitimate issue of comparative insignificance in order to demonstrate to the community that he or she has the authority and the will to use it. But with the exception of such ethical contrivances, the veto is a sign of failure.

ADDRESSING THE ASSEMBLY

There are other guidelines for presidential behavior vis-á-vis assemblies. Do not attend all faculty or student assembly meetings, and rarely stay for an entire meeting. The first item on the assembly agenda should be the president's report on campus activities and conditions, followed by questions. The president should not chair the assembly; the assembly should elect its own chair, usually a faculty member who meets with the president occasionally and the academic vice president regularly. A faculty chair protects the president from accusations of unfairly trying to control the assembly while allowing dissent about both the system and issues to be registered. (Take no more heat than necessary.) At the one-on-one meetings with the assembly's elected chair, consult with him or her about important presidential decisions that could have campuswide reverberations, and discuss things in general and become professional friends.[3]

The president should not even sit in the area designated for assembly members. After an invitation to speak from the elected faculty chair, the president should rise from the gallery. Presidential remarks should usually reinforce the "State of the College/University" address given in the fall at the opening faculty meeting (also attended by all administrators). Candidly inform the assembly about off-campus activities, problems, and strategies as

---

[3]On some campuses, the faculty assembly's executive committee meets with the president. Depending upon the circumstances, this, too, can be effective and win friends.

well as successes. Speaking to the assembly openly and in depth implies confidentiality and trust and keeps the audience's interest. If a president does this well, the charismatic ripples of trust and confidence will extend throughout the community.

FINAL AUTHORITY IN MORE COMPLEX INSTITUTIONS

Some institutions, especially the largest, have multicameral campus governance bodies, typically featuring separate organizations for students and faculty that independently make recommendations to the president. Other campuses have tricameral systems, assemblies for faculty, students, and administrative staff, each of which make recommendations to the president. A few institutions even break these groups further down into subgroups. If possible, a president in this situation should try to bring representatives of these groups together on occasion to reduce conflicting recommendations, but should not attempt to do away with the groups themselves.

Obviously, the key word here is recommendation. Regardless of how many formal groups exist on a campus, they must all make recommendations to the president. Although multiple assemblies can diminish campus unity and ignore political realities, the fragmentation of campus opinion can enlarge presidential power. In effect, the president becomes a broker, adjusting one faction's position to compromise with another and attempting to integrate all into the president's objectives. If ever forced to play one group against the other, the president should do so gently. Although the literature is not specific on this subject, a unicameral governance body probably best serves the president's interest and the special interests of the several campus constituencies.

COLLECTIVE BARGAINING

At an institution with mandated collective bargaining, nonacademic staff representation, or inappropriate trustee involvement in campus governance, the new president should either be assertive on the subject shortly after assuming office, or attempt to make the best of a bad situation by gingerly applying the tested concepts of power. (The presidential honeymoon is a time to accomplish wonders.) Sitting on such problems will only make them worse.

With collective bargaining, you should know and attempt to establish warm, personal relationships with union leadership, but you should not discuss the specifics of working conditions with them. When the time comes to negotiate, always send in an experienced negotiator and do not go yourself. In most instances of collective bargaining, you will not even have the opportunity. The president of a New England institution whose faculty voted for collective bargaining became actively involved in negotiating the first collective bargaining contract—always the most difficult one, and nearly always an adversarial negotiation that produces bad feelings. The president believed he would make friends by showing his interest; instead, he made enough enemies to fatally wound his presidency.

Remember that collective bargaining differs from more traditional patterns of shared governance. Do not make the mistake of the New England college president of thinking you are still colleagues in all things, but neither should you assume a harsh adversarial role. You are two distinct groups (management and employees) pursuing essentially the same goals from a different perspective. If you don't have collective bargaining in your institution, you can best preserve your charismatic leadership potential by designing a system (usually salary and personal perquisites) that is sufficiently attractive to staff to discourage faculty unions.

CAMPUS GOVERNANCE: A SUMMARY

The campus governance machinery can harness the collective intelligence of the campus community to common advantage, and also can serve as an effective channel through which the president inspires confidence, trust, and support. The surest way to cause campus governance to become adversarial is to treat campus constituencies in an adversarial fashion. Be patient, complete in your presentations, open in your answers, genuine in your respect for faculty-student representatives, unified in your administration, and spare in your attendance. You will be rewarded beyond your expectations.

FINAL THOUGHTS

- Never allow any group on the campus to make final decisions; everything must be recommended to the president.
- Attend the meetings of the internal governance assemblies periodically; be first on the agenda, provide remarks, answer questions, and then leave.
- Be brilliant, but failing that, shut up.

- Because you will not attend all campus governance meetings, you should have an observer at all meetings who can provide information, but who makes clear that he or she does not speak for you unless specifically instructed to do so.
- There is nothing wrong, and much right, with the administration doing a bit of politicking and making its point of view known to campus assemblies.
- Learn to lose, but don't like it.
- Be wary of unstructured give-and-take discussions on campus that assume the nature of a press conference. Some presidents can enhance their charisma and demonstrate their expertise in such a situation. Most, however, do not handle these situations well. Remember, you no longer enjoy the luxury of taking a chance on spontaneous brilliance or foolishness.
- Never play your cards for pennies in petty displays of presidential authority.
- Never allow the internal governance process to compromise the fundamental neutrality of the university; the university cannot be temporarily irrational and maintain the respect of society. Our collective irrationality during the past is one of the causes of our problems today.

CHAPTER
nine
• • • • • • • •

The President
and the Faculty

The faculty is the University.

John Cardinal Newman

*The faculty culture is risk averse. You don't publish in the leading jour-
nals if you threaten the intellectual standing of the referees, or suggest
that they don't see the world correctly.*

David Sweet

*The possession of unlimited power will make a despot of almost any per-
son. There is a possible Nero in the gentlest human creature that walks.*

Thomas Aldrich Bailey

Faculty members are the body and the heart of a college or university. It is
they who must produce, and they who are the most measurable test of a
president's leadership, influence, and mission. Faculty members must be
autonomous in their disciplines, respected in their governance role, and
gently reminded from time to time that the final authority is the president.
The president must lead, remind, and inspire the faculty beyond themselves. Concerning the presidential role vis-á-vis the faculty, recall the daily

adage used by the former vice chancellor of Cambridge University, Sir Eric Ashby: "I am a necessary evil."[1]

The degree to which the president is respected and admired by the faculty will be the extent to which he or she is able to inspire trust and confidence, the extent to which he or she is believable and can deliver (in relative terms). Faculty members are frustrating, fretful, cynical, and critical, but also supportive, brilliant, and even magnificent. Only they can transform the president's vision into reality. They must be cajoled, challenged, and, at times, faulted, but, most of all, respected and appropriately included in all important decisions affecting the institution.

FACULTY LEADERS

Many faculties meet exclusive of the primary campus governance body. In such cases, to make the elected leader of the faculty a voting member of the assembly is a valuable practice for both parties. It allows a faculty check on the assembly, and permits the administration to dilute the impact of negative faculty positions by providing a second chance to influence the deliberative process before resorting to a presidential veto.

The president or chair of the faculty should be viewed by the institution's president as the primary conduit for faculty opinion. Regular and frequent meetings with this person and serious efforts to cultivate his or her trust and friendship are in order. Here again, as is the case with the elected head of the campus governance body, consultation prior to important decisions is vital. Prior discussion not only helps reach decisions, but also obliges the faculty leader to stay on-board should problems develop after the presidential course is set.

However, other contacts with faculty are essential to establish and maintain presidential charisma. These less formal activities can help a president avoid a situation where so many voices speak for the institution that none does so effectively. Those frequent contacts with faculty convey to their elected leaders that you have other conduits to faculty opinion. Once again, the sensitive balance between distance and familiarity is an issue. There are ways to measure the pulse of the faculty accurately and, at the same time, to spare the president from overly ambitious faculty leaders who purport to speak for the faculty as a whole.

---

[1]Necessary, indeed. In 1919, a group of faculty in New York City gathered together to establish the New School for Social Research. Idealistically, they decided not to elect a president, and instead opted for governance by faculty committees. Within two years, they abandoned this model as unworkable and appointed a chief executive.

STAYING IN TOUCH WITH FACULTY

Many valuable techniques allow the president to stay in touch with faculty opinion and avoid exclusive dependence on elected faculty representatives. Staying in touch with the nonactivist, less political faculty members will provide valuable and often essential leverage in dealing with their elected spokespersons, who often are not a representative sample of the entire faculty. Indeed, keeping lines of communication open to nonpolitical faculty will facilitate effective use of all the forms of power discussed in chapters 1 and 2.

The president can use many informal methods to stay in touch with faculty aspirations and problems. Occasional invitations to a group of faculty to have lunch with the president usually are appreciated, as are invitations to the president's office sent to randomly selected small groups of faculty for "how's it going?" sessions (every six weeks or so). These informal gatherings should always begin with a statement from the president that reviews conditions, especially off-campus, and includes a note of inspiration (the vision). After establishing a frame of reference in the opening remarks, invite questions and comments and treat them candidly. However, to insure an optimistic session, the president should both maintain center stage and be a good listener. Whenever else these meetings are scheduled during the year, they should always be held toward the beginning and end of the academic year. At the beginning of each year, faculty members and the president have more to be optimistic about; at the end, people can always look forward to the next fall. More of these sessions may be more important early in a presidency than later on, but they are always helpful, particularly when an institution is experiencing financial problems. Faculty, for good reason, want to know that their president is in touch.

The same kind of meeting—not under the auspices of the faculty, the assembly, or even the chief academic officer—should be scheduled for all new faculty (if you have any). These meetings should follow essentially the same format as above, but should especially emphasize the institution's mission and your presidential vision.

Weekly campus tours provide an opportunity for everyone to see the president walking through classroom buildings. If invited, the president may even visit classes, and, on occasion, deliver a guest lecture. Dropping in on faculty members' offices for a brief conversation over coffee can also be worthwhile. Show up at least once a week where you are least expected.

Consider the unfortunate case of the western liberal arts college president who, in a well-attended governing board meeting, described all the campus classroom and office buildings as "air conditioned." The truth was that hardly any building or office on the campus, except his own, was air conditioned. The faculty, who long had believed that the president was out of touch, used this example to convince the board of trustees that the president had to go. He left shortly thereafter, never understanding both the reality and the symbolism associated with being seen on the campus.

Frequent and visible attendance at campus functions is important; this means getting used to feeling on view. At campus theater events and musical productions, mingle during intermissions, and go backstage afterwards to congratulate the performers. On occasion, visit the institution's intercollegiate athletic teams before or after a game—but take care not to do so too often, lest you be regarded as the apotheosis of most faculty members' fears, the "jock" president. Every event should be viewed as a leadership role—an opportunity to foster trust and confidence.

Attendance at departmental social functions is not always a good idea, especially those for the president's own discipline. At such gatherings, faculty press you overly hard on departmental affairs; when you attend one, keep moving. Try to avoid sit-down dinners; no function is purely social for a president. Never miss a retirement party, funeral, or memorial service; whenever possible, accept an invitation to speak at such times. These events are rare opportunities to unify people as well as to express sincere appreciation or condolences. Better to be late for official meetings, even board meetings, than to miss a special occasion of great happiness or sorrow. Also visit faculty, staff, and students in the hospital. They never forget, and you feel better about yourself.

Staying long at departmental or administrative parties is a mistake, and presidents relaxed by liquor should not drink. To limit your stay, imply that you have at least one more social function that evening. An experienced president can make appropriate remarks and the rounds in 20 to 45 minutes. Besides, people enjoy themselves more without the president; your absence gives them something to talk about.

The president who plays bridge, chess, or better yet, poker, or who was an athlete, can take the opportunity to play with faculty and staff, provided the stakes and egos are small. Mix on-campus and off-campus types in these events, and, in sports like basketball, even students. These activities are great levelers that do not sacrifice position when done occasionally. They are better than most social events because everyone is too involved to pressure the president to talk business.

FACULTY MEETINGS

Faculty meetings are not the best way to stay in touch with faculty opinion. Indeed, they can become so familial and leveling that the president is reduced to little more than a coordinator, and an ineffective one at that.

Although custom demands general meetings of the faculty on most campuses, they are of little value in terms of institutional direction, conflict resolution, or presidential leadership. If held too often (two a year should be enough), they can, all in the name of better communication, do great damage to the effective conduct of the institution and your presidential vision.

With the five sources of power in mind, call one meeting of the faculty in the fall to present a "State of the Institution" address and a charge for the year, and perhaps a second at midyear when the chief academic officer speaks. No other general faculty meetings should be called except during periods of emergency that provide you a charismatic opportunity. Do not attempt to resolve a serious problem at a general faculty meeting; the result will almost invariably be no solution or an uneasy solution, and a frustrated and less effective president.

BE THE PRESIDENT WITH THE FACULTY

As already suggested, presidents can scarcely afford the luxury of taking a chance on spontaneous brilliance and should arrange their presentations to the extent possible. Thus, a president should be wary of unstructured situations that can deteriorate into special pleadings on behalf of individuals or programs, or produce "off the wall" questions designed less for information and more for embarrassment. A president who holds an "open forum" with faculty and students (a popular, but risky enterprise) should by all means control the agenda and the forum, and ensure that his or her expertise and that of supportive colleagues, such as vice presidents, is more than sufficient to handle any foreseeable eventuality. These sessions can contribute to charisma by demonstrating expertise and providing the president with excellent opportunities to express his or her vision. On the other hand, they can degenerate into whining, adversarial denouements that reduce effectiveness.

Only an exceptional president can succeed continually in unpredictable, unstructured fora, and even those exceptional individuals sometimes rue their own desire for increased communication and openness when unrehearsed statements are later misinterpreted. President Bill Clinton's frequent unstructured, off-the-cuff encounters with citizens and the media aptly portray both the advantages and disadvantages of unstructured public encounters for U.S. presidents and college presidents alike. The faculty may love such encounters, but presidential statements made in haste or without proper reflection are difficult to take back or alter. Presidents no longer have the freedom to make strong statements over coffee with faculty, and then seek to "take it all back" the next day.

A president should look for other opportunities to demonstrate his or her public participation in the intellectual ferment of the day. For example, a president can offer seminars on subjects about which he or she feels comfortable and qualified, or write book reviews, but never on a book written by a member of the faculty. He or she can write opinion pieces for newspapers, and testify before appropriate committees. Occasionally, the president can attend campus seminars and (hopefully) ask penetrating questions, but should take care to avoid irrelevant debate or controversy. The effective president should take visible positions on the important academic issues of the day; however, he or she should seek to minimize involvement in the lacunae of such eternally controversial campus issues as parking and food. In such cases, there is much to lose, and little to win.[2]

On finite and well-chosen occasions, the president may choose to commit his or her own prestige, and that of the institution, in support of stances on issues that ring with special intensity for the campus. Consider the case of the public university president whose campus was invaded by nonstudent "white power" racists who sought to intimidate both his campus and the community. The president organized a march that involved both the campus and the community, and expressed the university's moral opposition to the white power advocates; while doing this, the president defended the right of the racists to state their views, however obnoxious, as long as they did so peaceably and without attempts to intimidate specific members of the campus community. This principled stand galvanized and united the campus community, and the white supremacists soon left for other pastures.

A president must be careful, however, in committing his or her institution to partisan stances on political and social issues and should resist any faculty impulses to do so. The presidency is a bully pulpit that should not be abused. The task of the university is to promote, not stifle, discussion on the issues of the day. The university must remain neutral except when its own structure, policies, personnel, and academic values are threatened. There is a profound difference, then, between speaking out against white racists whose views, if implemented, would violate university policies, and taking a

---

[2]The president should show interest, but neither express strong views, nor be a responsible decision maker. Someone else in the administration should deal with such matters.

partisan position on issues such as abortion or health care that have no special impact on the campus community.[3]

Other activities, including an appropriately modest program of teaching and research, can enhance the president as a leader in the faculty's eyes. Whatever the activity, the president must remember that he or she is not "one of them" while occupying the presidential office, regardless of past achievements in a discipline, or what they say. It is only natural for faculty to try to keep or make you one of them; if they succeed, it will be your fault, and you will be less effective as their president.

Recent research on faculty attitudes and presidential styles indicates that of the four styles identified—bureaucratic, intellectual, egalitarian, and counselor—the one most directly associated with faculty insecurity and perceived presidential ineffectiveness is the intellectual president; and, interestingly, this is the president "who most frequently communicates with faculty" (Astin and Sherrei, 1980). The intellectual president usually experiences the most frustrations and disappointments with faculty and is least "trusted" by fellow administrators. This president should probably have stayed on the faculty, for he or she lacks the confidence and commitment to establish sufficient distance from the faculty to lead them.

Nonetheless, David Riesman (1980) reported that faculty members serving on presidential search committees prefer candidates for president who have the characteristics of someone they would most like to have as a colleague—an interesting set of contradictions. Faculty favor presidential candidates who look like themselves, at least in background, if not in other attributes. However, once that individual actually is appointed president, most faculty regard his or her academic views as mildly or substantially irrelevant. Clark and Clark (1994) voice this warning: "Even though the faculty insist on a president with an academic background, the president who dares take the lead in academic reform is seen as meddling in academic affairs, claimed by the faculty as their own turf."

Notwithstanding faculty preferences, one of the major deficiencies of modern academic institutions is the lack of leadership provided by presidents on the pressing curricular issues of the day. The curricula of many American colleges are in tatters precisely because of a paucity of presidential involvement.

Even more than administrative associates, faculty must be credited for successes, and you must assume responsibility for failures. Faculty support is

---

[3]This does not mean, however, that the president, as a private citizen, cannot take positions on these issues. He or she should make it absolutely clear in such cases, however, that he or she does not speak for the institution.

fickle, never to be taken for granted. In commenting on the faculty, one administrative assistant recounted the following:

> I remember one state university president staring contemplatively out his window at a swarm of faculty coming out of an adjacent building following a general faculty meeting. "Look," he said, "there go a couple thousand people who are convinced that they know more about how to run this university than I do." (Carbone, 1981)

Notre Dame's Father Theodore Hesburgh (1979) observed that "Every day of every year, year in and year out, the president must prove himself to the faculty." With many faculty, their relationship to the president can be characterized by the classic question, "What have you done for me lately?" The wise president must understand that the typical faculty member regards the president as an equal, perhaps even an inferior, in academic wisdom and understanding. Hence, frequently they do not look to the president for academic leadership, and instead are primarily interested in the president's ability to deliver raises, buildings, equipment, travel money, and teaching and research support.

Friendships between a president and a faculty member can result in the friend supporting the president in hard times but arguing about every substantive decision or course of action. Such friendships can erode leadership because good friends simply know each other too well for any of the power forces to be effectively used. For the president who has been appointed from within the institution, the best advice is to be as "presidential" as possible without violating your obligations to close friendships. Do your best not to discuss the institution and its problems with them. Bear in mind, when tempted to become too personal in your relationships, that strong leaders who can deliver results are more admired and supported than leaders who are more friendly and democratic but who, because of their egalitarian natures, cannot back up their friendly stance through effective action.

CRITICISM AND REVENGE

According to the *Chronicle of Higher Education*, the average faculty member believes that the average administrator (presidents included) is slightly below average in performance. Faculty can be extremely disparaging of presidential performance, often being unfair and even contradictory. If the president balances the budget, she is stingy; however, if she runs a deficit, she is irresponsible. If another president maintains distance, he is perceived as being aloof; however, the president who dives into campus social life and becomes personally involved with faculty is seen as interfering.

Perhaps with some faculty, a president cannot win, even if he or she walks on the Biblical waters. This can be disconcerting to many presidents, especially "inside" presidents and former colleagues of the faculty who are accustomed to praise and friendship.

As a consequence, these and other presidents can become testy, defensive, and revengeful. Punishing faculty tormentors is almost always a mistake. After the initial satisfaction of revenge disappears, the president realizes that he or she has left Saint Simone's platform and joined the crowd below. Further, campus reaction to retaliatory behavior is nearly always negative; regardless of the facts, the president will be viewed as the Leviathan, and the individual faculty member as principled and powerless, even if a bit odd. The wise president keeps in mind the observation of Woody Allen that "You can never get even with the world; it takes too long and there are too many lawyers." You never can get even with unreasonable or abusive faculty; don't try. Your satisfaction must come from other sources.

FACULTY RECEPTIVITY TO CHANGE

Several national surveys have revealed that the typical American faculty member is politically more liberal than the average American citizen. This has inspired decades of mildly derisive punditry about faculty revolutionaries who wish to turn the world upside down, but "have never met a payroll." Faculty are viewed as radicals by their detractors—individuals who prefer societal change to the status quo.

Campus reality is different. Many faculty members may be ready to vote in the next election for a modern incarnation of Karl Marx, but they usually are remarkably conservative insofar as the nature of their own work is concerned. Most professors are comfortable with traditional academic staples such as the 50-minute lecture, tenure, academic departments, and credit hours. Many are uncomfortable with self-paced learning, televised instruction, electronic libraries, and credit for life experience. Further, in contrast to workers in most other occupations, faculty essentially are their own managers and have considerable ability to frustrate, alter, or stop changes they do not like or feel threatened by. Thus, change often does not come easily to the faculties of higher education.

Outside of higher education, in organizations such as Caterpillar, Ford Motor, Merck, or Hewlett-Packard, employees either change in response to management dictates, or they lose their jobs. This is not the tradition (or law) of higher education, where tenured full professors who are so minded usually can find a way to avoid changing their methods of doing things, regardless of what the dean prefers. If their college loses enrollment as a result, and some faculty must be terminated, it will be junior, temporary, or part-time faculty who go, not tenured faculty.

The innate academic conservatism of tenured, senior faculty at American institutions of higher education reflects many things, including their own significant managerial role and their insulation from the forces of the marketplace. Faculty often resist change, particularly change proposed by presidents and caused by forces external to their institutions. This resistance has resulted in numerous calls for restructuring higher education, declining political support, and several highly critical "exposes" of faculty and university behavior (for example, Sykes, 1988). Faculty and the institution of tenure are viewed as the heart of the problem. Even a friend, such as Robert Rosenzweig (1992), former president of the American Association of Universities, has concluded that "It is absolutely true that faculty are a major part of the problem. They are innocently or willfully ignorant of the real world."

Even though faculty are often risk averse and resistant to change, little of consequence can happen on a campus without at least their implicit agreement. It therefore behooves the president to work with faculty to increase their flexibility and responsiveness to changed conditions. In order to do so, the president must use all the sources of power outlined in earlier chapters. The president must articulate an attractive vision from a platform of legitimate power, demonstrate expertise, provide incentives for faculty to change, and create a sense of mission.

Of course, not all colleges have the same mission. In 1973, Sister Joel Read led Alverno College in Milwaukee through a discussion and change agenda that resulted in an "ability-based" curriculum that almost immediately captured national attention (and the interest of students). Sister Read worked with faculty, communicated a vision, and found ways to make that vision attractive to her faculty.

Faculty can and will change, but they require much convincing, many carrots and a few sticks, and, most of all, strong and capable leadership by a visionary president who is opportunistic, energetic, and willing to take risks. The president who succeeds in harnessing faculty power and enthusiasm behind his or her vision is virtually guaranteed success.

FINAL THOUGHTS

Faculty are the heart of the institution; they can be both a presidential bane and a blessing. They should be granted the right to interpret their disciplines as they will, subject, of course, to peer and student evaluation. In all other matters, their role should only involve making recommendations, although they should play a significant role in virtually all campus affairs. If you conduct yourself wisely, you can be their leader, benefit from their insight, and enjoy their company. But always remember—you are the president.

- If you have close personal friends on the faculty (and you probably will), be careful.
- Teach now and then. Better yet, also ensure that all qualified senior administrators teach periodically.
- Keep faculty well informed about the major initiatives of the institution.
- To schedule more than two faculty meetings a year is an exercise in intellectual anarchy and will yield a thousand directions, an unhappy faculty, and a frustrated president.
- You will never know for certain if you are liked by faculty; therefore, do not lose much sleep over it.
- Listen to everyone, and seek out the quiet performers.
- The president who spends too much time in the faculty dining room remains or becomes a member of the faculty and should return there.
- The extent to which you are one of the boys (or girls) is the extent to which you are one of the boys (or girls).
- Almost inevitably, you will be criticized, perhaps unfairly, by faculty. Get used to it. Do not seek revenge; it usually backfires.
- The value of your presidency will be the extent to which you maintain fidelity in individual relationships with faculty, students, associates, and all others.
- Always convert every complainer into a supporter, and try to do the same with your adversaries.
- Faculty may be liberal politically, but they are profoundly conservative in terms of their receptivity to changes in the traditional ways of doing their work.

CHAPTER
ten
· · · · · · · ·

The President
and the Students

The first flush of power is done in caricature.

C. Richard Gillespie

*We have to. . .become student-centered. It's not what you think they
need, but what they think they need.*

M.A. Guitar

What is the end of study? Let me know.

Shakespeare, *Love's Labour's Lost*

The best interests of each individual student should be the criterion
against which the president evaluates virtually every decision. This criterion tests presidential motives and heightens the trust and confidence
placed in the office by the community.

The time that you spend with students will be of exceptional value to
you. They are, after all, the primary reason the university exists and no
president can truly be considered a success if he or she does not serve
students well. Students also are a valuable source of information about
everything an institution does. While their point of view can be narrow and
fail to take account of the larger picture, students are nearly always candid
and less likely than other campus constituencies to harbor selfish motives.
Students can also be superb ambassadors. Their good opinion of you and

your institution will extend to all your power objects.[1] Hence, a president has good reason to spend considerable time listening to what students have to say.

Yet, many presidents take little time for students, probably because of rationalizing that there are more pressing concerns. However, students, along with support staff, can be the most enthusiastic, courageous, and valuable source of presidential support, for students will go right down to the wire with a president they admire.

Many students are idealistic, bold, uninhibited, and, unlike many of their mentors, not too sophisticated to give open admiration and affection. But students' trust must be earned. The president should take steps to gain student support early in his or her administration. Initial impressions are significant and carry on from generation to generation; alumni will warmly remember and financially support the president and the institution that pays attention to them and provides them with considerate, personal service.

CHANGING CAMPUS DEMOGRAPHICS

Fewer than 15 of every 100 college students in the United States today are full-time undergraduate students who actually live on the campus. The "New Majority" on college campuses today consists of part-time and commuter students who frequently also are employed, and graduate students. The two most rapidly growing segments of higher education enrollment today are community colleges (where on-campus residential living is rare) and distance learning (where students hundreds or thousands of miles away from the home campus use television and other technologies to access higher education).

In 1900, only 0.3 percent of the American population attended college—only 232,000 students, nearly all Caucasian men. By 1993, however, fully 14.99 million students attended college, of whom an estimated 55 percent were women (U.S. Department of Education, 1994). Women now earn more associate, bachelor's, and master's degrees than men.

At the same time, the student population of African Americans, Asian Americans, and Hispanics has burgeoned, as has the census of interna-

---

[1]An acknowledged example of a student body serving the ambassadorial role is Virginia's James Madison University, where enthusiastic student reports on their experiences there have been an extremely important factor in James Madison's move over two decades from a small, single-sex teachers' college to a "hot" institution of choice that is ranked favorably in many national periodicals. James Madison's highly successful president, Ronald Carrier, deliberately positioned the institution to produce this result.

tional students, which now numbers almost 500,000. Almost one in every four American college students now is non-Caucasian—African Americans lead the way with an estimated 10 percent enrollment (U.S. Department of Education, 1994).

But more has been changing than simply the sex and race of college students. Between 1970 and 1990, the number of part-time college students doubled, while the number of full-time students increased by only one-third (American Council on Education, 1994). By 1990, only 31 percent of students completed their baccalaureate degree in four years, down from 45 percent in 1977 (*Change*, 1993). Because many campuses have devised facilities, programs, and activities on the basis of the needs of full-time, residential students, these new demographics should give us pause for thought.

Students, part time or not, now often have jobs and children, whether or not they are married. Thirty percent of all children born in 1993 were born out of wedlock (Smith, 1994). When such individuals approach the campus, they have different needs than single, residential students who usually fall within the 17- to 21-year-old bracket.

Just as Mr. Chips long since has disappeared from American college campuses, the cinematic model student played by Van Heflin or Cary Grant who puts a tie on every day and sings "Boola" is far divorced from reality. Today's student is more likely a woman nurse with an R.N. credential who wishes to obtain a bachelor's degree, or an African-American male who will take six years to complete his bachelor's degree because he must work to pay his bills, or a graduate student with a family and children.

The upshot for the modern college president is that this New Majority student body has different interests from those of the traditional undergraduate, resident student body. The New Majority student likely is more interested in the amount and quality of the institution's child care or Saturday office hours, than he or she is in the football team or the next rock concert. Bus service, campus safety at night, telephone registration, electronic bill payment, child care, computer modem access, and the ever-present problem of parking are topics that surge to the fore.

Many presidents make only a cursory wave of acknowledgement in the direction of the New Majority students, for they seldom are as visible or

well-organized as the full-time undergraduate students, and they participate in campus governance less frequently. Yet, they pay their fees, take
classes, and deserve attention and services just as the traditional student
clientele does. And they have distinctive problems and ambitions. One
urban independent college president, after literally stumbling into a meeting of part-time and evening graduate students, emerged to declare that she
had discovered more about her institution and the quality of its services in
that one-hour session than in 10 years previous.

The president must seek out the New Majority students, for the very
welfare of the institution may depend on such communication. In at least
40 of the 50 states, demographic trends dictate that the supply of traditionally aged students will decline for at least 10 years. Already, about 45
percent of all students are aged 25 or older. Institutions that fail to
recognize this will find their clientele disappearing and face painful retrenchment, to say nothing of a dissatisfied group of recent alumni who will
refuse to provide financial support for an institution that they believe
ignored them.

The most difficult challenge in this regard will face those campuses that
continue to enroll significant numbers of traditional students even while
they attract much larger numbers of nontraditional, New Majority students. The president will have difficulty sensing the pulse of the student
body in such a situation, for there are many pulses. Stretching the institution's
resources to provide the different range of services and attention that each
group prefers will be especially difficult. But the president who falls out of
touch with the New Majority student body will regret it.

ACTIVITIES WITH STUDENTS

Surveys consistently indicate that students would like to see more of their
presidents (Astin, 1981). No student activities, roles, or moods are unimportant to a president. Starting with the orientation program for new
students, be present whenever possible. Use a color videotape for orientation programs when you cannot attend. In time, you may find that the
videotape is an excellent substitute; the association with television and
movies inspires an extraordinary sense of presidential importance.

Presidential talks to large groups of new students should be inspirational
and elevating, although one-on-one sessions with students are also important. Academic regalia at a fall orientation or convocation, as at other
campus ceremonies, can contribute to the aura of leadership. Such things
set the mood for the year, and that mood could be important by the
following spring.

The astute president knows that an hour in the residence halls in September could be worth literally weeks the next spring when trouble may strike. When students are moving into the halls, show up for a part of each day to welcome parents and students informally, help carry some luggage or boxes, or just sit on the curb in front of a freshman residence unit and visit. Here again, the key is not to get off the presidential platform. Do not carry luggage all day; just show people that you are not so impressed with yourself that you can't carry luggage. Most parents as well as most students and staff never forget these gestures, and they will give you more credibility during periods of difficulty than a spate of presidential proclamations.

Student residences are best considered the students' home. With few exceptions, only go there when invited. Invitations can come from individual students as well as from residence hall leaders and councils. Indeed, the popcorn and Pepsi sessions where the president sits on the floor with a group of students at 11:30 at night are usually the best (except on your stomach).

At primarily nonresidential institutions (including community colleges, commuter student schools, and institutions with heavily graduate student bodies or advanced professional schools), spending time at the student union or center, graduate or adult housing social centers, book store, or registration serves the same purpose. Most presidents will find a combination of residence hall and other campus social centers (including well-chosen visits to international and campus religious organizations) valuable, but the best advice is that each president should select multiple activities with students which he or she feels comfortable attending. One Midwestern liberal arts college president serves food to students in dormitory lunch lines; President Edward Malloy of Notre Dame plays basketball in the annual campus tournament; another president is a member of a jazz quartet; and President Bill Merwin of SUNY-Potsdam regularly buys pizza for his students and is overwhelmed by student requests to be part of the group. Whatever the activity, it should not subject the president to ridicule, for, as Father Hesburgh (1979) has put it, students "have an extraordinary radar for detecting double talk and the irrelevant." Stay in touch, but avoid the ludicrous.

Eating and drinking with students is a way to evaluate the quality and efficiency of the campus food service and to visit informally with students. To increase your impact and exposure, take your food tray and go up and ask to join them; most will be delighted. You, of course, must take the initiative. One president wondered why he could not relate effectively to students, complaining "I even go out on the campus and sit on a bench, and nobody joins me." This president could have learned from the large public university president who became famous on his campus for offering any student a "free lunch." Students were delighted and a half-dozen at a time would take him up on his offer. He learned a great deal from these sessions, and his reputation with students for openness soared.

A good check on the registration program is to ask a cross-section of students how long it took and what their impressions of registration were. Better yet, talk to a sample of students as they emerge from the registration process. If there are problems with the people or the process, you can trust students to let you know.

Knowing the social centers of the campus and regularly making the rounds is also good leadership. Both research and everyday observation reveal that modern American campuses are increasingly characterized by a diverse and changeable set of student social groups that seldom communicate seriously with each other. In a typical student union, the Greek-affiliated students sit with each other, as do the African Americans, the Filipino Americans, the athletes, the artists, the libertarians, the gays and lesbians, the computer jocks, the granolas, and so forth. Usually, this campus sociogram develops within the first few weeks of school, and by knowing where these students congregate, a president can take the pulse of the student community each morning before going to the office. If you regularly make the rounds, it is no surprise to students when you occasionally stop for coffee and a brief chat. It takes no more than a half hour to visit a sample of the student nerve centers every morning and still be in the office by 8:30 or 9:00, regardless of the size of the campus. (Vary the time of day occasionally.)

Attend student dances, debates, theater, and sports events, and make drop-in appearances at residence-hall or student-union bull sessions. Wherever you go, be visible. If you are at a dance, dance, or at least try; if you are at a football or basketball game or at the theater, be seen and circulate. Visits to players and coaches in the locker room after losses are ill-advised unless the team is particularly heartbroken. On the other hand, the president should be around for major victory celebrations. Whether made in defeat or in victory, the visit is best kept short.

STUDENT LEADERS

Characteristics of student leaders change with the times. During periods of relative tranquility, they are usually moderate to conservative, even inclined to refer to the president as "sir" or "ma'am." During campus unrest, they are almost invariably more challenging. Every meeting with the president is a confrontation or, at least, they try to make it one. Often they will go to great lengths to avoid a one-on-one session with the president. They usually know, at least intuitively, that if the president closes the distance between them, they will risk compromising their goals. If you cannot get them alone on campus, pursue them to their lairs; they can usually be found there late at night. Recognize that most student leaders (including those who edit the campus newspaper) assume office with the intention of reforming the institution. They usually have an agenda; find out what it is and how you can blend that agenda, and their enthusiasm, into accomplishing the goals of the institution.

Generally speaking, student body and class officers are more conservative, malleable, and less influential than student newspaper editors and experienced reporters. The leaders of Greek groups and other campus organizations are typically the most conservative and supportive of all. Obvious exceptions are radical and extremist organizations, especially troublesome during periods of unrest. During such periods, more traditional student leaders may want to help offset extremists. If so, use them. The president must know leaders of all important student groups, regardless of how fractious, and attempt to establish an honest rapport.

Rapport with the president of the student body and the editor of the campus newspaper is especially important and can be easily established, assuming commitment and sincerity on your part. Invite each to your office for a private session immediately after his or her election or appointment. If possible, initiate private meetings with all the candidates for these key posts before the winners assume office; such meetings will provide links with virtually all activist or potential activist groups on campus. Avoid forums where you are put on the spot by student leadership hopefuls; regardless of their brilliance, presidents always lose in such settings.

Assuming the student body president is elected in the late spring, it is often helpful to appoint the winner to a summer internship in the president's office. This practice is not so cynical as it seems. It gives the president an advantage when school starts in the fall because of the opportunity for rapport, but, more important, it also helps the new student body president understand the nature, procedures, and problems of a college or university. This understanding results in better student government and usually also produces an impressive and informed ambassador for the institution.

In the fall, establish frequent private meetings with the student body president and the newspaper editor or their representatives; put these meetings on the calendar and try always to be there. Talk about everything from your agenda to the student's personal plans. This kind of relationship almost invariably proves valuable for everyone, but especially during periods of difficulty.

SAYING NO

Although most bad news should be conveyed by deans and vice presidents, at times the president also has to say no to student leaders. A decisive no will be respected and usually adhered to, but should be explained in person rather than through messages or notes. Really poor student leaders, if of limited influence, are best ignored. If such a student holds a key campus position, any dealings the president has with him or her should be candid and direct and not veiled with false acceptance. The student's impact can also be diminished by cultivating his or her associates—vice presidents, assistant editors, and the like. One of the authors once challenged such a student body president to debate in the University Union, hoping that he would not accept. He did not, and resigned a short time later. Relief in the president's office was great, since this session could have backfired in a major fashion.

OTHER WAYS TO INFLUENCE STUDENTS AND THEIR LEADERS

Some of the best ways to insure presidential influence with student leaders, including those on the campus newspaper, are to hold regular and well-advertised student office hours each week, attend student social functions and stay a while, speak to student groups, and get out on the campus and be seen. By showing student leaders that they are not the president's only conduits to student attitude and opinion, their furor and even their influence can be greatly reduced. Students will be unusually inclined to work cooperatively with your administration, and rarely will they display a "we/you" attitude.

Generally, student leaders are motivated by the same things that motivate a president; they are just not as sophisticated. The great measure are good, decent, concerned persons with a sense of mission, anxious to advance their cause and themselves. Real zealots are rare, except in fringe groups, and caution has already been recommended in dealing with these people, whether they come from the right or left. Most student leaders will respect and like the president, given half a chance. They will listen, even change their positions, if you make sense, and line up right behind you when the chips are down. Respect is more important than friendship, for, contrary to conventional contemporary assumptions, a leader/follower relationship is still what students, and most other people, expect. The president who establishes genuine and close relationships with students will have a legion of supporters for life.

STUDENT UNREST

From time to time during a president's tenure, he or she may be required to deal with hostile student groups, which often contain a sprinkling of faculty and off-campus hangers-on. Whenever possible, the president should send the appropriate vice president, usually the student personnel officer, to talk and negotiate with such groups. Too many presidents feel that they have something to prove and go into these situations without regard for the chain of delegated responsibility. One of the surest ways to lose whatever presidential mystique you have is to louse up during a student confrontation. Remember, an important key to an effective presidency is presidential charisma, and charisma is best fostered in structured situations.

If there is an occasion where your reputation has been placed on the line, you may feel bound to meet a group of hostile protestors. In such a situation, if at all possible, the group should come to the president's territory, preferably in or near the administration building. The venue should be a public place, a meeting room or lounge, not the president's office. (If students forcefully occupy that office or anywhere else on campus, they should be *carefully* arrested after being so advised and given a reasonable amount of time to vacate the premises.)

The president should meet the group alone—without the usual protective entourage of staff and associates. Invariably, this will take them off guard. A few trusted associates should be scattered throughout a large and hostile crowd, but these individuals should not participate in the dialogue. In such settings, with your supporting structure virtually gone, it is best to divest yourself completely of your presidential appointments; such an appearance will disarm the protestors and give you a better opportunity to establish a "charismatic moment."

Always try to confront the full body of protestors rather than agreeing to meet with representatives of a protesting faction. Because a college president is likely to have more experience making presentations to a group than student leaders, the president has an advantage. The president can also spot opportunities to divide the group and get factions debating one another. By contrast, meeting with representatives allows the president's adversaries to present themselves as legitimate opponents, and to interpret even a written presidential message as they will. Resist the temptation to meet with what, at the moment, may appear to be a smaller and therefore less threatening group.

If possible, obtain the group's demands in advance of the meeting. This gives you the advantage of speaking first and tends to diffuse the group's solidarity behind its goals. Any president should absolutely refuse to respond to nonnegotiable demands, without casting judgments as to their intrinsic legitimacy.

Speak extemporaneously or from notes, but do not use a prepared text. If possible, the session should be unobtrusively taped. Prepare a press release before the session to be edited quickly afterwards. Speak for at least 10 minutes, calling as many students by name as possible. Explaining the president's role and responsibility, lead with remarks that draw you together with the group and only then address their demands. In most cases, a president will be able to evade actually answering the demands by pledging to present in writing reactions within a mutually agreeable time period. The president who can do this may be able to end the session as a hero and dissipate the group's hostile energies at the same time. If the leaders haven't read or remembered Sol Alinsky's *Rules for Radicals* (1972), the president is home free, at least for the moment.

Insist on civility throughout your remarks. Questions should be invited after the president speaks but neither long speeches nor attempts to cut short answers should be tolerated. (If interrupted, keep talking.)

Accepting a little abuse is actually not a bad idea. Some members of protesting groups may hurl names, be rude, or say things that would ordinarily prompt a strong response. Do not overreact to this behavior; you can actually gain support from otherwise unsympathetic members of the audience.

After a reasonable period, no more than an hour, simply thank the group for their attention and leave. When leaving, be joined by an associate or two to prevent the possibility of continued discussion during the departure. The idea is to keep the entire session under your control, not theirs.

After the confrontation, encourage members of the group to talk privately; most of them will feel guilty. Some may even tearfully come to the president's office to apologize. Regardless, if you spot them alone or in small groups on campus, talk to them. Other administrators cannot do this in place of the president. The aftermath of confrontation is an ideal time to build strong relationships and inspire understanding and support.

Finally, do not hold a grudge, regardless of what has been said or done. Within the bounds of ethics, enlisting members of dissident groups can produce valuable allies for the future. Their presence during meetings brewing radical causes can often prevent problems. One president hired as his assistant the student leader who spoke most vigorously against him during a campus strike; that student is now a college president. Another president finally won over a student who had once declared the president an "incarnate evil." Since that time, the student has become a prominent journalist and has written more than a half-dozen flattering personality profiles of the president in major local and regional publications.

THE CHIEF STUDENT SERVICES OFFICER

Another critical communication link to students is the chief student services officer, the president's in-house superego, a conscience against which to weigh decisions affecting students. The longer a president's tenure in office, the more likely he or she is to take for granted or forget the primary importance of students. So, regardless of the president's background, a highly placed person in the administration should be charged with student advocacy.

The role of a professional student advocate is too important to be delegated to just another manager. Loyalty and competence are of course important, but the person must be able to speak effectively for students and accurately assess their moods. "Company" types do not work well in this position. The chief student services officer must be willing to argue with a president, yet be steadfastly loyal to whatever position is decided upon. Within the terms of loyalty, the chief student services officer must be free to advocate, and, during periods of difficulty, his or her position may be in conflict with the advice you get from your other vice presidents. Remember personal chemistry when making this appointment; you may often hear things from your chief student advisor you would rather not hear. Listen thoughtfully, and then strike your own course.

Student services, student affairs, and student personnel areas have grown significantly during recent years. They often include such areas as counseling, remedial programs, residence halls and off-campus housing, student unions, and student organizations, as well as admissions, financial aid, health centers, and intramural and intercollegiate athletics. We personally question this plethora of responsibilities because it tends to make administrators out of student services officers who ought to be "in touch" advocates. If you have such an arrangement, or a similar one, your chief student services officer must also be a capable manager who understands fully the principles and practice of delegation and accountability. The very nature of student services work, and the characteristics of individuals who gravitate to work in these areas, make this a challenge. To find a person who combines the attributes of student advocate and manager is difficult, but you must find that distinctive individual who can do both. If you appoint only an advocate, you have a constant administrative mess. If you appoint the manager, you find yourself unadvised or ill-advised about students during periods of difficulty.

FINAL THOUGHTS

Faculty are the body of the university, but students are its lifeblood; a good and successful president recognizes this, honestly cultivating them, understanding them, striving to earn their respect and affection, and never taking them for granted. After you have left office, few things will make you feel better than a former student who meets you and warmly says, "We miss you."

- *Listen* to students! They have something to say.
- An hour in the residence halls in September is worth a week in April.
- Test your convictions on each new student generation. In the process, you will change and stay honest.
- Never act out of uncontrolled anger; be ashamed when you do.
- Make decisions based on the best interests of the individual student, not the department, the institution, the state, or the church—or even the pressing demands of student politicians.
- Never countenance the violation of the duly constituted law.
- If you want an irresponsible student generation, grant them amnesty when they violate the law. When the campus is viewed as a refuge from the law, both you and the students are in trouble.
- Do not be afraid of group confrontations. They can be fruitful and exhilarating, but never go into them unprepared.
- Try to be out of the office and on campus during the first week and last week of school; you can be gone the rest of the time and not be missed.
- When students start calling you by your first name, you probably need a haircut.
- Never consider nonnegotiable demands.
- Dance with students, play basketball and chess with them, go to lunch with them, participate in a step show, or play in a jazz quartet with them. Have fun, but never become ludicrous.
- Remember that more than 85 percent of today's students are not full-time undergraduates living on their home campus. On many campuses, the old demographics and old models of student interests and behavior are passing away.

CHAPTER
eleven
•••••••

The President and Off-Campus Constituencies

Anyone who isn't heard outside the campus isn't worth being heard inside.

Father Theodore Hesburgh

God is usually on the side of the big squadrons against the little ones.

Roger DeBussy Rebutin

Always do right. This will gratify some people, and astonish the rest.

Mark Twain, 1901

To become influential, a president must be visible. To become visible, a president must be bold. To be bold, a president must risk being controversial. To remain at all comfortable and retain the presidency under such conditions, you must know what you are talking about. Such knowledge requires reading, listening, and, above all, surrounding yourself with superior persons. To keep superior persons, a president must take care of them and be exciting. Being exciting means being visible and bold. And so it goes.

The president is vital in insuring the success of off-campus ventures—the cultivation, enlistment, and involvement of external constituencies. Historically, most books on presidential style and leadership effectiveness have paid less attention to external affairs than to any other relevant topic (Astin and Scherrei, 1980; Benezet, Katz, and Magnussen, 1981). This view of the relative importance of the tasks of the presidency has begun to change in recent years (Crowley, 1994) because no responsibility is more important to presidential success than the responsibility for external affairs (Fisher, 1980b).

Too many presidents underemphasize or neglect their off-campus responsibilities, usually because their backgrounds (usually academic) make them more knowledgeable and comfortable on-campus than off-campus. Many presidents rationalize their lack of attention to off-campus challenges by saying that they are bogged down with more important matters on campus, or by confessing that they are just plain uncomfortable dealing with off-campus people and conditions. This lacking so diminishes the potential of their presidencies, that individuals who do not understand (or who fear) off-campus presidential responsibilities and opportunities should not be appointed president.

THE INTELLECTUAL PRESIDENT

Presidents who have arrived at their office through academic chairs are especially prone to minimize their external responsibilities. Indeed, many presidents of this type never make it onto the presidential platform because they are unable to draw sufficiently far away from the comfort of their academic backgrounds (Astin and Scherrei, 1980). The "intellectual" president (whether or not from academe) also often has the most serious problems with faculty and staff. This occurs for two reasons. First, academics are often cynical, and sometimes condescending and patronizing in their attitudes toward nonacademic types. An individual at all inclined this way, thrust into the "outside world" as a solicitor, may well have an unsettling (and unsuccessful) experience. Second, the lack of success by such a president on the "outside" almost immediately leads to a decline in his or her charisma and power internally. Faculty respect presidents who have power and contacts that they do not, and who can produce results. Presidents whose "outside" performance is mediocre will not produce results that faculty respect (and expect); soon these presidents find that even their academic judgments are questioned. The reason for this situation has much less to do with their academic virtues, and much more to do with their off-campus performance.

INSTITUTIONAL ADVANCEMENT: THE PRESIDENT'S EXTERNAL ARM

Most colleges and universities have a line division called development, university relations, public affairs, or institutional advancement—or some combination of these. It usually includes professionals in public relations, fund raising, alumni relations, publications, and government relations who can help a president relate to external groups. This division should rank just behind the academic affairs division in terms of presidential priorities and attention. Academic affairs and institutional advancement are the basic determinants of the charismatic president's administration. Indeed, the degree to which a president is able to make wise use of the professionals in institutional advancement[1] may well represent the difference between the presidency being bland, colorless, and undistinguished or exciting, significant, and stimulating. Make no mistake, however, the president remains the key player in the external affairs program.

External affairs officers can be a president's greatest asset in the systematic quest to enhance his or her public presence and influence; treat them as such. Of course, like presidents, advancement professionals can sometimes lose sight of the goal in a forest of unrelated particulars, and may need reminding.

A president must be able to negotiate smoothly and effectively the external forces that will determine the future of the institution. To take these for granted, or to assume that someone else can or will completely handle this role for a president, is complete folly. Chapters 11 through 15 consider the rationale, systems, and techniques of external relations in greater detail. These chapters concentrate on how to use the various forms of presidential power with each of the following external groups: influential persons and benefactors, trustees, politicians, public figures and bureaucrats, the media, and alumni. Complete information on each aspect of administering an institutional advancement program is available from the

---

[1]Strong institutional advancement personnel are invaluable, but difficult to identify and retain. The very nature of the positions sometimes attracts individuals who are "salesmen" in the most traditional sense. More than one president has been "sold" a virtual bill of goods by institutional advancement personnel whose verbal skills greatly exceeded their actual ability to perform.

Council for Advancement and Support of Education (CASE), 11 Dupont Circle, Washington, D.C. 20036.

THE PRESIDENT AND GENERAL PRINCIPLES OF EXTERNAL RELATIONS

There are some general principles to adhere to in all external relations. Here again, the charismatic characteristics of distance, style, and perceived self-confidence that produce a significant public presence for the president must be cultivated, for most presidents have little legitimate and reward power and almost no coercive power in external situations. The degree to which a president is able to establish the charismatic qualities that produce a public presence is, in large measure, the degree to which he or she is able to use expert power effectively and advance the institutional mission.

Remember the following points from the research reported in chapters 3 and 4:

1. Too much informal behavior may reduce effectiveness; the president is always the president. Stay on the platform.

2. Although the president should be involved in many external activities and arenas, the involvement should not be too deep, for deep involvement risks virtually all your power forms as well as exhausts an inordinate amount of time. Your first and primary obligation is to the institution; spread yourself around, be visible, be brief, but genuine, and you will be charismatic.

3. The president's effort to influence external conditions to the advantage of the institution should not be equivocal. People in the external community expect and need to hear your vision as much as those on campus.

4. When speaking to groups, individuals, or the media, know the subject and try to be the only expert on it in the group. Ordinarily, presidential panels are to be avoided, especially on television.

5. Trappings are just as important to a presentation off-campus as on-campus.

6. A small entourage can be important with off-campus groups; at least take along an assistant. Make your solo appearances disarming, rather than the rule.

7. Speeches to an external audience should be delivered from its perspective, not the president's. Merit does not necessarily triumph in speech-making. (More on this later.)

8. It is important that those off-campus *like* the president. Within the limits of your nature and code of ethics, try to be attentive to, and interested in nonacademic types. In time, you will like them.

9. The president must always at least appear energetic. Never tell a reporter, a trustee, or a politician that you are tired or harassed, and do not tell anyone that you have a cold or need sleep.

THE NEWLY APPOINTED PRESIDENT

The first, essential order of business in external affairs for a newly appointed president is to begin immediately to seek and accept community speaking engagements that are important enough to be reported in the local media. Speak to everyone, from the American Legion to the World Federalists— the right and the left, social and service groups, political and professional organizations, religious and recreational groups. The larger the group, the better. Appearances on radio and television and quotation in newspapers and magazines should be sought.[2]

If possible, write regular features for local newspapers on any subject the papers are willing to print, providing you actually have something to say. Or, do a regular radio or television show. Never turn down an opportunity to appear as a principal on a show or to be the subject of a feature article (again, providing the topic is legitimate and you will not be subjecting your presidency to ridicule). An institutional leader who is not a good public speaker or feels unusually uncomfortable on television, should talk to a public relations professional about getting help. These public appearances should be candidly critiqued by the president's assistant and advancement staff, and their objective responses should not be confused with disloyalty.

Although debatable among public relations professionals, your staff might issue news releases on all your significant formal appearances. Several years ago, a friend called one of the authors with the happy news that he had just been appointed to his long sought college presidency. After sharing the joy of the moment, he asked the awkward question, "Should I write my own press release?" The answer was an unequivocal "Yes," and he

---

[2]If given a choice between a newspaper feature and an article in a professional journal, always take the newspaper. Remember that your effectiveness will not be primarily determined by publication in distinguished academic journals.

was reminded that he was not going to Harvard and of the importance of those first presidential steps. Further, he was advised to have his draft release edited by the PR officer (whom he knew well) at his present institution and to have the PR officer send the release to his new PR office.

For the most part, institutional news releases are only picked up by small local or weekly papers, but these are useful. Occasionally, major dailies may print an item. Typically, large newspapers must be "sold" a story and convinced that it is significant before they will print it. That process constitutes one of the most important tasks confronting your news and publications staff, which, if sophisticated, can use recent technological developments such as "Profnet" to place stories in national outlets. Releases should also be sent to television and radio stations, which sometimes pick up stories missed by the newspapers. They should also be sent on a selective basis to members of boards and others you influence. Providing they are sent meaningful material, community leaders appreciate being informed about the institution, especially when they receive news before it appears in the media.

Invitations to appear at celebrity events and tournaments, even the "right" fashion shows, are best accepted. The aim is to become known and admired by the general public. Do not assume, however, that presidential advancement is the only dimension of college and university public relations—far from it; a good public relations program includes media cultivation by staff, feature stories about campus programs, people, unusual scholarly and research activities, and other things.

In the course of time, presidents take chances, and upon occasion, become controversial. Whatever the controversy, the cause must be worthy and the case sound and above logical contradiction. (Another reason why the president's associates must be superior is to enable them to critique presidential generalizations.)

With a good external relations program, politicians will assume their constituents admire the president, bureaucrats will think that politicians do, trustees and influential persons will assume that everyone does, and the media will find you interesting. What the president must never forget is that this image is largely undeserved and must regularly be reviewed, refueled, and refined by more objective advisors. Pity the president who takes his or her image to heart; but have one you will, so shape it as carefully as possible.

YOU ARE THE STAR

Many presidents are uncomfortable with the notion that they should to some extent portray "star" qualities. With rare exceptions (e.g., Princeton, Stanford), the president, rather than the institution, must be the star. While others will receive major public recognition, none must, for long, exceed the president's; the president must lead, and publicity fuels the president's charismatic image and ability to lead. Credit must be shared with colleagues, but ultimately presidential leadership and authority cannot be shared.

Because charismatic distance is an essential component of long-term presidential effectiveness, successful presidents learn to avoid social relationships that diminish distance, charisma, and "star" quality. Often, this is easier said than done, as all presidents have a need to unburden themselves from time to time. However, while president, do not expect to speak to anyone on nonpresidential terms. If you do so, you and your presidency likely will suffer.

Presidents learn to cherish the rare anonymity they find and become ever more grateful for the friends they have. They must never forget, however, that they remain the president in the eyes of students, faculty, alumni, and citizens—often disconcertingly so. Most presidents are not anonymous, even when they believe they are. Consider the following examples:

- Author James L. Fisher was vacationing in Greece. Walking down a village lane singing with friends, beer in hand, he came face to face with a student from his home campus (Towson State University) who said, "President Fisher, what a surprise seeing you here."
- Author James V. Koch and his wife were enjoying a hamburger and a libation in a cowboy bar some 600 miles from his home campus (the University of Montana). They were enjoying their too rare time together, believing themselves completely anonymous. Hardly. As they departed, Mrs. Koch left her jacket (which had no identification on it) in the establishment. When the Kochs arrived home two days later, they were flabbergasted to find that the lost jacket already had been returned to the president's office. An unknown friend in the saloon had recognized them and sent it back to the university.

You are never anonymous when you are president. You may think you are, and may, to your detriment choose to act that way, but you kid yourself. You are always on stage. The authors have been recognized by alumni bicycle riders in Oxford, tourists in Japan, and soccer players in Bermuda. Their automobile license plates have been recognized in parking lots near and far from home. A presidency is a high-visibility occupation, and the incumbent must come to terms with this fact or pay, along with the institution, a high price.

The president must use "star" status intelligently. George Bernard Shaw said, "You get a man through his religion, not yours." Whether talking to a potential contributor, reporter, trustee, Rotary Club, legislative committee, or alumni group, never be so thoughtless or so absorbed in conveying your vision and message that you fail to appreciate the conditions that motivate the audience. Including in the presentation the listener's power centers, especially in the case of politicians, will almost invariably win your cause. The merit of a cause is never sufficient; it may win sympathy, but rarely the day. A speaker who ignores the listeners' concerns is likely to become known as that "nice guy who is completely unrealistic," a person few treat seriously off campus—and, in time, on campus as well. He or she is also the president who becomes bitter and hostile toward off-campus decision makers, feelings that are hard to hide.

THE EXTERNAL INFLUENCE POWER HIERARCHY

To succeed in external relations, the president must identify and cultivate the people with the money and power to help the college or university reach its goals. With this important group, charismatic and expert power are in order, with a measure of legitimate and reward power and virtually no coercive power. This hierarchy of wealthy and influential people can be more important than the governor, the education and editorial writers for the major newspaper, and, in many instances, even the trustees. If a president can come to be viewed as one of the hierarchy, he or she will be able to command the admiring attention of all the others. This is particularly true in the case of independent institutions.

In spite of proclamations and protestations to the contrary, the leadership hierarchy nearly always ranks at the top of the socioeconomic scale in all communities. They are corporate leaders, newspaper publishers, political and foundation leaders, and the wealthy landed families of the local aristocracy. Several decades ago, these individuals almost never were *nouveau riche;* today these individuals may well have recently assembled their wealth because of their entrepreneurial, technological, or scientific expertise. Bill Gates of Microsoft is a prime example.

Some members of the new power elite, however, are neither "well born" in the usual context, nor wealthy. Instead, they hold influence because of their political power or moral suasion. The Rev. Dr. Martin Luther King was a power broker both because of his message and because "he could get things done." The changing demographics of American society have gradually, but continuously, altered societal power relationships. Today, a senior African-American legislator or clergyperson may exercise as much influence as a traditional Caucasian male member of the landed gentry.

This latter group of power brokers—those newly endowed with power—did not necessarily graduate from the nation's most select academic colleges and tend to be geographically and institutionally mobile. They have not, therefore, developed deep loyalties to traditional academic institutions and causes, and may even have developed some suspicion of such. As a consequence, they represent unexploited opportunities that require skillfully developed entrees and cultivation. The president must find ways to meet them, include them in institutional events, and demonstrate to them that they can meet their own goals through becoming involved with, and supporting, the president's institution.

Whatever the source of their influence, you have an advantage with these leaders, for they tend to have more respect for a college or university president than for most politicians, trustees, and (especially) the media. They derive a certain self-enhancement from being associated with you and the university's mission, and your presence with them is reassuring about the general order of things.

Once again, distance, style, and perceived self-confidence are crucial. Regardless of your own social background, do not be obsequious or obviously uncomfortable. Comport yourself with dignity and as much grace as possible without contrivance. Presidents who have already incorporated these charismatic leadership qualities into their style can just be themselves. Failure to do so soon means being ignored, for your presence can become an uncomfortable embarrassment for them.

Ultimately, however, cultivation of the power elite requires that the president be able to offer an appealing, substantive vision that these individuals deem attractive. Otherwise, the president shortly will appear to be manipulative and shallow. Substance must be present; yet, many presidents have developed solid, substantial programs that never garnered the support of community and state leaders because the presidents did not understand how to persuade those who could make a difference.

WHO'S WHO

The president who did not come from the local power aristocracy should have the advancement staff put together a book on the local hierarchy. Each entry should include as much as possible about each person: photograph, education, assets, interests, persuasions, politics, family, and so forth. Absorb this to the extent that you rarely have the sense of meeting a person for the first time.

With this "Who's Who" prepared and learned, the president is ready to cultivate these people in nonstressful, nonproblem settings. They should not be asked for anything specific until a relationship has developed, which means spending numerous evenings attending civic functions, serving on hospital and symphony boards, giving speeches, attending cultural and athletic activities, and spending hours on the tennis court or golf course. The after-activity conversations and drink breaks will pay off. Anyone uninterested or unable to do most of these things is probably the wrong person for the job.

SERVICE CLUBS AND COUNTRY CLUBS

Unless the setting is a small town, it is generally not a good idea to join either social or service clubs. Vice presidents and other administrators can belong to the Rotary and Kiwanis; the president should speak to them. After joining a club or other group, some of the advantages of distance are lost. Join only the top organizations, if you join at all. A better policy is to "attend all, speak periodically, but join none."

Although joining a country club may seem attractive, it can jeopardize credibility among some constituencies. This is especially true when the country club has a past history of denying membership to women and minorities. When the president's memberships and social activities differ from the president's words, the memberships speak louder.

Although there are notable exceptions, a president should rarely be publicly identified as a member of a group or even a political party. The president of an institution can best gain the support of those who count if he or she has few such encumbrances.

APPOINTMENTS TO BOARDS AND COMMISSIONS

Appointments to community or statewide commissions, task forces, and the like can be of value. If the mayor, governor, or other public official extends such an invitation, it is usually because a president is achieving a significant public reputation, or, alternatively, because the official needs a respected public person to buffer an unpopular decision. The president's staff should carefully research and critique all the possible consequences before responding, but, if possible, these invitations should be accepted. Nonetheless, avoid no-win situations, such as the governor's invitation to serve on a commission to recommend new abortion legislation, or a commission to locate a new prison site.

On the other hand, membership on a state high technology board, or a prestigious federal commission, can be both interesting and productive. Ordinarily, you should not accept membership on a board or commission whose meetings you are unlikely to be able to attend.[3] The wise president will strike an appropriate balance between serving on everything (and gaining the reputation of never being present) and serving on nothing (and having no influence).

GETTING THE HIERARCHY INVOLVED ON CAMPUS

Although the reverberations of public activities and speeches will eventually result in invitations, a president shouldn't wait that long to begin cultivating the local hierarchy. One of the best ways to attract their interest is to elevate the cultural and athletic events sponsored by the institution. Arts balls and exhibits, special events, speakers and musical performances that appeal to influential individuals, and major tennis or golf tournaments are possibilities. Several of these activities can also generate additional revenues.

Meals are good situations for meeting members of the hierarchy. Luncheons are better than dinners, and breakfasts are best. For the most part, extend luncheon and breakfast invitations and accept dinner invitations. Until in office for a while, few presidents can induce many truly important people to come to dinner and end up wasting valuable time and institutional money entertaining faculty, staff, and friends who cannot help the institution much.

---

[3]Exceptions include the president allowing his or her name to be used on the letterhead of short-term community endeavors organized for specific purposes, for example, a testimonial dinner for an important local citizen or the diabetes foundation, etc. Such activities, even when the president cannot attend, contribute to presidential power and influence.

ONE ON ONE IS BEST

By far the best way to establish good relationships with others is one on one in informal and relaxed settings. There are as many ways to relax as there are human beings. Some prefer tennis, sailing, or golf, but watching sporting events, playing chess, attending concerts, playing computer simulations, hunting, fishing, jogging, and walking have all been used effectively by presidents to establish rapport with individuals of influence.

Two techniques have worked especially well for the authors in establishing strong personal relationships. One involves inviting targeted guests to breakfast in the presidential board room. The guest is invited to come any time between 6:30 and 9:00 A.M. With the help of a good assistant who is out of sight by the time the guest arrives, the president prepares breakfast, seats the guest, pours coffee, and calls his or her attention to reading materials beside the breakfast plate. These materials should include the morning newspaper on the bottom of the pile, and the president's most important message on top. At the appropriate time, breakfast is served, and the conversation almost invariably will gravitate to the informal agenda set by the pile of materials the guest has perused while the president finishes preparing the meal. Guests will be impressed that the president does the cooking, which is usually not difficult in this era of "healthy" breakfasts. Breakfast prepared by the president usually costs less than breakfast prepared by staff. The invitee almost always comes because few people extend breakfast invitations, and through the years typically becomes one of the institution's most constant supporters and contributors.

The other technique involves making a visit to the individual's place of business and asking for a detailed tour of the establishment's operation or production line. (This will work best if an appropriate dean or faculty member has prepped you for the meeting and tour.) Your host will be surprised that you want to know more about his or her business and will be delighted to find that you already know something about it—a comparatively rare occurrence for academics. The conversations you have with the host after the tour, and all subsequent encounters, usually will be productive because you broke out of the mold. Successful professionals and businesspersons enjoy talking about what they are doing; when you provide them with the chance, you vastly increase the chance that eventually you will be rewarded with a gift, a series of student internships, or political support.

DRESS

With persons of influence, dress is another sensitive subject. Local aristoc-
racies everywhere are virtually the same in their interests, values, activities,
and clothing styles—Brooks Brothers or clothing that looks like Brooks
Brothers. They can spot kindred souls anywhere by their dress. Many
college and university presidents look like they just stepped from the pages
of an old and wrinkled J.C. Penney or J. Crew catalog; others foolishly try to
affect the latest student styles. It is all right to economize, but a president
ought to buy the right look.

In Chapter 2, we discussed "the presidential look" in terms of clothing
and accessories. Dress has become progressively less formal in American
society in the 1990s, and today many organizations sponsor "dress down"
days, typically on Friday. Further, appropriate dress on a Boston campus
bears little relation to what is suitable on a campus within sight of Waikiki
Beach in Honolulu. Nonetheless, every president should follow two rules
with respect to dress. First, dress as well as the people of influence in the
area. Second, dress appropriately for the occasion. Do not acquire a reputation as a stuffed shirt because you consistently overdress for an occasion,
but take care not to underdress either because it will label you as an
individual who does not know better.

One of the best ways to insure a cold reaction from most of the members
of the local hierarchy is to look like you do not know better. Poor appearance can mean that important invitations are not extended. With people
who do not care, what you wear will not matter; with people who do, it can
often make an important difference. Why risk compromising a good case
over something so easy to change as the color of your suits?

FINAL THOUGHTS

Because of their academic background, many presidents are so facile and
clever with words, and so attracted by the campus milieu, that they deceive
both themselves and others on campus about the importance of external
affairs. They consider off-campus matters to be beneath or beyond them,
and some even think such matters are unimportant or trivial. Do not think
this way! Such a view results from fear and a lack of sophistication, both of
which can be overcome with an adventuresome attitude and a top advancement staff.

Remember the following:

- Excellent institutional advancement personnel are hard to find, but essential.
- If people are not fair, honest, decent, and good, say so.
- The president's main job is off-campus; do not be afraid to mingle with strangers.
- Do not make the mistake of believing that you are anonymous; even when you are far away from the campus, you are usually not.
- Academic freedom is precious; guard it, and do not allow those whom you seek to influence to compromise it.
- The university is a sanctuary for the presentation of any idea. Do not be afraid to say so, even when those of influence complain.
- Unless in a small town, speak to but do not join service clubs.
- You will acquire a reputation among the power elite as a charlatan and social climber if you do not have a captivating vision for your institution. If you do not really believe in that vision, you will not succeed.
- Dress as well as the local individuals of influence.
- Spend entertainment money to boost your stock, not your ego.
- Speak to everyone!

CHAPTER
twelve
• • • • • • • •

The President and Politicians, Public Figures, and Bureaucrats

Power is the great aphrodisiac.

Henry A. Kissinger

We can't do without dominating others or being served. . . .Even the man on the bottom rung still has his wife or his child; if he's a bachelor, his dog. The essential thing, in sum, is being able to get angry without the other person being able to answer back.

Albert Camus

All men are motivated by self interest: man should play his friends as pawns on a chessboard, one against the other.

Niccolo Machiavelli

Politicians and public figures are among the easiest to cultivate of any in the hierarchy of wealthy and powerful people. In most instances, they are highly sensitive to the attitudes of their major supporters and to their own reading of popular opinion. Of course, the college or university president also has access to these supporters and to the public, and politicians realize this—their supporters are your supporters, and their public is your public. In this sense, college presidents and public figures are much alike.

Few members of a legislative body are profoundly influenced by the intrinsic virtue of any request that you may place before them, by its importance to your institution, or by its vital nature to you as president. Your case ordinarily must be presented in terms of its importance to their major supporters and to the public at large, those people on whom the public figure depends. Do this and you will increase your chances of succeeding in the political arena. The key to doing this is to win the support and confidence of the general public—that is, to establish yourself as a charismatic president with a public presence.

BECOMING POLITICALLY POWERFUL

Power plays a key role in decision making in any arena (Pfeffer, 1981). Centuries ago, John Locke observed that "the great question. . .has been, not whether there should be power in the world. . .but who should have it." If you wish to wield political power as a president, then you must build influence with those individuals upon whom elected officials rely and depend. One of the most direct and fundamental ways to begin that process is by speech making. Make speeches in public figures' districts to all kinds of groups, including political clubs and organizations such as the Rotary and Kiwanis, the American Legion, local and regional economic development organizations, real estate professionals, the Urban League, Boulé, and religious organizations. Such speeches will place a president in contact with the people who form the backbone of most political organizations.

Another opportunity is the political fund raiser. Political fund raisers on both sides of the aisle are important to attend, and many times complimentary tickets are surprisingly easy to obtain. The candidate will be pleased to see the college president there and probably will not realize that the president is doing the same thing the political leader is doing—building a base of support. This advice is especially important for the presidents of community colleges and four-year public institutions. Author James L. Fisher once served as a president in a state with 26 public institutions; he saw only two other college presidents with any consistency at such functions and they were both successful in the state legislature. The other presidents wondered why.

Take along a small entourage to mix with people and learn names, interests, and positions. If possible, a public introduction should be arranged subtly through the politician's aid by an assistant or friend in the group. Everyone should know that you attended, although not because you announced it.

Newspaper columns or articles and television and radio appearances can be especially helpful in influencing politicians and public figures. A president with a three-minute radio commentary on the most listened-to local station will find that no one, including local politicians and newspaper publishers, has more public influence. (More on this later.) At least no one will be perceived as having more public influence. People will always be in when that president calls.

CAMPAIGN CONTRIBUTIONS

Contributing to political campaigns is not a good idea, but if you do, use your own funds and contribute to both candidates. Early in his presidency, one of the authors got into difficulty by allowing himself to be pressured into buying tickets to an expensive political fund raiser. He rationalized that it was justifiable, for the moment at least, to draw funds from the university foundation to pay for the tickets.[1] The ensuing newspaper publicity dramatized the mistake.

POLITICAL EGOS

Politicians have among the largest egos of any influential group, with the possible exception of talk-show hosts. Some are friendly, considerate, and thoughtful; others are impervious to reason and inordinately sensitive. Nearly all politicians react quickly to slights from anyone outside their hierarchy, and most do not forget quickly. Some are abusive, condescending, and rude, but only until you become "somebody" to their constituents.

However you feel about them, elected political officials are absolutely essential to the welfare of colleges and universities, and can make or break them. For example, Senator Robert Byrd of West Virginia, while often criticized for his "pork barrel" activities on behalf of West Virginia's public and private institutions of higher education, may well have done more for these institutions than any other single individual, including their presidents. At the state level, powerful elected officials can lavish support upon, or starve, specific institutions of higher education, both public and independent, by their actions or nonactions. A mid-South newspaper editorial

---

[1]Note that recent legal developments strongly suggest that the tax-exempt ("501-c-3") status of collegiate foundations is in jeopardy if the foundation's funds are used to support political candidates.

writer once suggested, not so facetiously, that a hitherto struggling independent institution ought to be renamed after a powerful regional politician
because of the tens of millions of dollars that this elected official had routed
(sometimes surreptitiously) to that institution. Thus, courting (and, more
important, influencing) politicians and pivotal public figures constitutes a
"must do" item on the job description of a modern college president.

Almost without exception, elected political officials appreciate a president who is willing to come to their office or home for a significant
conversation during a time period well removed from legislative sessions. If
the legislative session begins in January, make these visits in the summer.
You will receive their undivided attention and usually have the opportunity
to talk substance. As one legislator pointedly observed to author James V.
Koch, "most of your friends (the other presidents) don't want to get their
shoes dirty."[2] If you are willing to get your shoes dirty and visit the farms,
homes, and offices of legislators, you can make long-term friends.

Do not make the mistake of believing that because you are a college or
university president, you are automatically important to politicians, public
figures, and bureaucrats. To most of them, a president counts for little until
he or she actually enters the greater public domain, makes contacts,
acquires influence, and is known and perceived as being admired. Once
this happens, attitudes will suddenly change and the institution's budget
proposals pass more easily through city and state legislative committees, as
will any other reasonable legislation the president favors.

Author James L. Fisher's first appearance before the Joint House-Senate
Committee on Budget in the Maryland General Assembly occurred only a
few months after he took office. He was told that he had only 20 minutes to
represent the condition, aspirations, and interests of the state's second
largest institution to the state's elected representatives. He wrote out every
word and rehearsed carefully in front of his bathroom mirror. The presentation was a perfect 18 minutes, and he thought it was grand. After respectful
amenities, he began a splendid address, glancing only occasionally at his
prepared text, which he had memorized by that time. He soon noticed that
some committee members were reading newspapers. A little later, the
chairman seemed to be engaged in some kind of amorous activity with an
attractive administrative assistant. As he launched, disconcerted, into his
crescendo, he noted that one committee member was actually asleep.

---

[2]One university president became legendary when an apocryphal story circulated that he
had been willing to climb under a tractor to talk with a hard-working farmer who doubled as
the chairman of a state appropriations committee. According to the story, the chairman was
so impressed that he promised the president a million dollars on the spot. Although not
accurate, the story did wonders for the president's reputation.

Shaken, he finished to the sonorous tones of the now disengaged chairman saying, "Thank you, doctor, for those eloquent words." On the way back to campus, Dr. Fisher told his associates that they would never again treat him that way because he was going to do the things necessary to ensure that he would be taken seriously. Relying upon the type of program outlined in this book, he soon succeeded.

POLITICIANS AND PUBLIC FIGURES ON CAMPUS

Invite public figures to the campus for events that will have large audiences. They often enjoy the activity and always appreciate being introduced. People on campus will be impressed that their president can attract such noteworthy public figures.

On such occasions, a photographer from the institution should always be present to photograph everything. Virtually all the shots should include the president: in the locker room with the senator and the basketball team, at the reception before the show, playing tennis, or shaking hands at the Christmas party. There should be pictures taken of the president and members of the faculty, student body, and staff. (Always smile, and never be photographed with a glass or cigarette in your hand.)

Afterwards, depending on the degree of community sophistication, brief reminders of the occasion can be penned by the president on photos and sent out. Some presidents even frame the photographs before sending them. In time, a president will probably see his or her face hanging on walls in studies, offices, libraries, and dens. When others do the same thing to you, however, do not hang the photograph. To do so would simply tell people who visit your office the people you know who are more important than you.

PRESIDENTIAL OFFICES AND MEETING THE POWERFUL

The physical character of the president's office is a legitimate subject for discussion, especially when it is used to meet influential civic and political figures. The decoration and configuration of the office transmit a message about its occupant just as much as speeches and public appearances. A presidential office should set a serious, dignified, but almost understated tone that subtly suggests leadership, power, and a substantial incumbent. If possible, it should include tasteful paintings and other art objects that the president personally enjoys and can discuss knowledgeably, but few school symbols, and only a few memorabilia that personalize the office. Campus, state, and American flags can be combined tastefully with wood furnishings and attractive carpets (dark blue is preferred to pastel colors) that evince both substance and taste.

In fashioning your presidential office, note well that the object is not to spend money ostentatiously, but to convey an atmosphere. An attractive plaque reciting John Masefield's "The University" might provide the final touch for a setting that will assist the president in influencing people and transacting important business.

COMPROMISING PRINCIPLE

Most politicians are sincere, outgoing, public-spirited individuals who, as a matter of course, regularly find it necessary to compromise on particular issues and positions in order to be productive and remain in office. These individuals, and the accommodating roles that they fill, are honorable and necessary for the body politic to function effectively and fashion consensual legislation that can pass.

Such compromise, however, is not the same as compromising basic *principles* that relate to equal treatment before the law, fundamental concepts of equity, and vital performance standards. The longer a politician serves, the more likely it is that he or she will have compromised otherwise sacred principles. Rare is the legislator who has not cast a "clothes pin vote"—a vote in favor of something so objectionable that a figurative clothes pin is required to avoid being overcome by the smell. This, however, is the nature of the American political process.

Because compromise is at the heart of that process, most politicians find it easy to ask the president to compromise his or her institution's rules and standards. When politicians get to know a president, many will not hesitate to ask for everything from residence hall rooms with a view, to jobs, special admissions, and special consideration for the sons and daughters of constituents. Treat such requests with the utmost respect, but resist gracefully and firmly if you are being asked to compromise fundamental rules and standards. Regardless of how important a particular political leader's vote seems, his or her support is never worth inappropriate concessions. The president who has successfully gained a reasonable base of popular support will be less tempted to make such concessions.

The president who compromises basic institutional policies is on a slippery slope and has taken a few steps on the road to exit from office. It is one thing to provide basketball tickets, obtain a library book, or to provide a courtesy check on the status of a hiring process for a legislator. It is quite another thing to adulterate the institution's academic standards, or to compromise its academic freedom in order to cater to the passing whims of political figures.

Most governors and national officials will also test presidents. Treat them with the courtesy and respect due the office, but resist any inappropriate requests gracefully and try to provide some noncompromising favor instead. Remember that these people stay in their positions at least partially because of the patronage they can give. Nonetheless, a president who is gullible enough to allow them to use an institution inappropriately will regret it. The trust and confidence of associates and people on campus is more important to a presidency than a favor for the governor or any other powerful figure, but you can gain the trust of both groups and maintain your integrity in the process if you understand and establish a public presence that results in charismatic power.

BUREAUCRACY

Bureaucrats are often in the company of politicians, but have little in common with politicians other than an interest in power. Many government bureaucrats have the power to break the president of a public institution and distress the president of a private one. They can be unctuous, officious, and humorless, but usually are intelligent. They enjoy being courted, and a discerning president will show them respect and keep them well informed. Generally, they convey little respect for college presidents or their associates and many delight in forcing a president they believe to be overcompensated to toe the line on a small issue. Although there are exceptions, most bureaucrats pay attention to you only after you become "somebody."

Although essentially the same, federal bureaucrats and congressional aides in Washington, D.C., are sufficiently different from their state and local counterparts to warrant further comment. Because of the size and complexity of the government, their ability, and their staying power, congressional aides in Washington often develop influence beyond that of even some elected officials and should be accorded respect consistent with their achievement. They are usually exceedingly well informed, sophisticated, and occasionally sympathetic. Although a few are interested in a professorship or administrative position, they are usually impervious to a college president's power and must be approached from a base of expertise. Always know what you are talking about when making a presentation to an experienced congressional staffer. His or her job is based on tenure and expertise, which you can increase by making the staffer look good. Do not be obsequious. Although some congressional staff will act as if they expect such behavior from you, they will not take you seriously if you are obsequious. Comport yourself with confidence, charismatic distance, and surety, but be especially certain that the surety is impeccably accurate and substantial.

CATERING TO BUREAUCRATS

Presidents and business officers both in public and independent institutions often are advised to cater to bureaucrats and to invite them to campus golf courses, football games, and private parties. Such events can be highly productive opportunities to explain your institution's needs. Many bureaucrats come in response to such invitations, but the smart ones minimize such occurrences because they want to remain free of obligation, personal or otherwise.

Often bright, sometimes informed, and usually completely honest, career bureaucrats seldom feel great job or performance anxiety because government policies usually make them immune to dismissal, except at the highest levels. It can be a waste of time to curry favor with nonpolitical, career bureaucrats, who will not respond to charm or flattery, but will develop, at best, a grudging affection. Presidents who grant them special favors often discover that the bureaucrats do not expect to reciprocate and only feel more contemptuous of their benefactor, and deservedly so.

On the other hand, treating bureaucrats with respect and keeping the most influential of them informed of the institution's plans and programs (by timely visits, especially prior to budget-making and legislative sessions) can pay off handsomely, for these individuals are the "invisible hand" of government. Political leaders often rely heavily on key legislative and executive branch staff members and the astute president must take steps to be known and respected by these aides.

HOW TO BEAT THE BUREAUCRAT

Higher level bureaucrats and top department heads ordinarily are appointed by elected officials, and therein lies the key. If not caught up in the labyrinth of a multi-layered state system, the president can beat the bureaucrat by cultivating the private citizens of influence behind the elected officials, thereby winning the top elected officials, the top appointed officials, and the bureaucrat. These people are easily identified by reading the newspapers and asking people who have been around a while. They are most effectively impressed by how a college president has cultivated the general community and the media and may even begin to court him or her as a political candidate. These powerful figures are easier to deal with than their politicians, because they are more secure and therefore less guarded and more candid. Politicians come and go, but bureaucratic power figures often stay on from administration to administration.

CULTIVATING THE POWERS BEHIND THE THRONES

Treat respectfully those legislative and gubernatorial staff people and close advisors who are "powers behind the thrones," but meet them on your own terms whenever possible. They respect a well-prepared president who is not brazen and will often grant favors to the president who recognizes their position of influence, has taken the time to seek their opinions, and has gotten them involved. Many presidents do not take the time to do so.

The "powers behind the throne" believe that the president who will not compromise his or her principles is at once admirable, naive, and educable—particularly if they see latent political potential. If you have established a public presence they will see, respect, and even fear latent political potential even if it is the farthest thing from your mind.

Many key individuals who congregate around the centers of power enjoy being around college presidents (especially when the president has established a public presence) and this presents numerous opportunities for advancing your cause. If you cultivate such companions carefully, these individuals will carry the word around that you are charismatic, politically astute, well informed, and able to marshall public opinion. As a result, public institutions will find their budget documents less extensively revised, requisitions and requests for new positions approved, impressive buildings budgeted and built, and budget hearings smoothly run. Independent institutions will find fewer questions raised about public aid to private colleges, cost comparisons, and special capital construction grants. These results come from an institution's president being viewed as "somebody."

FINAL THOUGHTS

In summary, politicians, public figures, and bureaucrats are important to the presidents of both public and private institutions, but especially to the presidents of public institutions. They need not be catered to, or feared, but they should certainly be respected and deliberately considered by the president. Because of the great public vulnerability of the politician and the public figure, and the dependence of the bureaucrat on both, they as a group can be recruited as allies. The key is for the president to win the admiration of the persons upon whom they depend. Do not spend excessive time courting the politician or public figure alone, for your worthy cause will simply not measure up against their need for public acclaim. Instead, find ways to augment your public presence and thereby cause many different individuals to carry your case for you.

Carefully establish a public presence, which is a most important component of charisma. Be with their voters, for they are your people too. The next chapters will suggest more specific ways to develop and shape your presidential image.

- If politics is dirty, you will always need a bath.
- Cultivate the people off-campus and the people who control the people whom the people think represent them.
- Never deny convictions for the sake of peace and equanimity.
- Do not allow political figures to compromise the fundamental principles of the institution.
- Fight issues, not people; never personalize combat.
- Beware of the bureaucrat in a drab suit and a government-seal tie clasp. He is conscientious, usually intelligent, without humor, and often insensitive to academic matters.
- Treat bureaucrats with respect and keep them informed. It will pay off.
- Do not get overly serious at social functions unless you are invited to do so by a person of influence, and, even then, it is wise to adjourn the conversation to a more private setting.

CHAPTER
thirteen
• • • • • • •

The President
and the Media

The greater the power, the more dangerous the abuse.

Edmund Burke, 1771

People everywhere confuse / What they read in the newspapers with news.

A.J. Liebling, 1956

Omnipotence is bought with ceaseless fear.

Cinna Corneille, 1639

Four hostile newspapers are more to be feared than a thousand bayonets.

Napoleon I

I hate television. I hate it as much as peanuts. But, I can't stop eating peanuts.

Orson Wells, 1956

The president's off-campus image is composed of a jumble of impressions formed by a relatively inattentive public. However, this image is the major factor in developing a public presence and an aura of charisma. In the great majority of cases, print and broadcast media (and especially television) are the prime instruments for creating an image. Play these forums as a virtuoso plays a violin, although, like most virtuosos, you may seldom be satisfied with the reviews. A direct connection will not always exist between your public image at any moment and the immediate response you wish to receive, but the general public's prevailing impression of a president's standing will set the tone and determine the limits of what faculty, students, staff, alumni, trustees, politicians, public figures, bureaucrats, and potential benefactors will do for the president. Even the most experienced, important, and sophisticated people make judgments based on how many people admire an individual.

REPRESENTING ALMOST ALL PEOPLE

Although a president should be alert to his or her standing with the faculty, students, staff, trustees, politicians, and other public figures, these groups are often a distorting mirror of the president's image or prestige among the public at large. Each group has limited and different constituencies and priorities and will typically claim to speak for "their" people, and purport to be more effective and committed representatives of the people than the president is. They are not. Not if you are doing your job. A president must never even imply this to be the case, even if at any given moment it is, for to do so would obliterate your charismatic potential with whichever group these individuals purport to represent. From that point on, you will be dependent upon the whim of the representatives, for they will clearly know that with "their" people, they will be your master. Remember, they are your people, too, or at least potentially they are.

DEVELOPING A PRESIDENTIAL IMAGE

Unless the leader of a Northwestern or a Johns Hopkins, a president's first moves may not send out ripples that extend far, but they are nonetheless vitally important to the presidency. The public image takes shape the day an incumbent is first perceived by anyone as the president. This is different from being seen as a scholar, dean, vice president, or public figure in another arena. Once an image of a president is formed, it changes slowly, if at all. The president who starts off low-key, waiting a while to study conditions before determining a course of action, is almost irreversibly stamped as indecisive and anxious, regardless of what is done later.

The public at large is almost always too preoccupied to be easily impressed by a university president. Public attention is drawn to many issues: country, kids, sex, crime, schools, pocketbook, or pleasures. Anyone who can present these common concerns as "ours" will gain public attention and then proceed to convey his or her own particular mission.

A president makes more of an impression by doing than by telling. If a president speaks of challenging antiquated and unproductive conditions, then he or she must challenge them. If you are not prepared to do something, then do not raise the subject. A president who asks people to give time and effort and does not give of him or herself to the extent possible, should not expect significant contributions. A president should try to find a way to express his or her purpose through personal action that has special meaning to the public, and do so early in the administration. This aspect of leadership is a formidable assignment, for it competes with daily pressures in the lives of the public as well as with a president's earlier, sometimes too visible performances.

MANAGING PUBLIC ISSUES

Although a president can control few of the events that command the attention of the people, some issues can be managed and turned to advantage. Some issues can be used as a stepping stone to an ever-widening audience by calling attention either to that issue or to another legitimate and timely issue.[1] Such issues in higher education are government ineptitude, bureaucratic inefficiency, tuition and fee levels, the economic impact of higher education, faculty teaching loads, excessively democratized curricula, uneducated students, declining job markets, student unrest, and reduced government support. Get people where they are, and proceed to take them where you will, assuming that the cause is legitimate and worthy. (Sadly, these techniques work whether it is or not.)

USING THE MEDIA

The media, the prime instrument for cultivating the greater public, will at times appear as a simultaneous bane and blessing. Presidents are misquoted, misrepresented, distorted, exaggerated, and sensationalized—if they are lucky. When the institution is in trouble, the president is responsible and must explain. For better or worse, in the last analysis, the institution's voice is the president's. The president will have an image regardless, so every effort should be made to insure that the image is accurate and enhances the institution's mission and the president's vision.

---

[1]Even so tragic a campus event as a murder of a student can (and has) been used to convince the campus constituency to behave more safely, to garner additional funds for campus security from the legislature, and to convince a surrounding city to increase its police coverage of the campus.

Here are some guidelines for effective media relations. First, hire a good public affairs professional. To the astute president, this person is almost as important as the chief academic officer. In an emergency, the public affairs officer (sometimes called the public relations officer or public information officer) is the president's single most important conduit to the public on and off campus. The importance of the president being free to concentrate on the issues at hand can be offered as the reason for designating a spokesperson.

From the first day, this person should be the institution's official voice. This in no way distracts from the president's identification in the public eye with the institution. A good public affairs officer is so finely tuned to the presidential role and personality as to quickly develop an almost intuitive sense about the president's best interests—when to speak and when not to. This person is more objective than the president, a presidential assistant, or spouse. The public affairs officer is the only person fully informed regarding the president and the institution who can also take the pulse of the media accurately and sensitively. He or she writes well and quickly, performs happily in crises, and is completely and totally the president's. If your public affairs officer cannot be so described, hire another one. The public affairs officer does not pretend to be neutral and, whether or not he or she reports directly to the president's office, has a tested loyalty beyond question.

The good public affairs professional can assume responsibility for all the institution's publications and periodicals, be involved in the president's formal and informal "friend-making" activities, keep an eye on the campus newspaper, and serve as a scapegoat and solver of other communication problems that are bound to present themselves.

Like the president's assistant, the public affairs officer should be encouraged to be ruthlessly frank and candid and to say "you are wrong." Honesty is not disloyalty. Some people are always waiting for a president to lose composure or get angry. Under ordinary circumstances, anger might be justifiable, but a president only displays emotion publicly after careful thought. The student press can be provoking, but the normal tendency to lash out should be controlled. The public affairs officer will caution a president and help stay the natural need to justify and defend oneself.

SPEAKING DURING PERIODS OF CRISIS

The question of when to speak is always answered primarily by feeling and intuition. In the last analysis, the president has to make the judgment. The advice and intuition of the public affairs officer, however, should be heeded above all others.

During periods of difficulty, neither impetuosity nor reluctance should determine when to speak. During campus crises or unrest, the president should speak at the peak of the drama, but always let the staff know what he or she plans to say before they have to handle the reverberations. Soldiers should see only stirring and inspiring flashes of the general during combat; to be there all the time invites the loss of their attention and perhaps their support.

Another good practice is to touch base with leaders on and off campus before announcing major decisions or changes in direction. A president should not appear to be asking what to do too much, but rather, should be more informative than questioning. Tell them why. If this is done effectively, most will be supporters or at least remain silent if a strong negative backlash results from a presidential action.

MEDIA APPEARANCES

To the extent possible, public media appearances are best staged. Perform on your terms, not theirs. Press conferences and "media days" are good if media representatives will attend. Calls to sympathetic reporters to offer a story break (about all a president can give a good reporter) will often lead to a favorable story. Regardless of what is written later, people remember the first story. For this reason, a call from the president to previously neutral or even unsympathetic reporters is both surprising and more effective than waiting for them to call. Finally, virtually all invitations to appear on television, radio, or in print should be accepted unless the situation is obviously and completely biased. Try to go on radio and television live rather than taped unless you are assured of a sympathetic reporter.

REPORTERS

A reporter's job is to report a good story and not to promote an institution or its president. The final test with experienced members of the media is expertise and truth: expert power. Except for the most callow and inexperienced reporter, charisma will buy little with them. Indeed, of all a president's constituent groups, reporters and writers are probably the least impressed by any of the standard measures of power. Legitimate power means little to them unless a president is on intimate terms with their publisher, senior editor, station owner, or manager. Even then, a good reporter will not be affected.

Most reporters are inured to rewards. The most professional ones from major news outlets will not accept them; others often take everything from free meals to special passes and even trips, and simply accept the treatment as a matter of course. The rule of thumb is, "The more you give, the less you get." Good reporters think less of those who ply them with rewards, and this lack of respect will somehow creep into what they write. Let relationships with reporters and media personalities be polite, but never obsequious, and let them develop naturally.

Many colleges and universities are located in geographic areas covered by a single daily newspaper. More often than not, a single reporter will cover most higher education topics. That reporter may be smart or dumb, honorable or deceitful, ambitious or slothful. Whichever the combination, he or she is a powerful individual whose reporting can have a major impact on the institution and the president. A good working relationship with this individual is essential for the president. Above all else, the president should be truthful with this reporter, and as helpful as is reasonably possible. Let this reporter know when he or she has written an especially good or bad story and provide unemotional suggestions.

One subtle, though important way to influence a reporter's coverage is to meet with the editorial board of the newspaper periodically to update them on institutional developments and to provide them with fodder for editorials. A reporter who knows that the newspaper's editorial stance is in favor of, say, a land acquisition by the college is less likely to write inflammatory prose about that process. Once again, however, this will work best if the editorial board visit occurs before the anticipated event.

EDITORIAL BOARDS AND RADIO TALK SHOWS

Regardless of whether you are attempting to influence a reporter's coverage, periodic visits to newspaper editorial boards are a good policy, as are occasional visits with television commentators and radio talk show hosts. Surveys suggest that relatively few newspaper subscribers actually read editorials; however, the people of influence in the community do. Positive editorials are important in establishing your public credibility and presence among these shakers and movers.

Radio talk shows constitute the proverbial horse of a different color. Radio talk shows have taken America by storm in the 1990s, and many shows have acquired listenerships that are large, highly opinionated, and prone to deluging public officials (including college presidents) with complaints if they have been inspired to do so by the talk show host.

Most local radio stations have a talk show host who may function as an imitation Rush Limbaugh, but who also sees him or herself as a type of ombudsperson for listeners. The president who goes on such a show takes a risk. The questions can be fair and coverage superb; however, many talk show hosts are past masters at posing loaded questions, interrupting their interviewee, and providing incendiary commentary that incites listeners. The result can be a debacle.

Nonetheless, media economics and coverage have changed dramatically in the past decade. Newspaper readership continues to decline in most communities, and today more and more individuals acquire their news by television, radio, or even the Internet. A single radio talk show host demonstrably exercises more power in many situations than the daily newspaper. Thus, a shrewd and sagacious president is well advised to find ways to capitalize on this increasingly important (though volatile) molder of public opinion. The president who does not develop a personal relationship with the most powerful radio talk show host in the area likely will regret that fact when an event arises that the talk show host can exploit as a means to attract and excite listeners.

UNFAIR TREATMENT BY THE MEDIA

In case of unfair treatment or misquoting, offending reporters will usually be curt, editors only slightly more polite, and publishers equivocal. It is preferable to talk to those people before rather than after a storm. Although libel charges may seem tempting, try to let the feeling pass as quickly as possible. Newspapers and stations have insurance, and as a semi-public figure, a college president probably will not win anyway. Further, if your relationship with the media already has deteriorated to that point, you are probably on your way out as president anyway.

One approach to unfair treatment is to meet with members of the editorial staffs to discuss concerns, take them to lunch or dinner, or invite them to social functions—but here again, the good ones usually will not come. Far better, of course, that you have visited with these individuals beforehand. This is much more likely to avert unjust coverage than an anguished session after the fact. Whatever, with representatives of the media be scrupulously honest, be as candid and complete as you can, and do not expect favored treatment. Remember, regardless of what they say, you do not have to talk with them.

The only way to insure fair treatment and perhaps even inspire positive media coverage is to become one of the media yourself and command their attention as a competing power force. To complain repeatedly about offenses committed by the media gains nothing except a suspicious reputation. On the other hand, the president who has a platform from which to address regularly the same public to which the media appeal implies the threat of retaliation. Some reporters have developed arrogant and conde-scending attitudes because they know there are few effective checks on their style or substance. A president who emerges as a well-known, ad-mired, and fair-minded public figure, whether as a commentator on an important radio or television station, a newspaper columnist, or a public speaker, will gain power in any dealings with the media. Editors will speak to you with respect as a peer, reporters will no longer interrupt you in mid-sentence, and publishers will come to hear your speeches.

LESS DEPENDABLE WAYS TO INSURE OBJECTIVE MEDIA TREATMENT

Some presidents cannot do these things, sometimes because they have no opportunity, but more often because they lack confidence or expertise. There are, however, other reasonably effective ways to accomplish fair and impressive media coverage. To begin, a president must, of course, be honorable and correct, and his or her institution must be engaged in impressive and noteworthy activities. The first and most fragile way to improve an institution's standing with the media is to attempt system-atically to cultivate the publisher and the people who influence the pub-lisher, including major advertisers and the local landed gentry, if the publisher is one of them. But most publishers are sensitive to such ap-proaches and often are inoculated against such blandishments, however subtle.

Another potentially hazardous approach is for the president to work for the establishment of a regional or state council to which a person could petition if badly treated by the media. Minnesota has one that has operated effectively for many years. Such a council would consist of prominent people generally beyond the power of the media, e.g., major advertisers, retired persons, and religious leaders. Some states, like Florida, have passed redress laws to protect vulnerable public figures, but for the most part the public and particularly those who seek power remain at the mercy of the media unless they enter the arena and gain power for themselves. Further, the media will predictably denounce any attempts to develop such councils or laws as having a "chilling" effect upon their first amendment freedoms. Hence, a president should be careful in his or her advocacy in this area, however justifiable such innovations might seem.

A president need not become a media personality, but an effective presidency is more likely if he or she does. If the president does not, media relations can still be successful; the process will simply require more care and the allocation of even more resources to the public affairs or institu-tional relations office. Good news releases will be even more important, as will special campus features prepared by the public affairs staff. (A special feature on the president, however, will only get published in the alumni magazine because it is too obviously self-serving.)

A number of universities and colleges have established impressive ways of regularly and quickly conveying newsworthy items to a broad range of print and broadcast media. They use audiocassettes, videotapes, feature idea sheets, opposite editorial page columns, and many other techniques, in addition to standard news releases. (CASE has available specific information and advice regarding techniques to consider in communicating effectively with a diverse public.) Regardless of the method used, the institution's public information officer will usually need to provide a "story hook" for the media outlet, one that provides them with a local or topical interest reason to cover the story. This is one of the most important tasks of the public information officer. Many stories do not sell themselves.

Some college and university publications and periodicals are so well done that their readership extends beyond alumni and friends. Many institutions are hiring, as public affairs officers, people who are not only educated in journalism and experienced in higher education but who have held responsible positions in the media. Such individuals usually have a well-developed sense of how to provide a "story hook" for the media.

AS YOUR IMAGE DEVELOPS

As a presidential image begins to develop through the media, do not expect to shape it completely yourself, for no one can fully control what people write or say. Presidents have been called "opportunistic" when they thought they were courageous. A reporter may interpret as "outspoken" a comment the speaker thought was simply truthful. A president may be considered outgoing and assertive where he or she is basically shy and private. The image that comes out may surprise or offend or amuse you. What matters is that you face yourself each morning in the mirror and respect what you see, knowing that you are improving the condition of the institution and the people you serve.

FINAL THOUGHTS

The media can make or break a president. As Judge Learned Hand noted during World War II, "the hand that rules the press, the radio, the screen, and the far-spread magazine, rules the country." In single newspaper towns, the attitudes of that newspaper, and the single reporter the newspaper likely has covering higher education, are critical. The media must be cultivated in an atmosphere of mutual respect; you need them, but they also need you. Always tell the truth (or, if you can't, say "no comment"); treat even the most irritating media representatives with respect, and let them know without anger or rapture when you think they have failed or succeeded.

- Do not fall in love with the image of yourself in the first publicity. That way, you can more easily handle what comes later.
- Remember, you do not have to talk to the media, but it is usually a good idea.
- Do not get carried away with your own rhetoric.
- For the president, a feature article in a newspaper is infinitely better than a scholarly piece in a professional journal.
- Do not take media criticism or praise too seriously. Your fundamental worth as a human being cannot be changed by the views of a single reporter.
- When they stop calling you outspoken, you have stopped speaking.
- Never apologize for your convictions. However, if you cannot explain them without getting defensive, re-examine them.

CHAPTER
fourteen
· · · · · · · ·

The President and
the Alumni

*If I were the head of a penitentiary instead of a university, I would have
no trouble with the alumni.*

A. Lawrence Lowell

*Power is the ability to show up late for a meeting and have the people
thrilled when you arrive.*

Louis XIV

Keep 'em a little nervous.

Robert Forman

Alumni are the constituency a president is most likely to take for granted.
Yet, without a strong and positive base of alumni support, a president is
bound to fail in virtually any effort to enhance his or her charismatic power.
Whether alumni are of modest achievement and means or rich and powerful, they must not be overlooked in favor of other external groups. Without
their interest and involvement, a president can not gain lasting friends
among nonalumni, generate a broad base of public support, raise money
from nonalumni benefactors, or significantly influence trustees, politicians,
or the media.

Alumni are "grown-up" students, and whatever else they become, remain students until the day they die. Indeed, it often seems as if a cycle were
at work. Many undergraduates become intensely committed to their insti-

tutions, and when they leave, that commitment is not lost. Even students who were strongly critical of an institution while attending it, or who appeared to have no more than a passing interest in its welfare, often go through a remarkable transformation. Studies indicate that no more than a few years later, even those students who flunked out tend to remember their undergraduate institutions fondly. As time passes, they usually return to their alma mater fired with appreciation and interest. A president should ethically exploit this spirit to the fullest.

A wise president communicates honestly and completely with alumni, even if the news is not always popular. That is why the initial contacts with alumni are so important. Most alumni remember their alma mater as it was, and they usually want it to stay as they remember it. The president's plans must be presented as ways to make the alma mater even more excellent while preserving and respecting many of the old traditions. Alumni tend to resent dramatic changes, and a new president may symbolize dramatic change. Therefore, warm and convivial relationships with the alumni leadership are not always immediately established by a new president.

WHY WORRY ABOUT ALUMNI?

More than one president has taken the view that there is no reason to cultivate alumni unless they are going to raise or contribute money, support the institution politically, help recruit students, find students jobs and internships, or otherwise help it meet its goals. Taken to its extreme, this view suggests that in essence, one may forget about alumni after they graduate unless they are going to do something positive for the institution.

Wise presidents realize, however, that unhappy and dissatisfied alumni can do a host of negative things to an institution and its president. They can reduce political support, ruin fund raising, disrupt meetings, put a damper on student recruiting, and (ultimately) cause the president to be fired. Presidents that go to war with their alumni soon regret it, even when the presidents are on the side of the angels. Several years ago, the president of a large Midwestern university moved to abolish the institution's existing alumni association and substitute another new and approved association in its place. This move resulted in legal action, wretched media coverage, and a severe headache for both the institution and its president.

Properly appreciated and cultivated, alumni can provide magnificent financial support, help recruit students, find jobs and internships for students, provide critical political support, and serve as invaluable sounding boards for the president. An alumni association can also serve as a political polling organization for an astute president. They can let the president know what is going on, and how the institution, its programs, and he or she are perceived.

Twenty percent or more of all alumni typically make financial contributions to their alma mater. A president who does not cultivate this potential is not just short-sighted, but negligent. Thus, a president should not focus on the negative things that alumni can do (including attempting to run the institution and select its president and intercollegiate athletic coaches), but concentrate on the many productive things that properly motivated and appreciated alumni can accomplish for a charismatic president with an attractive vision.

ALUMNI ASSOCIATIONS

Most colleges and universities cultivate their alumni communities through the creation of alumni associations. Alumni organizations are phenomena peculiar to American higher education. They are practically unknown in the rest of the world. For example, in Europe, when a student graduates the institution is assumed to be through with the student, and vice-versa. In many Western European countries, alumni give loyalty to discipline, fraternity, or club. In Germany, *burschenschaften* (student fraternities and clubs) command far more loyalty than the universities in which they were organized, and a student *verein* (union) in an academic discipline exerts a much stronger pull on a graduated student than his or her former university. Outside the United States, therefore, alumni associations generally do not exist and the tradition of alumni supporting their institution financially is almost completely absent. The irony of this circumstance is that in most foreign countries the cost of higher education to a student is small compared to the United States. Despite this, American students, who pay much more to their colleges and universities for their own educations, are much more loyal to them after they graduate. Only in recent years have European institutions, such as Oxford University, realized that they should cultivate their alumni and that these alumni can provide significant financial support to the institution.

Alumni associations in the United States are staffed by professional officers charged with representing either the alumni, or the institution, or both. This is an easy relationship until there is conflict, an inevitable circumstance between alumni and a changing institution. For this reason, the alumni officer at a dynamic institution has perhaps the most schizophrenic position of anyone on the institution staff. Regardless of the nature of the alumni association, for a president to constrain the officer to the same absolute conditions of staff loyalty expected of other staff is to render the alumni officer ineffective in working with this key constituency.

Whatever your experience with, and attitudes toward, alumni associations, do not rush off pell-mell upon appointment and abruptly change its nature. Any changes in this area should come only after strong relationships are firmly established with key alumni leaders. Presidents who encounter difficulties with alumni are not saved by the support of the institutional governing board. To seek their assistance may actually cause greater harm. Alumni do not fear trustees, staff, faculty, big givers, politicians, or a president, for none of these groups has any control over them.

The alumni have vested their hearts in the institution. Presidents who have offended alumni have literally been driven from office. A president has legitimate, reward, and expert power with alumni only so long as they agree with him or her. Coercive power is virtually nonexistent. A president must rely almost exclusively on his or her ability to develop charismatic power. Initially, alumni grant the new president a certain grudging respect, but their affection and support must be won. Perhaps more than anyone else, alumni must trust and like the president before really giving their support. Without it, a short term lies ahead.

INDEPENDENT AND DEPENDENT ALUMNI ASSOCIATIONS

Most alumni associations depend on the institution for support and staff. Others are partially independent, and a few provide for themselves completely. In most cases, the prime source of support for the alumni association does not matter. What counts is to have alumni involved in a serious and constructive manner in the affairs of the institution.

With independent associations, the primary risks are reduced organizational efficiency and an association developing so much autonomy that it becomes an unrestrained adversary. The staff officers of independent alumni associations do not report to the president, but to their alumni boards, and this can cause problems. However, while independent associations can produce anxious moments, they are in reality to the president's advantage. If a president is willing to gamble on his or her charismatic skills, an independent alumni association can become the most effective milieu for cultivating alumni support. Alumni of public institutions will often give more under such a relationship. If the president is perceived as a more confident and open president, the alumni association, the institution, and the president will prosper.

Should the more comfortable, dependent association structure be chosen, the result need not be dramatically less productive. The imperative here is that the president realize that the paid alumni officer must honestly render to the president or a delegate the attitudes and opinions of alumni. While the alumni officer may be expected to represent the interests of the institution to alumni, he or she must also be able to represent the interests of the alumni in a way that is reassuring to them. Although alumni do not mind being influenced or persuaded, they will not accept coercion. Information and persuasion must be applied to convince alumni that the president's way is best. The presentation should not invite disagreement, but inform convincingly.

Alumni and especially alumni officers realize that their interests are better served if the incumbent president of the alma mater receives their support. Rarely has an alumni association taken the first step towards a hostile relationship with a new president. Most alumni associations will let the president do as he or she pleases, so long as it is done with thoughtfulness and care.

CULTIVATING ALUMNI

The charisma presence established on campus and with other external groups will be helpful in developing good relationships with alumni. The president must make alumni know how important they are. This applies regardless of whether alumni are genuinely accomplished or of modest achievement and means. Of course, the president should be presidential with alumni, and distance, trappings, ceremonies, and other charismatic qualities apply as much to alumni as to other groups.

A variety of approaches to alumni are effective, such as special letters and off-campus speeches to alumni groups, but should not be so frequent or regular as to be taken for granted. Occasionally, a president can attend part of an alumni board meeting to make a brief presentation. One-to-one sessions with important alumni leaders include visits to their homes and offices. Attending virtually all campus alumni functions, campus athletic activities, and other events where large numbers of alumni may be present will help build support.

THE ALUMNI OFFICER

If a president inherits a chief alumni officer of senior tenure, then he or she should try to keep the person aboard. Experienced alumni officers will often respect a new president and are prepared to be supportive. However, more than anyone else on the staff, alumni officers have a deep and abiding affection for the institution, and a new president wisely makes serious efforts to convey the same feeling to them. They often have closer ties in the alumni community than anyone else on campus or off.

Should the inherited alumni officer be inexperienced, educate him or her as quickly as possible. Send the alumni officer to professional meetings and especially to special conferences designed to instruct alumni officers in appropriate techniques. Encourage them to read professional magazines, articles, and books. (Further information is available on this subject through the Council for Advancement and Support of Education.) Send the alumni officer to visit highly regarded alumni offices on other campuses. Foster the continuing education of alumni staff, and alumni will soon be contributing as never before.

If a president needs to appoint a new alumni officer, alumni must play an important role in the selection process, even in dependent associations in which the president makes the final decision. (An independent association should be so structured that the president has a voice in the appointment of a new alumni officer.) The important condition is that a committee on selection be created to which the college president has an appointment. If one person cannot represent a president's interests, then either serious mistakes have already been made with alumni or the wrong person is on the committee.

ALUMNI PUBLICATIONS

The alumni publication may be put out by the alumni office or the publications staff. This valuable public relations tool should be furnished sufficient resources for excellence. It need not be elaborate or expensive, but the writing and design should reflect the quality of the academic program. Have someone talk with the editors about ways the president can be prominently portrayed in the publication. "A Message from the President" in every issue could get boring unless the incumbent is an exceptionally skilled writer. Instead, strive for a variety of coverage: a picture at a newsworthy campus event, an article by the president, and a report on a presidential speech. The president wants to be prominent, but a skillful editor can help insure this conveys "leadership" rather than "ego."

If the association is independent, the same kind of coverage is desirable, but more subtlety may be required to obtain it. Presidents have no editorial authority over "independent" alumni association publications, nor should they have. But if a president is becoming a public figure and providing strong leadership, he or she will naturally make news that the independent alumni association periodical will want to cover. An unfettered alumni press inspired by a dynamic president will yield better results than a restricted editor putting out what amounts to a tired house organ—such censorship is always obvious.

ALUMNI AND ATHLETICS

Few areas of a college or university excite alumni more than intercollegiate athletics. Unfortunately, this excitement often can cause problems and on occasion even result in the termination of a president who antagonizes important alumni on this subject. For example, it was commonly reported in the mid-1980s that a precipitating reason for the dismissal of the president of a large public university in the southeast was his attempts to exercise greater control over the university's intercollegiate programs, athletic director, and coaches. Unhappy alumni constituted a majority of the members of the president's board, and he found that they would not support his moves toward reform and control, despite the fact that the National Collegiate Athletic Association had investigated and penalized the institution for its athletic malfeasances. The import of this incident was not lost on other presidents.

Whatever one believes the role of intercollegiate athletics should be in a modern college or university (and we believe that they are overemphasized on many campuses), they usually constitute the single most visible and unifying activity that an institution undertakes. Intercollegiate athletic contests, especially football and basketball games, attract many visitors to the campus, including alumni, citizens, legislators, and individuals of influence. For example, by 1994, the University of Michigan football team had played in front of 117 consecutive sell-out crowds of 102,000+ fans in Ann Arbor. Tens of thousands of proud alumni sang "Hail to the Victors" at each of these games. Yet this phenomenon is not limited to "big-time" intercollegiate athletics. Even on small campuses, football Saturdays and winter basketball games typically provide numerous possibilities for cultivation and presidential conversations with old grads.

The opportunities for an ambitious and entrepreneurial president to exploit the larger-than-life character of intercollegiate athletics are both large and mesmerizing. The problem, of course, is that the beast that is intercollegiate athletics often has a voracious appetite and can devour the president. Many of the institution's alumni, abetted by the media, may insist not only on winning teams, but also upon being heavily involved in selecting coaches. Alumni who support the intercollegiate athletic teams of an institution think nothing of offering advice to a president on a plethora of other topics as well, including admissions and grading standards, degree requirements, and athlete behavior.

The task of the president is to remain in charge, visibly so, in the eyes of the alumni and the public. To the uninitiated, this may seem a routine task, but it is far from that once an institution's teams become big winners or losers, for that is when the pressure to compromise becomes most intense. The three most important links to presidential control are strong relationships with alumni, an athletic director who is absolutely trustworthy and evinces high standards, and a board of trustees that has been educated on these issues and will support the president. The president who cannot fire his or her football coach will gradually be recognized as powerless—or be on the way out.

Many presidents have talked about reformulating intercollegiate athletics. However, the task of reforming intercollegiate athletics in the United States is comparable to cleaning the Augean stables; few presidents who have much at stake will attempt it, although most probably should. Those who do make such an attempt are well advised to first establish a warm rapport with their alumni, who in most campus situations are the primary proponents of bigger and more expensive intercollegiate athletic programs.

Only a truly charismatic, transformational president—one who has already established a recognized track record of sterling performance in many different arenas—usually possesses the power to do anything other than affect marginal changes in his or her institution's intercollegiate athletic programs. Presidents whose institutions sponsor intercollegiate athletic programs in the NCAA's Division III (where no athletic scholarships by that name are allowed) are not exceptions. More than one president of a small liberal arts college has emerged chastised from a session with alumni, some of whom are members of his or her board, who ignore academic matters and instead complain bitterly that the alma mater has lost to Ol' Siwash too many times in a row.

The president should keep a close eye on intercollegiate athletics, for they contain large upside and downside risk. This means that the president must maintain close contact with alumni, who typically exhibit the most long-term interest in an institution's teams and their success and therefore are most likely to compromise the institution and the president. If alumni vocally disagree with a president's stance on intercollegiate athletics, that president already must have established a charismatic, successful presidency, or he or she will find him or herself in the proverbial heap of trouble.

FINAL THOUGHTS

Alumni are older students over whom a president has no real authority but who, mobilized and committed, can be a crucial force in achieving institutional goals. Alumni are educated and, in most circumstances, rational people, except when it comes to their alma mater. Never forget that the old school can bring tears to alumni eyes. Respect, include, and understand alumni. In almost every group a president addresses, someone will hear the words in that context. When addressing a group exclusively composed of alumni, a president should not talk only about the university or the college today, but also of history, tradition, and customs, as well as former faculty and even presidents. Show slides and films, but always include monuments and reminders of the past. Do these things, and alumni will love you.

When dealing with alumni, do not forget the following things:

- Your alumni want to love you. Provide them with reason to do so.
- Remember that the first loyalty of nearly every former student is to the institution, and not to you.
- Never compromise principle, no matter what the temptation.
- Drink club soda and lime, or a diet cola, at most alumni functions. You are on stage whether or not you realize it. Afterwards, take a stiff belt if you need it.
- With alumni, try to discuss travel, children, the weather, and almost anything else, but be careful of athletics (unless you have just won the national championship) and politics.
- When addressing alumni, always begin by reattaching them to their roots; only then should you talk about new developments.
- Always wait overnight or longer before posting a nasty letter to anyone, particularly an alumnus/alumna.
- Remember, dignity can also be fun. Do not try to be "one of the boys" by "misbehaving" with the alumni at the big football game.

CHAPTER
fifteen
•••••••

The President, Philanthropy, and Fund Raising

We often excuse our own want of philanthropy by giving the name of fanaticism to the more ardent zeal of others.

Henry Wadsworth Longfellow

Who will not feed the cats must feed the mice and rats.

German Proverb

It is better to light a candle than to curse the darkness.

Chinese Proverb and Motto of the Christophers

You are a newly appointed college president. You are pleased, even excited, but also a bit confused and uncertain; it is only natural, then, that you do a little posturing. Because you are an educated and practicing academic, this situation makes you uncomfortable. After all, at least *some* things that you are presumed to know as you begin your presidency actually are completely foreign to you. This is especially true in the area of development. Yet, no one asks whether you might need a little time to learn anything. From the first day, you are expected to be off and running—a combination of Abraham Lincoln, Mother Theresa, Nicholas Biddle, and Father Hesburgh.

You make some phone calls to a few presidential friends, take a few trips, and even attend a three-day seminar for new presidents; but you are still unsettled. You know that some of your first steps will probably be mistakes, but you intend from the start to keep errors to a bare minimum. You also know that those first steps can ultimately spell the difference between presidential success and failure, whether your administration is a plus or a minus, bland or piquant. What if you appoint the wrong vice president, offend an important donor, create the wrong office (or fail to create the right one), or postpone confronting the reality of a difficult decision that only festers when put off? So many "what ifs"! Nonetheless, you remain pleased and excited about your presidency because in your entire life you have never had such an opportunity to play a major role in realizing your dream. And that is worth all the anxiety.

This chapter is designed to help obviate at least some of your anxiety and to give you a higher degree of confidence as you address one of the most important areas of your administration: development, or fund raising. In this area, you simply cannot afford to make serious mistakes. However, it also is the area about which most new presidents know the least.

INSTITUTIONAL ADVANCEMENT

Institutional advancement, the area of college and university administration that usually includes development, public relations, and alumni activities (and sometimes also mistakenly includes athletics, admissions, and even placement), is the area with which most newly appointed college and university presidents are least familiar. Yet this area, more than any other, will determine the extent to which your administration is deemed worthy or unworthy.

The idea of asking for money makes many individuals uncomfortable. Perhaps you know little about the history of philanthropy and its important role in human institutions. There are few courses or books on the subject and you are not sure where to start—or whether you should start at all. Of course, if you survive the first three years in office, your attitude will change. But is there time?

The contention of this book is that your institutional advancement area, if handled thoughtfully and seriously, can not only be extraordinarily successful, but also one of the most rewarding and most intellectually stimulating of your presidential responsibilities. The key is to approach fund raising head-on, with both eyes open, using all the mental faculties at your command at *the beginning of your term.*

Colleges and universities in the United States and Canada employ nearly 9,000 full-time development officers, over 7,500 public relations and publications professionals, and about 4,500 professional alumni administrators. Assuming that, like you, other presidents are the chief advancement officers of their institutions, then another 3,000-plus can be added to the list. Thus, more than 24,000 persons are engaged in institutional advancement activities for colleges and universities in North America. Although a number of other countries (United Kingdom, Ireland, Germany, Mexico, Brazil, Australia, Hong Kong, Indonesia, India, and others) are beginning to fashion development programs on the American model, most are still rather primitive. Papers, meetings, special conferences, and (recently) Fulbright grants promise that within a few years many American-type fund-raising programs should be in full operation around the world.

ESTABLISHING A SUCCESSFUL FUND-RAISING PROGRAM

What follows is a simple, concise, research- and experience-tested formula for college presidents to follow in establishing and maintaining a successful fund-raising program. Although there are a number of variations on this approach (some of which are discussed elsewhere in this book), you should test any significantly contrary ideas on at least one experienced, trusted, and candid friend before seriously considering them.

1. Start a Personal Fund-Raising Library

In addition to Frances Pray's *Handbook on Educational Fund Raising* (1981), Wesley Rowland's *Handbook of Institutional Advancement* (1986), and Michael J. Worth's *Educational Fund Raising* (1993), read everything you and your assistant can find on philanthropy. Robert Payton is the reigning expert in the field and all college presidents should have his book *Philanthropy* (1988) on their bookshelves. An excellent primer for new presidents in the area of fund raising is Fisher and Quehl's *The President and Fund-Raising* (1989). You should also become familiar with the seminars and programs offered by CASE (Council for Advancement and Support of Education) and by AGB (Association of Governing Boards of Colleges and Universities). You will then be ready to use what you have learned.

2. Keep or Replace an Incumbent Vice President

You will probably have in place a vice president or director for development, college and university relations, or institutional advancement. You must intelligently, but quickly, determine whether that person should go or stay. The imperative here is that you examine his or her accomplishments before you get to know the incumbent so well that you cannot comfortably and objectively make a change. Many new presidents assume that because incumbent vice presidents are experienced, they also are qualified. Because of uncertainty, you may want to wait before making any dramatic move. However, by the time you confirm what you knew instinctively, you might already be hostage to the sticky tenure of politics and friendship.

Because faculty members, students, and even board members are generally as unsophisticated as college presidents about fund raising, that is often the area where presidents appoint friends, political compromises, or "music" men or women who make grand promises. If you are not exceedingly careful in choosing your chief fund raiser, you could rue your decision. Unfortunately, more than a few unproductive charlatans inhabit the ranks of chief development officers today, even in the most prestigious institutions.

The track record of the development or institutional advancement division[1] of your institution is the most documentable of any of the conventional line divisions. Either the institution has raised money or it has not. If it has not, regardless of whether yours is a public or private institution, look critically at the incumbent vice president and all the reporting offices. Do not easily accept statements like "People won't give to our college; we do not have the potential" or "We are not ready for a capital campaign" or "Your predecessor would not allocate sufficient resources for us to do much" or "President So-and-So did not expect us to raise much money."

Whatever the case, if your institution has not raised much money, you have a presidential problem. If your incumbent vice president does not enthusiastically endorse your assessment, then immediate change is in order. There are other indices of effective community and public relations activities, but for the new and relatively inexperienced president the best index is "How much money has been raised?" *Every friend-making activity should be translated directly into fund-raising terms—cash or kind.* You will receive advice that contradicts this statement. Ignore that advice.

---

[1]"Institutional advancement" is the title currently in vogue; however, "development" may more nearly suggest bottom-line evaluation.

3. Appoint a Fund-Raising Consultant

Shortly after you assume office, and before you name a new vice president, appoint a fund-raising consultant. After discussing your plans with your board chair, call CASE in Washington, D.C., at (202) 328-5000 for advice about consultants. Get the names of four or five. Approach fund-raising consultants as you do the entire advancement area—based on track record. Find out for whom the candidate firm has worked, and then phone fellow presidents. Unless other presidents view you as a direct competitor, they will almost always be candid.

If you are completely (or even a little) befuddled about your advancement area, and do not know where to start, visit CASE and talk with the professionals in each major division there. This is much less expensive (and probably much quicker) than inviting all of them to your campus, and will give you a better idea of how to organize and operate your development/ advancement area and the kind of vice president you should have. But even having made such a visit, you still will need to appoint a consultant.

Your consultant should come to the campus one or two days every month, and always be as near as the phone. Rates vary, but they usually go from $1,500 to $3,000 per day. Some will charge a flat $10,000 or so per year, with a prearranged contract calling for a specific number of visits and accomplishments within the contract period. Most consultants are full-time, and you should select a tested professional from among this group. However, a number of able and highly qualified persons who hold campus positions do consulting. If they are experienced, they will advise you about both their time and interest limitations. Often, particularly in short-duration assignments, they can be both exceedingly helpful and less costly. Many newly retired persons fall into this category. They have expertise and time, and are not highly driven by financial needs. *A good consultant is usually worth the money. Only a naive president tries to raise money without one.*

If you have a satisfactory vice president in place, you will hold that person accountable for accomplishing your fund-raising goals, so you must grant him or her authority and involvement consistent with your delegation. *But stay involved yourself.*

4. Conduct a Feasibility Study

Assuming you have a written fund-raising plan, your consultant will usually suggest a feasibility study and develop a case statement. Today, some respected authorities suggest alternatives to the classic feasibility study, but by and large these "alternatives" are simply more equivocal ways of achieving the same purpose. The study will determine the extent to which your various institutional publics have the capacity and willingness to give (cash or kind) to your institution. Either your consultant, or yet another firm, may conduct it. Be sure of sufficient experience because you must place great confidence in the results.

If you are at a more sophisticated institution that already has such a study, ask to see it. Most institutions should update a feasibility study every five or six years. Your vice president will be surprised and impressed that you know about these studies. At the very least, update the study consistent with the time of your appointment and your own particular dream or mission for your institution. Be sure the study is conducted according to your terms, not the consultant's or the vice president's—whatever came before, this is your administration!

A feasibility study usually will cost between $10,000 and $50,000. Do not blanch at the amount; if you hire a good consultant, it will be worth it. If yours is a new development program, your consultant, after reviewing the results of your evaluation/audit, may advise you to announce your new direction through a modest fund campaign (perhaps only $1-$5 million). This campaign can get you up and going within 15-20 months, and a thorough feasibility study can follow your campaign. But whatever the advice, *listen to your consultant.*

5. Develop a Case Statement

The best research indicates that a formal, written, concise case statement characterizes an "overproductive" fund-raising program. It provides evidence of a clear sense of mission: where you were, where you are, and where you want to be. It also provides tangible evidence of a well-managed institution that seeks to control, rather than be controlled by, its environment. Here again, *appoint a consultant.* The best course is usually to talk with a good writer on your staff about your ideas for a case statement, and ask for a draft. You should edit the draft and present it to your consultants (who may recommend dramatic changes). You can get this done for $2,000 to $8,000.

6. Appoint an Extraordinary Vice President

Campus considerations probably will require that you use a search and screen committee to advise you as you appoint a new vice president for development or advancement (should you need one). Do not allow the participatory system on your campus to intimidate you. If the vice president does not work out, it will be your fault; but if he or she turns out to be brilliant, be sure to give your advisors all the credit.

The search and screen committee (do not call it "selection") should probably include representatives of the faculty, the student body, the alumni association, and perhaps even trustees. Be careful not to appoint lower-ranking advancement professionals to the committee; they will only inhibit candidates from speaking candidly about a modestly successful program. If you must have any administrators on the committee, appoint one from another line division of the institution (preferably business affairs).

Although your college councils (faculty, student, alumni) will want to play a role in your search and screen committee appointments, you must have at least one appointee or agent on the committee (if one cannot do the job for you, then you have the wrong agent). Your appointee should ordinarily be your presidential assistant, or someone else in whom you have complete confidence. The committee should recommend to you three to five qualified candidates, not in rank order (although somehow you will know the rank). This leaves you free both to *make* the selection and to be *perceived as* making the selection (both are important). Here again, most experienced presidents will employ a search consultant to work with themselves and the committee. CASE can give you the names of several top firms or individuals. These consultants usually charge from one-fifth to one-third of the first year's salary.[2]

The twin criteria for a vice president for development/advancement are (1) a strong track record (once again) and (2) his or her chemistry with you. Note the word "twin"; one is not more important than the other. We have known presidents who feel so foreign in the company of fund-raising activities and people that they appoint to their top position a person with an impressive resume, but who makes them uncomfortable. Almost invariably, they later regret their choice when they engage in the even more uncomfortable task of getting rid of the person. Our advice is this: If you don't find a qualified person who makes you feel comfortable, then go with chemistry over experience.

Should you decide to go the limited- or no-experience route, be sure the person is bright, educated, enthusiastic, and has a past record demonstrat-

---

[2]Beware, however, the tendency of some search firms to supply you with "warmed over" lists and candidates who have failed, for good reason, in other recent searches in which the firm has participated. Your campus needs are unique and there is no point in paying a search firm for work already performed. On the other hand, do not cast aside a candidate simply because another institution did not select him or her. Their needs probably are different from yours.

ing extraordinary motivation. Also, be certain that, *during the first few months* in office, your inexperienced vice president attends a CASE Summer Institute in Fund Raising and two or three conferences on especially pertinent subjects (annual fund, capital campaigns, planned giving, and so on). The vice president will both learn about the field, and meet key professionals who will become part of a valuable information directory.

You should pay the vice president what you must to get the one you want.[3] And, if you decide to appoint an experienced professional (which is usually your best bet), you may have to pay this person more than you do several of the other vice presidents. Go ahead. For the right person, be bold. You are the president. But remember that your appointee must, after a period of time, demonstrate productivity; such highly visible expenditures will attract attention.

7. Give the Vice President an Attractive Office Near Yours

Why do we mention something so apparently pedestrian? Because so many presidents make the mistake of putting vice presidents in the wrong place. The position and look of an office make a difference. The vice president's office should look attractive and prestigious, but reserved. Preferably, it should be adjacent to your own suite. It should be tastefully decorated, without a lot of school rah-rah (save for the alumni office). Quiet understatement is in order. For instance, quality pieces of art that have been given to the institution convey a number of messages.

Ideally, the other offices in the development/advancement area (with the possible exception of the alumni office) should be near the vice president's. If this is not possible, put the vice president alone in an office near yours. Obviously, this office placement speaks to lots of inquirers—skeptical faculty and staff members, potential contributors, and visitors who ask "What is development?"

8. Make the Vice President a Member of Your Top Advisory Council

Like the vice president's office, the key to making your fund-raising program a success is to recognize its tenant as an integral part of your chief

---

[3]A serious problem faced by some state colleges and universities is their inability to pay competitive salaries for development personnel, usually because of a state personnel system that is inflexible, not oriented toward merit, and out of date. The result can be mediocre personnel who do not perform.

advisory group. Too often, this vice president is not included—especially in "kitchen councils." If these vice presidents are invited, their opinions may be discounted during mainstream discussions about the institution. This not only makes them feel less important, but is a sure way to create a disenchanted, superficially knowledgeable, and less productive advancement area. A good officer, when treated this way, will begin quietly to lay plans to move on, and you will have committed a basic presidential mistake.

First and foremost, advancement professionals *should be* educators, be they in development, public relations, alumni administration, or publications. Even if some of them do not initially believe it themselves, you must make them educators. Only then will they be able to approach their maximum self-esteem and professional achievement. Hence, you must include your fund-raising vice president in all substantive discussions about the institution and its affairs. If you cannot do this, then you have appointed the wrong vice president, and either you are already in trouble, or you are headed that way.

In time, your message about the importance of development will filter down. You will see it in your publications and hear it at alumni meetings, over coffee and cocktails, and in presentations to potential benefactors. Your respect and appreciation for your advancement staff will energize the entire division. Do not think that you can "respect" them by simply appreciating the number of dollars they bring in or the number of people they affect. We feel this way about good carpenters. Advancement officers are not tradespersons; they are professionals. In higher education, the only sure way they can be truly committed to the mission is to be considered full-fledged members of the team.

Off-campus, and with your board of trustees and the alumni board, this vice president should be perceived as your surrogate. These groups should view your vice president as so important that they feel, in speaking with the vice president, that they virtually are speaking with you. Obviously, you can delegate this much responsibility only to an exceptional person, and so you must invest a great measure of presidential trust and confidence in your vice president. This is the main reason you must have an extraordinary relationship with your vice president. Perhaps more than any other of your top associates, he or she can hurt your career. This person must have such a well-integrated and healthy personality that there is little or no discomfort in identifying with you. (Identifying with the institution is not identifying with you.) This is especially true when you are not present.

Watch for the tendency of your vice president to use the first person singular—a bad practice you should nip in the bud. If you do not, you will soon lose the reins. On the other hand, if you choose not to grant surrogate status to your vice president, you will not have this potential problem (at least not to this degree). But, neither will you be free to exercise yourself as freely in the conduct of your presidency, nor will the vice president be as effective as you would like. It is a trade-off, and we encourage you to take the chance. Talk about it now and then with your vice president.

9. Approve a Budgetary Allocation That Generously Reflects the Great Potential of the Activities in the Area

Because a president should adopt a general style designed to get more for less, your thinking in institutional advancement, particularly development, should be investment-oriented and long-run. Of course, you will likely "get more with more," at least initially, unless your development personnel are severely deficient. Nonetheless, the payoff to excellent development activity may take several years to appear.

The most "overproductive" programs invest more money in development. Be aware that you will have great difficulty in carrying out this philosophy if you have a new, unsophisticated program—one that does not raise much money, regardless of what "they" say. As a rule of thumb, you can expect to take three years before you break even, which means that you may have a real selling job to do on all your potential critics (the board of trustees, the faculty, other staff, and most notably your business officer). In time, your average fund-raising cost per dollar raised should be approximately eight cents in a private institution and approximately twelve cents in a public.

Author James L. Fisher vividly recalls repeatedly telling his chief development officer, "Next year," when pressed to allocate additional funds for a planned-giving officer. If Dr. Fisher had listened more intently to this plea, his institution would have raised several million additional dollars in unrestricted funds. Since that time, the same officer has been responsible for raising more than $300 million for other institutions. Dr. Fisher asked him recently why he had not raised that kind of money for Dr. Fisher. He responded, "Jim, it was because you wouldn't let me."

Do not let this happen to you. If you take these words seriously, it will not. Although this statement could be stretched to a fault, we make it nonetheless: *Every college or university, regardless of size, should have a full-time planned-giving officer.* The only exception is a new institution with mostly younger alumni.

Of course, in making what appears to be a generous allocation of resources to your development area, you will need both to defend and evaluate zealously. Other vice presidents may carp, and some may resort to questionable behavior. Stop this sort of thing quickly or, in time, the criticism will erode popular confidence in your development program. It is your job to buoy their spirits and stay their tongues when resources are scarce. Only the president can do it.

Do not tolerate even casual informal asides that belittle your development efforts. If you do, the criticism will surely grow, and you will regret your tacit support. It is easy to become disenchanted in the first and last stages of a fund-raising program (campaign). No matter how you feel in the heat of the particular fiscal moment, be as enthusiastic as you are bottom-line oriented. Be tough and specific in tracking the fund-raising program, even during the three-year grace period. A good vice president will anticipate this action, yet be persistent. Find out what you are getting for the money spent. Do not accept generalizations, cliches, or vagaries as answers. In the end, this style will make your advancement staff feel better. In the beginning, however, be prepared for anxious defensiveness; most presidents are not so demanding.

Use development as a model to evaluate more rigorously every advancement activity (alumni, public relations, and publications). Money raised may be a rather gross index to some, but even the most sophisticated programs use this measure. That is the reason we prefer to put a development officer in charge of the advancement division (as the vice president). For obvious reasons, these officers are by nature more inclined to accept and expect performance indices relating to the amount of money raised.

An extraordinary public relations or alumni officer can also do a good job as your vice president, but you must be careful to stress from the start the importance of written measurable objectives for which that person will be accountable. In addition to financial objectives, you can also establish measurable objectives in alumni and public relations areas. Anything that you can count, weigh, or otherwise measure should be included in the annual mission goals.

10. Be Lean in Organizing and Administering Your Advancement Area

Our earlier suggestion to be generous in the budgetary allocation to your development area may seem to contradict this suggestion to be lean. It does not, and here is why. After you start making impressive strides (and you will) in your development efforts, you may tend to (1) accept any proposal for additional positions or programs and (2) become more amenable to solving personality conflicts and other problems by adding staff or building around them. These things happen most in wealthier and larger institutions where predecessors have already incorporated the fat and the inefficiencies. Because of your lack of experience, you could find yourself in danger of simply accepting such arrangements or situations.

Development expenditures are worthwhile only if, in the long-run, they produce more revenue than alternative expenditures, say, investments designed to generate research grant funding, or advertising expenditures designed to expand or improve the quality of the student body. There is nothing intrinsically virtuous about development offices and their expenditures. Performance is the ultimate criterion.

If an established development program costs more than 15 percent of the total dollars raised, you have a problem, and you certainly should ask for an explanation. However, rarely do people ask questions—so the institution continues practices that should not have been accepted in the first place. (Remember, revamped programs, like start-up costs, cost more.) This wasteful and less effective condition also occurs in liberal arts colleges and similar public institutions. They are often smitten by the "big time," and quickly adopt some version of the Harvard, Stanford, Michigan, or Berkeley models, all of which are more inefficient than you can probably afford.

The most obvious costly practice is to create separate vice presidencies in both development and public affairs (or public relations). Some institutions even have alumni vice presidencies. This practice is most evident in major private and public universities. There is no evidence that such organization makes things better, more successful, or more efficient. We are convinced that these operations would raise more money than they do (and they raise staggering sums) if they had more efficient organizations. Unfortunately, even some consultants support the practice, usually to mollify the president and staff. If you are inclined this way, go ahead; but be aware of the price. At the very least, you will spend money that could have been allocated to your academic program (or perhaps better spent on a management seminar). Such an arrangement also makes it more difficult to conduct and evaluate your advancement activities with the bottom line in mind.

Here especially, beware of the advisor who counsels you that "public relations is valuable for the sake of public relations." This position is sheer nonsense. Your public relations program exists to enhance the ability to generate resources for your most precious activity, your academic program. The idea of not attempting to cash in on your cultivation activities is naive and mistaken.

There *must* be a reason for every public relations activity you undertake. Conduct your development (advancement) program to raise money; the cause is more than worth such a candid assessment. Do this, and you will find all the critics of your program converted to enthusiastic supporters. This same style should apply to every social event, every president's party, every news release, and all publications. If you do not insist on such accounting efforts, chances are no one will, and you will have generated less support for your institution.

Some presidents have created separate vice presidencies in public relations, development, and alumni affairs because of personality conflicts or because of perceived or real limitations of the incumbent officers. Every situation like this that we have known occurs because the sitting president does not want to make a tough decision about which officer should be subordinate to the other, or which should go. Once this arrangement is in place, it usually remains.

Not long ago, author James L. Fisher spoke at a prestigous campus that had gone this route. After his speech, he spent some time talking with staff, all of whom disliked their arrangement. Why did they feel that way? Well (to cite an unusually pertinent example), the next day, Bob Hope was coming to be involved in the institution's public relations and fund-raising activities. Despite the fact that the institution had vice presidents, each highly respected, there was no way, short of involving the president as referee, to coordinate effectively Bob Hope's activities for the advancement, public relations, and alumni offices. Everyone was relieved when Hope left two days later.

Understandably, important activities in development, and particularly in public and alumni relations, will not be readily measurable. Results of many valuable public relations activities often are difficult to gauge, and all your advancement offices participate in them. These activities include such apparent disparities as sending out news releases, producing publications, media relations efforts, parties, alumni meetings, and tours and trips. On your part, they include appearances on TV and radio, speeches, newspaper and magazine articles, political fund raisers (both sides of the aisle), and countless parties with the landed and the shakers and movers. All these goings-on influence your fund-raising program.

Another of the less financially measurable activities is the work that advancement offices do with the academic and administrative departments. These efforts will seldom bear immediate results, but they are valuable and should be carried out under the direction of your advancement division. Include in this arena everything from departmental brochures and college catalogs to faculty participation in development, public relations, and alumni activities.

Sooner or later, your public relations and alumni officers will have to work more closely with the admissions office to enhance efforts to match the institution with prospective students. Although the prime authority and accountability for admissions "marketing" activities should remain in the admissions office, it is wise to bring the expertise and involvement of these advancement functions to bear on the ever-important area of admissions.

ALUMNI ASSOCIATIONS

Although early alumni associations focused upon serving their *alma matris*, alumni social activity and fellowship, and continuing institutional service and education, are considered legitimate alumni activities. These activities are difficult to reduce to fund-raising specifics. Recognize them as important and legitimate activities but, at the same time, press for closer (regardless of the present condition) relationships between the alumni and development offices. Some presidents have found it worthwhile to assign the annual fund to the alumni office. Often this arrangement can set a better tone for all alumni activities.

As discussed in greater detail in Chapter 14, most newly appointed (and some experienced) presidents do not understand the differences between dependent and independent alumni associations. Most alumni associations are dependent—funded largely by the institution. While the dependent association may charge dues and engage in other revenue-generating activities, this office clearly is an institutional activity, and staff are expected to conduct themselves within the same professional and management context as other advancement professionals. They must recognize that they are primarily accountable to the incumbent officers of the institution rather than to some vague college or university tradition and a vested alumni board.

The roles of independent alumni associations are not as clean-cut or easily explained. The independent association usually is significantly, if not completely, funded by its own activities. Its board of directors appoints and evaluates the staff. Its publications and other activities and programs are more autonomous than those of dependent associations. While the chief alumni officer must work closely with other advancement professionals in development and public relations (and with you), his or her prime allegiance is to the alumni board. Because of this relative autonomy, many presidents are wary of independent associations. Some attempt to make them dependent, even though this could cost the institution more.

If you inherit an independent association, do not jump too soon. Although the arrangement is suspect from a presidential perspective, many of the top alumni associations are independent. Their programs are impressive. Their suggestions to the institution usually are as helpful as they are uninhibited, and they contribute generously to your development program.

We are not suggesting that you go one way or the other. Just wait until you know the territory before you leap. Some presidents have moved hastily and regretted it leisurely.

These indirect activities will cost, and the amount will be difficult to determine. But you must never cease trying and pressing your associates to quantify these costs. This is the reason that bottom-line dollars and cents raised serve as such a good starting and ending point. When the bottom line becomes vague, you should know why and how it will ultimately tie in with the amount of money raised for the institution.

WHAT BELONGS IN THE INSTITUTIONAL ADVANCEMENT AREA?

Another important trend in institutional advancement is the move to assign admissions, placement, athletics, and other externally related activities to the division. Except for rare instances, you should avoid this situation. The rationale may appear logical, for each of the areas engages the external public, but the problem is one of efficiency, costs, and philosophy. These areas take too much management time from your vice president, who is (or should be) primarily responsible for raising private support for the institution. While it makes sense to tie your public relations (and publications are a part of your PR program) and alumni programs to your fund-raising effort, you reach a point of diminishing returns when you add other areas and thereby become less efficient.

If yours is a larger institution with colleges and professional schools, do not establish autonomous development offices in each of them. If you do so, you will soon find these autonomous offices going their own way, and your institutional fund-raising priorities will be ignored. It is not inappropriate to locate centrally trained and centrally reporting development officers in individual colleges and professional schools. This can be a productive way to raise funds. Nonetheless, they should not be autonomous and individual colleges and schools should not have their own separate foundations.

If you have inherited an autonomous arrangement, quickly appoint an outside consultant to make enlightened recommendations. All advancement activities, however remote, should report to your vice president or to his or her delegate.

A Bare Bones Model for Institutional Advancement

Although the size and nature of your institution may necessitate modifications, the following model suggests an efficient and effective general design for your fund-raising program. Be skeptical about anything that calls for additional staff, even though in time, with success, you will need to add them.

You cannot do without a vice president and director of development, a public relations officer, an alumni officer, a professional to do initial research and cultivation and begin your annual fund, and a planned giving officer. This is a bare bones total of five professionals. As your operation grows, you will want to consider recommendations from your vice president calling for additional development, public relations, and alumni staff. If you discriminate, do so on the side of the development staff. In time, you will need to approve an additional position for the capital campaign that your unprecedented success will demand and merit. After such success, most institutions err on the side of too many staff, especially in public relations. Many public institutions have a number of public relations professional and absolutely no fund-raising staff. This practice should be unacceptable to you.

FINAL THOUGHTS

Keep your enthusiasm high, take the advice of experts, keep your eye on the long-run, and, above all, hire good people. Consult Appendix A for a history of fund-raising that will provide you with perspective on the challenges and opportunities that you face. But remember, the long-run is not forever and accountability in your development/advancement efforts is critical. A reasonable estimate of the time necessary to mount an effective fund-raising program that pays off is three years, but even that estimate assumes that you are starting virtually from scratch.

Even at a public institution, you should immediately involve your board of trustees and other good friends of the institution in your fund raising, for they should be among your principal fund raisers. If you do things correctly, you will be able to create confidently a trustee development committee that will carry this message to the full board "Give, get, or get off." The committees and the board will view you, your vice president, and staff as sufficiently sophisticated to merit their being gently orchestrated. And you will be on your way to a distinguished presidency.

PART
4

Governing Boards
and the President

CHAPTER
sixteen
••••••••

The President and
the Trustees

Yes, power corrupts, but absolute power is absolutely delightful.

Anonymous (Book of Wisdom)

Confidence is the only bond of friendship.

Publilius Syrus in *Moral Sayings*

Trustees are the most important formal link to a president's supporting public. Most of the more than 60,000 trustees who serve on college and university governing boards in the United States do so because of their special commitment to the institution or the incumbent president, or both, and deserve the definition of the name trustee, which is "to hold in trust." In the very best sense, they wish to achieve "good" things, and are committed to supporting their institution and making it better.

On the other hand, some board members serve for reasons of prestige, patronage, power, and personal advantage. Some are appointed only for political reasons, and may place their own agendas ahead of the welfare of the institution. To them, the president is useful only as he or she can help them achieve those personal agendas.

Whichever the case (and most boards are a mixture), few things are better for a president and his or her institution than having the confidence, respect, and admiration of a powerful group of trustees. You will obtain that position primarily by means of your charismatic power and public presence.

When you establish these, you will enjoy a bonus—the opportunity for your expertise to come to the fore. If this propitious mixture of power sources is present, your chances of being a successful president increase vastly.

TRUSTEES IN PUBLIC COLLEGES AND UNIVERSITIES

The trustees of public colleges and universities are sufficiently different in several respects from those of independent institutions that comment is necessary. Public trustees are usually elected by the people of the state, or appointed by governors or other elected officials as a reward for special service. To suggest that the prime criterion for appointment as a public trustee always is the quality and commitment of the candidate is as naive as to suggest that all trustee appointments to the boards of independent institutions are made without regard to the personal wealth or influence of the candidate. For these reasons, public trustees are sometimes less committed to their trust and less influential than the trustees of private institutions.

Most public institution board members are appointed to their posts, usually by the governor of the state. In recent years, most governors have taken this responsibility seriously and the general quality of appointees has increased. Hence, in many states, public university boards boast a clear majority of members who are astute, visionary, public-spirited, and strongly motivated to support and promote their institution. Both authors have benefited from many such board trustees.

Unfortunately, some public trustees, especially those who are elected, can be parochial and pedestrian, not the least because they feel that they come to their post with their own political power base. Sometimes these individuals have little long-term interest in the institution, but, in other cases, they bring with them a specific agenda.[1] Their votes can be influenced by political, business, and personal factors. From time to time, sudden shifts in state political winds can result in dramatic changes in board membership and attitude, resulting in internal arguments between and among board members and considerable presidential indigestion. More than one president has felt the axe as a result of a change in board membership. Further, some public institution board members may regard their membership on the board as "public service" and be reluctant or totally unwilling to support the institution financially.

The same situation can hold for independent college board members. Good and bad trustees exist on both public and independent college

---

[1]In the 1950s, a group of trustees elected to the Board of the University of Illinois were united by an interest in ridding the university of its Keynesian economists.

boards. However, the method of appointment and motivation of public institution board members usually differs in critical ways, and this can produce distinctive selections and behavior.

MULTI-INSTITUTION PUBLIC BOARDS: A SPECIAL CASE

The quality/motivation problem for board members is especially prevalent on multi-institution public boards that are responsible for several different colleges, or perhaps even an entire system. Experienced presidents learn not to expect helpful support from such a board, and they realize that their influence with such board members is likely to be small. Such boards tend to treat the numerous presidents with whom they deal as supplicants whom they line up for occasional cameo appearances at hectic, crowded board meetings. The president in such a situation gradually assumes a role not unlike a teenager asking parents for the family car. Such a situation is almost always detrimental to the institution as well as to the president, for the president's charismatic potential is slowly reduced to the level of those persons who serve on the board. Further, the president's ability to demonstrate expertise, project a vision, or hold a substantive conversation with such a board is severely limited.

Yet, these boards are the final authority, and the president is obliged to show the board its due respect, and effectively represent his or her institution in what usually becomes a mediocre concept of public institutions (everything is reduced to a midpoint). It is especially important in such situations for the president to acquire the public presence and external power that will allow him or her to establish a somewhat independent image. The members of multi-institution boards, and the bureaucratic staffs that serve them, will fight this development, for it reduces their own power and authority. For these individuals, the venerable advice given to an up and coming Chicago machine politician applies to presidents—"Don't make no waves and don't back no losers." In such a circumstance, the president's task is to avoid antagonizing the multi-institution board members and staff, but nonetheless cultivate sufficient external support for the institution to become exceptional—a rather sensitive and difficult balance to achieve.

Many multi-institution boards have neither staff nor trustees sufficiently able, influential, or interested to help an individual institution. Because of this, they develop unimaginative "cookie cutter" rules that force all institutions within their purview to behave identically, usually under the guise of "avoiding duplication" or "promoting accountability." The essential sterility of this situation is apparent to all seasoned observers, for in most states it has led to undistinguished institutions.

More often than not, key state decision makers—politicians, state bureaucrats, the media—are aware that the campuses controlled by such boards are neither particularly distinguished nor innovative. Consequently, few would argue with the conclusion that these boards amount to little in the power hierarchy of the state or region, and this in itself is one reason why the appointments to such boards tend to be lackluster.

For the president to be obsequious with such boards is to appear inept and impotent by association and eventually to lose the respect of faculty, students, and associates, as well as off-campus decision makers. In this situation, you must be extremely careful: respect your trustees, but remember they are charged to govern several institutions, and you are charged to lead one. At times, these functions can appear mutually exclusive. Whatever the case, maintain the respect and support of your campus community and the general public, and the sometimes counter moves of the multi-institution board will not extend too far into your territory.

Not all public trustees are poorly motivated, ill-qualified, or unwilling to devote the time and risk necessary to serve a public institution. Author James V. Koch has worked with public university boards in six different states, and can vouch that some states, and some governors, have assembled outstanding records of filling collegiate boards with intelligent, powerful, and visionary individuals who are truly interested in higher education and the public welfare rather than their own personal agendas. In other states, the initially committed trustees often end their terms in frustration and cynicism or with a strongly worded letter of resignation. Others just quietly slip away in disgust.

PRESIDENTIAL POWER AND TRUSTEES

In dealing with trustees in both private and public institutions, the president must rely almost exclusively on charisma and expertise, but especially charisma. Charisma is generated and made obvious to trustees by strong campus support, and by the admiration of the local, regional, or national hierarchy of the wealthy and powerful. Other external constituent groups—politicians, public figures, alumni, the media, and even bureaucrats—also contribute to the power a president has with a governing board. If trustees perceive the president as effective on campus and respected and influential beyond the campus grounds, and if the president is not arrogant or overtly disrespectful, they will give their respect and support and grant considerable executive privilege.

Board members are admiring and respectful when others perceive their president as a caring individual, a good manager, an inspiring leader, and an influential person off campus. Trustees learn these things from others, not from the president, whose energies will be better spent building a base of support. The president who does these things well does not have to worry much about the board. He or she is able to join them as a peer and a leader, and to inspire them to serve a high cause; if not, the president is at least able to silence those who would work contrary to his or her interests.

THE ROLE OF TRUSTEES

The roles and functions of the trustee are essentially the same in public and private institutions. Exceptions are primarily in the public sector, where elected and other political figures can influence the decisions of trustees. Although the private sector has instances of undue attempts by church members, generous givers, and alumni to influence trustees, these pale when compared to episodes in the public sector. Fortunately, in either case, incursions are usually to gain personal and financial advantage rather than to influence academic matters.

Beware of trustees who spend too much time exercising office, especially those who visit the campus frequently and meet in private with administrative officers and faculty. They can do much to reduce virtually all forms of presidential power (legitimate, reward, coercive, expert, and charismatic). Nothing can compromise a president's charismatic power on campus so readily. Virtually no one is as deeply invested in the institution as its president. Faculty members have their disciplines, and trustees are usually at best part-time laypersons committed to the best interest of the institution. The president is at the pinnacle of a career and must be the person in whom the trustees place their authority and much of their power, always excepting, of course, the power to replace the president.

One of the authors once served as a consultant to a community college president who was having serious leadership problems. The chairman of the board had an office on campus where he spent several hours a week. He visited and discussed college affairs with top administrators, faculty, staff, and students. Of course, he was viewed as beyond presidential authority and, in time, his activities significantly undermined the president. The president got into trouble with the faculty and staff of the college and was asked to resign during his third year in office. Four years later, the college was on its third president, and the chairman of the board still had his office on campus.

Such examples are not limited to community colleges. Upon election, the chairperson of the board of a large, national university consistently mentioned in national surveys as one of the best in the U.S., moved to the hometown of the campus so that (according to the newspapers) "he could do his job better." Ironically, he was applauded for his commitment, even though it predictably led to major mischief and a visible reduction in the effectiveness of the institution's president.

Other examples of trustees' over involvement include the following:

Case 1: *At a midwestern liberal arts college, a wealthy woman who was expected to make a major gift to the college lived in the community and attended most student functions and all student council meetings. At each meeting of the board, she presented a lengthy and even charming report on student behavior at the college and students' relationships with the dean of students and the president. The president and the dean of students sat in board meetings and cringed.*

Case 2: *At a private women's college, the trustee chairing the development committee did not like the vice president for development, so she worked directly with the several officers who reported to the vice president. She saw the president and all but ignored the vice president. The president did nothing to reinforce the vice president who was fired for being ineffective. The vice president's successor seems to be having the same problem and is already in trouble with the president.*

Case 3: *At a southern Catholic college, several trustees constitute a committee that regularly comes to the campus, has its presence announced, and encourages members of the student body, faculty, and staff to come in and discuss their problems. The trustee committee then reports to the board, and the board does not understand why the president "cannot lead."*

Case 4: *The chairman of the board of a Middle Atlantic public university has the habit of inviting groups of faculty to his home for cocktails, dinner, and stimulating conversations. The president of the university not only is not invited, but he must listen during public board meeting to frequent comments by the chairman about what the faculty think. The chairman has started discussing the president's limitations with other board members.*

These cases are not intended to denigrate the role of the trustee, nor to imply that most are not committed and able. It is a mistake, however, to consider trustees an omnipotent, all-powerful body that must be pleased and adhered to regardless of other considerations. The notion is foolish.

There are almost as many definitions of the proper role of the trustee as there are college presidents and trustees. Nonetheless, the president who understands effective leadership prefers completely informed trustees who are not involved in any way with the administration of the institution. He or she will so state before accepting a presidential appointment and, if necessary, will occasionally remind the board of this condition. (Astute trustees may do this for the president.)

Rather than becoming involved in the administration of the institution, the proper function of trustees is to approve policies, evaluate and support or discharge the president, advise the president, and contribute financially or otherwise to the institution. The board members should be well enough informed to have a good feeling for the institution and what is happening there, but they must not be so involved that they are moved to do things for which the president is ultimately accountable. Some presidents lean toward the belief that trustees should meet to appoint the president, adjourn, send money, and then reassemble only when the president resigns. This stance is much too strong, but a more modest version is appropriate and should be impressed upon trustees who might otherwise be tempted to get involved in daily college or university affairs.

The president's role with trustees should be both professional and personal, but this does not mean sharing everything, either personal or institutional. At the same time, a president should keep no secrets from trustees. The president should tell them more than they want to hear about significant issues, but refrain from discussing personalities and administrative procedures. Such discussions lead to an over-involved board and an institution with uncertain direction.

The good president has one-to-one sessions with each of the trustees, and unless the board is unusually large, does so more than once or twice. Playing golf or tennis, attending cultural events and social functions, inviting them to campus social functions (particularly those with the president in the limelight), and performing small noncompromising favors are all worthwhile.

No trustee should be permitted to pressure a president into violating college or university policies, or into endorsing obviously inappropriate practices such as changing grades or censoring professors or speakers. Once headed down this treacherous road, a president cannot go back, and the trustee served by the compromise will not expect to reciprocate, but will simply assume that favored treatment comes with the trusteeship. As is the case with similar requests from legislators, the president must resist this pressure with grace.

Respectful strength is the most effective presidential posture with trustees. Trustees should be cultivated as well as informed but obsequious deference will not enhance a president's effectiveness. If you catch yourself laughing too loudly, rising too quickly, or being overtly attentive, stop; such behavior wins nothing. Your success and survival depend on the extent to which you are able and willing to define yourself in terms of the interests of people on campus and how well you maintain the distance necessary to lead. Because one of the authors has been a trustee of seven liberal arts colleges, we do not write only from a presidential perspective.

THE PRESIDENTIAL POWER BASE

The college president who knows and uses the concepts of leadership and power presented in this book will soon have sufficient stature and influence to be able, if necessary, to disagree respectfully with individual trustees and, if need be, even with the entire board. Trustees make mistakes, as do presidents, and at times those mistakes will not be effectively corrected by other trustees and must be addressed by the president. If not, things will only get worse.

Some presidents have achieved a position of power beyond the collective power of their trustees. In one state, the president of a public institution wanted a separate board of trustees rather than continuing to report to the board that ineptly and corruptly governed seven different universities. His politically appointed board did not agree, yet the strong president was able to generate sufficient support to get a bill passed through the legislature and signed by the governor that created a separate governing board for his university. In this instance, the president had become so influential that he was able to name most of the new trustees. Throughout the apparent conflict, the president's image and influence appeared so strong that the original board chose not to make a public issue of the matter. The newspapers wrote about it, but the board did nothing.

The fundamental consideration of the president must always be the best interests and welfare of students, faculty, and staff; these considerations clearly stand above the sometimes selfish interests of some members of governing boards. While conflicts with trustees should be handled sensitively and the president certainly should not be pushed into a display of bravado, neither should a president pretend that conflicts will go away or that they do not exist. The extent to which you will be effective in such conflicts will depend almost exclusively upon your ability to foster trust and confidence—public presence and charismatic power.

You must establish a broad personal power base that is recognized and subtly acknowledged by the trustees; the extent of this power base will determine the degree to which you are able to comfortably maintain your obligation to your faculty, students, and staff. The president must feel able to speak candidly and confidentially to all the people, and that ability is only insured through achieving a high degree of charismatic power.

Too many presidents sell out their campus constituency to those off campus. This ethically questionable practice will produce a short-term president. This chameleon-like president is either soon detected or, at best, has a mediocre presidential tenure fraught with anxiety and problems. Too often, this president later writes, usually for publication, that he or she did not enjoy the office. However, the temptation to compromise convictions in the presence of an influential trustee or another off-campus power figure is great. Those who succumb will find the off-campus power broker's respect short-lived and will in time lose the respect and support of other constituencies.

In the final analysis, the trustees have the authority to do virtually anything. What the effective president must do is demonstrate by his or her behavior the extraordinary ability that inspires the confidence and respect of the board, and confidence and respect are not earned either by obsequiousness or intimidation.

ACCESS TO THE BOARD

The principal informant of trustees should be the president, not other administrators or faculty. There are exceptions, particularly in the independent sector, where many development officers, especially the vice president, need to spend considerable time with trustees. This is another reason why the appointment of a development officer can be crucial to your good administration. But even the development officer's contacts should be strictly limited to development topics; he or she should not be seen as someone who is "reporting on" the president and the remainder of the administration.

The wise president guards his or her relationship with trustees carefully and grants access to them on a discriminating basis. Too much direct contact with the board by others reduces the president's legitimate and charismatic power, as well as the board's legitimate power; it also makes the use of all other power forms by the president more difficult. In the best interests of all concerned, the board simply must not usurp the president's responsibilities or in any way replace the president as the chief operating officer of the institution, nor must it give the impression of doing these things.

Keep the board distant from campus people—administrative staff, faculty, and students. Speak of trustees in general, rarely in particular. Conveying a sense of the board's legitimate authority will prove to a president's advantage during periods of difficulty; the president is the key to the trustees' approval, the expert on trustee relations, and the prime determinant of trustee involvement. It is also legitimate for a president to use the board as a source for unpopular decisions. A president takes the heat for enough unpopular decisions, so if the opportunity presents itself to use the board, go ahead. Just don't do it too often. Discerning trustees understand this.

THE APPOINTMENT AND ORIENTATION OF TRUSTEES

At both public and private institutions, presidents should play a primary role in the recruitment and appointment of trustees. While building a good board is generally considered a major responsibility of a private institution's president, in the public sector it is often considered presumptuous. A public president, like any other, should do what he or she ethically can to influence the appointment of trustees. Indeed, presidents who are doing their jobs will constantly discover new and attractive board candidates. If trustees are appointed, then the president should by all means suggest attractive, viable candidates, even to the governor. If trustees are elected, a president can speak of the qualifications of a good trustee. Once a trustee is on the board, the president must live with the choice for a long time; so regardless of custom or method, it behooves a president to be involved.

The education of trustees is as important as their appointment, and the president's task, regardless of resistance, is to insure that they are oriented and informed, a process that begins the day a trustee says yes. Excellent material available on this and other dimensions of trustee responsibility is available from the Association of Governing Boards of Colleges and Universities in Washington, D.C.

FUND RAISING AND THE TRUSTEES

Trustees should be exploited—in the best sense—to the advantage of the institution. The president should so inform new trustees and not be reluctant to remind old ones. Whether an institution is public or private, the chair of the board and the president's behavior should diplomatically convey the conviction that the trustee who does not contribute to the institution is unworthy of the appointment. Although some trustees are obviously able to give more than others, all should contribute money, in addition to time and talent. A president who does not gently but firmly convey this to the board will not be well supported. On this, it is imperative for the chair of the board to reinforce the president.

People generally give because of who asks them. Your good cause is important and so is the sense of obligation or debt a person feels toward your institution, but there is nothing like being asked by the right person. Many times this will be you or your development officer, but often it will be a person of status and influence more closely akin to the potential contributor's world. Use trustees and other friends of the institution who have already given (preferably more than the person they are going to ask) in this capacity. They can usually raise more money faster and more directly than the grandest case prepared by you, your staff, or a consultant.

A president begins the effort to raise money for an institution with the trustees, for, in spite of the important fund-raising role of others in the local hierarchy of the wealthy and powerful, the core of all really successful fund raising is the governing board of the institution. If trustees are not accustomed to giving or feel no responsibility, the president's task is to educate them to the fundamental importance of this role and to be certain that they are asked to give. Trustees simply must give to the institution and any who do not should be counted as presidential failures. Trustees should be deeply involved in, but not accountable for, everything from annual funds to capital campaigns to planned giving and even phonathons.

THE BOARD MEETING

The executive committee of the board should meet or consult prior to the board meeting and should usually meet, albeit briefly, at the time of the meeting itself. The executive committee should include key and experienced members of the board who have the confidence of both the president and the chair of the board. Always be certain that the executive committee, especially the chair of the board, is fully informed about all potential problems. Do not assume that they do not want to know or that you should not tell them. They will come to know you almost as well as your vice presidents and presidential staff, and will be a significant test of your charismatic leadership, for you have virtually no legitimate power with them. If you are successful with your other constituencies and you bear in mind the prime charismatic feature of distance, you will have a good and happy relationship with your key trustee leadership.

Board committees should meet at the time of the board meeting. This insures good attendance, continuity, and saves time and money. The committee meetings should precede the board meeting, and the trustee chair of the committee should report at the full board meeting rather than the vice president or other administrator who staffs the committee. Some presidents include the committee chairs on the executive committee, although this can lead to cumbersome and unwieldy executive committee meetings. Some use steering committees that include the committee chairs and the executive committee.

The opening session of the board should begin with an inspiring and brief presidential report on the state of the institution. The agenda materials that you send to your board, or your written presidential report to the trustees in advance of the meeting, should always include sections on each of the major activities (usually the line divisions) and cover other general subjects affected by board policy. Oral reports on each division should be presented by the trustee chair of each committee, which occasionally the president may amend or call on an appropriate vice president to explain further.

"Sunshine" laws and open meeting legislation usually require public colleges and universities to hold public meetings of their boards of trustees (except for closely prescribed executive sessions that deal with personnel decisions, legal matters, and real estate transactions). The same legal strictures may not apply to independent institutions, but the perceptual environment has changed mightily in recent years, and even independent college board meetings held *in camera* inspire suspicion and can be counted upon to provoke media criticism.

Board meetings should be structured to satisfy the law (or public expectations) and still be productive. Two principles should govern public participation and access. First, unless scheduled by the president or the chair of the board, no individual other than a board member or the president should speak during a meeting of the board or its committees. (A sample board policy on this matter is contained in the Appendix B.) A wise president will not arbitrarily or frequently withhold from interested parties permission to speak at a meeting. At the same time, such a provision will protect both the board and the president from being blind-sided by unrelated topics,[2] and also will protect them from being bombarded by the emotional proponents of the current hot issues.

---

[2]An example suitable for the "Hall of Shame" of board meetings is contained in the habit of a board chair, who at the end of each meeting, would look out into the audience and ask, "Is there anyone here who wants to talk with us or add anything?" Needless to say, once knowledge of this practice became commonplace, a succession of crackpots and campus malcontents used this invitation to introduce irrelevant material, excoriate the board and president, discuss inappropriate personal situations, and detract media and campus attention away from the major achievements of the board meeting. It was good entertainment (for some), but an irresponsible way to run a board meeting.

Second, faculty, students, and alumni should not be members of either the board of trustees or its committees. Such board memberships, although increasingly popular in recent years, erode the president's influence and charismatic potential with nearly every constituency. If anything, have such constituencies report to board committees or invite them to lunch with you and the board on the day of a board meeting. The invitation should be a valued privilege extended by you.

Unfortunately, many boards consistently violate these principles in the belief that they are being democratic or "staying in touch." The evidence does not support these beliefs. Such practices do not lead to positive results. There are better means by which a board can become well-informed. Boards that violate these principles should not be surprised when their president gradually loses effectiveness as faculty, students, and alumni find that they do not need to deal with or through him or her.

If you are unable to honor these principles, be aware that your power with both the board and the campus will be somewhat compromised, and executive sessions with the board will become even more important for you (if indeed they are legal).

EXECUTIVE SESSIONS OF THE BOARD

At formal trustee meetings, an executive session that excludes the vice presidents and others is important. During these sessions (if they are legal), you should discuss whatever strikes you at the moment as being of sufficient weight,[3] although occasionally there may be nothing to report. Include the item on the board agenda anyway; it keeps the vice presidents and others aware of their president's mystique and exclusive authority. Executive sessions of the board may also be called during emergencies.

TRUSTEE DISAGREEMENTS AND SPOKESPERSONS DURING TROUBLE

Unless there is absolutely no alternative, a president should never get involved in disagreements among trustees. Playing mediator or taking sides

---

[3]In many states, the law may prohibit public college and university boards from discussing in executive session items that do not involve legal actions, personnel matters, or land acquisitions and sales.

may be tempting, but in the end, the president will suffer. If trustee conflicts become so serious that the president's office cannot be effectively conducted, call the Association of Governing Boards or your national presidential association for advice about choosing an outside consultant.

Should an institution's troubles command media attention, the president or an agent—not board members—should speak to the media. Try to obtain an understanding or even a policy from the board that asks trustees to make "no comment" and refer inquiries to the president's office. If possible, the only times a trustee should speak to the media are at the request of the president and when the president is under fire and needs support. In these unusual circumstances, the trustee should speak at a press conference arranged by the president's press officer. Except in rare instances, the speaker should be the board chair.

FOUNDATIONS AND FOUNDATION BOARDS

Careful trustee selection and orientation is critically important, and a wise president will spend considerable time identifying, cultivating, and promoting appropriate candidates. For public college and university presidents, influencing the appointments to their institutional board of trustees may be difficult or impossible. Nonetheless, they can help select the members of the boards of their institutionally related foundations that exist for the sole purpose of generating private resources for the institution. In both the public and independent college sectors, institutions often create foundations to raise money, hold real estate, support intercollegiate athletics, and sponsor research. Presidents should take seriously the membership of these boards. One or more members of the board of trustees for the entire institution should be members of these specialized foundation boards.

FINAL THOUGHTS

Trustees should be respectfully dealt with as the designated representatives of the supporting and concerned public of the institution, but the approach should be that of one in the company of peers. This can only be accomplished with any degree of confidence if the president has built a base of support that includes the campus constituency and the off-campus individuals and groups who are of special importance to the trustees.

Here are some additional things to remember:

- All trustees should give their time and money. If they do not, it is your fault.

- When tempted to compromise by governing boards, politicians, or others in power, keep faith with the fundamental academic verities. You will feel better the next day (and five years from now) because you have done so.
- Strong, interested, competent board members are gold. Search for them, mine them, and treasure them.
- If you have vision and establish a powerful public presence, you will be able to attract strong members to your institution's board, and they will enable you to achieve repeated successes.
- Board meetings are not open forums; participation by faculty, students, alumni, and citizens in board meetings is not a right but a privilege, to be extended by the president or the board chair.
- Do not be afraid to admit mistakes to your board; just do not make them often.
- Use consultants to deal with "sticky" board-related and governance-related issues. They have expertise and they can say things you cannot.
- Those with vested interests in the institution should not serve on the board (faculty, students, staff).

CHAPTER
seventeen
••••••••

Responsibilities of the Governing Board

Unto whomsoever much is given, of him shall much be required.

St. Luke

Our privileges can be no greater than our obligations.

John F. Kennedy

The five most fundamental responsibilities of a governing board are presidential appointment, presidential review or evaluation, presidential support (notably compensation), board policies and institutional governance, and institutional evaluation. In this chapter, we also consider other important responsibilities that can contribute to the restoration or establishment of a more accountable and productive college presidency.

The board chair and the president must insure that the trustees understand these paramount responsibilities. Indeed, the education of board members is essential to their constructive participation. Many assume that otherwise sophisticated board members need no further education regarding the governance of a college or university. Quite the opposite is often true. Many individuals simply do not understand the proper role and responsibility of college board members. Indeed, the most sophisticated board members typically are most in need of special orientation in enlightened higher education governance because they usually hold well-developed opinions and are used to getting their own way. If board members are not oriented properly, things may go smoothly until problems arise, then it is too late.

Author James L. Fisher once was invited by a board chair and president to do an orientation session for the board of a midwestern public university. The reason for the session was one trustee's insistence on meddling in administration. Dr. Fisher went to the session primed for rational conversation. The offending trustee did not show up. As it turned out, he was advising the vice president for academic affairs about how to organize the academic services of the university. The moral of the story: schedule orientation sessions *before* problems develop.

The offerings of the Association of Governing Boards of Universities and Colleges (AGB) are so widely known that AGB's list of governing board responsibilities has come to be almost generic for colleges and universities. This list, with noted modifications, serves as a point of departure in the following presentation. We discuss these responsibilities by emphasizing transformational leadership, that is, change-oriented leadership.

As with corporate boards, boards in higher education are both the highest authority and the body ultimately accountable for the conduct of the institution. The following are the appropriate responsibilities of a governing board:

1. to appoint the president
2. to evaluate the institution
3. to assess board policies
4. to support the president
5. to review the performance of the president
6. to renew the mission
7. to approve the long-range strategic plans
8. to oversee the programs
9. to ensure financial solvency
10. to preserve organizational independence
11. to represent both the institution and the public
12. to serve as a court of appeal
13. to determine board performance

This list closely parallels the AGB list, which is wanting in two respects. First, it does not mention the need for a board to periodically and formally evaluate the condition of the institution. Second, AGB includes "to ensure the well-being of faculty, students and staff" as a trustee responsibility. This policy may seem unobjectionable, but it has often compromised the authority of the presidential office and the ability of a president to perform effectively and be fairly evaluated. Faculty and students are protected by law. The long-standing AGB policy that calls for boards to insist on "clearly established and publicized codes governing faculty status and student behavior" ensures due process for all members of the community.

We will discuss all these responsibilities in this chapter in order to increase understanding of the conditions necessary to produce a more legitimate presidency. These responsibilities are designed to facilitate significant participation of all concerned parties within the provisions of the AAUP *Statement of Principles on Academic Freedom and Tenure (1940)* and the 1966 *Joint Statement on Governance of Colleges and Universities* and, at the same time, allow for a transformational and fully accountable presidency.

BACKGROUND

Colleges and universities are essentially corporations formed for the purpose of education. Like other institutions that serve the public good, they are unique in that they are governed primarily by laypersons who are not educators and who serve without compensation. Such has been the case since the seventeenth century.

The lay governing board is not unique to the U.S., but was used previously in Italy, The Netherlands, and Scotland. In England, Oxford and Cambridge were governed by senior faculty who allowed the institutions to decay until the universities called for government intervention to address their problems. Since that time, no English universities have been established without lay boards.

Today, lay control has come to be the preferred form of governance in higher education. Ideally, this control is not so closely involved that board members can meddle and arbitrarily terminate faculty, but not so far away that board memberships and board policies can be abruptly changed by the shifting winds of politics (government).

The lay board of control model in the United States has worked well, primarily because governing boards have accepted the principles and practices of academic freedom and shared governance. Academic freedom guarantees the faculty the right to teach and to interpret their subjects without interference, and shared governance gives the faculty the privilege of participating in institutional decision making. The main governance problems in higher education lie in the interpretation of these two principles. Governing boards have increasingly granted to faculty, staff, and students prerogatives that were traditionally privileges granted by the president, and they have allowed the essential and important notion of academic freedom to be bastardized and used as a defense for a variety of unreasonable faculty behaviors and statements that bear little relationship to the original concept. The result has been a trend toward ineffectual college presidencies and drifting, unproductive institutions.

At first, these inappropriate and unwise governance conditions (usually advertised as having increased "campus democracy") appeared in a few institutions, but through the years their numbers multiplied. Eventually, their proponents moved into the mainstream of higher education and their positions began to be reflected in the programs and publications of national organizations. AGB is the most obvious example at the national level; some believe that AGB, despite its many positive contributions, often represents the interest of the faculty to the detriment of the president and the board.

TRUSTEE RESPONSIBILITIES

We recognize that there are other views on these issues and therefore the following discussion of trustee responsibilities attempts to suggest a range of possible interpretations. Our position is that AGB has been the most responsive national organization in higher education, and, rather than withdrawing, institutions whose leaders are dissatisfied should actively participate in the organization and press for their particular positions. Current principles and practices can be changed if all the participants have a better understanding of leadership theory and empirical evidence relating to leadership, and then are willing to subject their ideas to the rigorous scrutiny of the free and open marketplace for ideas.

1. Appointing the President

Failure in this, the most important responsibility of the governing board, is among the major problems in American higher education today. In general, the appointment process has become so compromised that it is bound to produce a questionable appointment. Often the wrong committee is appointed, outside consultation is not used, searches take too long, referencing is done poorly, and confidentiality is breached. Once the wrong committee has been appointed, nothing can be done, short of abolishing the committee, to correct the course.

Without deliberation, many governing boards have abrogated their responsibility for presidential appointment by granting a disproportionate role in the process to faculty. In many institutions, faculty make up a majority of the search committee and play the major role in developing the search policy and directing the search process. In a number of cases, faculty committees screen all presidential candidates before any are reviewed by the board. Many institutions have modifications of this usually unfortunate practice.

As the role of the board has become increasingly less important in the presidential appointment process, the status of the presidential office has declined, academic standards have become equivocal in many institutions, public confidence has diminished, and higher education has been unable to make the changes necessary to restore itself. If there is to be a restoration process, it must start with the presidential appointment procedure. This procedure should be, at least initially, under the exclusive authority of the board.

The key features of an effective and efficient presidential search are

1. the appointment of consultants, especially a general consultant before the appointment of the search committee;
2. the membership of the search committee;
3. the right search process;
4. complete confidentiality from beginning to end;
5. an institutional review or audit;
6. an emphasis on referencing over interviews with the search committee or the board; and
7. a compensation package tailored to the needs of the final candidate.

We discuss these matters in greater detail in Chapter 19.

2. Evaluating the Institution

Unless the governing board or a newly appointed president insists, institutions are rarely evaluated by external review. In part, this may be due to a lack of emphasis on the part of AGB, which speaks of the importance of institutional assessment, but does not give it a place on its list of governing board responsibilities. The good condition of the institution is the primary trust of the governing board. Accreditation does not do the job, for it is primarily a confirmation of minimum standards. Most institutions go unexamined except by those who are self-interested (faculty and staff) and who often cannot be relied upon to take the necessary Olympian view of the institution.

There are indices a board can follow to determine the general condition of the institution, such as trends in enrollment, standardized test scores, external support, faculty credentials and publications, job placement, and recency of curriculum changes. However, these indices are contextual and often imprecise and incomplete. Most boards never have a full expert and objective evaluation of their institutions; they simply assume that things are good (or bad) and proceed from there. Virtually the only way a board can get a reasonably accurate reading of the condition of the institution is to commission an outside "authority" who assembles a team to examine the entire institution.

No board should undertake a presidential search without a thorough assessment of its present condition in order to intelligently determine its needs for the next presidency. With extraordinary exceptions, most boards seem to believe that a search committee can accurately determine the condition of the institution and its present needs, or that a search consultant can come in for a quick assessment. The idea is ludicrous. In one distinguished university, the board felt that the institution had been resting on its laurels and might be slipping. During a presidential vacancy, the board engaged an outside consultant who conducted a complete evaluation of the institution. The evaluation concluded that the board was correct—the institution was slipping. The search committee and its search consultant appropriately adjusted the presidential selection criteria, and a president was appointed who probably would not have met the initial criteria.

Newly appointed presidents commonly commission an outside institutional evaluation if the board has not already had it done. The institution is then able to both unearth and address issues and conditions that otherwise might continue unattended, or that might inspire unproductive conflict if initiated by the new president. Sitting presidents and boards use institutional evaluations for the same purposes, or as a check on how things are going, and as a solid way to develop strategic initiatives. Most importantly, it is a basic responsibility of the governing board to ensure that periodic institutional evaluations be conducted in order that the board can more nearly determine its effectiveness.

3. Assessing Board Policies

The policies of a board may change through practice and emendation, or a board may make no alterations in policy in spite of challenging institutional needs. Both conditions set the stage for serious problems.

A board can prevent these problems by insisting on a periodic review of its bylaws and practices. An outside consultant is clearly in the best position to conduct an objective review, but the important point here is that the board commission regular and complete reviews of all governance documents and board policies.

A typical occurrence is the following: Although the board's original policies called for a clear relationship between the board and the president, over the years these policies became muddied by practices that have dramatically reduced the authority and the accountability of the president. The institution drifts into a contentious torpor in which no one is happy and things continue from bad to worse.

In one instance, a board went through four presidents in nine years before realizing that the primary fault was in its policies and practices rather than in the presidents who had been deposed. In another institution, the governing board was able to secure its leading presidential candidate only because its bylaws had been reviewed and its policies revised. The candidate would not have taken the position otherwise.

Many of the problems of higher education in the United States today could be averted if only governing boards operated in accordance with appropriate written policies. Too often, board policies dangerously compromise the legitimacy of the president, and arrogate to the faculty, students, alumni, and other constituencies the power that is necessary for a president to be effective. The irony of this is that boards, in adopting the counterproductive policies that lead to these situations, believe that they are accomplishing just the opposite. Usually, only a knowledgeable expert on collegiate governance can point out the contradictions in the board's policies and practices.

A board should commission an outside review of its governance documents at least every five years. The full board should discuss the resulting recommendations and consider changes that may be appropriate.

4. Supporting the President

The board should give the president both psychological and substantive support. Both are essential and often overlapping, but are too often unappreciated or taken for granted by a board. The result can be an unhappy and less effective president and shorter presidential tenures.

When a board appoints a president, it accepts the responsibility of being—and being perceived to be, both on and off campus—solidly behind that president. Board members should resolve any reservations behind closed doors, either in one-on-one meetings or in executive sessions. A board must be prepared for the controversy that is a certain by-product of a dynamic president. Even the most mundane circumstances often involve conflicting positions that only the president can resolve. However the issues are resolved, some people are bound to be unhappy.

If the board has properly delegated to the president the responsibility and authority for running the institution, the president will be perceived as the agent of the board and as holding its complete mandate. If faculty and others sense that the board, or even certain members of the board, do not back the president, these uncertain relationships create role confusion and unnecessary and unproductive conflict. Finally, the president becomes a scapegoat for all parties and is judged ineffective. Every president deserves the opportunity to succeed or fail on his or her own merits and not because of ambiguous or wrong board practices and policies.

The board should tell the president, from time to time, that it appreciates that things are going well, if in fact they are. The board should make these kinds of affirming statements in official board meetings as well as in less formal settings.

The second dimension of presidential support is substantive, that is, presidential compensation. Too often the board takes it for granted that presidential compensation is sufficient. Indeed, compensation is often an afterthought in presidential searches, seriously considered only when the board is about to negotiate with the first-choice candidate. Although this would be hard to document, countless interested candidates have surely been lost at this point.

The astute board will have a special compensation committee charged with thoughtfully attending to the needs of the president, and this not only includes salary and other prerequisites (everything from special annuities to rabbi contracts), but also the president's physical and emotional health. Today, many boards insist that their presidents take annual vacations and have regular physical examinations. Some institutions engage executive compensation firms to conduct compensation studies and make recommendations.

Too often, boards merely look at last year's package, do a quick review of national compensation studies (which are invariably misleading), and then decide what to do for the president. Many good presidents are also lost in this way. Indeed, we hazard that more able presidents are either lost or decide to decline the position for reasons of compensation than for any other single reason. Although presidents and presidential candidates rarely admit to a board that compensation is the primary reason they leave or decline a position, in time this truth comes out. For that reason, we devote Chapter 20 to the intricacies of presidential compensation.

5. Reviewing the Performance of the President

Although this responsibility is second in importance only to appointing the president, most boards do a poor job of it. Either they do no presidential evaluation, or they do it poorly. In spite of the importance of presidential evaluation, it is infinitely better for a board to do nothing than to do a poor evaluation.

Informal evaluation may or may not include contacts with faculty and others by the board. Evaluations that include faculty or administrators who report to the president lead to less effective presidents, even if the president passes with flying colors.[1] The process itself diminishes the presidential office. According to leadership research, it is far better for the board to interview *no one*, confining its activities to an annual evaluation of the president according to mutually acceptable objectives in an executive session.

Approximately every five years, the board should commission a more formal presidential evaluation to be done by an external authority. The selection of this person is most important. A poor choice can also lead to a diminished presidency. The board should consult the president and gain his or her concurrence before appointing a consultant. The key to an effective formal evaluation is that members of the faculty and staff *are not* systematically included in the process. In no way must the staff, faculty, and students gain the impression that the president is up for vote. In most instances during recent years, this has been the case, and the result has been a visible diminution of presidential effectiveness.

Both informal and formal evaluations can be invaluable to both the board and the president. The board should, in return, invite the president to express opinions about its conduct. Evaluations provide for the president and the board a regular assessment that makes for thoughtful and reasonable consideration of their mutual effectiveness.

6. Reviewing the Mission of the Institution

At least every five years the board should ask the president to commission a review of the objective of the institution that will be presented to the board for discussion. The board should not do the review, but should ensure that it is done.

---

[1] In recent years, the distinguished president of a land grant university accepted another ostensibly less attractive presidency after an apparently positive evaluation conducted according to the conventional wisdom. He privately explained that he left because the methods used in the evaluation, notable public systematic faculty judgement, so diminished the presidential office that he knew his good future there would be in jeopardy.

The review should answer these kinds of questions: What is our mission? Do we teach different subjects from other institutions? If so, at what levels? How can we improve the curriculum? the student body? the faculty? our overall effectiveness? our efficiency? Do we have obligations to special interests and groups?

The president should include faculty, staff, and students in this mission review, which becomes increasingly refined as it proceeds through the institution. This review may be accomplished as part of a strategic planning exercise. Finally, the president presents the reviewed and possibly revised mission to the board.

Once the board has reviewed and approved the mission, it should be distributed widely to the campus community to give faculty, staff, and students the opportunity to invest or reinvest in the grander mission of the institution and to define more accurately their own roles in these terms.

7. Approving Long-Range Strategic Plans

Long-range (or "strategic") planning is the road map for achieving the mission of the institution. "It is a process that articulates institutional mission, weighs external opportunities and threats, gauges internal strengths and weaknesses, and determines appropriate action" (Shirley, 1988). The appearance of Keller's *Academic Strategy* (1983) set off a flurry of strategic planning exercises on nearly every American campus, and devotees of strategic planning began to preach its virtues, almost to the exclusion of other concerns (the organization of governance being one).

Approximately every five years, institutions need to ask fundamental questions about their mission, environment, strengths, weaknesses, opportunities, and goals. These discussions may result in intelligent and articulate plans, but the mere discussions themselves are valuable, for they force campus constituencies to come to grips with reality and to think about their futures. The process may generate specific outcomes that will determine the institution's future ("We will offer every student an internship or cooperative education experience," "We will seek nationally recognized status in aerospace engineering"), or it may simply clarify and underline the institution's current commitments ("We will continue to be regarded as one of the top 10 liberal arts colleges in the Midwest"). In either case, the planning process usually forces individuals from disparate regions of the campus to come out of their offices and talk in detail about their prospects and problems. That is the ultimate payoff to strategic planning.

Strategic plans are made to be broken. The whirlwinds of accelerating technological change, constantly changing job markets and student tastes, and the vagaries of state and federal budgets are among the reasons why any strategic plan is soon out of date. Indeed, if you find that it is not soon outdated, then it did not say anything of importance! That is why the plan should be reviewed and updated annually, although with much less fanfare than is associated with the five-year version.[2] The strategic plans should be prepared under the direction of the president in consultation with administrative associates and faculty, staff, and students. In some public institutions, state officials are also included in long-range planning, but in most instances this practice has not proven particularly fruitful.

If there are differences on campus regarding the strategic plan, the board should not reconcile them (as advocated by AGB). The president should consider the differences and make the final decision. The president should explain to the board the opposing sides in an unresolved conflict, but the board should publicly support whatever decision the president makes. Except in the most unusual circumstances, the board itself should never be the final arbitrator because such a role would diminish the legitimate position of the president. Should there be compelling arguments on both sides of a conflict, the president will probably seek counsel informally from key members of the board. The ultimate test, of course, is the performance of the president and the prosperity of the institution; these things will reflect the long-term wisdom of the president's choices.

8. Overseeing the Educational Program

Teaching, scholarly productivity, and public service are the core activities and raison d'être of an institution of higher education. They are the basic and unavoidable tests against which all things should be measured. Unfortunately, the academic programs of American colleges and universities have become the most nearly sacrosanct areas of these institutions. As faculties have assumed (or presumed) a virtually inviolate role in establish-

---

[2]Experience indicates that strategic plans with a time horizon exceeding five years tend to exhibit characteristics reminiscent of Buck Rogers novels, and therefore risk having little connection to the institution's current reality. It is entirely appropriate in a planning exercise to talk about phenomena with a time horizon beyond five years, but it is unwise to assume that today's conditions will be replicated in 5 or 10 years. Strategic plans ordinarily should focus on no more than a five-year horizon and be sparing in recommendations that might bind the institution thereafter.

ing curriculum and setting academic standards, both presidents and boards have acquiesced in this situation. The adverse consequences of this forfeiture of responsibility and leadership by presidents and boards have been several, but include watered down, bloated, and irrelevant curricula; lax academic standards; distorted promotion and tenure standards; and a disdain bordering sometimes on contempt for quality teaching of undergraduates.

Although this incongruous and puzzling academic condition is fairly recent (this century), it is now considered in many important quarters to be part of the historic fabric of American higher education. Only faculty, it is said, can talk about curricula and academic standards. Unfortunately, this attitude has led some campuses to academic bankruptcy. Several years ago, at a large land-grant public university in the Midwest, a commissioned report by its own personnel took the institution severely to task for its twisted value and reward systems, careless attitude toward academic standards, seeming disparagement of effective teaching, and abandonment of undergraduates. The report noted pithily that "this bed was made over a long period of years by us, the faculty, and now it is too smelly to sleep in."

To be sure, faculty opinion in the areas of curriculum and academic standards not only should be sought, but also should be accorded great respect by presidents and boards. Presidents and boards should not place themselves in situations where they end up rendering judgments on whether a course in sociology is a better fit in a curriculum than one in psychology, or whether a course should be four hours rather than three. The overall size of a liberal education program, however, as well as its general makeup and goals, are within the proper purview of both presidents and boards.

Neither the president nor the board are properly exercising their trusts if they stand mute while faculty slowly stray from the fundamental purposes of the institution. Faculty stray because the reward structures of their institutions and disciplines encourage such behavior and because presidents and boards fail to exercise leadership. Undergraduates are ignored because professors face inadequate incentive and reward systems, a lack of presidential and board leadership, and a lack of accountability.

How can a board maintain its academic trust if it denies its primary and accountable agent, the president, any real authority over what the institution does? Realistically, it cannot. Today, institutional bylaws frequently contain passages like the following, which deprive presidents, boards, or both of any effective role in the academic program:

> The formulation and implementation of academic policy shall be the responsibility of the faculty. It shall discharge this authority under the Board of Trustees.
>
> These by-laws may be altered, amended, or repealed by the Board only after consultation with the principal legislative body of the University [the faculty]. . . .

Institutions controlled by academics are seldom more democratic than institutions whose presidents and boards ignore the views of faculty. Any change in faculty-controlled institutions is all but impossible. To give the faculty complete authority over academic matters is comparable to turning the government over to the bureaucrats, the Department of Defense over to the military, or religious institutions over to the clergy. The answer is to fashion a form of shared governance on campus in which everyone affected by decisions, especially the faculty, have a voice in making decisions.

Teaching and scholarly and public service activities *should* be the primary responsibility of the faculty; that is what they are appointed to do. There is a vast difference between responsibility, authority, and *accountability*. Although a faculty can assume all the responsibility and a large measure of the authority, it can assume virtually *none* of the accountability. This is an important reason why totally faculty-driven institutions become paralyzed.

The president and the board are accountable for the conduct of the institution. The president, as the delegate of the board, takes a calculated risk in granting authority to the faculty, who cannot be held accountable. While this is advisable in the case of academic affairs, the president, the board, and ultimately those to whom the institution is dedicated, will pay the price for any academic misconduct. The collective faculty cannot be held accountable for anything.

The board should not meddle with the details of the curriculum. It should be concerned with such questions as the comparative emphasis on teaching and research, the qualifications of students who should be admitted, and the general content of the curriculum. While academic freedom for the faculty embraces both the courses to be taught and how they are interpreted, the board should be informed of methods of evaluation and their results. The board should make the final decision regarding the addition or elimination of academic programs.

The board retains final authority for academic matters, but it delegates to the president virtually everything but that final authority. On academic matters, the president recommends and the board listens thoughtfully, objecting only in extreme cases. The board should regularly review academic matters, including the curriculum.

9. Ensuring Financial Solvency

No one objects to the board's responsibility for financial solvency. While others want to run the institution, they quickly and confidently turn to the board for financial support. Board members are generally more comfortable dealing with financial and business affairs, and most boards spend a disproportionate amount of time on finances and related areas. In our experience as presidents and board members, most boards are too involved in financial affairs (excluding fund raising) and insufficiently informed about the academic program of the institution.

The board must see that the budget is balanced, and that income equals expenditures. The board must also be concerned about the property of the institution and the investment of institutional monies. Some administrators tend to let deficits accumulate in the hope of a brighter tomorrow, rather than making cutbacks in programs or personnel. In prosperity, institutions are usually less attentive to costs and expenses. In both instances, close board review is necessary.

When a budget is out of balance, trustees must find a way to correct the condition, either by reducing costs or increasing income. An institution can increase its income by adding students, engaging in institutional entrepreneurial activities, increasing tuition and fees, and launching fund-raising efforts. Many believe that there has been a disproportionate emphasis on increasing tuition and fees during recent years, and there is some evidence that particular institutions have injured themselves by excessive tuition and fee increases. The counterpoint is to increase financial aid for those who cannot afford the tuition increases, if that is an option. It is difficult to reduce costs and to raise private support. Yet, contemporary experience suggests that there are abundant opportunities to do so.

Entrepreneurial activities on the part of colleges and universities have been used by more and more institutions to generate revenues in recent years, but are subject to question on several counts. Institutions that act as entertainment bureaus, landlords, private business operators, business and technology advisors, dental hygienists, and hoteliers may run afoul of both public opinion and the law. The primary danger, however, is that these activities may detract from the fundamental academic purposes of the institution. Thus, they must be considered carefully and controlled closely.

Raising money for the institution is a basic board responsibility that can only receive proper due by frequent reminders from board leadership. In this case, the initiative is the board's rather than the president's. The traditional mandate that a board member would provide "work, wealth, or wisdom" has been replaced with today's order to "give, get, or get off." Every board member should be concerned with raising financial support for the institution. Not only should every board member contribute, but board members should also ask for additional ways to be involved in fund raising for the institution. Board members should be optimistic in the face of difficulty and recognize that "People give because of who asks them." When staff of the institution ask for involvement, every board member is obligated to respond enthusiastically, regardless of whether or not they "like to raise money."

10. Preserving Institutional Independence

One of the great sources of strength for American colleges and universities has been their relative independence from outside control, which gives them the freedom to pursue their own mission. By nature, a college or university is controversial as well as important, and outside groups often try to use an institution for special purposes (political, bureaucratic, personal, business, etc.). Because it is also vulnerable, an institution needs a strong board to protect its independence. The very knowledge that such a board exists is usually sufficient to ward off the contractor who wants special consideration, the influential citizen who wants special admission treatment for his son, the important elected official who feels that the institution should more nearly represent her political interest or who needs a job for a friend, the government bureaucrat with a penchant for running colleges and universities, or the donor who wants to attach inappropriate conditions to a major gift.

A key role of a college or university is to take exception with the conventional wisdom, from both the left and the right. The institution is a sanctuary for the free expression of ideas, some of which will disturb specific individuals or groups. However, as Justice Oliver Wendell Holmes put it, the test is "not free thought for those who agree with us, but freedom for the thought we hate."

While the university ensures the right to express ideas that may be unpopular, it is also bound to see that the laws are enforced. Every board must insist on policies that protect the institution from extremists from both inside and outside. For instance, if, in the course of dissent, students or staff violate the duly constituted law (for example, denying an individual the right to speak, or destroying property), the institution is bound to have them prosecuted. Institutional forgiveness cannot be given for reasons of youth, motivation, or sympathy. In the case of civil disobedience, if the student or staff member has the right to violate the law, the institution has the obligation to see that the law is enforced. It is the responsibility of the board to see that it is done.

11. Representing the Institution and the Public

Colleges and universities are bound to be controversial, and the duty of a trustee is to explain, defend, and enhance the institution under this condition. A college or university that is not at times controversial is not worthy of the name. Truth is never absolute and rarely comfortable[3] and, as the primary function of a college or university is to pursue and interpret the truth, a board should never find comfort in a smooth course.

The trustees interpret the campus to the external community and provide the legitimate link to those who might otherwise object. It is easy to sing the praises of an institution in ivy-covered moments; it is quite another thing to defend it when it is in trouble. To do these things effectively, trustees must be informed about the institution—they must know its mission, its programs, and its plans.

Trustees may at times be called upon to defend things they do not personally support, such as the appearance on campus of a controversial speaker or the performance of an avant-garde play. These situations are the test of the effective trustee. The time for questioning institutional practice is in the privacy of a board meeting. In public, the trustee either champions the institution or supportively states that the chair of the board or the president will speak on that particular issue.

Conversely, trustees represent the views of the external public to the staff and, in so doing, enhance the breadth and view of the institution.

---

[3]Max Weber put it well: "The primary task of a useful teacher is to teach students to recognize 'inconvenient facts.'" Board members also must recognize that their institution's pursuit of the truth may result in alleged "inconvenient facts" being put forward about the state of society, or even their own personal portfolios or activities. However objectionable and off-target these episodes may seem, board members should firmly resist the urge to discipline or silence faculty members or students who utter such thoughts, providing, of course, that they do so without violating the law or the rights of others.

Representing society to the institution is an important trustee responsibility. As societal changes occur, colleges and universities, like other institutions, are invariably reluctant to change. Colleges often tend to live in relative isolation or to feel that the outside holds questionable values and is unworthy of serious consideration. In a shrinking and high-technology world, colleges and universities are woefully slow to embrace the importance of requiring foreign languages, full computer literacy, or an understanding of non-Western cultures. Trustees cannot themselves make these changes, but they can insist that officials of the institution be aware of the academic and management implications of the greater society.

12. Serving as a Court of Appeal

On rare occasions, a board of trustees may be pressed to sit in judgment over an institutional dispute. We have become a litigious society, and ever more frequently staff or faculty or students will question judgments against them. Contrary to the conventional wisdom on this subject, unless there is clear evidence that the institution's policies have been violated or that the law has been broken, the board should support the president pro forma. If the issue is pressed, let it be in the courts of law. To do otherwise not only reduces the legitimacy of the president, but also establishes a most unfortunate precedent. When members of the campus appeal to the board, a president cannot survive if the board overturns his or her judgment too frequently.

This kind of situation can best be prevented if the board insists on well-publicized policies and procedures regarding faculty appointment, promotion, and tenure, and expected student conduct. Further, the board should insist the president and the administration follow these policies, as well as applicable law. As potential problems develop, the president should consult informally with the board chair.

13. Determining Board Performance

Once a year, in executive session, the board should ask the president, "How are we doing?" Some boards appoint a board committee (not the executive committee) to consider the annual performance of the board. This might be the presidential compensation committee (if it is not the executive committee). This committee should also evaluate the president.

At least every five years, the board should engage an outside consultant to help answer questions regarding the performance of the board. While board performance is usually addressed in an institutional evaluation and in a presidential review, the board chair should specifically ask the outside evaluator to assess the board itself.

FINAL THOUGHTS

The model we have proposed enables each of the most important segments of the university community—board, president, faculty, students, alumni—to play its proper and effective role in governing the institution. At the same time, the interpretation of these responsibilities allows the president to play the key role in the institutional leadership and to be measured fairly in that performance. This model is in accord with leadership theory and empirical evidence, as well as with all recognized governance statements adopted by national higher education organizations. If pursued, it will not guarantee either a successful president or a prosperous campus, but it will maximize the possibility of these things occurring.

- A board membership is a trusteeship; board members hold the future of the institution in their hands.
- It is irresponsible for either the president or the board to assign all responsibility for academic programs and curricula to faculty.
- The failure of most boards to pay much attention to their constitutions, bylaws, and campus government documents leads to presidential failures and disrupted campuses.
- Boards should evaluate themselves.
- Continuous, predictable turnover in board membership usually is a good idea; it avoids the problems that arise when one board member uses longevity to place his or her personal stamp on the institution.
- Board members should "give, get, or get off" the board.
- Many boards damage their presidential searches irretrievably by providing faculty with a majority of the slots on the search committee.
- An astute institutional evaluation is of supreme value to the board, presidential candidates, and the eventual new president.

CHAPTER
eighteen
·······

Evaluating the Institution

A man must serve his time to every trade / Save Censure—Critics all are ready made.

Lord Byron, in *English Bards and Scotch Reviewers*

He can see a louse as far away as China, but is unconscious of an elephant on his nose.

Malay Proverb

Increasingly, governing boards choose to commission institutional evaluations (called "reviews" because this term is less pejorative) as a first step toward establishing or re-establishing a solid foundation for the institution and more legitimate premises for the president. Boards and search committees often find these reviews indispensable during presidential searches. Presidents, particularly newly appointed presidents, find that institutional reviews can help them start their presidencies on a solid footing. Sitting presidents find reviews useful in providing them with an unbiased picture of "how things really are." This enables them to plan for the future and, as the need arises, to initiate certain difficult, but necessary, campus conversations by citing (and perhaps even blaming) the review team.[1]

---

[1] A liberal arts college in the Pacific Northwest developed several graduate programs, but without giving proper attention to academic standards and requirements. For example, admission standards were minimal or nonexistent. This practice was, however, popular with graduate program directors who were able to exercise (and sometimes abuse) their huge discretion in this area. The college's president used the institutional review to begin a conversation about these issues that led to the establishment of respectable academic standards and an eventual commendation from the Northwest Association of Colleges and Schools when the college was reaccredited.

Indeed, institutional reviews are often considered of greater value and validity than accreditation reports, which are sometimes merely exercises in back-scratching or efforts to check the behavior of the unconventional. Few regional accreditation reports are as truthful and useful, as institutional reviews conducted by well-chosen, knowledgeable reviewers.

WHAT IS AN INSTITUTIONAL REVIEW?

An institutional review is an evaluation of the entire institution, with special attention directed toward strategic positioning.

An institutional review is conducted by a team of outside recognized authorities who, over a two- to four-month period, assess the condition of an institution through interviews and data. The review is finally presented to the board and/or the president, and it may be used as either a public or a confidential document, although certain benefits are lost in a confidential review. A public review often serves as a tonic for the entire institution. Initially, some in the campus community are skeptical, believing that no outsider could really know them; others may be anxious at the thought of discovery; but most are pleased at the prospect of an objective evaluation that will verify their worth and improve their condition. A good review will nearly always meet the test of all concerned parties, including the initially skeptical.

The review evaluates every dimension of the institution. The final report should include an institutional profile plus separate chapters on academic programs, faculty, students, administration, budget and finances, and governance. Analysis, observations, and recommendations should be included for each of these areas.

THE VALUE OF AN INSTITUTIONAL REVIEW

Of course, not all institutional reviews are good, but most clarify the condition of the institution being reviewed and provide a useful set of suggestions for future action. Consider the comments of the chair of the board of a major public university who reported:

> We would never have found the president we did, nor gotten him under way so effectively, without an institutional review.

The chair of the board of a liberal arts college said:

> The review was a breath of new life and honesty for our entire college community and it served as the format from which we interviewed and evaluated our presidential candidates.

At the end of his first year in office, a university president declared:

> The review was the wisest thing I did. It gave me an expert, objective assessment of our condition and it served as the basis for my presidential strategy.

Another college president said:

> It would have taken me years to find out what we learned from the review in three months. Even though it was candid, it was celebrated by our entire community.

A sitting president reported:

> It's the only way we could overcome our own opinions, which had become encrusted by special interests, personal obligations, and preconceived opinions.

A review prepared in anticipation of the search process offers the following benefits:

1. It is valuable to prospective candidates.
2. It enables the search committee to establish more than messianic criteria.
3. It helps the board address conditions during and before the appointment of a new president that will make the position more attractive to first-rank candidates. (For instance, a number of boards make changes in governance policies and practices between presidencies.)
4. The institution will develop more realistic expectations and plans.
5. In the case of public reviews, faculty, administrators, students, alumni, elected officials, benefactors, trustees, townspeople, and all other concerned parties are encouraged—indeed, bound—to consider a legitimate opinion of the institution that might differ from their own.
6. The region, state, and the entire universe of the institution gain a heightened awareness of, and interest in, the college or university because of their involvement in the review and their reading of the

results. (At one major university, the local newspaper published the entire 100-page review, and nearly every daily newspaper in the state did feature stories and editorials.)

For a newly appointed president, in addition to the above, a review can do the following:

1. Ensure a better informed and more enlightened board by bringing to the board's attention important issues and potential problems affecting the institution.
2. Help establish a tentative agenda for the institution and provide a more objective foundation for strategic and long-range planning.
3. Serve as a dispassionate way to evaluate the organization and administration, the quality of academic programs, and the faculty and student body of an institution.
4. Advise on the attitudes of all constituencies, including alumni, media, political bodies, and townspeople, as well as faculty, staff, and students.
5. Help determine the potential for increased private support.
6. Provide a valuable substantive dimension to the inaugural year by informing the internal and external publics of the institution of the present condition of the institution and the forthright style of its new president.
7. Prevent the new president's leadership potential from being diminished by not forcing him or her to make what might otherwise appear to be arbitrary judgments on important but controversial issues.

A sitting president finds an institutional review of value for the following reasons:

1. As an assessment of how things are going and what future plans (both institutional and personal) should include.
2. In preparing for accreditation and outside evaluation—a good review usually is far more valuable than the most thoughtful self-assessment.
3. As a check on other outside evaluations that may have been conducted from different or even opposing premises.
4. As a precursor to a presidential evaluation by the board.

The accomplishment of all these conditions need not risk the acceptance, credibility, or leadership of the president because institutional problems and prospects are addressed by an outside authority who is not (or should not be) threatened by alienation, vested interests, or subtle reprisals from inside or outside the campus. Problems of funding, morale, personnel, organization, and governance can be addressed candidly without being colored by provincial interests and without diminishing the leadership potential of either the president or the board.

WHO CONDUCTS THE REVIEW?

The most important decision regarding an institutional review is who should do it. The appointment criteria should include experience, legitimacy, chemistry, and cost. Cost should not be the overriding criterion; a good review usually is worth many times the price.

The person or firm you have in mind should have sufficient experience and provide you with copies of previous institutional reviews or assessments conducted, along with references. This is an important consideration. The quality of the review will be the primary way to determinane the value of the effort. Do not be misled by the spoken word; ask to see evidence. The review team should include from three to six persons with impressive credentials; one person surely cannot do the job.

The person who chairs the team is of primary importance. He or she will organize the effort and finally write the report. This person must have experience in conducting such efforts. He or she should assemble the review team. Too often, the president, and sometimes the board, want to name the people on the team, thereby raising questions about both validity and process. Presidents or board members should feel free to suggest names, but should not press. A good chair cannot be party even to the appearance of special interests.

How you feel about the person in charge of the review is obviously important. You should spend one-on-one time discussing the prospect, and you should consider the record of the individual (not the firm). If the chair has publications in the field, read them and make sure you are in general agreement with the author before proceeding further. Some authors write about the college presidency from the position of a strong presidency, while others take the "collegial" position. A team headed by a collegialist undoubtedly would take a somewhat different approach in many areas, particularly administration and governance. You make the choice, but never assume complete objectivity by the reviewers; the most you can expect is honesty, sophistication, and freedom from influence by your vested interest groups. Again, cost should not be a decisive deterrent when an institution is deciding whether to undertake an institutional review. A good review nearly always is worth it, even if it initially seems rather pricey. A complete review can run from $40,000 to $500,000, depending on the amount of time, the number of persons interviewed, and the reputation of the individual or firm conducting the review.

PREPARATION FOR THE REVIEW

Although the core of an institutional review is the visit to the campus and surrounding area by the review team, the preparation for the review begins at least one month before the visit. After meeting with the commissioning authority (the board or the president), the chair of the review team takes charge of the process. He or she sends the following materials to each member of the team for reading in advance of the visit:

- all catalogs, brochures, applications, and promotional information
- all media coverage and press releases for the preceding 12 months
- budget and finance information (including procedures and recent audits)
- past accreditation reports and any other outside evaluations
- an institutional membership list
- a profile of the student body (including five-year entering test scores and enrollment figures)
- private support figures for the past five years and organizational and promotional materials
- the constitution and bylaws of the governing boards, the campus governance body, the alumni association and private foundations (if any) associated with the institution, along with names, titles, and home telephone numbers of all trustees and directors
- state-of-the-institution addresses and other papers of the incumbent president
- promotional materials on the surrounding community
- institutional and other planning documents
- organizational chart(s)
- faculty, staff, and student handbooks
- compensation figures for all employees

- institutional research reports and surveys conducted by or about the institution
- information on the library, honors programs, placement records, and graduate success of students
- faculty publications
- any other information that may be of value to the team in conducting the review

Finally, the chair of the team should ask key institutional officers to prepare confidential papers on the status of the institution; these will prove invaluable in preparing for the campus visit.

HOW A REVIEW IS CONDUCTED

After the appointment of a review team chair, he or she selects prospective team members on the basis of their particular strengths and on the special nature and needs of the institution. The team chair discusses the names and credentials of prospective team members with the president and board, and, if acceptable, they are invited to serve on the team. Ordinarily, they are paid by the chair.

During a two-day or three-day visit to the campus(es), the review team conducts confidential interviews, both individual and group. The interviews are the heart of the visitation and of the final report. The team interviews not only persons who have a special interest in the institution, but also outside authorities (e.g., persons in scholarly disciplines and national organizations). All interviews should follow a standardized format that allows an opportunity for interviewees to express any additional thoughts. Interviewees are selected because of position (trustees, faculty senate chair, senator) and at random. The team should select faculty by stratified random sample as well as at random and by position in campus governance.

No time should be scheduled for social amenities, but some ostensibly free time should be allowed for spontaneous interviews of people selected completely at random.

The team should receive the materials noted above at least two weeks prior to the visitation. They should also receive orientation materials from the team chair at an on-site meeting the evening before the interviews begin.

The team should work in a comfortable, but neutral, area (not the administration building) and should receive on-site assistance organized by a campus coordinator. The ideal on-campus coordinator/assistant is an experienced staff administrator or secretary who schedules interviews and makes arrangements for the office space, transportation and lodging, and secretarial services.

Interviews are typically 50 minutes, and team members may interview by telephone those people who cannot conveniently come on-site. Frequently, the team will do telephone interviews after the visit to assure that no important persons are left out of the review process. This is key; everyone should be allowed to buy into this activity. If the team has the expertise, it can hold group sessions with separate groups (8 to 15) of faculty, students, alumni, and staff. These should follow the interview format.

At the conclusion of the visit, the team should have a brief private meeting, and then the chair of the team should meet with the commissioning authority.

After the visit, the team continues its evaluation of the institution, now including both written materials and the opinions of a hundred or so diverse parties. After six to nine weeks, the team submits a final written review. This is best done without additional comment. In-person presentations of such a document can lead to dialogue that obscures positions carefully considered and formulated after much thoughtful deliberation.

FINAL THOUGHTS

The value of a well-organized institutional review has seldom been questioned by boards, search committees, or presidents after the review has been completed and digested by the campus. The results typically are embraced with progressively growing respect and enthusiasm, for the observations and recommendations provide the building blocks of a stronger institution. On occasion, of course, a review is so critical that it leads to changes in institutional leadership, sometimes at the presidential level. More often, however, the review provides even a mediocre president with the tools to improve his or her performance and stimulate the institution.

- The identity of the reviewers is the most important determinant of the quality and usefulness of an institutional review.
- An institutional review is *not* a review of the president, although the quality of presidential leadership must be addressed.
- Reviewers must take great pains to avoid giving the impression that they are there to review the president; if the campus believes it is "voting on" the president, the president's effectiveness will plummet.

- Institutional reviews may cost from $40,000 to $500,000, depending upon the complexity of the institution. Despite this cost, they are nearly always worth the price if the appropriate reviewers have been chosen.
- One of the best times for an institution to commission a review is just before it begins a search for a new president.
- Institutional reviews are not just for colleges and universities that are in trouble.

CHAPTER
nineteen
• • • • • • •

Searching for
the President

The many may err as grossly as the few.

John Dryden in *Absalom and Achitophel*

Most committees get everybody together and homogenize their thinking.
The result is mediocrity, which may have been the aim in the first place.

Robert Bell

Ironically, as the presidential search process has become increasingly sophisticated, the presidency itself has become a major dilemma in higher education. Harvard's David Riesman has referred to today's presidential search as "the search and destroy process." The process has not been working as it should, and the result has been a decline in the number of transformational, visionary presidents.

Many scholars and most national associations are candid about the issue. We believe that presidential leadership is the main imperative for the revitalization of higher education. Certainly no commission or study group has concluded that the search process is the prime culprit in the decline of the presidency; rather, it is only another symptom, although an extremely important one, of the leadership dilemma in higher education. We believe that the presidential search process is the unfortunate beginning of the compromised presidency in American higher education.

The presidential selection process was an early victim of the twentieth-century drive to disperse power on American campuses. Without effective dissent, presidential selection became popularized. As faculty members and students achieved closer and formal ties with governing boards, both the process and the result of presidential searches gradually changed. The process of presidential selection became more important than the outcome. Increasingly, the weight of the people was felt in the process of presidential selection, and the effective, transformational presidency got lost in the democratic shuffle. Once appointed, few presidents have had the ability or the desire to object to the new power-diffusing policies and the conscious reduction in presidential authority. The typical president either covets the position so much that he or she hopes all will work out anyway, or silently rides the tide.

Strong presidential candidates often have been unwilling to participate in searches in which confidentiality cannot be maintained because of "open" meetings and widespread campus participation. A majority of states now have "open" meeting and "sunshine" laws, some of which require that all presidential search meetings for public institutions be open to the public.[1] Most agree that sunshine laws have had a generally beneficent effect upon the quality of overall governmental activity; however, their effects upon presidential selection processes have been substantially negative.[2]

The direct consequence has been that many top people have become increasingly reluctant to be candidates. Those who do often drop out because of the threat (or certainty) of breaching confidentiality. Compounding this is the tendency of zealous faculty-dominated search committees to eliminate any candidate who is associated with strong stances or controversy. Amidst all this, most governing boards have scarcely noticed that their institutions have lost momentum. Left with neither rational form nor order, presidents have come and gone, or have quietly sat on the bench as custodians while boards and faculties have tried to run the institutions.

A FLAWED SEARCH PROCESS

The compromise of presidential legitimacy begins, and in too many cases continues, with the presidential appointment process. If the first steps in

---

[1]Florida requires that all candidates and all nominees for public university presidential positions be made public. This latter feature of Florida law has been enough to cause some sitting presidents to fear receiving an otherwise flattering nomination for a presidential post in that state.

[2]Unwise requirements for destructive disclosure in presidential searches should not be confused with much more defensible "sunshine" provisions that dictate that actual board meetings, including the meeting where the president is formally appointed, be open to the public.

this crucial process are unwise, regardless of subsequent outside counsel and the most sophisticated material, the outcome is likely to be mediocre. Indeed, a good candidate usually slips through by accident rather than by sound intention. The institution will most likely end up with a "faceless" managerial president who sits by passively while the institution fails to meet the tests of the time.

In most institutions today, the search process is fundamentally flawed. Either a good committee is doing the wrong things, or a poorly constituted committee is doing the right things. In either case, the next president is a compromise.

In the first case, a well-constituted, though inexperienced, search committee chooses to establish a "new" procedure: *A poor process is the result.* Such a committee often focuses on the process rather than the outcome, attempting to involve virtually all interested parties. These committees often do such questionable things as create additional faculty and even administration committees, cater to the media, take too long to get the job done, design committee stationery, invite the outgoing president to join them, appoint a faculty/student screening committee, assign a faculty member to handle the administration of committee matters, hold public interviews with final candidates, appoint all sorts of advisory and subcommittees, and, most unfortunately, decide that they can do the job without outside consultation.

In the second case, a poorly constituted search committee includes a disproportionate number of faculty, members of the administrative staff, and board members. These members of the academic community are inexperienced with executive searches and typically prefer "least common denominator" candidates who stand for little and have offended no one. In no case should the number of faculty on a search committee exceed the number of members from the governing board. A board must realize that the appointment of a president is its most important responsibility, or it is heading for trouble.

Occasionally, top candidates do survive this happy egalitarian process. Their native ability, plus a pleased search committee, are enough to lull a governing board into acceptance, at least initially, of the new president. In time, if the governing board becomes too involved in campus administration and external relations, it begins to question the president, all the while forgetting that its problems started with the presidential search process.

What *should* a board do when there is a presidential vacancy? This chapter describes a tested presidential search procedure, fashioned after careful review of the research on effective leadership.

WHAT THE BOARD SHOULD NOT DO
WITH A PRESIDENTIAL VACANCY

Let us assume that you are the board chair and your president has just informed you of his intention to leave office in 15 months. What is the first step? You should *not* convene the board and appoint a search committee. Although it may seem the reasonable thing to do, a review of what was done previously should not automatically be undertaken. The review of old minutes will result in "new" procedures that really are "old-fashioned" retreads. Following precedent can get you in trouble.

The ignorance of the past is given new life by a well-intentioned board that does not know what else to do.[3] A mistake made in the appointment of the search committee is usually irreparable. Consider search committee membership. Riesman and McLaughlin (1984) found that more than 50 percent of the institutions they surveyed reported that less than one-half of their search committee members were trustees; 16 percent responded that no trustees served on their search committee (Riesman and McLaughlin, 1984). These data reflect well-meaning, but unknowledgeable boards who later will pay for their obliviousness.

The key features in an efficient and effective presidential search are the following:

1. the use of outside consultants (probably more than you think you will need)
2. the right search committee
3. the right search process
4. complete confidentiality
5. an institutional review or audit
6. an emphasis on referencing rather than interviewing
7. a finely tailored compensation package

---

[3]Curiously, searches generally are ignored in the literature on leadership and presidents. For example, two recent books on these subjects (Clark and Clark, 1994; Crowley, 1994) do not discuss presidential searches even though the nature of the search process has a tremendous influence on the identity, power, and success of the individual appointed.

WHAT THE BOARD SHOULD DO

The five steps described below should take approximately two weeks.

1. Appointment of a General Consultant

To ensure a graceful departure for the out-going president, the single most important thing a board can do is engage an experienced general consultant. Engage the consultant *before appointing a search committee.* After discussions with the chair of the board, the consultant should speak to a meeting of the full board or the executive committee.

A prestigious middle-Atlantic university prepared to appoint a 17-member faculty screening committee to review all candidates before they were reviewed by a board search committee. The board chair was prepared to do this even after acknowledging that the same screening committee process had last time produced a president who lasted an unhappy four years. After discussion with a consultant, the board changed course. The chair changed the design and involved the faculty in a way that was helpful, not compromising, to the search.

At this point, you do not yet need a consultant to run the forthcoming search. You need someone who is broadly experienced in higher education, a scholar or a successful CEO. This consultant should speak about the general condition and future prospects of higher education, particularly as related to institutions similar to yours; review recent research on the college presidency; and discuss the presidential appointment process, placing special emphasis on your search for a new president.

2. Appointment of the Search Committee

The general consultant should advise you about whom to appoint to your search committee. *It is absolutely vital that you hear from your consultant (or read this) before appointing the search committee.* Appointing the search committee first usually leaves the selection process hostage to a committee heavily loaded with faculty staff, and students. Before the consultant can begin, campus politics have already infected and contaminated the search process. The committee should consider the various vested interests of the campus community, but those interests should not be heavily represented on the search committee.

One of the authors' experiences as a consultant for the presidential search committee of an eastern liberal arts college illustrates what all too often happens. The committee of 13 (too many) included four trustees, four faculty members, three administrators, and two students. This group asked him to advise them about a selection procedure that would result in a wise choice. After a day and a half during which a candid rapport was established, they finally agreed that regardless of what process they followed, they were unlikely to make a desirable presidential choice. They realized that even if they followed the most sophisticated presidential selection procedures and used the most astute consultants, they were likely to appoint the wrong person. Their conclusion was based on their gradual realization that the search committee would have a highly politicized character. Except for the outnumbered trustees, every member—faculty, staff, and student—was tacitly but finally obligated to a particular vested interest within the college. If the committee followed a one-person, one-vote regime, it was bound to end up with a compromise candidate—a negotiator, a manager, the average rather than the exception. In spite of initial protestations to the contrary, they finally concluded that, while they might all be involved in the presidential appointment process in some other way, the college would be best served if their search committee was dissolved, and it was.

You can minimize the politicization of your search committee in two ways.

1. Adhere strictly to the message of the research on effective management and leadership, which clearly calls for no automatic and titular representation of members of the community on the search committee (i.e., no faculty senate representative, no one elected or appointed by anyone except the governing board).

2. Appoint a committee with a distinct majority of strong trustee members and only modest representation from the campus community. This plan is the wisest choice for higher education, according to a survey by David Riesman and Judith McLaughlin (1984) on search committee composition.

The general consultant may advise you to opt for the committee composed largely of trustees. Regardless of institutional politics, the ideal size for such a search committee is nine (but never fewer than 7 or more than 15), and will include five strong trustees, two faculty members, one student, and one alumnus. As chair of the board, you should also chair the search committee. If you choose not to be chair yourself, appoint (never elect) your strongest board member.

There should be no administrators on the committee. Administrators are members of the president's team, and no candidate should be given the impression that the administration plays a role in selecting the president. The leadership research also indicates that committee members should not be chosen by institution-wide election. Nonetheless, if the faculty governance body is asked to name faculty representatives, they usually will choose to elect them. While it would be better if faculty spokespersons were appointed by their council, let *them* choose how they will do it. This issue is not worth a disagreement with the faculty as long as board members constitute a majority of the search committee.

After you decide on committee membership, ask the chief academic officer or the interim president (*not* the outgoing president) to act as your agent in discussions about how the faculty will choose their representatives. This will allow you to maintain the necessary distance between the board and the faculty and will not threaten the leadership of your next president. Remember, close that gap and you risk diminishing your president in other things after the appointment. *Always* play up the presidential office. In the long-run, things will run more smoothly if you do.

In most situations, the chief academic officer or interim president should also ask the primary faculty governance body to appoint a special advisory committee consisting of one faculty member from each school, college, or division and, perhaps, a student and an alumnus. This request will satisfy faculty expectations. Toward the end of the presidential search, this committee should be asked to interview *in complete confidence,* the top choices of the search committee. Each member of this advisory committee should then evaluate the candidates on a special form prepared by your consultant. At the conclusion of the candidate interviews, the assigned chair (usually one of the faculty members of the search committee) should collect the forms without discussion and give them to you to share with the full board as it makes the final decision.

3. Committee Staff

You need to appoint a loyal, discrete staff member who will serve as the administrative officer and secretary for the search committee. This person takes notes, makes meeting arrangements, staffs the search office, handles correspondence, maintains files, and provides other services to the committee. He or she does not vote or, except in an objective role, participate in the discussions of the committee.

After talking with the general consultant, have the news office on campus prepare a press release announcing the general time frame (two months to a year is acceptable, but four to six months is best) and stressing the confidentiality of the search. You should also make it clear that all future comments on the search process will come either from you or from the chair of the search committee.

4. Confidentiality

The importance of absolute confidentiality *cannot* be overemphasized. More good candidates are lost, or are never attracted, because of a lack of confidentiality than for all other reasons combined. This is particularly true of states with strong sunshine laws, but it happens in others as well. Confidentiality means confidential *to the end.* Many believe that the final stages of the process should include public interviews on campus. The idea is without foundation. Not only are good candidates lost in this way, but personal interviews, including public interviews, are one of the *least* effective variables in predicting job success. The key to your best candidates will be the institutional review and careful referencing by the committee and the consultant. Interviews have gained currency in higher education simply because of a kind of politics vested in collegiality and because governing boards do not know what else to do.

5. Charge to the Search Committee

The next step is preparing a board charge to the search committee (see Appendix C). This charge will probably include, among other things, a statement about the departing president, the names of the search committee members, the general time frame of the search, and how many candidates should be recommended (three to five in *no* order of preference). The charge should emphasize again the importance of confidentiality.

The board should approve all the appropriate conditions. Once the charge is approved, you are ready for the first meeting of the committee.

6. First Meeting of the Search Committee

Appendix D provides for a concise step-by-step process of a four-month search.

The first meeting (held during the third week) should be brief, instructive, and carefully planned. A suggested agenda is found in Appendix D.

1. opening remarks by the chair
2. presentation by general consultant
3. consideration of search consultants
4. consideration of institutional audit or review
5. consideration of compensation study
6. consideration of specific time frame
7. consideration of public hearing
8. presentation by affirmative action officer
9. advertisements: design and posting
10. special letters
11. presentation by outgoing president
12. office space, secretary, correspondence[4]
13. other matters

Your opening remarks should be brief but inspiring. Do not assume that committee members recognize the profound importance of their task. After everyone takes a blood oath to confidentiality, read the board's charge to the committee, review the agenda, and then proceed.

The presentation by the general consultant (item 2) should include a review of the condition of higher education, specifically that of the presidency; a review of the research on effective leadership, emphasizing the college presidency; a presentation of a generic search process; and a discussion of items three through seven on the agenda. Committee members should be invited to ask questions.

Although the third item on the agenda calls for consideration of search consultants, the board chair can appoint a search consultant before the first committee meeting, as long as he or she first discusses the matter with the general consultant first. Although there may be institutions whose trustees

---

[4]Some boards have found it helpful to determine these things *prior* to the first meeting of the search committee. They are fairly routine but can sometimes consume an inordinate amount of the committee's time.

and staff are sufficiently involved and informed to be sophisticated about presidential search, we have never known of any. Many members of search committees believe that they know a great deal about how to conduct a presidential search; few actually do.

You should avoid, at all costs, the common tendency to dig out old files and personnel (board or staff) who have participated in past searches. If you want to do the best job possible, you must appoint an outside search consultant. This is true even for state systems that have full-time officers assigned to conduct searches. Increasingly, boards of trustees are appointing search consultants to help in this fundamental task. Good search consultants know both the process of presidential searches and the universe of prospective presidents. They also have their reputations on the line each time they accept an assignment.

To choose a search firm from the variety of possibilities, make a few calls, but always interview at least three prospects. The general consultant can provide the names of top search firms and can help monitor the work of the one you select.

There are two basic kinds of search firms, not-for-profit and profit. Using either kind is better than doing the search yourself. The not-for-profit firms have been criticized for concentrating too much on the search *process*. While they seem to invariably leave the people involved happy, some feel they should focus more on the project at hand, which is the appointment of the best possible president. Although nonprofit firms usually take longer to do the job, their fees are generally lower.

The for-profit firms are more concerned with outcome, take less time (four to six months), and charge more (usually a third of the first year's salary). Both the profit and the nonprofit firms are sometimes faulted for a lack of substantive knowledge of, and experience with, effective leadership in universities and colleges. There is also concern that these firms sometimes draw on a common pool of candidates for all institutions and that they will accept without enlightened critique any design for a search, so long as they win the contract.

Because one of the authors has frequently served as a general consultant to governing boards and search committees, he has probably heard more presentations by more search firms than anyone else in the country. He has yet to be completely satisfied with any. Few, if any, are thoughtful students either of current issues or leadership research in higher education, and few boast successful former college presidents among their principals. They naturally tend to represent the parochial interests of the search committee and do not provide the committee with objective information that enables the members to form impressions and make decisions. Still, using these firms is infinitely better than doing the search yourself (even with this book in hand) because of their higher efficiency and greater knowledge of the candidates in the field.

We lean towards the for-profit firms because most are more goal-oriented, but many boards have been completely happy with the nonprofit firms and have saved themselves several thousand dollars in the process. However, the very nature of nonprofit firms often causes them to experience frequent and large turnovers in personnel; it is therefore difficult to assess their prospective worth to you.

Whatever you do, stay in touch with the process; you will feel better and keep your consultant alert. It is not at all unusual for a search committee chair to talk with the search consultant three to six times a week.

If you decide to use a search consultant, the general consultant should first present a brief on each firm you will be inviting for an interview. If you interview three firms, at least one should be not-for-profit. Your general consultant can recommend a number of highly regarded profit and nonprofit firms. You and the committee members may wish to add to this list.

The most important consideration at this stage is that you check references on each firm and that you talk with their past clients. You and your associates on the committee should feel good about the person making the presentation for each firm, and you should also make sure that the persons doing the presentation will be assigned by the firm to do this search. Boards and search committees have been known to sign contracts under the belief that they would be working with the person who made such a powerful presentation, only to find later that another person is assigned to do the job.

After introductions, ask the representative of the firm to make a brief presentation (no more than 20 minutes) and then answer questions from the committee. Consider asking the following questions:

- How long will it take to do a thorough search?
- What is your opinion of our institution?
- What experience have you had with similar institutions?
- What kind of president do you think we need?
- What role will we, the committee, play in the search process?
- How do you reference candidates? Do we help?
- Why shouldn't we do this ourselves?
- What do you, or others in your firm, know about higher education?

- Are any members of your firm former college presidents?
- Are you associated with any scholars in higher education?
- How do you evaluate the campus and its needs before focusing on candidates?
- If so, how? Tell us more about the process.
- How many searches do you conduct simultaneously?
- Should faculty be represented on a search committee?
- Should students be represented? If so, how heavily?
- How do you feel about the use of screening and advisory committees to assist the search committee?
- Is confidentiality really important? If so, how is it maintained?
- What about public interviews?
- How do you decide that a search has failed? What do you do then?
- What is the difference between a profit and a nonprofit search firm?
- Why do you ask us to pay your fee in installments?

After all the presentations, the committee should discuss the firms with the general consultant and then make its selection. From this point on, the search firm is your primary instrument in the search process. However, you may choose to continue to involve the general consultant as your surrogate. You will need to decide the extent to which he or she will be involved. In some instances, telephone contact is sufficient; in others, the general consultant continues to attend all committee meetings to advise on procedures, the institutional review, and media and public relations, and to review the activities of the search consultant.

The fourth agenda item is the institutional audit or review. Many boards (including those of prestigious institutions such as the University of North Carolina at Chapel Hill) have found of indispensable value an institutional audit or review conducted by the general consultant or by another person from outside the institution who is considered an authority (see Chapter 18). This commissioned consultant appoints a review team of four to six people of stature. Through interviews, campus visits, and reading materials, the team reviews all areas of the institution (academic programs, faculty, students, administration, budget, finances, fund raising, public relations, and governance) and presents you with a written report. The report of the evaluation team can be either confidential or public, but most agree the report is more valuable when made public. This review is the basis for both a profile of, and a tentative agenda for, the next president.

Boards find institutional reviews helpful in stirring the interests of top presidential candidates and in conducting interviews with finalists in the search process. Indeed, some leading candidates, including finalists, have not been interested until they have read the institutional review. A thorough review can take from 8 to 10 weeks. Commission it early so it will be of maximum value in the search process.

If the board has not already commissioned one, the fifth agenda item calls for considering a presidential compensation study (see Chapter 20). If your outgoing president has been in office five or more years, and you have not undertaken an outside compensation study during that time, you need one badly. Some searches have broken down at the end because the board has taken for granted the subject of presidential compensation or has assumed the validity of ancient conditions.

- One state institution lost its first-choice candidate because its presidential housing allowance was $6,000 per year (a board policy from 1967), and the board could not get a policy change approved by the state in time to keep the candidate.
- A western state university lost most of its presidential finalists when these candidates finally learned of the institution's compensation package.
- In a highly publicized situation, the University of Hawaii lost a strong and experienced individual who already was president of another major institution when the Hawaiian legislature refused to support a compensation agreement that the University's board had signed with the new appointee.

If you are in doubt about your compensation package, have a good executive compensation firm run a two-phase study, the first to study your opening package, and the second to develop a defined package tailored to the needs and the situation of your final choice. This could just be the clincher for a top candidate. It demonstrates that you are thoughtful, and it provides the kind of security a president needs, but rarely mentions. Whatever you do about compensation, think about it seriously and specifically in advance.

Your time frame (item 6) preferably will be about a year, but a thorough search can be conducted in much less time. The average search takes approximately seven and one-half months, and you can do a better job if your search does not lag. Too much time makes for a sloppy search in which the task of finding a top president runs a greater risk of becoming obscured by politics and breaches of confidentiality. A number of boards have found it wise to announce a longer time period, but to shoot for less. This will get better results and more readily satisfy the media and other pressing interests as you proceed. Whatever the time frame, the process should be broken down into four sections: (1) promotion, (2) review, (3) interviews, and (4) recommendations.

Unless it has already been established by the board, another matter on the first meeting agenda should be the consideration of a public hearing (item 7) on the appropriate characteristics of the next president. This hearing should take place on the campus and all potentially interested parties should be invited, by letter and through the public media, to register *in advance*. As many members of the search committee as possible should sit quietly on the panel, which is presided over by the committee chair. Committee members should usually not engage in dialogue with presenters or others in the audience. The purpose of these meetings is to encourage all interested parties to advise the committee. The chair announces the rules, and the meeting continues until all presenters have spoken. The secretary of the search committee is present, and the entire proceedings are taped for future reference. This practice serves two purposes: the committee has the advantage of additional insights, and the members of the community and others have the opportunity to become significantly involved in the search for a new leader. You should hold the public hearing the day before the second search committee meeting, with as many search committee members as possible in attendance.

Next, the affirmative action officer makes a presentation (item 8). The committee must be sensitized to, and informed about, the importance of affirmative action considerations. No matter how enlightened the committee may be, this presentation should be made by a staff member who is especially well-informed on the subject. He or she usually has the title "affirmative action officer" and can advise the committee about conditions on campus, the law, and sources of good candidates.

The promotional period includes placing advertisements (items 9 and 10) in the *Chronicle of Higher Education* and national newspapers, such as the *New York Times, Washington Post,* and *Los Angeles Times;* in major regional newspapers in your area; and in publications commonly read by women and minorities. Put the advertisements in quickly and run them in multiple issues spread over a month. It is entirely proper to do this before the search committee is appointed, although not before you have consulted with your affirmative action officer concerning the legal and ethical ramifications associated with the advertising and language that you use.

You *do not* need to be overly specific in your advertisements and announcements. Many committees labor over the wording of newspaper and journal advertisements that are rarely read in detail or taken seriously even by the most interested candidates. Such labor takes up an inordinate amount of time and delays the posting of your vacancy. All you want to do at this stage is get the word out that your presidency is open.

Your consultant will suggest a list of persons, organizations, and groups who should be invited to submit nominations for the presidency. The committee should send a letter to these persons and any others the committee may wish to add: all college presidents in the region or state, presidents of the same type of institution, presidents of impressive national reputation, key figures in higher education in the state and nation, scholars on the presidency, and the presidents of important national associations in higher education.

The individuals just mentioned may or may not be capable of producing a diverse candidate pool for you. To include women and minorities in your candidate pool, you should ask your campus affirmative action officer for the names of individuals and groups most likely to know such candidates. The circles in which some national higher education figures circulate are sometimes surprisingly narrow, especially those based in Washington, D.C., and those writers on higher education who seldom leave their institutions. Such individuals will produce good names for you, but you should also go beyond them to less well-known sources.

Later, you should send all these individuals another letter, inviting additional nominations and containing a copy of the institutional review. Frequently, the institutional review will inspire application of additional top candidates.

At this first meeting, the committee should approve a letter inviting members of the university community, including faculty, staff, students, and alumni, to submit nominations. The letter should be included in campus and alumni publications. Remember, you cannot do too much in inviting interested parties to submit nominations.

Unless the outgoing president is leaving with bad feelings, he or she should be invited to prepare a paper on the condition of the institution (item 11) to present to the full committee. At the close of the president's remarks (no more than 30 minutes), encourage committee members to ask questions. Finally, after no more than 50 minutes, the president should be excused from the meeting, never to be heard from again unless a specific instance arises where he or she can provide helpful information. Too many search committees muddy their efforts either by inviting the outgoing president to sit on the committee or by snubbing the president altogether by not inviting him or her to make a presentation.

After the president speaks and is thanked and excused, the members of the committee can feel completely free to speak about anything concerning the institution, including the outgoing president.

Finally, after selecting a search consultant, consider any additional matters the committee may wish to raise (such as office space or secretarial help) and adjourn the meeting.

At this point, the efficient search committee now has three meetings in order to complete its task. During the interim before the second meeting, nominations and applications begin to arrive. Each candidate should receive a letter of acknowledgment on discrete letterhead, requesting him or her to list three to six references. During this period, the consultant does a preliminary sort and selects those candidates who most nearly meet the criteria for the position. This number is usually between 30 and 40. Members of the committee are encouraged to come to the search committee office and evaluate all applications and review correspondence. Only the consultant should be allowed to take candidate files out of the search office. During this period, thank you letters should be sent to nominators, applicants, and other candidates.

Also during this time period, the institutional review should be completed so that committee members will have time to assess the report. Finally, the search committee secretary should collect all media comments concerning the search and provide copies for the next meeting.

7. Second Search Committee Meeting

A suggested agenda for the second meeting should include the following items:

1. opening remarks by the chair
2. review by chair and consultant (stress confidentiality)
3. discussion of institutional review
4. committee review of files of top 30 candidates (allow two to four hours, and be prepared to respect the judgment of the search consultant in most cases)
5. discussion by committee and consultant of candidates to reduce list to 15 to 20
6. reference assignments given to committee members (they will use interview forms developed from the institutional review, if one was conducted)

The chair opens the meeting (item 1) by stressing confidentiality; the consultant presents a report on activities since the last meeting, including the results of the institutional review.

The chair explains that the consultant was asked to pare down the candidate group to between 30 and 40 (item 2). The committee spends 90 minutes or so reviewing and evaluating candidate files. After asking the committee for additional names (and usually getting none), the chair asks the consultant to lead discussion on the top candidates.

This discussion may last for an extended period of time, but should not be allowed to drift. It should reduce the list to between 15 to 20, and members of the committee should be assigned certain candidates to reference, using a form prepared by the consultant from the findings of the institutional review (item 3). However, no candidate on the list of the top 30 to 40 is eliminated at this time. The consultant and the committee chair will do in-depth referencing of all candidates, going beyond the references provided by the candidates. This is precisely the point when consultants with broad experience in higher education can be of great value through the personal relationships they have formed over the years.

During the interim period preceding the third search committee meeting, the committee and the consultant are engaged in referencing, and the consultant continues developing prospects. To heighten the interest of the top candidates and evoke the interest of new people, send the institutional review to persons in strategic positions in higher education, as well as to the top 30 to 40 candidates.

8. Third Search Committee Meeting

A suggested agenda for the third meeting should include the following items:

1. opening remarks by the chair (stress confidentiality)
2. consultant's review of new candidates and prospects and his or her update on others
3. discussion of referencing on remaining 15 to 20 candidates
4. reduction of list to 7 to 10 candidates to be reviewed (preferably out of the area)
5. other business

During the interim before the fourth and final meeting of the search committee, the committee and the consultant continue referencing. The single most reliable predictor of a president's performance is that individual's performance in previous positions. Previous performance is more trustworthy than a candidate's performance in a one-hour interview. If deemed necessary, site visits may be conducted with the knowledge of the candidate. During any site visits, confidentiality is essential. If such visits are considered necessary—and their value is highly variable—the consultant and one member of the committee should make the visit.

Note again that thorough, exhaustive referencing plus the consultant's contacts provide by far the most valuable considerations in the decision making of the committee. Site visits sometimes result in more show than substance, but if you need show, and some committees do, carefully make the visits.

9. Fourth Search Committee Meeting

The major function of this meeting is to interview the 7 to 10 semi-finalist candidates. Schedule this meeting in an out-of-town location to diminish the possibility that you will have to contend with curious media representatives or campus members not on the search committee. The meeting should occur in a high-quality hotel of sufficient size to prevent candidates from encountering one another.[5] This meeting will take at least one full day, and may take two days, depending upon the availability of the candidates. Arrange specific times for the interviews and tell candidates that they will be called in their rooms regarding where to join the committee.

A suggested agenda for the fourth meeting should include the following items:

1. opening remarks by the chair (stress confidentiality)
2. review by consultant
3. candidate interviews (approximately 50 minutes each)
4. reduction of list to three to five candidates to be recommended without preference or ranking to the board

At this meeting, the committee interviews the candidates referenced since the last meeting. Occasionally a reference eliminates a candidate, and infrequently additional candidates are found. As the search progresses, however, the standard for "late" inclusion in the search should rise continuously. By the time semi-finalists are interviewed, only truly exceptional candidates should be added to the pool. Last-minute additions to the pool often are not as thoroughly referenced as other candidates, usually because they bring with them some degree of fame. Fame does not necessarily imply actual excellence of performance, and not examining a prospective late addition as closely as other candidates is a mistake.

---

[5]Strange dynamics can emerge from such encounters. Candidates may assist or mislead each other; neither circumstance benefits the search committee. The committee should attempt to give every candidate the feeling that he or she is distinctive and special, not one of a mob. Presidential searches are an important way to advertise an institution.

Candidate interviews follow the same format as the one used in referencing. If you assign a specific item of the interview to each member of the search committee, you will ensure that all interviewees are asked essentially the same questions. This will make comparisons easier during the committee discussion following the interviews. The consultant can be sure that all areas are covered in each interview. The chair should welcome the candidate and ask the first question, a fairly easy one to get things off to a smooth start: "Please tell us something about yourself, where you were born, your family, schools, and your career." After that, the committee can ask other questions, both planned and spontaneous. A good interview will take about an hour; interviews become stagnant and nonproductive if they last much longer.

In the discussion of the candidates, the committee must finally agree on all the candidates to be recommended to the board, i.e., the committee must pledge itself to support enthusiastically any candidate selected by the board. You may sense which candidates are the first, second, and third choices, but do not rank them.

FINAL INTERVIEWS AND APPOINTMENT BY THE BOARD

We are now back at the beginning, with the board about to exercise its most important responsibility, the appointment of the next president. If you are being pressed to hold public campus interviews, resist the temptation! Many searches break down at this point, and many candidates withdraw because confidentiality has been breached. Confidentiality is impossible if public interviews are undertaken. Strong candidates do not want to be portrayed on their home campus as "trying to get out," or, if they are not the person appointed, as the "loser." Rather than confront these circumstances, they will not become candidates or will withdraw.

Consider the case of one of our colleagues (whom we will call Jones) who was considered for a prestigious presidency, but was not appointed. He was thrilled to be a finalist for the position, but mortified when he returned home and read a front page headline, "Jones Rejected." The lengthy story accompanying the headline described interviews by an enterprising reporter with several members of the search committee to ascertain "what was wrong with Jones." Several witless and unethical members of the search committee provided the reporter with their views of Jones' shortcomings.

Not surprisingly, Jones left his heretofore highly successful presidency shortly thereafter.

What you should do instead, if you have organized things astutely, is ask the chief academic officer (or the acting president) to invite the faculty senate (or whatever it is called on your campus) to name one highly respected faculty member from each unit of the institution to serve on an advisory, completely confidential committee that will interview the final candidates. This will provide faculty with input, and you have maintained confidentiality. You may also invite the student government organization and the alumni association to each name a representative. Ask a faculty member of the search committee to chair this special meeting and, after you have given the committee a brief orientation, leave them to undertake their interviews. Ask this committee not to reach a consensus on each candidate, but instead to have each member independently fill out the candidate interview form used by the search committee. At the close of the committee meeting, the chair should bring the forms to you where the board is meeting so that the board can consider the reactions of the faculty committee before making its final choice.

You should stagger the interviews so that each candidate is interviewed by the faculty committee before he or she appears before the board. This practice will test the stamina of the candidate and give the board the benefit of the faculty impressions before it makes its final decision.

The board interview should follow the same format as that used by the search committee in the first set of interviews. After your initial question, board members from the search committee can take the lead. The interview should take no more than 60 minutes. Ask the candidate for questions, thank him or her, and say that you will be in touch. At this stage, observe everything about the candidate: language, presence, dress, posture, eating or drinking habits. Remember that the personal interview is one of the least valuable predictors of job success; the most important is the referencing of past performance that has already been done by your committee and the consultant. Many presidents whose previous performance was mediocre have charmed such committees and won appointments. The ability to shine in a one-hour interview is not synonymous with the ability to be a successful president.

After the interviews, rank your acceptable candidates. Get to your first choice as quickly as possible, but do not dismiss any candidate until a contract is signed. Sophisticated candidates know that a board usually moves quickly after final interviews, and if too much time passes, the finalists who are not contacted will withdraw to save face, and you could find yourself in an awkward situation.

Be prepared to offer your top choice precise terms. Have a compensation package prepared well in advance (see Chapter 20); you can lose precious time and even your best candidates if your package is not sufficient to acquire your choice. (The search consultant should have discussed the general nature of the terms and have ascertained the specific needs of each finalist before this meeting. At this point, you should begin to think seriously about the spouse of your candidate. Spousal happiness is important, and you should consider everything from household appointments and services to employment prospects. (See Chapter 5 for more on this important subject.)

Once you have your president signed, make the public announcement as soon as possible.[6] This not only lets the public know the final selection, but also it more seriously ties in the candidate, now the president-elect. Ask the candidate to approve the press release and any plans for a news conference. This is really the beginning of his or her presidency and should be planned carefully.

Next, inform all other candidates, on the same day the announcement is made. If possible, close and store the files and have the finance records audited. Because you have gone about the process the right way, you have a new president who will bring increased distinction and status to your institution.

Finally, have a party for the committee.

FINAL THOUGHTS

The most important responsibility of a college governing board is the selection of a vigorous, energetic, visionary, transformational president. Despite popular opinion, this cannot be accomplished by any process that approaches a campus opinion poll. Because of the turnover that occurs in the membership of boards, relatively few board members have extensive experience in searching for a president, and their memories may be occluded. Therefore, engaging consultants to guide the search is essential. If the search is conducted in conformance with the principles outlined in this

---

[6]Do not forget that the person you are appointing is leaving another campus or organization. He or she may need to tend to the public relations impact of your announcement on his or her home campus or organization. Be understanding and consider appropriate language and arrangements that will minimize problems.

chapter, you will maximize the possibility of appointing a winning, successful president who will make a significant, positive difference in the life of your institution.

- Most faculty members and most board members know very little about presidential searches, although they may believe they do.
- Past performance in increasingly responsible positions is a much better predictor of presidential success than interviews.
- Thorough referencing of candidates to discover and evaluate their past performance is critical.
- A knowledgeable, experienced consultant is essential to appropriate referencing.
- Most experienced consultants are Caucasian men. You must provide them with specific guidance if you expect them to produce a gender- and race-diverse pool of candidates.
- If you cannot maintain strict confidentiality in your search, you will lose some sterling candidates.
- The members of the board of trustees should constitute a majority of the search committee.
- *How* you conduct a search not only sends messages about the institution, but also has a great deal to do with the nature of the candidate pool from which you eventually can choose.

CHAPTER
twenty
•••••••

Presidential
Compensation and
Related Matters

Nothing is to be had for nothing.

Epictetus, in *Discourses*

I can't get no satisfaction.

Mick Jagger

W e believe that more presidents are lost to other institutions (or cannot
be hired in the first place) because of noncompetitive compensation than
because of any other factor. Boards kid themselves when they think otherwise. It is true that many presidents shrink back from discussing their
compensation package with their boards. Such a topic is awkward and in
the eyes of some carries with it the scent of self-aggrandizement on the part
of the president. Nonetheless, compensation is vitally important to attracting and retaining nearly any president and boards are well-advised to take
this into account.

Most board members do not know how much, or in what ways, presidents typically are compensated. Because they are not academics, they are
more than a little bit at sea when presidential compensation is considered.
As a consequence, they tend to rely upon national salary surveys (for
example, those produced by the National Association of College and

University Business Officers) for information. These data, however, are seldom strictly comparable and are usually at least a year out of date. Also, these studies nearly always exclude any meaningful nonsalary compensation such as deferred compensation agreements.

Add to this mix the current financial status of many institutions of higher education. Most public institutions of higher education have experienced substantial cuts in their state-supported budgets, and many independent institutions are struggling. When presidential salaries are revealed in the press (and even independent colleges must reveal those salaries to the Internal Revenue Service, whereafter they will be published in the *Chronicle of Higher Education*), individuals ranging from legislators to faculty and students can be counted upon to gasp and suggest that the president may be overpaid. Even though the president may be the key to progress (and even survival) of the institution, increasing the president's salary in difficult times will seldom meet with approval.

Because compensation is awkward to talk about, many boards simply do not know what options are available and what principles they should follow. We attempt to remedy this situation in this chapter.

ISSUES AND PRINCIPLES

The following postulates should guide board deliberations about presidential compensation:

- Regardless of what they say, more presidents leave their posts (or turn down offers) because of dissatisfaction with their compensation than because of any other factor.
- The chair of the board of trustees should review the president's compensation package on an annual basis. The chair should not wait for the president to raise the topic because he or she may not do so until another offer already is in hand.
- At least once every five years, the board should commission an experienced outside consultant to examine the compensation package offered the president.
- Salary is an important part of any compensation package, but the truly enticing items to most presidents are deferred compensation, presidential leave, spousal accommodation, and their status upon leaving the presidency.
- Salaries must be publicly disclosed. Many other items, including deferred compensation, need not be disclosed if they are provided

via 501-c-3 foundations, or other devices. The wise board and president will place considerable emphasis on these other items not only because they create fewer public relations problems, but also because they can bind a good president to an institution more effectively than salary.

- It is both prudent and possible to construct a presidential compensation package that exhibits "golden handcuffs" characteristics that make an excellent president unlikely to leave.
- Some boards assume that they cannot compete with other, more wealthy institutions insofar as presidential salaries are concerned and therefore essentially give up and allow other institutions to bid away their effective presidents. This is both incorrect and self-defeating because salary is but one of many items that a board can consider in constructing a compensation package.
- Published national salary surveys are of limited use because few presidencies are truly comparable and there are too many other items that constitute compensation for salary to be used as the primary indicator.
- The vast majority of boards fail to consider the "exit" conditions for their president when they construct their compensation package. Boards do so at their peril, for presidential exits often are more difficult to manage than searches and appointments.

PROCEDURES

The board that wishes to develop an enticing compensation package to attract or retain a president should begin by appointing, with the concurrence of a sitting president, an outside executive compensation firm of impressive reputation. If the package is being developed to offer to a new president, the board should retain the firm at the start of the presidential search, and the package ultimately should be tailored to the special interests of the final candidate. Although top presidential prospects rarely speak at length about compensation, they are mightily impressed by a board that makes such special efforts in this sensitive but important area.

The consultant should make final recommendations to the board in executive session. The recommendations should be based on a sophisticated analysis of comparative compensation conditions and the particular needs of the president.

Boards should not be overly impressed with the results of national presidential compensation studies, regardless of the source. Average figures in such studies, as well as the range of compensation, are invariably low because unusual prerequisites are seldom reported. Since deferred compensation agreements, annuities, and rabbi trusts sponsored by private foundations are frequently part of the compensation mix today, most salary surveys are misleading. Internal Revenue Service records can be checked, but these usually carry information about current income only and do not include deferred-income plans, which the astute president may find even more appealing than current earnings. For all these reasons, the board should give strong consideration to employing an experienced presidential compensation specialist who can separate the wheat from the chaff.

COMPENSATION PACKAGES

In recent years, boards have implemented a number of innovations to attract and retain presidents. Items in many presidential compensation packages often include, but are not limited to, the following:

1. Salary
2. Retirement System Contributions
3. Insurance (Health, Life, Accident, Disability)
4. Vacation and Sick Leave Time
5. Memberships and Entertainment
6. Automobile
7. Presidential Home and its Maintenance
8. Deferred Compensation, Annuities, and Trusts
9. Provision for Presidential Leave
10. Faculty Rank and/or Tenure
11. Tuition Assistance
12. Spousal Accommodation
13. Board Memberships, Consulting, and Honoraria
14. Post-Presidential Responsibilities, Title, and Compensation
15. Nature of the Presidential Contract(s)
16. A Graceful Presidential Exit

We will consider each of these topics in turn.

PRESIDENTIAL SALARIES

A good (or bad) president usually will make millions of dollars of difference in the fiscal condition of his or her college or university. Hence, a truly effective president is easily worth what he or she typically is paid. This needs to be placed in perspective. Several years ago, the authors carried out an institutional evaluation of a small liberal arts college that had been struggling before a dynamic new president arrived who completely turned things around. All agreed that he was primarily responsible for a multi-million dollar improvement in the college's financial condition. In such a situation, is it not both equitable and responsible for such a president to be paid well?

The president of a medium-sized university today typically is in charge of a budget that exceeds one hundred million dollars annually. It is a highly responsible position and many lives depend upon the wisdom of such a president's decisions. Such an individual should be paid well if he or she is successful; if not, then he or she should not be paid well, and the institution's board should find a new president.

The parallel in the private sector is the successful CEO of a $100 million firm. Such individuals typically are paid $250,000 to $1,500,000 in annual salary, plus many other fringe benefits, including stock options. This is considerably more than most college presidents are paid.

We do not draw this comparison to suggest that college presidents should be paid the same as corporate executives, but to point out that payment for responsibility and successful performance is hardly un-American and is considered good business practice. Boards should keep this in mind as they consider presidential compensation in academe. Performance should be rewarded, just as lack of performance should be noted and appropriate action taken.

The ideal presidential salary is competitive,[1] but not ostentatious. A few seeming anomalies exist. Salaries paid at independent institutions generally exceed those paid at public institutions of similar size and mission, the major exceptions being independent institutions that are small or church-related. Many presidents of large institutions are paid less than their medical school, law, and business deans, and less than many medical school faculty members.

Few firm rules can be stated with respect to presidential salaries; however, we offer the following advice:

---

[1]By "competitive," we mean sufficient to attract and retain a talented and successful individual.

- Use national surveys to approximate competitive salary levels, but do not confuse these salaries with total compensation.
- Salary increments in particular send signals to the campus and the public about presidential performance. If the president is doing well, he or she should receive a generous raise, but not so large that it causes problems.
- The best way to reward a successful president is via deferred compensation and other nonsalary items. Annual salaries attract too much attention and invite invidious comparisons.

RETIREMENT SYSTEM CONTRIBUTIONS

Retirement system contributions can act as "golden handcuffs" for many presidents and provide them with strong incentives to remain at their institution. At nearly all public institutions, a state retirement system exists and is constructed such that the financial penalty for leaving the system is great. This tends to bind presidents to their institutions and their presidential positions. Depending upon the success of the president, this can be either good or bad. In some state systems, a board can purchase additional years of credit in the system for their president, which can be attractive to some presidents. Typically, these systems are "defined benefit" in nature; this means that the president's eventual pension is based upon his or her salary and years of credited experience, and is not dependent upon the performance of the system's investments, which the president usually cannot influence.

The vast majority of independent institutions (and an increasing number of public institutions) participate in the Teachers Insurance and Annuity Association (TIAA) pension system. TIAA is a "defined contribution" system; participants eventually receive payments based upon the magnitude of their contributions and how profitably these contributions have been invested. The number of years a president has served is irrelevant, except as it eventually influences the size of the president's total contributions to TIAA. A TIAA participant may choose to retire at any time and begin to draw his or her pension; how much the person receives depends upon how much has been contributed to his or her account, how well those funds have been invested, and how long the recipient is expected to live.

Most presidents prefer TIAA because contributions to it on behalf of a president immediately "vest," i.e., become the immediate property of the president, even when the institution has made the contribution.

In addition, a presidential TIAA account is "portable." This means the account moves with the president as he or she moves from one institution to another and contributions from multiple employers can be included in the same individual account. The effect is to make an institution that already participates in TIAA a more attractive site to which a prospective president might move. Conversely, a president can more easily consider a move from an institution when he or she need not worry about losing pension contributions.

In the public sector, pension contributions to a state system often do not vest for five years or more. This can discourage individuals from joining that system initially, but also can have the effect of encouraging them to stay once they have completed the vesting time requirement.

Presidents do think about these things when they contemplate taking a new position, or leaving an existing one. Boards should act accordingly.

Recent changes in federal law have made it difficult, if not impossible, for institutions to make proportionately larger pension contributions on behalf of top executive employees than for other employees. Thus, if an assistant professor's compensation includes a 10 percent contribution to TIAA made by the institution, it typically is not permissible for the institution to contribute 15 percent to TIAA on behalf of the president—unless the president declares that additional contribution as income. Boards should use qualified consultants to define precisely what they can do in this area.

INSURANCE

Compensation packages can include health, life, accident, and disability insurance coverage. An institution is well-advised to offer a competitive insurance package to its president. Among other reasons, these benefits usually are nontaxable if the option is offered to all employees, and therefore a dollar spent here by the institution is more productive than a dollar spent on salaries.

Do not neglect disability insurance. One highly successful, but modestly compensated, state university president who became permanently disabled was not covered by disability insurance. Given his relative youth, he had only an exceedingly small retirement stipend. The result was a semi-public tragedy; the president and his wife lived in virtual poverty. Both the institution and the president were embarrassed, but neither took steps to do anything about it. When a board hires a president, it assumes an obligation to that individual, who forever after is connected to the institution. By the same token, only a foolish president will neglect to purchase appropriate insurance coverage, especially disability insurance.

VACATION AND SICK LEAVE TIME

The ideal president works like a demon for 48 to 50 weeks a year, and then relaxes—completely—for the remaining 2 to 4 weeks. Presidents must take vacation time in order to recharge and refresh, and a wise board will insist that they do so. One of the authors was a colleague of a president who bragged that he never took vacation days and that the state received more than its money's worth from him. Newspapers reported this in a favorable light, not recognizing what others closer to the situation could easily see— over time this individual exhibited the classic signs of burnout. His institution languished as a result. Presidents should resist mixing work with vacation; they really need to get away from the campus. Communing with nature in the Adirondacks, rafting the Colorado, or reading murder mysteries in Italy may be highly profitable activities for a president and his or her institution. Getting away from the campus brings new perspective and more than one president has exclaimed that serendipitous solutions came to them as they were relaxing and watching a baseball game or sitting on a far away lawn listening to a pops group.

Sick leave is necessary because presidents, like other individuals, get sick. Where possible, boards should consider starting a new president with a bank of sick days so that he or she does not immediately lose income if he or she becomes ill shortly after coming to campus.

Allowing departing presidents to "cash in" their unused vacation and sick leave days may subject presidents and boards to criticism, especially if the amount of the payment is large. A contract that includes deferred compensation or annuity payments is better than one containing a provision for a large vacation/sick leave payout.

MEMBERSHIPS AND ENTERTAINMENT

A successful president must see, be seen, and entertain. This implies a number of carefully selected memberships for the president in organizations and clubs that will enable the president to carry out institutional business satisfactorily. The adage "you must spend money to make money" applies here, for most donors and friends of the institution require cultivation.

Both the president and the board should, however, insist that the president's membership and entertainment activity—on and off campus—

be audited on an annual basis. From the president's standpoint, this will reveal if memberships actually are being used, how the president is using his or her time, and, retrospectively, how productive specific events actually were. Of course, such audits also serve the traditional function of ensuring financial integrity, which every president (and board) must insist upon without qualification. Several dozen college presidents have fallen by the wayside because they fudged financial regulations and spent institutional dollars inappropriately. Witness the *Chronicle of Higher Education* headline, "President resigns after audit finds he spent college money lavishly."

Presidents should not be deceived; any pattern of inappropriate behavior is certain to be discovered eventually anyway. Annual audits serve the dual purpose of discouraging such conduct and allowing the president to declare (with emphasis) that he or she operates according to the rules and expects others to do so as well.

AUTOMOBILES

Rarely can a president get along without having an automobile available for the conduct of institutional business. Hence, virtually every presidential contract includes either an automobile, or a cash automobile allowance.

The president's automobile should transmit a sedate, dignified message that the president is an individual of substance. This suggests an upscale sedan capable of transporting at least five individuals comfortably. The automobile should be American-made unless the president wants needlessly to court criticism. Buicks, Mercuries, Oldsmobiles, and Pontiacs fill this bill, but Cadillacs and Lincoln Continentals do not because (true or not) many individuals believe they are too luxurious.

Some presidents choose to drive unadorned, fleet-level Fords and Chevrolets in order to drive home the message that they are frugal. This is a point worth making in some quarters, but might transmit a less useful message when the president uses it to court members of the power structure, as he or she must.

Other presidents choose to use a driver or chauffeur, especially on longer trips. This practice enables the president to work while traveling and to arrive less tired and more composed. However, in certain locations, the appearance of a driver can provoke negative reactions and inspire the student newspaper to portray the president as aspiring royalty. The wise president will not use a driver to move on or near the campus.

Today, automobile telephones (and perhaps even a fax machine) are almost a requirement for active presidents.

The value of the mileage the president drives for personal purposes in an institutionally supplied automobile constitutes taxable income and must be reported by the institution to the Internal Revenue Service. More than one president has suffered embarrassment and substantial tax penalties from the failure to do so.

A HOME AND ITS MAINTENANCE

The vast majority of presidents are provided with a home by their institutions or, more frequently in a community college situation, a housing allowance. Unless the rental value of the home is truly exorbitant, the president need not report that value as taxable income, provided that the home is used substantially for entertainment and other purposes connected to the institution's business.

The institution customarily pays for the maintenance and cleaning of a university-supplied home and the grounds around the home, or provides workers to accomplish these tasks. Because an effective president will use the home for entertainment, the board and the president should resolve, in writing, who will prepare the meals, pay for the food, set up the tables, and clean up after the meal. In most cases, the institution bears all these costs, provided that the entertainment event is institutional business.

Many individuals envy presidents who have a home supplied to them because they know that such an arrangement eliminates what otherwise could be steep monthly mortgage payments. This seems like a good deal because the value of a typical president's home and attached services could be $20,000 to $50,000 per year. There are two problems with this view. First, presidents who occupy a college-supplied home may not own their own home. When they stop being president, they may find that they have a sharply limited ability to buy into a housing market that may have inflated rapidly while they were president. Second, if they do own their own home, they must find a way to care for that home and meet the mortgage payment on it while they serve as president.

Presidents who serve for long periods of time often do not own, or have claim to, appropriate housing when they leave office. An intelligent board will take this into consideration and attempt to develop deferred compensation and other arrangements that will enable a highly successful president to find appropriate housing when his or her service is done. Otherwise, the president may end up in an embarrassingly genteel state of poverty despite having given years of distinguished service.

DEFERRED COMPENSATION AND ANNUITIES

Increasingly, both independent and public institution governing boards develop deferred compensation agreements with their presidents. These agreements may take the form of an agreement sponsored by a foundation, an annuity that later becomes property of the president, or a trust that will make payments to the president at a certain time in the future. The agreements defer the president's compensation until some time in the future, provided the president fulfills certain expectations. The longer the president serves with distinction, the more deferred compensation he or she will eventually receive. Boards use such agreements to lure outstanding presidential prospects, to retain outstanding performers, and as a safety valve should problems develop along the way. In the latter situation, both the board and the president need not be plagued with confrontation or acrimony if the board has developed a relatively easy way out for the president by means of deferred compensation and other items. (See Appendixes G, H, and I for sample deferred compensation agreements.)

Particularly noteworthy is the so-called "rabbi trust," initially used to keep winning football and basketball coaches on board (see Appendix H).[2] A rabbi trust guarantees the beneficiary a pot of gold at the end of a prearranged period, usually 5 to 10 years. The trust assumes certain conditions (for example, a "noncompete" provision stipulating that the president will not leave and go to work for a perceived competitor and that he or she continues to be a "winner"). The president must continue to fulfill the expectations of the governing board and to meet or exceed all the evaluation criteria. The trust should make it increasingly profitable for the successful president to remain in his or her position—hence, the notion of "golden handcuffs."

The terms of a rabbi trust are not fulfilled until the president has completed a prescribed period of effective service as determined by the board. For tax purposes, this trust is designed so that there is "no significant evidence of ownership" (no constructive receipt of the funds) on the part of the recipient.

The method of funding such trusts is important, particularly within public institutions. Funding of any deferred compensation agreement in such institutions is usually under the aegis of a private foundation operating in conjunction with the institution and is sometimes made contingent upon the president procuring an increased level of private support. This avoids using otherwise designated funds for this purpose.

---

[2]This is, however, another example of an imbalance in higher education: these pioneering efforts came first as a way to attract and retain intercollegiate athletics coaches.

PROVISION FOR PRESIDENTIAL LEAVE

Successful presidents give their all to the position, which one of the authors has described as "a rugged, all-consuming, draining experience" (Koch, 1994). Although few presidents admit to "burn out," many are subject to this phenomena. If a board wishes its president to serve for an extended period of time, it should consider granting a leave to the president to renew, refresh, and reflect (including writing).

If the board chooses to grant presidential leave, this should be built into the president's contract. Optimally, the president will be able to take a semester's leave (or a summer) every five to seven years. That leave should, however, be dependent upon (1) excellent performance; (2) the return of the president as president after the conclusion of the leave; (3) a leave plan being approved by the board; and (4) a presidential report to the board after the leave is finished. The leave should be with full pay and include those fringe benefits not directly connected to work activities (for example, the presidential automobile should not go with the president on leave, but pension payments should continue to be made). Travel and research expenses can be paid by the board as it sees fit.

The entire notion of faculty leaves and sabbatical experiences is not one the general public understands or appreciates. Hence, the board may find it necessary to explain, even defend, a presidential leave. The board that is not willing to do so should not grant the leave in the first place.

FACULTY RANK AND/OR TENURE

Most presidents hold faculty rank and receive tenure as faculty members (though never as presidents), even though some presidents do not boast the credentials necessary to merit rank and tenure. Most new presidents will insist on rank and tenure, citing such arguments as their need to appear to be one of the faculty, the fact that they probably already hold rank and tenure at their current institution, and their need for security.

All these arguments are valid, but boards should not grant rank and tenure too readily. Prudence is required for the following reasons:

- Many presidents have not functioned as faculty members for many years, and faculty members know this. Granting the president rank devalues the concept and will often be cited by unhappy faculty members when the president makes unpopular promotion or tenure decisions.

- An increasing proportion of presidents (often from outside of academe) have no practical experience at all as faculty members.
- Few situations match the unhappiness associated with a terminated, unsuccessful president placed on the faculty of a department that neither wants nor appreciates him or her. Such an appointment is humane only in a restricted sense, usually generates bad publicity, and is typically expensive.

We advise boards to grant faculty rank and tenure to new presidents only when the president's credentials merit that appointment and the board feels that it could live with that individual as a highly paid member of its faculty for an extended period of time. If the board does grant rank and tenure to the president, it should insist that he or she teach on occasion and undertake minimal scholarship to demonstrate that the rank and tenure have meaning. There are other more appropriate ways to reward presidents than to use tenure as a means to stuff them down the mouths of a cynical and unaccepting department faculty.

TUITION ASSISTANCE

The boards of independent institutions commonly provide a president with tuition assistance so that he or she can pay the tuition of a spouse or children who attend this or other institutions of higher education. Tuition assistance is much less common for presidents in the public sector, and in such institutions often is limited only to the home campus.

Tuition assistance is a particularly attractive fringe benefit to presidents who have college-age children and can function as a powerful set of handcuffs on an otherwise mobile president. Also, because it is nonsalary, and promotes higher education, it attracts less critical attention than other fringe benefits of equivalent worth.

SPOUSAL ACCOMMODATION

We already have dealt with this topic in some detail in Chapter 5. Suffice it to say that despite rapid societal change, most presidential husbands and wives are teams. They function together and an unhappy spouse generally implies an unhappy president. A wise board will attempt to find out what spousal arrangements (employment, volunteer activity, travel with the president) would be most attractive to the president and do whatever it can to satisfy those needs. The board that does not do so is much more likely to face a presidential departure, divorce, or visible lack of enthusiasm.

Having said this, we caution boards from agreeing to arrangements whereby the president's spouse works for the president's institution. Only in rare cases can this work out, and, even then, it often is misunderstood. Our advice is to find spouses meaningful activity outside the institution. That will provide them with a life of their own and avert misunderstandings.

BOARD MEMBERSHIP, CONSULTING, AND HONORARIA

Well-chosen board memberships can do many things for presidents—place them at the center of the power structure, broaden their outlooks, and provide them with income. Generally, the same can be said for highly selective consulting activities, and strategic speech making. Of course, the board cannot guarantee a president a paying board membership or consulting opportunities, not the least because the president's own credentials describe the range of possibilities. Yet, these devices can accomplish a quantum increase in presidential satisfaction and bind a successful president to an institution more effectively than a highly visible increase in salary.

Unfortunately, as is the case with spousal accommodations, many boards neglect to consider memberships, consulting, and honoraria as highly effective possible additions to a presidential compensation package. Along with deferred compensation, they are the most neglected aspects of presidential compensation packages.

POST-PRESIDENTIAL RESPONSIBILITIES, TITLE, AND COMPENSATION

Most governing boards concentrate upon what is necessary for them to attract and retain their president. Few pay much attention to what their presidents will do after they are finished serving as president. However, post-presidential responsibilities, title, and compensation are important because if they are sufficiently attractive, they, too, will act as "golden handcuffs" for the skillful, productive president. The right combination of post-presidential circumstances provides incentives, generates loyalty, and demonstrates both commitment and humanity. Also, should the unlucky occasion arise, an attractive set of post-presidential circumstances will make it easier to convince a president to leave the post without creating problems. All these things are more likely to occur if the agreement underpinning them was negotiated years previous when the individual first assumed the presidency.

The most widely used practice in academe involves boards providing presidents with special post-presidential professorships if they are qualified to do so, and interested. Ordinarily, a president must serve capably for a minimum number of years (at least five) in order to qualify. Of course, many institutions grant a tenured faculty position to the president at the time of his or her presidential appointment. A "named" professorship with perquisites should depend upon extended, valued service as president unless the president already possesses the scholarly qualifications to merit that post. Such a position might carry with it the following provisions:

1. faculty rank and tenure
2. at least 80 percent of the salary earned by the president upon departure from the presidency
3. a full-year sabbatical to be used for transition and retooling
4. a teaching load of no more than four to six courses per year
5. comfortable office space and clerical assistance
6. a reporting relationship directly to the chief academic officer of the institution to ensure that any teaching or other service for an academic department would be considered a bonus by the department
7. the title of president emeritus or distinguished professor (if merited)
8. an agreement that the former president will not interfere or meddle in the operation of the institution.

The above discussion assumes that the president is an academic who is qualified to perform as a faculty member, and is interested in doing so. As noted above, an increasing proportion of presidents do not necessarily fit this mold. After concluding their service as president, such individuals might be accorded a term contract as a distinguished lecturer or "businessperson/public official" in residence, plus other attractive fringe benefits and connections to the institution.

In either case, a president, even one who has not set the world on fire, should not be cast into the outer darkness. Presidents who know this will exhibit more loyalty throughout their careers and, if so unfortunate as to be asked to step down, will resist less.

In state systems, departing presidents are sometimes assigned to other campuses or to the system office. The quid pro quo is that the former president must not be involved in institution-wide efforts or in other ways "get in the hair" of his or her successor.

The key here is that the sitting president can, in effect, gracefully and without controversy, choose to move to a professorship or other designated role, for this option is "writ in stone" in board policy long before the fact. Had these policies been in effect earlier, they would have saved the dynamics of countless institutions, as well as the dignity of their presidents. Indeed, to get an ineffective president out of office in such a comparatively effortless manner would be cheap at many times the price. Yet, most boards continue to be sustained by the thought that the president can go on forever with the hope that serious problems will not develop.

ENSURING A GRACEFUL EXIT

The clean and timely separation of the former president should be accomplished before the new president begins. This separation is the job of the board. Countless boards have neglected this sensitive relationship. In one situation, a former president continued to receive mail in the president's office for 10 years and came around personally to pick it up! In another, the former president continued to live on the campus and to be visible and obvious at campus events. In a third, the former president became a member of the board; indeed, in at least one situation, five former presidents sat on the board!

Former presidents should get out of the way, literally as well as figuratively. Ideally, they should leave the community, at least for a year, preferably at institutional expense. This year-long hiatus should also apply to the former president who assumes a professorship upon leaving office. The job should ensure that this transition is accomplished smoothly. Without question, any transition will be easier to accomplish if the president's post-presidential responsibilities, title, and compensation have been fixed ahead of time.

PRESIDENTIAL CONTRACTS

The board's expectations should be spelled out in at least two contracts, a letter of appointment at the time the new president is employed, and a standard employment contract (perhaps multiple year) containing such stipulations as the period of employment, duties, salary, additional entitlements,[3] termination, and presidential evaluation or review. (See Appendixes J and K for sample contracts.)

On occasion, the authors have encountered presidents who brag that "my contract is a hand shake" and that they are not employed under the terms of a written contract. This is a recipe for disaster, even though some well-meaning, honorable individuals may survive, and even prosper, under such an arrangement. The president (and the board) who fail to set down their rights, privileges, obligations, and expectations in the form of a contract are begging for trouble. Verbal agreements may suffice for some period of years; however, innumerable things can change over time, including the membership of the board. Thus, a retiring president suddenly may find that the retirement home that he or she believed the institution would provide will not be provided (this represents an actual instance). Or, the board may find that its ability either to retain or to terminate a president has been seriously reduced by the lack of a written contractual agreement.

When in doubt, write it down, but not before both parties consult experts.

FINAL THOUGHTS

All too often, presidential compensation is an afterthought to a virtually completed search and screen process. In fact, detailed consideration of presidential compensation should occur at the beginning of the search and screen process in order to develop the outlines of an attractive, competitive compensation package that will be discussed with the finalists. Under no circumstances should candidates be invited to the final interviews without knowledge of the broad framework of the compensation package that the board will offer. After all, this may determine whether the individual actually is a serious candidate.

Then, in a final flurry of activity, the board and the anointed (but not yet appointed) candidate should iron out particular details that tailor the compensation package to that individual. As we have seen in our discussion, some compensation items will be more attractive to one candidate than to another, and the board should maintain a flexible attitude toward the final composition of the compensation package.

---

[3]Additional entitlements that can be listed are hospitalization, disability insurance, retirement provisions, vacation, sick leave, residence and expenses, sabbatical leave, entertainment reimbursement, automobile, and other special considerations such as professional employment conditions for the spouse.

Having appointed a successful president, the board must continually review and discuss with the president his or her compensation package, for most presidents will be reluctant to broach this topic directly with their board. If the board has appointed an unsuccessful president and needs to terminate that individual, it should exit the president gracefully and should already have in place the process and incentives to do so without squalor. In either case, the president's compensation package should contain provisions that specify his or her post-presidential responsibilities, title, and compensation. The easiest time to accomplish this task is at appointment.

- More presidents leave because of compensation problems, or are not appointed in the first instance, than for any other reason.
- The key to retaining a successful president is a set of "golden handcuffs" that make it increasingly attractive for him or her to stay.
- The strongest handcuffs are nonsalary in nature, and typically involve a combination of deferred compensation agreements in the form of annuities or trusts, plus attractive post-presidential circumstances.

CHAPTER
twenty-one
● ● ● ● ● ● ●

Evaluating the President

Intelligence is not to make no mistakes, but quickly to see how to make them good.

Bertolt Brecht

Trifles make perfection, but perfection is no trifle.

Italian Proverb

That which is common to the greatest number has the least care bestowed on it.

Aristotle, in *Politics*

A successful presidential evaluation should accomplish two things: (1) fulfill the board's responsibility to evaluate the president and (2) increase the legitimacy of the presidential office. Most evaluations fall woefully short in this last area. Increasingly, boards employ evaluation techniques that compromise the ability of the president to lead. This chapter describes a method that can objectively determine the performance of the president and at the same time enhance the importance of the presidential office, that is, make it more possible for the president to lead and be held accountable.

The evaluation of the president is the most sensitive and delicate responsibility of the governing board; none of the evaluation methods currently offered in the higher education literature or by mainstream organizations is adequate. Although accountability is basic to the idea of granting more legitimacy to the presidential office, the need for accountability should be satisfied by the governing board in a way that does not diminish the presidential office in the process. For this reason, we label our recommended procedure a "presidential review" because (as is the case with an institutional review) other terms tend to have pejorative connotations.

Equal in importance to the appointment and support of the president is the presidential evaluation. It is an even more complex responsibility of the board, for poorly conducted presidential reviews frequently compromise otherwise effective presidencies.

Most presidential evaluations *are* poorly conducted. Far too often, a board of trustees, while conscientiously trying to satisfy its important review obligation, effectively reduces the authority and potential of its chief executive officer. Indeed, distinguished presidents have resigned from office on the heels of ostensibly "objective" presidential evaluations, and others have left in even less comfortable circumstances.

THE HISTORY OF PRESIDENTIAL EVALUATIONS

Formal or systematic presidential review first gained credence in 1969 when a besieged Kingman Brewster, then president of Yale University, endorsed the idea in an article entitled "The Politics of the Academy," published in *School and Society*. During that period, an unprecedented number of governing boards and presidents were making concessions to the pressing wave of democratization described in preceding chapters. Faculty and students began to appear on governing boards, usually with presidential endorsement, or at least acquiescence. Faculty, students, and staff soon came to expect as rights conditions that presidents formerly had granted as privileges. In many instances, what governing boards did not give away, faculty and staff organizations, and unions, were able to gain by negotiation, threat, and intimidation.

In the 1970s, many institutions achieved the epitome of collegial leadership, a completely accountable president with no real authority. In many institutions, the president was no more than a symbol in higher education's "shared governance," subject to faculty evaluation and removal. According to national panels, commissions, and scholars, presidential leadership in colleges and universities was at its nadir.

The same period of dramatic decline in leadership gave birth to informal and formal presidential evaluation or assessment, a practice now followed by more than 85 percent of colleges and universities. Today, many believe presidential evaluation, particularly "formal" presidential evaluation as currently presented by mainstream publications and national organizations and practiced by most governing boards, has been a significant factor in the decline of the American college presidency.

The practice of presidential evaluation is relatively new. For a procedure so critical to the conduct of an institution, there is a dearth of literature and virtually no significant substantive research. Since Brewster's article in 1969, scarcely more than a dozen people have written on the subject and only a handful with any regularity. The only "authoritative guide" on the subject is John W. Nason's *Presidential Assessment* (1984), a publication of the Association of Governing Boards of Universities and Colleges (AGB) in Washington, D.C.

CONVENTIONAL WISDOM ON PRESIDENTIAL REVIEW

Nason writes of two methods for presidential assessment: informal and formal.

> Informal evaluations tend to be more frequent. . .at least once a year. . . .They are conducted by the board as a whole or by the executive committee—occasionally there may be an individual board member or special committee appointed for the specific purpose. The trustees may or may not make inquiries of faculty, administrative officers, students, alumni, and others, but such inquiries are likely to be casual and unsystematic. Their information may come largely from rumors floating about the campus. . . .They have a confidential character. . .and are certainly not heralded nor their results publicized. (Nason, 1984)

> Formal evaluations are regularly scheduled every three, four or five years. They involve an organized and systematic effort to get objective evidence. . . .Sometimes questionnaires are distributed widely to faculty, students, alumni, and others. . .and they are public. (Nason, 1984)

Nason suggests that formal evaluations are likely to generate as many negative consequences as positive ones. Although he does not say so, he seems to believe the same is true for the informal method. He then provides a glimpse of an "Ideal Design" based on his survey of college and university governing boards (Nason, 1984). But, the reader is left wondering about this attractive prospect, for Nason devotes most of the remainder of the book to describing how to conduct these same questionable methods of "evaluation." While he advises caution, he concludes that formal evaluations seem to be the order of the day and offers everything from procedural advice to sample letters, questionnaires, rating scales, and evaluation instruments. Regardless of the outcome of such a process, all of these techniques lead to a significantly reduced presidency. While generally well-motivated, they are an absolute contradiction of what we know about the conditions that ensure effective leadership.

THE PROBLEM WITH CONVENTIONAL WISDOM

Most formal and many informal evaluations achieve the exact opposite of their intended effect. While the presidents who receive poor evaluations are usually eased out of office, those who continue do so with less stature and less authority. Faculty members and even staff and students are led to believe, at least implicitly, that they have a "vote" in the president's tenure. Board members (and often presidential evaluators) frequently establish undermining contacts with faculty, staff, and students. When the State University of New York fell to this state, it replaced formal assessment with informal periodic review. Our contention is that SUNY, like many others, was simply doing formal evaluations the wrong way. Indeed, in order to do its job properly, the governing board should commission formal evaluations at least every five years.

Periodic formal review is by far the most effective way for the board to accomplish its basic responsibility of evaluating the president. The question then is how to do it, not if it should be done.

The major problem with most methods of presidential review is that they publicly involve members of the president's primary leadership constituency (faculty, students, and staff) in the review process. Involving these people diminishes, albeit unintentionally, the status of the presidential office and the leadership ability and potential of the president.

Why are most presidential assessments diminishing, polarizing, and, in the long-run, demoralizing to the entire community? When faculty members, students, and staff are given reason by a board to believe they control the leader, the resulting attitude compromises both the presidential position and the president's potential for leadership.

Leadership is not rooted in collegiality. As Max Weber concluded years ago, "Collegiality is not democratic; rather, it is as elitist as a monarchy. It is simply that a select group of people share in the power. Indeed, if the collegials can wrest all the power away from the leader, they will prove every bit as self-serving as the most dissolute monarch" (Weber, 1947). The problem is that a board cannot hold a group of collegials accountable, but it can replace a president. Unaccountable conditions give rise to irresponsible representations that force collegiality to break down under conditions of tension and conflict.

Leadership is rooted in the leader's ability to empower others by inspiring trust and confidence. In order to achieve trust and confidence, the leader must be professionally qualified and must be invested with sufficient legitimacy (authority) to lead. A president so invested can be both engaging and giving in conducting the presidential office. The president can grant privileges to members of the community, faculty, staff, and students. The president can be benevolent because the president is, in fact, *the president*.

Some assume that members of the college or university community must be involved in the board's presidential review. If not, the faculty will begin its own evaluation.

If a board believes that it has an objective method of evaluating the president, it should not respond affirmatively to self-motivated faculty evaluations. Beyond academic freedom, which should be rooted in a board tenure policy, the institution owes faculty no other unique conditions.

Although shared governance is a desirable and potentially effective condition, at most institutions it was originally a privilege that presidents granted to faculty members and, to a lesser extent, students. These groups were encouraged to participate in the decision-making process, subject to the final authority of the president.

This system worked well. Faculty and students became importantly involved in decision making, and a dialogue was established that almost invariably led to a better institution. But through time and societal circumstances, the role of the president in this decision-making process became more and more a token one. The time came when most presidents could not question the prerogatives of the faculty. Academic freedom had been extended beyond the individual to include the collective faculty, and today few presidents can afford to take serious issue with the faculty.

Many governing boards and even respected national associations assume the faculty is autonomous in academic affairs and entitled to an authoritative hand in all matters affecting the institution. Under such circumstances, presidential accountability is impossible. As we established in chapters 8 and 9, there are two primary reasons why the faculty cannot, in fact, be autonomous. First, whatever authority the faculty members may have, they ultimately bear no responsibility for the institution. Second, no law, tradition, or hallmark document calls for absolute faculty authority even in academic matters.

Proof of this current unbalanced condition is the idea that, if you do not involve faculty in presidential review, they will demand to be involved, and it will happen anyway. Governing boards must resist such logic and stand above any debate. If need be, they must declare that there is only one chief executive and he or she is accountable for the conduct of all affairs of the institution. If this means changing board policies, then they should be changed.

Should the accountable president choose to delegate responsibility and authority (and the wise one will), then so be it. That decision must be the president's. Only under these conditions can the president remain the truly accountable officer and be evaluated in that light. This also means that there are no formal relationships between the board and faculty, staff, and students, except those that are recommended by the president. Under these conditions, as discussed in the preceding chapter, shared governance can work beautifully; affected people are involved in decision making, yet the president is clearly the final and accountable authority.

HOW TO CONDUCT AN EFFECTIVE PRESIDENTIAL EVALUATION

A board conducting an annual informal presidential evaluation should consider the following procedures.

Annual Evaluation

1. The president drafts a Modified Institutional Management by Objectives (MIMBO) for presentation to the governing board in the spring of each academic year. This draft should precede the informal evaluation, which ordinarily should take place in the months of May or June. The MIMBO is the most important dimension of an informal presidential evaluation. The president may do the initial draft in consultation with close associates, but in the final analysis, the draft is the president's. The document should include both specific and general goals; the specific goals are more readily measurable, and the general goals allow and, indeed, inspire the president to conduct the presidential office in pursuit of the grander vision of the institution. Concentrating exclusively on specific goals would force the president to adopt management tendencies and would reduce his or her leadership potential.

2. The president presents the MIMBO to the board chair. The chair and the president then have a thoughtful private discussion during

which the MIMBO may be modified, subject to the acceptance of both. At this point, the MIMBO can be presented to the full board as a document endorsed, at least tacitly, by the board chair, representing the goals of the president for the coming year. The presentation of this document affords the president a wonderful opportunity to talk with the board about the successes, problems, challenges, and prospects of the institution, and to seek the board's advice and counsel.[1]

3. A year later, the president prepares a written statement responding to the MIMBO. The statement is discussed with the board chair and then presented to the full board as a part of the next year's annual evaluation. Thus, each year, the president reviews the past year's MIMBO and presents the next year's MIMBO. Note that all this should occur in executive session. An executive session (without the public or staff, faculty, or students) fosters a dialogue that can prove helpful to both the board and the president without threatening the importance of the presidential office. If an executive session with the full board is not possible, the president should make the MIMBO presentation to the executive committee of the board.

4. The board meets in executive session without the president.

5. The president then meets with the board or the executive committee of the board for a more specific discussion of the past year's MIMBO and the next year's MIMBO.

6. Interviews should not be conducted in conjunction with annual evaluations, nor should board members have "informal" chats with staff or faculty.

7. Outside consultants are generally not used in conducting informal presidential evaluations.

Formal, Complete Evaluation

The board should commission a formal presidential evaluation about every five years. Whatever the method used, the evaluation should not include the public involvement of faculty, students, and staff. *This condition is crucial to the preservation of the legitimate presidency.*

---

[1]Because this potentially far-ranging discussion is being done as a part of the president's annual evaluation, nearly any topic can be broached without violating most open meeting laws. This is an important consideration, since many open meeting laws render it nearly impossible for a president to conduct a meaningful private discussion with more than two board members at a time.   Thus, the annual evaluation provides the opportunity for a substantive president/board conversation.

The board should conduct the evaluation in confidence and with the endorsement of the president. If the evaluator interviews faculty, staff, or students, he or she should represent the interviews as a review of the condition of the institution, rather than as an evaluation of the president. (In reality, a formal presidential evaluation *is* a mini-evaluation of the institution.) A board that plans a formal presidential evaluation should do the following:

1. Use outside third-party consultation. If a thorough and fair evaluation is to be done, it must be done by a tested outside consultant. The board chair should engage the consultant with the approval of the president.

2. Review the annual MIMBOs of the president and his or her performance relative to those MIMBOs. If MIMBOs have not been used in the past, then move to point 3.

3. The president should prepare a confidential self-review for the consultant following guidelines provided by the consultant. Among other things, the self-review should include the president's response to whatever goals have been pursued during the time frame of the evaluation.

4. Several weeks prior to the campus visitation, the consultant should receive a package of pertinent materials relating to the institution and the president (see Chapter 18).

5. Interviews should be conducted with trustees and members of the nonprimary leadership constituency (for example, all board members, alumni, newspaper editors and publishers, elected officials, appointed officials, benefactors, businesspersons, leaders of minority groups, and so forth).

6. After arriving on campus, the consultant should select faculty, students, and staff to interview. Any other approach seriously compromises the legitimacy of the presidential office and reduces the potential of the incumbent. The consultant should select the interviewees by position (for example, the chair of the faculty senate), stratified random sample, and at random.

7. The consultant should write an evaluation report and present it to the chair of the board, with a copy for the president. Preferably, the consultant presents the president's copy in an off-campus setting. The evaluation should include the following sections: (a) overview, (b) academic programming, (c) faculty, (d) students, (e) adminis-

tration, (f) budget and finance, (g) private support, and alumni, public, and government relations, (h) governance, (i) presidential effectiveness and style, and (j) observations and recommendations. The full report *should not be* made public because of the unnecessary and potentially harmful dimensions of public exposure. Note, however, that if the presidential evaluation is being done as part of a larger institutional evaluation (and this is preferable), then the larger institution evaluation (sans presidential review) should be made public.

If the board handles the process sensitively, it will gain a valuable assessment of the institution, its people, policies, practices, and its president. The incumbent will be closely and objectively evaluated, and the presidential office will be enhanced.

THE PRESIDENT WHO SHOULD LEAVE

Virtually all presidents know when their time is up. The problem often is that they have no comfortable or satisfactory alternative. The declining president continues in office, and the institution and its people pay the price for want of a graceful way out. To compensate for inattention or ineffectiveness, the president usually appoints additional staff, making the institution administratively top heavy and even more costly and ineffective. The appointment of an executive vice president, or some other title, ostensibly to manage the internal affairs of the institution is sometimes a sign that this is happening. The life and vigor of the institution diminish. Others of lesser station and perspective fill the leadership vacuum ineffectively. The institution and its people suffer.

Another scenario that frequently accompanies a president who has lost effectiveness and enthusiasm is a pattern of presidential authoritarianism. The president who has lost energy and fervor may fall into a pattern of ruling ex cathedra without consulting faculty or taking the time to explain and sell his or her vision. The authors are foursquare in favor of strong, transformational presidents, but nonetheless, a president will have difficulty in transforming an institution if its constituents are consistently ignored, are not made part of the vision, and are not asked for their advice. The substance of the president's decisions may be wonderful, but those who have to carry out the decisions may resist, obfuscate, and dally in order to frustrate a president whom they believe is dictatorial or insensitive.

If the leadership of the governing board is astute, it recognizes these truths, but may reason that things are not really bad enough to make a case for dismissing the president. Besides, the president may have only a few years to retirement. The situation continues in a frustrating, endless maze as the board treats the symptoms rather than the real problem—the president. The great wrong is that both the board and the president know there is no fail-safe mechanism for the president to gently and gracefully leave the office. Both have neglected to do anything about it, and now it is too late.

Examples

Case 1: *A well-meaning board was convinced that its nine-year president, who was four years away from retirement, was hurting the institution. With the knowledge and support of the president, the board appointed an executive vice president. The president did not know that the board had asked this new executive vice president to really run the university and to report in confidence to the executive committee of the board. Within months, virtually everyone knew what was happening. The board was confronted with an incredulous president, unhappy alumni and benefactors, and a divided faculty. The president retired, and the executive vice president resigned. At last report, the board had been forced to extend its presidential search for want of good candidates.*

Case 2: *In another situation, the president of 17 years asked to be relieved of his presidential duties and be appointed chancellor, primarily for external and fund-raising purposes. This was done and now, eight years later, the institution has had three presidents whose every move has been overshadowed by the omnipresent chancellor. The faculty has been demoralized, private support has gone down, yet the chancellor continues on.*

Case 3: *A 14-year president of a small private college was wavering. A compassionate board thought it could carry him to retirement by assuming an increasingly larger portion of the presidential burden.*

The executive committee met more often, and the board chair, a strong woman, moved into a more prominent position in center stage. Three years later, the staff and faculty, initially happy to have such close contact with the board, were demoralized. Both the enrollment and the endowment had gone down. The president, ostensibly the one to be served by the arrangement, retired—dispirited and undignified.

Case 4: *A seven-year president of a medium-sized public university knew he was running out of gas. When he became president, morale was at an all-time low, the academic program was in disarray, accreditation was in trouble, and the reputation of the institution was definitely second-rate. His first years had been dynamic and productive. Spirits soared, and everyone was filled with the excitement of his enthusiastic leadership. The president appeared tireless. It seemed he spoke some place every night and always made an appearance at the important social and civic functions. Yet, he was also highly visible on the campus to faculty, staff, and students.*

His work days were usually 15 hours or longer. During one three-month period, he was not able to have dinner at home with his family even once.

The curriculum was tightened, a greater number of better students enrolled, faculty and staff were energized anew, and private support developed significantly. The region and the state took special pride in their university. The university was often noted for excellence and listed as outstanding among institutions of its type.

This situation continued into the seventh year when the president began to tire. He wanted out. Not interested in another presidency, he continued in office as problems went unattended and his enthusiasm waned. The university gradually returned to its former sleepy, unhappy state. Ten years later the unhappy president was still in office.

Case 5: *A distinguished state system president of long term was forced to resign in a power play by a politically ambitious new board chair. The now former president, out of a job, did all she could to undermine efforts by the board to appoint an able successor. Finally, the board appointed a "home-grown" business type to the position. Ten years later, the state still suffers from the damage done.*

For confirmation and perspective on the subject, we asked a distinguished, long tenured president to comment on our observations. He wrote the following response:

> I have read and reread this material a number of times. On Sunday afternoon, it was raining and I started again, this time from a different perspective. I outlined the thirteen presidential changes, entries, and/or exits I have observed closely and looked at at them as dispassionately as possible in terms of your proposals and examples.
>
> I would have to say that the majority fit, in one way or another, the substance of your contention. Most smart of a brutality that was uncalled for under any circumstance, created long-standing scars within the constituencies and demeaned the board as well as the president. Two, on the other hand did not. Both were marked by two notable situations. In one, the outgoing president was given leave for one year as the new president

took office and, in fact, returned to the campus as a "distinguished professor" carrying, strangely enough, all of the perquisites you describe. The other was a retirement that followed another part of your scenario wherein the individual, in fact, was provided a very healthy annuity plan to allow retirement without a significant change in economic status.

The other eleven were clouded by poorly conceived, if not trumped-up, reasons for the president stepping aside stated by various members of the board. In short, I can't find a flaw in your observation or definition of the problem.

Realistically, an effective president, age fifty-five-plus, doesn't have many options unless they are created years in advance. Few are intellectually dead, and the professorship/retirement planning option seems to be a "best of all worlds" proposal for the institution and the president.

I think there is another scenario that is unspoken which can or could be created should the professorship route not be a viable long-term one. Your Case Four president in fact ought to step out after seven years. After age 55, one seeks not to look at another "top spot." With ten to twenty productive years still available, what the institution does in handling his stepdown has a marked influence on his return to the academy in a new role, even at another institution. In this case, the board has special responsibilities for the well-being of the president professionally. All too often the board doesn't choose to face them and lets it appear as a "forced stepdown." The institution suffers because of a real split in the institutional constituencies, and the ex-president suffers the consequences in the relocation process.

Your scenarios and solutions are completely applicable to the "older folk" among us who have served well and now should be cut loose for the good of the institution. I wonder how many young talents we drive away by not making the transition out a good one in the eyes of our colleagues.

THE EFFECTIVE PRESIDENT WHO MIGHT HAVE STAYED

Governing boards are too often confronted with able presidents who opt to move to other institutions for nebulous reasons. Although rarely discussed, compensation is almost invariably at the root of the presidential departure. How many presidents do you know who have gone elsewhere for less money? Yet, approximately 500 presidencies turn over each year, and more than half of those go on to other presidencies. In 1988, according to Fisher and Tack, most of those who moved were among the most effective presidents in the nation.

Case 1: *The president of a public institution, which had achieved a veritable rebirth under his leadership, has become a topic on the national scene. Invited to write articles, present papers, and provide informal consulting on the source of his success, the president is frequently contacted by search committees and head-hunters who try to tempt him with ever more attractive offers. Now in his fourth year, the president knows that his reputation will not suffer if he leaves, and he begins to consider other presidencies. One particularly attractive possibility offers a compensation package that is considerably better than his present situation. The president goes to his board chair, an experienced businesswoman, who feels that one should not compete with an uncertain outside bid. She tells the president that she will do her best the next time his contract is considered. The president leaves and is replaced by what the board considers a pale facsimile.*

Case 2: *A five-year president in a small liberal arts college has received an appealing offer from another institution. During his tenure, enrollment has increased, academic standards have gone up, and costs have gone down. The endowment of the college has increased from $12 to $35 million and is still climbing. When initially appointed, the president was of limited experience, and the board felt in no position to offer more than a minimum compensation package. Through the ensuing successful years, a few conservative board members who felt that the president's "call to serve" was sufficient to ensure his staying were able to lull other board members into doing little to increase presidential compensation. The president, a man with three children in school, felt "called" to go elsewhere for double his salary along with other compensations. After years in neutral, the board appointed a new president at essentially the same compensation level its former president earned at his new college. The impact of the new president is still an unknown to the board.*

Case 3: *The highly effective president of a land-grant university accepted the presidency of a small liberal arts college, declaring that he felt drawn to the serene, contemplative life of a small college in a small town, where a college president is still involved in the collegial life. The small liberal arts college also offered almost one-third more in salary than the land-grant university, along with a more generous retirement program, life and disability insurance, and a special annuity plan. Even though the land-grant university had a private foundation that could have legally provided an attractive compensation package, the president left.*

Case 4: *The board of a small private college is perplexed. It has gone through five presidents in 14 years, and four of them have left of their own volition, enjoying the full support of the board. Each has gone on to accept a presidency elsewhere. "It couldn't be the president's compensation package," stated the board chair. "We match all our figures with the national compensation studies."*

Case 5: *The universally admired president of a land-grant university leaves to accept the presidency of a regional public university in a neighboring state. In four years, the president had turned around the land-grant university, reduced costs, streamlined the curriculum, increased the percentage of state funds allocated to the university, and raised the morale of faculty and citizens. The regional public university quite literally used its foundation to buy away the land-grant president and then insured itself through an attractive pair of golden handcuffs.*

Virtually all these cases, as well as countless other variations on the same themes, could have been avoided if the board had considered the prospect of presidential departure before the appointment was made, or before the presidential nadir or job-change process began.

FINAL THOUGHTS

- One of the most frequent ways presidents are destroyed is by a board giving faculty and staff the notion that they "have a vote" in deciding if the president is retained.
- Board members who either openly or secretly solicit faculty input on their president (outside of a formal institutional evaluation) undermine that president and seriously diminish his or her legitimacy.
- During the annual evaluation, the board should measure the president primarily in terms of his or her performance relative to previously agreed upon objectives.
- The board must engage a knowledgeable, experienced outside expert to undertake a formal evaluation of the president.
- The formal evaluation of the president must be conducted within the context of the entire institution. If campus constituencies perceive that the president is on trial, some will attack a president who is now perceived as a vulnerable quarry.
- A board should not retain a president who is no longer effective; a weakened or ineffective president can inflict grievous injury on an institution in a surprisingly short time, both because of his or her own dismal performance and because of the negative example he or she sets for the rest of the campus.

PART

5

Summary

CHAPTER
twenty-two
•••••••

Summing Up

> . . .the academic ship rolls and careens with every wind, its topgallant is
> torn to shreds, its rudder turned to pulp, its compass whirls about under
> a thousand stray magnetic currents, and its decks are awash, but it still
> sails on. The brave captain. . .sings out to the ever loyal and faithful
> alumni that all is well. Perhaps it is. But there can be no doubt that we
> have blown very far from the old course and we are adrift.
>
> Somnia Vana ("Empty Dreams")

Somnia Vana (the pseudonym chosen by an anonymous author in 1922)
might have been writing about American higher education in the 1990s.
Denizens of the left, right, and center argue that higher education has failed
to meet many of the primary challenges of the day, and public opinion polls
suggest that confidence in higher education at large, and in professors and
presidents, is at or near post-World War II lows. By and large, the citizenry
no longer views higher education as the proximate solution to the most
pressing problems bedeviling society, but sees it as just another pressure
group and therefore part of societal problems no one seems to be addressing.

The critics outside the academy are many. Representative among them
are the iconoclastic and acrimonious views of Sykes, whose *Prof Scam*
(1988) places primary blame on the professorate for the demise of higher
education. More understanding, philosophic, and almost spiritual critiques
of higher education have been offered by Smith (*Killing the Spirit*, 1990) and
Jacoby (*Dogmatic Wisdom*, 1994). Best-selling works such as D'Souza's
Illiberal Education (1991) skewer alleged political correctness on campus
and claim that a profound and largely undesirable academic revolution has
occurred on American campuses.

To judge from the recent books written by those inside higher education (many of which are cited in this book), the problems afflicting higher education are largely exogenous in origin. In this view, higher education is a victim of inadequate funding, of a society in disarray, or of cyclical political problems. The implication is that higher education, if left to its own expertise and desserts, would bring Somnia Vana's meandering ship back on course and steer a true and steady heading.

There is a broad and nagging consensus that something is not right in higher education. Yet, there is little agreement on either the source or cure of the problem.

Our view is this: More than anything else, the problems of higher education involve a crisis in higher education leadership. Presidents have failed to lead, both because they do not understand what presidential leadership entails, and because their governing boards have not made it possible for them to lead. We do not doubt that the American college presidency is more demanding today than ever before, and we concur with those who decry the fiscal stresses imposed on higher education and the destructive impact that increasing societal discordance has had upon academic operations. Nonetheless, colleges and universities often have seen worse financial times than they see today (witness the 1930s). Intense and unpredictable social change has always characterized American society and rippled through higher education.

What is distinctive, perhaps unique, about American higher education today is the subtle changes that have occurred in the assumptions and practices that surround presidential leadership and campus governance. College presidents are the most critical (and endangered) species in American higher education today. Yet, too many presidents either do not know how to be a president, or they are fatally burdened by governance arrangements that dramatically increase their chances of failure. This book attempts to correct these problems by explaining principles that presidents and governing boards can use to vastly enhance the probability that individual campuses will prosper. The principles are based upon leadership theory, reliable empirical evidence, and our own experience as presidents and observers of higher education.

THE ROAD TO PRESIDENTIAL SUCCESS: THREE STEPS

All is not lost. Governing boards and presidents can turn the tide and make a difference. Consider the following three steps, which represent a distillation of our discussion in previous chapters.

Step 1: Establishing Legitimacy

The road to hell is paved with good intentions. So also it is with governing boards, which must establish the pre-conditions for presidential success. They want to do the right thing, which means establishing the legitimate conditions that will lead to presidential and institutional good fortune. But most boards fail to do so, perhaps because they do not understand the issues and do not know how to proceed. They distribute power throughout the campus, but demand accountability only of the president. They compound this by granting board access and audiences to a variety of campus constituencies, who soon learn that they do not need to deal with the president. Consequently, presidents founder and lose heart, with only a few choosing to fight admirable, but hopeless battles.

At a minimum, every governing board that wishes to have a successful president must provide that president with strong, legitimate power. The board must endow the president with authority and both its policies and practices must require all campus constituencies to deal with the president. The board that allows faculty, students, alumni, or any other group to circumvent the president is asking for, and eventually will get, presidential failure.

A significant part of establishing presidential legitimacy must be the insistence of the board that all internal campus governance bodies provide *recommendations* to the president on all topics. A wise president will consult widely with his or her constituents on and off campus. But the president must be seen as in charge, a condition that must be established and nurtured by the board. The board must support the president even when it might have preferred another course of action. The board that repeatedly disagrees with the president on important issues should either reexamine its views or get a new president.

In addition to legitimate power, the board must provide the president with sufficient coercive power and reward power. Presidents must be seen as having the ability to penalize and punish and be capable of rewarding members of the campus community. The astute president will use these powers (coercive and reward) intelligently and somewhat sparingly, for their exercise by him or her can stimulate undesirable side effects. Nonetheless, the president who is not *perceived* to have strong coercive and reward powers will soon be a eunuch. The board must ensure that the president possesses the necessary coercive and reward tools.

Along with presidential legitimate, coercive, and reward power must come presidential accountability, which cannot realistically be shared with any other group. It is axiomatic that the board must hold the president accountable, for neither the faculty nor the students can be held account-able for anything of substance. This ultimate lack of accountability is the persuasive reason why faculty and students cannot be entrusted with the ultimate power of the institution in any arena. Unfortunately, many boards do not understand this, and under the guise of being "democratic" or "sharing authority," they devastate presidential authority and effectiveness by treating a variety of campus constituencies as co-equal to the president in many areas. The almost inevitable consequence is a lack of institutional direction and finger pointing because no one is truly responsible for their actions.

Step 2: Presidential Activity and Behavior

The most important form of presidential power is the president's own charismatic power. Charisma is a widely misunderstood concept. John F. Kennedy exuded charisma; he inspired individuals to follow his leadership vision, even in instances when that vision seemed quixotic or unwise. Kennedy was handsome, engaging, articulate, and convincing.[1] Yet, political leaders as diverse as Hitler, Disraeli, and Kissinger; entertainers and athletes such as Michael Jackson, Roseanne, Hulk Hogan, and Ringo Starr; and media representatives such as Mike Wallace, Dick Vitale, and Barbara Walters all generate charisma. Charisma is a function of a fascinating variety of different influences, many of which can be learned and culti-vated, even by individuals who initially might seem uncharismatic. Cha-risma relates less to physical handsomeness (although that can be helpful) and more to an individual's ability to articulate a captivating vision or mood, to support that vision or mood with expertise/performance, to cultivate appropriate distance, and ultimately to establish a public pres-ence. A charismatic individual usually is capable of taking over a crowd by means of the power of his or her thoughts, his or her expertise or perfor-mance, and his or her carefully established public presence.

Clearly, charismatic ability can be used in support of either vice or virtue, but it is naive to pretend that charismatic power does not exist, or that it is necessarily illegitimate. Individuals as disparate as Benito Mussolini and Father Hesburgh have held in common singular charismatic abilities to

---

[1]Of course, these advantages, by themselves, are not sufficient to guarantee success. Many contemporary historians feel that President Kennedy did not always have command of the substance of issues, and that both his attention span and his "time on task" often were deficient. As a consequence, when his presidency ended so tragically in November 1963, he had few solid achievements to record.

inspire, inform, and persuade, even while their respective visions differed dramatically.

Charisma, then, is an important element of power, and power can be used in many different ways. But power and its exercise cannot be avoided and governing boards and presidents should not shrink from it. The president who wishes to succeed must learn how to enhance his or her charismatic power, primarily via a carefully cultivated public presence that recognizes the critical role of social distance healthily supplemented by expertise. This requires climbing on to Saint Simone's platform. In preceding chapters, we have outlined the primary ways in which that climb can be achieved, as well as how the presidential occupant can avoid being pushed off by the vagaries of campus and community life.

Charismatic power comes as a natural gift to some, but its secrets can be learned, and then cultivated and enhanced even by individuals who might at first seem unlikely candidates. But charisma and public presence cannot flower when a governing board has not first granted legitimacy to the president.

Step 3. Compensating and Evaluating the President

A president who possesses legitimate power, judiciously punishes and rewards, demonstrates expertise, maintains appropriate distance, and develops charisma and public presence is especially likely to be a success. But even successful presidents are sometimes flushed from their posts by unwise compensation and evaluation policies of governing boards.

More presidents leave one campus for another because of the inadequacy of their compensation than for any other reason. Boards must pay attention to the compensation packages they offer their presidents, and they are well advised to stress nonsalary items if they wish to apply a set of "golden handcuffs" to an exceptional president. Boards should establish the major facets of the "exit" conditions for their president at the time they hire him or her. Failure to do so nearly always leads to severe problems in the future.

About every five years, the board should formally evaluate the president, but only as part of an evaluation of the whole institution. An experienced and knowledgeable outside consultant should undertake the study. Under no circumstances should the governing board give the campus the notion that the president is being evaluated, or that somehow a vote is being taken on the president. Even the most successful president will find his or her power diminished after such an episode.

FINAL THOUGHTS

"The fault, dear Brutus, is not in our stars, but in ourselves," observed Shakespeare's Cassius in *Julius Caesar*. The problems that have diminished modern American college presidencies are not preordained and have not somehow been written in the heavens. Rather, the woeful state of the American college presidency is a direct and almost inevitable result of unwise governing board policies and presidents who do not understand the principles of leadership and power. In this respect, the fault *is* in ourselves. We have made our respective institutional beds, and now we must sleep in them.

But we can restore the American college presidency to its place of potential and prominence, if only we will pay attention to leadership theory, empirical evidence, and experience. The result will be revitalized institutions, climbing morale, and enhanced achievement by all constituencies. Fortunately, as W. Somerset Maugham sagely noted, "Failure makes people bitter and cruel [but] success improves the character of the man."

Whether governing board member or president, what is required is inquisitiveness, the ability to learn from the evidence, mental flexibility, ingenuity, the courage to swim occasionally against the tide, and the prodigious energy that comes from commitment to a worthy cause. We share the hope that you, the reader, having read this book, will be among the major suppliers of these scarce commodities over the next few years in American higher education.

APPENDIXES

· · · · · · · ·

APPENDIX
A

A History of Philanthropy

Any college president will be more effective in implementing the principles of effective fund raising developed in this appendix if he or she has an understanding of the nature and history of philanthropy. Successful fund raising does not occur in a vacuum; the philanthropic motives that result in successful fund raising are shaped by the history and traditions of a society and its attitudes toward philanthropy. This appendix provides a brief tutorial for the president in this area.

Philanthropy, or love of humanity, includes voluntary giving, voluntary service, and voluntary association, primarily for the benefit of others. What a wonderful term philanthropy is, and how in consonance it is with what a university is supposed to be! A university by whatever name (college, school, institute, and so on) exists for humanity, and its primary functions are to pursue truth, to interpret that truth gently with tentativeness and humility, and to create and appreciate beauty. There are no other fundamental purposes of a college or university.

Fund raising is a crucial dimension of philanthropy, and educational fund-raisers are completely engaged in the spirit and business and joy of philanthropy. Yet, few presidents think of philanthropy and fund raising together. Because of ignorance or inexperience, many presidents view fund raising as distant from philanthropy, rather than as a part of the philanthropic process. Yet, the worthy fund raiser is as much a part of philanthropy as the giver. They are both exhibiting a love of humanity and helping to reach a higher human condition. The president, more than any other, must illuminate the institution, its programs, and its people so that others who care may find their way to it (Simic, 1984). Fund raising *is* philanthropy, and therefore among the highest callings of your presidency.

CHARITY AND PHILANTHROPY: AN IMPORTANT DIFFERENCE

Although there is considerable historical debate about this, in Western society, philanthropy was born out of charity. The two terms have continued intertwined, although philanthropy is the more embracing term today (despite "charitable"-giving tax laws).

Charity is generally considered to be an act of goodness designed to reduce or eliminate human suffering, pain, or any other unfortunate condition immediately. Philanthropy is more general and long-term: It is an action directed at elevating humankind and preventing, rather than allaying, calamity.

Philanthropy is an activity that, if taken to its ultimate, eliminates the need for charity. Philanthropy is closely associated with the idea that the keys to self-sufficiency and freedom lie within the individual: Once the individual is independent, there will be no need for charity.

The following vivid and amusing illustration shows the difference between charity and philanthropy:

> A people lived in a village at the base of a great cliff. At the top of this cliff ran a much-used highway, and so many hapless travelers fell over the cliff that the kindly villagers were always busy picking them up and caring for their wounds. Finally, at great expense, the villagers bought an ambulance, which they kept ready at the base of the cliff to provide better care for the unfortunate wayfarers. One day, a thoughtful old man said, "Why do you not build a fence at the top?" But, the screams of the suffering were loud in the villagers' ears, and helping the injured kept them so busy that they could not take time to climb the cliff and build the fence. And, besides, they all knew, there is little charity in fence building. (Andrews, 1950)

Charity, then, is generally for the short run, and philanthropy for the long run. We will probably always need both, but we can hope not. In universities, our most profound commitment should be to a society wherein philanthropy is so widespread that only the most unfortunate need charity. The president who is fund raising must convince prospective donors that their gift will make a difference for his or her institution in the long run. Relatively few donors are comfortable in providing for the short-term operating expenses of a college or university.

Any discussion of the history of philanthropy requires us to acknowledge abuses in the practice of philanthropy. But even Robert Bremner, who has written the most candid (some say ruthless) historical assessment of philanthropy, proposes that philanthropy has been one of the principal methods of social advance. . . . The aim of philanthropy, in its broader sense, is improvement in the quality of human life. Whatever motives have animated individuals to become involved in philanthropy, the purpose of philanthropy itself is to promote the welfare, happiness, and culture of mankind. (1960)

THE ORIGINS OF PHILANTHROPY

Egyptian civilization yields perhaps the first Western evidence of charity. In the *Book of the Dead*, which dates back to around 4000 B.C., you can find passages praising those who give bread for the hungry and water for the thirsty (Budge, 1967). From the tombs of Harkhuf and Pepi-Nakht of the Sixth Dynasty (about 2500 B.C.) comes this record of giving and doing good because of a desire to improve the afterlife: "I desired that it might be well with me in the great gods' presence" (Breasted, 1962).

As the cultures of Egypt (and Israel) gave us charity, classical civilizations gave us philanthropy (Payton, 1988). In ancient Greece and Rome, the first clear extension of charity resolved into what we call philanthropy. Those societies behaved more or less kindly "toward people or society in general," rather than exclusively toward the poor. This kind of behavior was not relegated to alms giving, for it had little or no connection with poverty and was seldom motivated by pity.

Pre-Christian Romans followed the example of the Greeks. They gave for the benefit of any worthy citizen or for the state, rather than out of pity for the needy. Cicero (1967) wrote that all men were brothers, and "the whole world is to be considered as the common city of gods and men." Following this reasoning, the best example of morality would be a conscientious sense of obligation to this whole. In Roman terms, people owed it to themselves and to society to establish a sound economic base for their lives and subsequently to fulfill their duties as citizens (Cicero, 1967). These Roman thoughts are precursors of the philosophy of Rockefeller and Carnegie, without the religious fervor of Rockefeller. But charity itself found little scope in Rome. As Polybius reported, "In Rome no one ever gives away anything to anyone if he can help it" (Durant, 1944).

The Hebrews have a history of religiously motivated charity that dates back at least to the Egyptians. For them this sort of charity is called *tzedakah* and means "sharing what we have with the poor and doing good deeds" (Epstein, 1970). Indeed, their charitable practices were similar to the Egyptians' and suggest a strong degree of mutual influence that scholars have never closely examined. In the old Testament, Jacob saw a vision and promised to give a tenth "of all that Thou shalt give me" to God. The Mosaic Code required that all land be left fallow every seventh year (*Shemitah*); the crops that grew of themselves were for the poor, as were the "gleanings of the vineyards" every year. To give was a religious duty, and those who did not were "cursed." Today, in addition to being deeply involved in the broader charitable and philanthropic activities, *tzedakah* continues through efforts designed principally to serve Jewish interests.

The teachings of Jesus set up a high ethic for givers, a standard that has yet to be achieved by most who give or recognize (certainly including colleges and universities). Jesus taught that the spirit of the giver is more important than the size of the gift, and that the value of the gift is determined by the sacrifice of the giver; for the rich to merely tithe is not enough. In the Book of Matthew, Jesus advised the rich young ruler to "sell all that thou hast, and distribute unto the poor, and thou shalt have treasure in heaven."

Jesus taught that gifts should be given in secret and not for public acknowledgment: "Take heed that ye do not your alms before men, to be seen of them, otherwise ye have no reward of your Father which is in heaven." Note that Jesus promises the heavenly reward only for the secret gift. It is more blessed to give than to receive, he says—but only if we keep quiet about it and ask those who receive, if they must know, to hold it private.

THE CHURCH, THE RISE OF CHARITY, AND THE DECLINE OF PHILANTHROPY

With the advent of Christianity as an organized religion under Emperor Theodosius I in the fourth century A.D., Roman philanthropy ground to a halt. The more restrictive form of giving, charity, replaced it—continuing virtually throughout the Middle Ages. The Catholic Church depended for its support on charitable programs, which often were motivated more by secular and political factors than by religious ones. Charity helped the poor, the widowed, the aged and infirm, orphans, and others, but not adequately. Like the Romans, the church tried to provide cultural elevation, but there were few meaningful attempts. And so a period of little concern for the poor, and great attention to cultural elevation, changed to a period of almost exclusive concern for the poor, and little concern for the general betterment of the individual and society. One could only look to heaven for surcease. This was a period of all but unbounded religious authority. The

Catholic Church, together with an acquiescing state, tried to enforce payment of tithes, grant indulgences, and sell the use of other religious devices to fund their charitable programs. Perhaps the earliest such action was around A.D. 800, when the capitularies of Charlemagne commanded tithes to maintain the bishop, the clergy, the poor, and the general purposes of the church (Andrews, 1950). All these techniques assumed that you could buy salvation.

THE STATE AND THE NEW MIDDLE CLASSES

Religious motivation was considerably tempered by the reentry of a measure of philanthropy in the later Middle Ages. The first impetus was the rise of the secular state; the second, the rise of the new middle class. As the power and wealth of the state grew stronger, the church became less influential. In 1225, Louis VIII gave 100 *sous* each to the 2,000 leper houses in his realm.

Similarly, nobles and other wealthy individuals began to make gifts to charitable causes. Although religion continued to be a prime motive for giving, the church was no longer the exclusive conduit.

The coming of the Mercantile Age brought both preindustrial cities and a higher level of general sophistication. With these came a new prosperity that left in its wake social alienation and a growing number of people who had neither a job nor the institutions of family and church for support. The traditional charities lacked the resources and the vision to attend to new problems, and so the rising middle classes stepped in.

Endowments for schools, scholars, sermons, and orphanages began to spring up, particularly in England. Because such gifts were so widespread, legislation was enacted. In 1601, during the reign of Queen Elizabeth I, the Statute of Charitable Uses became law (Bremner, 1960). Its purpose was to create, control, and protect such funds. This statute stands to this day as the cornerstone of our laws concerning giving and as the legitimator of present-day American charitable foundations.

In England, the poor laws of the sixteenth century mark the real beginning of government assumption of responsibility for charitable activities. Indeed, Payton (1988) has concluded that the English poor laws marked the watershed between medieval and modern philanthropy. Under Elizabeth I, wrote Payton, poor laws "would suggest that the state had moved in to fill the vacuum (between church and nobility)." Early poor laws called for public collection of funds for the relief of the poor. These laws grew more specific through the years. They even came to include sanctions (mostly religious) for noncompliance. Eventually, the Poor Rate in the Act of 1601 established outright taxation (Andrews, 1950).

PHILANTHROPY IN THE UNITED STATES

Most would agree that organized philanthropy supported by systematic fund raising developed in twentieth-century America (Cutlip, 1965). However, the first systematic attempt to raise funds in America occurred in 1641, when the Massachusetts Bay Colony sent three clergymen to England to raise money for Harvard University. Until the twentieth century, however, philanthropy in America occurred on a small scale, largely financed by a wealthy few in response to personal "begging" appeals. The early years of the twentieth century finally provided the seed bed for today's philanthropic structure and success. During this period, institutions conducted the first major organized fund-raising campaigns, and universities hired the first fund-raising consultants and appointed the first development officers.

HARVARD'S EXTRAORDINARY ROLE IN AMERICAN PHILANTHROPY

From the initial bequest of John Harvard in 1638, and for almost 100 years thereafter, Harvard University commanded the major share of philanthropic attention (Curti and Nash, 1965). Although the College of William and Mary was founded in 1693, and the Collegiate School of Connecticut (later renamed for its first major benefactor, Elihu Yale) opened in 1701, the experience of Harvard set the pattern for philanthropic practices and problems that exist today.

A number of America's first colleges (such as Dartmouth College and King's College) received some public support, but the primary source was private, and the moral force religious. (The religious motives were little different from those of the ancient Egyptians.) In 1633, Reverend John Eliot (one of the first masters of the philanthropic appeal) wrote to Simonds D'Ewes, seeking funds for Harvard.

> God has bestowed upon you a bounty full blessing; now if you should please, to employ but one mite, of that great wealth which God hath given, to erect a school of learning, a college among us, you should do a most glorious work, acceptable to god and man; & the commemoration of the first founder of the means of learning, would be perpetuating of your name and honour among us. (Curti and Nash, 1965)

Although love of God was almost invariably the reason for a gift, even this lofty impetus was insufficient to stay selfish motives. The earliest example of questionable ethics in fund raising at American colleges came when Harvard tottered on the brink of collapse in 1641. Reverends Thomas Weld, Hugh Peters, and William Hibben went to England to raise what funds they could without engaging in dishonorable begging. Among the givers was the wealthy Lady Anne Mowlson, visited by Rev. Weld (Curti and Nash, 1965). Her gift called for the establishment of an endowment for the support of "poore schollar[s]," and Weld, apparently looking out for his own interests, stated that the first scholarship should go to one John Weld, his son. Young Weld never received the scholarship because he was arrested for burglary and expelled from Harvard. Despite this flaunting of moral laxity, however, the university was saved. (The gift money totaled 500 pounds sterling.)

A NAME TO REMEMBER: WHITEFIELD

Perhaps the most dynamic, and certainly the most successful, early college fund-raiser in America was the evangelist George Whitefield (1714-1770). In seven visits to the colonies, the young Rev. Whitefield preached philanthropy. Although he sought gifts for his other, more strictly charitable, causes, he also secured books and financial assistance for hard-pressed colonial colleges. Harvard, Dartmouth, Princeton, and the University of Pennsylvania all benefitted from his assistance (Cutlip, 1965). Bremner (1960) writes that if no single institution can be regarded as Whitefield's monument, it is because he helped so many.

PROMOTER PRESIDENTS AND SYSTEMATIC FUND RAISING

From the early days of the Republic through the Jacksonian period, there were several attempts at systematic fund raising. Most failed, but there were successes. In 1829, a British chemist, James Smithson, left an estate of a half-million dollars "to the United States of America to found at Washington, under the name of the Smithsonian Institution, an establishment for the increase and diffusion of knowledge among men" (Cutlip, 1965). In 1834, the indefatigable Miss Mary Lyon launched a fund drive to found Mount Holyoke College. She solicited subscriptions house to house for this women's seminary. She almost single-handedly raised $30,000 in less than two months.

Up to World War I, college fund-raising methods were much like Mary Lyon's campaign—"simple and homemade," dreams made real by extraordinary people (Marts, 1961). Western and southern colleges used "financial agents"—frequently the college presidents—and sent them to eastern cities to gather funds. Following the pattern of the original Harvard trip to England, Presbyterian financial agents went to New York City and Pittsburgh, Congregationalists to New England, and Methodists to New York State and Pennsylvania.

Throughout the nineteenth century, countless colleges stayed alive thanks to the personal fund-raising efforts of promoter-presidents. Even then, a primary task of the president was to secure the resources to maintain and improve the institution. Cutlip (1965) describes E.P. Tenney of Colorado College as typical of this group of effective presidents. When money was short, Tenney would board the next train for the effete East, to return with both money and students. As far as anyone knew, he never returned empty-handed.

In 1871, Smith College became perhaps the earliest example of how matching gift could stimulate public giving when the citizens of Northampton, Massachusetts, raised over $25,000 to meet the conditions of Sophia Smith's will.

Because of the role it was to play in later fund campaigns, we should also cite the founding of the American Red Cross. In 1881, a small group met in Clara Barton's house in Washington, D.C., to organize the "greatest venture of voluntary service in the world." This venture was destined to play an influential role in American philanthropy (Bremner, 1960).

CARNEGIE, ROCKEFELLER, AND LARGE-SCALE PHILANTHROPY

Large-scale philanthropy emerged when Andrew Carnegie and John D. Rockefeller created benevolent foundations. In a historic essay called "Wealth," published in 1889, Carnegie stated that millionaires should, instead of leaving their fortunes to their families, administer their wealth as a public trust during life.

In that same year, Rockefeller, a student of the old-fashioned school of religious motivation, gave $600,000 to help found the University of Chicago. This was the first of millions that he was to give to that university (Bremner, 1960). Out of this came both good and bad: Great amounts of money were intelligently administered, but the "tainted money" controversy grew out of accusations that the rich robber barons were trying to buy both public favor and heavenly rewards. Reverend Washington Gladdon's article "Tainted Money" and Ida Tarbell's book *The History of the Standard Oil Company* played major roles in inspiring strong public criticism of the new big givers.

WARD, PIERCE, AND THE FIRST FUND-RAISING CAMPAIGNS

During the early 1900s, colleges and other institutions seriously began to use the campaign as a means to raise funds. This method, developed by YMCA secretaries Lyman L. Pierce and Charles S. Ward, marked the beginning of philanthropy as a broad public enterprise rather than a hobby of the very rich. Arnaud Marts, president of Bucknell University and cofounder of the fund-raising firm Marts & Lundy Inc., documented this shift. He reported (1961) that it was not unusual in the early 1920s to see, at any given time, a half-dozen or more college presidents at New York City's Prince George Hotel. Each president was there seeking funds to meet campaign goals.

The essence of the Ward-Pierce Plan was to launch an intensive campaign to raise large sums of money in a short time. They did this by saturating the target public with appeals and by recruiting scores of volunteers to solicit many times their number. The first college to use the Ward-Pierce Plan was probably the University of Pittsburgh, in 1914, where the method succeeded in raising capital funds. In 1916-17, Ward and Pierce directed their famous $100 million campaign for the American Red Cross. This success prompted literally hundreds of colleges to use campaign techniques. Arnaud Marts' *Man's Concern for His Fellow Man* is a fascinating firsthand account of much of the work of Ward and Pierce.

HARVARD BRINGS REFINEMENT TO FUND RAISING

At the time Ward and Pierce were demonstrating their whirlwind campaign techniques, Bishop William Lawrence of Boston pioneered another effective, yet entirely different, approach. This son of a prominent New England family was repelled by the high-powered drives of Pierce, Ward, and their followers (Cutlip, 1965). In 1894, he became an overseer of Harvard, and in 1904 was elected president of the alumni association. In his presidential address that June, he called on Harvard alumni to give $2.5 million to increase the salaries of the faculty in liberal arts. Not surprisingly, Harvard president Eliot drafted Lawrence to organize the campaign to raise this great sum. Thus began the large-scale but less flamboyant alumni fund drive, which today constitutes a major financial activity in support of America's colleges, universities, and preparatory schools (Cutlip, 1965).

THE FIRST FUND-RAISING CONSULTANTS

The next major development in college fund raising was the rise of professional consultants. Interestingly, although professional consultants predated the first full-time college development offices, they gave life to them. But today, unfortunately, many college and university presidents appoint people with virtually no fund-raising experience to the chief development position, and then compound their problems by refusing to consider a consultant. These presidents wonder why they don't raise money.

In 1919, Charles Ward gave up his $8,000 annual salary with the YMCA to found the first fund-raising firm, Ward and Hill Associated. A few months later, the firm became Ward, Hill, Pierce (of YMCA fame), and Wells. The junior partners were Christian H. Dreshman, Olaf Gates, and Arnaud C. Marts (Marts, 1961). The first staff member of the new firm was George E. Lundy of Canton, Ohio, who had also been a YMCA secretary. After World War I, two young former army officers, Carlton and George Ketchum, opened Ketchum Publicity. From Ward and Hill Associated eventually came at least five of today's largest fund-raising firms—firms that have brought fundamental changes to American philanthropy (Cutlip, 1965).

JOHN PRICE JONES SUCCEEDS WITH STYLE

It was John Price Jones who, apparently without a plan, brought together the best of the schools of Bishop Lawrence and Ward-Pierce by codifying fund-raising principles and practice. His work included techniques of research and planning that were to elevate the field to a new level. A journalist by profession, he entered fund raising as a publicist in 1917 to work on the Liberty Loan Campaigns. The style of Bishop Lawrence at Harvard strongly influenced these campaigns. Jones, also a Harvard alumnus, blended his penchant for system, detail, and planning with the Lawrence technique. We have no direct report of it, but at this time he must have been aware of Ward-Pierce's extraordinary success.

In 1918, Robert F. Duncan, the Harvard Endowment Fund's first full-time secretary, appointed Jones to the Funds staff. Jones's appointment was to have far-reaching effects not only on Harvard, but also on the entire fund-raising profession. The university's $10 million campaign in 1919 made fund-raising history, and in fact changed the course of American higher education. Jones brought dignity and new techniques, as well as success, to fund campaigns. Cutlip (1965) says that Jones "sought to develop enthusiasm for giving to Harvard by dignified means without rough-and-tumble methods." The university raised $14.2 million in less than 10 months—a dramatic departure from the campaign of Weld, Peters, and Hibben.

THE COLLEGE PRESIDENT AND FUND RAISING TODAY

Today, $500 million campaigns are not uncommon. There are even billion-dollar campaigns. The patterns of philanthropy in American higher education seem set. The fund-raising drive is carefully organized—be it on behalf of capital, annual fund, or alumni (and even planned-giving) campaigns. Prestigious leaders, including college presidents, spearhead the campaign and professional and institutional development officers and consultants stand behind (but not too far). These development experts carefully pinpoint prospects, organize solicitation and large numbers of volunteers and help build a climate for giving. Such activities are the only *proven* ways to generate significant private support for a college or university. Individuals who interest *other* individuals in investing in an institution raise the funds. The primary initiative for this essential activity continues to come from the president.

Assuming that a thoughtful appreciation of the purposes of your institution and of the history of philanthropy undergird your program, you should have no uneasy feelings about fund raising. It is, after all, one of the grandest of presidential responsibilities, and one that has a long and honorable history.

APPENDIX
B
• • • • • • • •

A Policy for Participation at Board Meetings

It is the policy of the Board that there shall be useful exchange of information between the Board and the various constituencies served by the university. The purpose of this policy is to enable the Board to make informed judgments in taking actions that affect the governance of the university.

To that end, the President, as chief executive officer, is charged with the responsibility of maintaining communication between the Board and the various university constituencies, including faculty, staff, students, alumni, and members of the communities served by the university, as appropriate. These constituencies do not communicate directly with the Board, but through the President.

The President is expected to inform the Board in an accurate and timely fashion of the views of various university constituencies and to apprise and educate the Board concerning significant issues, opportunities, achievements, and concerns that have or will confront the university and those constituencies. To aid in that process, the President is encouraged to invite other members of the university community to attend and participate (as invited) in meetings of the committees of the Board. The President, in choosing representatives of constituencies to participate in meetings, may select representatives from existing support organizations such as the Faculty Senate, Student Senate, Alumni Association, and university-affiliated foundations.

In addition, when relevant and appropriate, the President may, from time to time, arrange for other informed faculty, staff, students, alumni, benefactors, friends, and interested parties to present their views to the committees of the Board.

Members of any university constituency who desire to make their views known to the Board on a particular issue should request the president to present those views to the Board, or request the President to provide them with the opportunity to do so in person at a future meeting of the Board or one of its committees. It is within the discretion of the President to determine the most appropriate way for those views to be communicated to the Board.

In order to ensure that the Board is conversant with the wide variety of issues, opportunities, achievements, and concerns that exist in the university community, the President is encouraged to provide the Board with broad exposure to university life. In addition to the foregoing, this may be accomplished by presentations by members of the university community at the meetings of the Board or its committees, and on-site meetings or informational sessions held in a variety of university facilities and locations, both on and off campus.

APPENDIX
C
• • • • • • • •

Initial Letter from Board to Presidential Search Committee

Date

Dear xxxx:

The Board of Visitors wishes to thank for your willingness to serve as a member of the Search and Screen Committee for the next President of xxx College. The Board is excited about the prospect of selecting a visionary and effective new leader for the campus and looks forward to your participation in the process.

Role of the Committee

The role of the committee is to assist the Board of Trustees in identifying and screening qualified candidates for the position of president and to advise the Board regarding the selection of highly qualified and acceptable persons for the position.

Specific Responsibilities of the Committee

1. To assess the present condition of the university and to develop a profile of desired characteristics and qualifications for the next president.

2. To develop an advertisement for the position.

3. To organize and promote an active search for qualified candidates for the position. This involves not only the placement of appropriate notices of the vacancy but, most importantly, a vigorous search for outstanding candidates from all appropriate sources, with special attention to seeking qualified women and minority candidates.

4. To review carefully all applicants and nominees in accordance with the profile and needs of the University.

5. To recommend to the Board by (date) the names of no less than two nor more than three candidates, without preference.

Procedural Guidelines

1. The search committee is established to assist and advise the Board.

2. The search process must be conducted within the letter and spirit of established affirmative action and equal employment policies and procedures.

3. Above all, the search committee should establish procedures that insure confidentiality regarding its work and the names of candidates. *Only the committee chair, or his/her designate, should make public statements regarding the search.*

4. The search process must be conducted in a manner that will enable the appointment of a highly qualified person to the position. It also should provide the basis for a successful transition into office for the person selected.

I look forward to working with you.

Sincerely,

APPENDIX
D
·········

Checklist for the Search Process

Steps in an Efficient and Effective Presidential Search Process (four to five months in length)

Weeks 1 and 2

Points 1 through 11 below can be done before the first search committee meeting and usually take from two to six weeks, depending on time constraints.

_____ 1. Knowledge of a vacancy or impending vacancy.

_____ 2. Employment of general consultant who speaks to board or executive committee.

_____ 3. Chair of search committee appointed by board (usually board chair).

_____ 4. Appoint search consultant (consider three to six firms, both profit and non-profit; interview at least three; cost from 20 percent to 33 1/3 percent of first year's salary, or flat rate plus expenses). Have general consultant sit in on interviews.

_____ 5. Consider an outside institutional review to obtain an objective assessment of the institution, define appropriate characteristics of the next president, and inspire the interest of top candidates.

_____ 6. Begin institutional review.

_____ 7. Consider an outside compensation study.

_____ 8. Budget ($25,000-$150,000 and more). Be generous, it will be worth it if you find the right individual.

_____ 9. Search committee appointed by board with distinct majority of board members (7 to 15 members: nine preferred).

_____ 10. Vacancy posted in _The Chronicle of Higher Education, The New York Times, The Wall Street Journal,_ significant minority and women's publications, et al.

_____ 11. Draft charge to search committee.

_____ 12. News release or press conference or both announcing general time frame, stressing confidentiality, and other conditions of the search.

Week 3

_____ 13. _First meeting of the search committee._

_____ 14. Opening statement by committee chair. Present charge from board: time frame—four to five months; three to five candidates to be recommended without preference; confidentiality, et al. Appointment of secretary, clerical assistance, permanent meeting and office space; stress confidentiality.

_____ 15. Blood oath by committee to confidentiality. Chair appointed as single spokesperson.

_____ 16. Presentation by general consultant.

_____ 17. Timetable adopted (median 7.5 months; most take entirely too long; a thorough search can be done in four to five months).

_____ 18. Presentation by outgoing president (and perhaps others).

_____ 19. Presentation by affirmative action officer.

_____ 20. Establish communication process with candidates and others (all through separate search office over signature of chair of search committee).

_____ 21. General consultant provides sample letters to be sent inviting nominations from significant persons in higher education.

_____ 22. Consider public hearing (faculty, staff, students, alumni leaders, community leaders, any interested parties).

_____ 23. Invite search consultant into committee meeting.

Between Meetings

_____ 24. Applications begin to arrive.

_____ 25. Letters of acknowledgement sent to candidates asking for three to six references.

_____ 26. Preliminary sort of applications conducted by search consultant and search committee chair.

_____ 27. All committee members encouraged to visit search office and study candidate files.

_____ 28. Public hearing conducted day before second search committee meeting.

_____ 29. *Institutional Review* completed.

Week 9

_____ 30. *Second search committee meeting.*

_____ 31. Review by chair and consultant (stress confidentiality).

_____ 32. Discussion of *Institutional Review*. Copies, with letters, sent to important persons soliciting nominations and top candidates.

_____ 33. Committee reviews candidate files (allow one and a half to two hours of private time at beginning of the meeting to review the top 30 to 40).

_____ 34. Committee discusses candidates. Reduces list to 15 to 20.

_____ 35. Committee members receive referencing assignments.

Between Meetings

_____ 36. Referencing by committee and consultants while continuing to accept nominations and develop candidate list.

Week 12

_____ 37. _Third search committee meeting._

_____ 38. Review by chair and consultant of new candidates and prospects and update on others (stress confidentiality).

_____ 39. Discuss referencing on top 15 to 20 and reconsider temporarily discarded and new candidates.

_____ 40. Reduce list to 7 to 10 candidates to be interviewed.

_____ 41. Other candidates kept in reserve. (No candidates are dismissed until the search is complete.)

Between Meetings

_____ 42. Further telephone checks, personal interviews, and possible site visits by consultant and/or committee members. (Usually consultant does the best job.)

Week 14

_____ 43. _Fourth search committee meeting._

_____ 44. Review by chair and consultant (stress confidentiality).

_____ 45. Interview top 7 to 10 candidates, preferably off campus, using forms prepared from the institutional review.

_____ 46. Committee discusses candidates. Reduces list to three to five finalists for off-campus interviews (three is the preferred) number.

Between Meetings

_____ 47. Further referencing and possible site visits by consultant.

Week 16

_____ 48. *Final interviews with board.* (At this point, there may also be non-public, confidential interviews with a special faculty screening committee shortly preceding the board interviews.) All interviews should be conducted off campus and use the same interview forms.

_____ 49. Evaluation of final candidates by board, possibly including additional interviews. The general consultant and the search consultant may or may not be present. (If no candidate is acceptable, return to step 41 or step 10).

After Board Decision

_____ 50. Job offer is made immediately with precise terms of employment, evaluation, separation. If rejected, return to step 48.

_____ 51. New appointee informs present employer.

_____ 52. Other finalists quickly informed.

_____ 53. Public announcement with press release approved by president-designate followed by press conference.

_____ 54. Release sent to other candidates.

_____ 55. Files closed.

_____ 56. Financial records audited.

_____ 57. Files stored.

APPENDIX
E
• • • • • • • •

Letter for Persons and Organizations Inviting Nominations

Dear President:

    The Board is seeking a president for (*name of institution*) who will be named in (*year*) and assume office in the summer of (*year*).

    We are requesting that you assist us in filling this position. We will be grateful for your nomination of one or more candidates. You may assure any nominees that the search will be conducted in professional confidence. Please write to:

    (*name, address: Search Committee Chair*)

    We appreciate your assistance.

                  Sincerely,

                  Name of Committee Chair,
                  for the committee

APPENDIX
F
•••••••

Letter to Persons
Making Nominations

Date

Name, address

Dear

   Thank you for suggesting (*nominee*) as a possible candidate for the position of president at (*name of institution*). We will contact him/ her in the near future and encourage his or her interest in the position.

   Thank you for your interest in (*name of institution*).

                        Sincerely,

                        Name, Chair
                        Presidential Search Committee

APPENDIX

G

• • • • • • • •

Tax-Sheltered Annuity/Other Benefits Agreement

THIS AGREEMENT, made the _____ day of *month. year*, by and between *institution* of *location*, (hereinafter called the "College/University") and *name of President*, (hereinafter called the "President").

WITNESSETH:

WHEREAS, the President has been employed this same date by the College/University to serve for *(number)* years as its chief administrative and executive officer, with title of "President," as evidenced by a separate document entitled "Contract of Employment"; and

WHEREAS, the Board, in order to retain the services of the President, and to compensate him/her for the loss of benefits and other income which he/she experienced so he/she might accept employment as President, is willing to provide additional and other benefits, as set forth below; and

WHEREAS, the Board and the President have agreed to the form of such benefits to be provided to the President or to his/her designated beneficiaries, and desire to reduce their agreement to writing,

NOW, THEREFORE, in consideration of the promises, covenants, and agreements herein set forth, and for other good and valuable consideration, receipt of which is hereby acknowledged, the parties hereto covenant and agree as follow:

1. *Retirement Privilege*

The College/University agrees that the President may retire from the active and daily service of the University upon the first day of the month following his/her eligibility for retirement under the existent pension plan of the College/University.

2. *Tax Sheltered Annuity and Tax-Free Income*

The College/University agrees to pay the President certain benefits outlined below:

   a. The College/University will purchase and maintain for each year of this agreement a tax sheltered annuity in the maximum allowable tax-free amount of 10 percent of the total salary per year, for the sole and exclusive benefit of the President, who shall choose the plan and select such payment options and designate such beneficiaries as he/she may desire.

   b. The College/University will pay the President an additional sum of (*amount*) for each year of this agreement in equal monthly payments or in one lump sum at the President's choosing. (*Note: This provision is especially appropriate in many public institutions with strict salary schedules. Some institutions provide this supplement as a deferred revenue plan assuming that it is tax-free and meets the current needs of the President.*)

   c. Neither the President, nor any designated beneficiary, shall have the right to sell, assign, transfer, or otherwise convey or hypothecate the right to receive any payments from the tax deferred annuity provided in subparagraph (a.) above.

3. *Term Life Insurance*

The College/University will pay the premium on a policy of term insurance upon the life of the President in the principal sum of (*amount*), which will be owned by the President, and the President shall have the right to designate the beneficiary thereof. (*The Board's ability to do so may be limited by what it does for other employees.*)

4. *Construction of the Agreement*

Any payments under this Agreement shall be independent of, and in addition to, those under any other plan, program, or agreement which may be in effect between the parties hereto, or any other compensation payable to the President or to the President's designated beneficiary by the College/University. The Agreement shall not be construed as a Contract of Employment, but shall be construed as fringe benefits given in addition to salary, nor does it restrict the right of the Board to discharge the President for just cause or the right of the President to terminate his employment.

The laws of the State of _____ shall govern this agreement. (*Especially for public institutions.*)

5. *Amendments*

This Agreement may not be altered, amended, or revoked except upon a written agreement signed by the Board and the President.

APPENDIX
H
• • • • • • •

A Modified Rabbi Trust

Deferred Compensation Schedule

| Year | Contributions | | Cumulative | | |
	End of Year	Cumulative	Value At 6%	Value At 7%	Value At 8%
1	$5,000	$5,000	$5,000	$5,000	$5,000
2	10,000	15,000	15,300	15,350	15,400
3	15,000	30,000	31,218	31,425	31,632
4	20,000	50,000	53,091	53,624	54,163
5	25,000	75,000	81,277	82,378	83,496
6	30,000	105,000	116,153	118,144	120,175
7	35,000	140,000	158,122	161,414	164,789
8	40,000	180,000	207,610	212,713	217,972
9	45,000	225,000	265,066	272,603	280,410
10	50,000	275,000	330,970	341,686	352,843

(Note: Cumulative value for each year includes accrued earnings, compounded annually, at an assumed constant rate of return shown, all on a pre-tax basis.)

APPENDIX

I

• • • • • • •

A Sample Trust Agreement

(Note: This is most appropriate for a public university, but could be modified for a private institution.)

THIS TRUST AGREEMENT, made and entered into as of this day of (year), between the (*institution*), (*the "Foundation"*) and (*name of trust company*) (*the Trustees*).

WITNESSETH THAT:

WHEREAS, the Foundation has entered into a contract this same day with (*name of president*), President of (*institution*) (herein to be known as the "President"), to provide certain benefits as an inducement to continue duties pursuant to an employment agreement with the College/University and remain so employed for a period of at least (*number*) years, from _____, 19___ to _____, 19___ (usually six to ten years).

WHEREAS, the Foundation, as part of its inducement to the President, has agreed to establish a trust fund to aid it in accumulating the amount necessary to satisfy its contractual liability to pay the President or the designated beneficiary such benefits; and

WHEREAS, the Foundation may make contributions to this trust from time to time, which contributions (if made) will be applied in payment of the Foundation's obligations to pay such benefits; and

WHEREAS, that portion of the Foundation's agreement with the President which relates to the Trust fund (also referred to herein as the "Plan") provides for the Foundation to pay all benefits thereunder from its restricted assets called "The President's Fund," and the establishment of this trust shall not reduce or otherwise affect the Foundation's continuing liability to pay benefits from such assets except that the Foundation's liability under this Trust shall be offset by actual benefit payments made by this trust; and

WHEREAS, the trust established by this Trust Agreement is intended to be classified for income tax purposes as a "grantor trust" with the result that the income of the trust be treated as income of the Foundation pursuant to Sub-part E of Subchapter 3 of Chapter 1, of Subtitle A of the Internal Revenue Code of 1986, as amended (the "Code");

NOW, THEREFORE, in consideration of the mutual covenants herein contained, the Foundation and the Trustee declare and agree as follows:

Section 1. Establishment and Title of the Trust

1.1 The Foundation hereby establishes with the Trustee a trust (the "Trust"), to accept such sums of money and other property acceptable to the Trustee as from time to time may be paid or delivered to the Trustee. All such money and other property, all investments made therewith or proceeds thereof and all earnings and profits thereon that are paid to the Trustee, as provided in Section 7.1 of this Trust Agreement, less all payments and charges as authorized herein, are hereinafter referred to as the "Trust Fund." The Trust Fund shall be held by the Trustee IN TRUST and shall be dealt with in accordance with the provisions of this Trust Agreement. The Trust fund payments to the President, or the designated beneficiary, and defraying reasonable expenses of administration in accordance with the provisions of this Trust Agreement until all such payments have been made; provided, however, that the Trust fund shall at all times be subject to the claims of the creditors of the Foundation as set forth in Section 8 of this Trust Agreement.

Section 2. Acceptance by the Trustee

2.1   The Trustee accepts the Trust established under this Trust Agreement on the terms and subject to the provisions set forth herein, and it agrees to discharge and perform fully and faithfully all of the duties and obligations imposed upon it under this Trust Agreement.

Section 3. Limitation on Use of Funds

3.1   Except as provided in provisos (1), (2), and (3) of this paragraph, no part of the corpus of the Trust Fund shall be recoverable by the Foundation or used for any purpose other than for the exclusive purpose of providing payments to the President or the designated beneficiary, and defraying reasonable expenses of administration in accordance with the provisions of this Trust Agreement, until all such payments required by this Trust Agreement have been made; provided, however, that (1) nothing in this Section 3.1 shall be deemed to limit or otherwise prevent the payment from the Trust Fund of expenses and other charges as provided in Sections 10.1 and

10.2 of this Trust Agreement or the application of the Trust Fund as provided in Section 6.4 of this Trust Agreement if the Trust is finally determined not to constitute a grantor trust; and, (2) the Trust Fund shall at all times be subject to the claims of creditors of the Foundation as set forth in Section 8 of this Trust Agreement; and, (3) provided, further that the President is able and willing to continuously serve as president of the Institution for not less than _____ years, commencing with _____, 19___, and has not been terminated for "just cause" pursuant to his basic employment agreement with the Board. If the President elects to leave the University prior to the completion of the aforementioned years, or his/her employment is terminated during said period for "just cause," the corpus of the Trust Fund, and all accumulations thereto shall revert to the Foundation.

Section 4.   Duties and Powers of the Trustee with Respect to Investments

4.1   The Trustee shall invest and reinvest the principal and income of the Trust Fund and keep the Trust Fund invested, without distinction between principal and income, in accordance with the directions of the Foundation investment guidelines as the Foundation may provide to the Trustee from time to time.

Section 5. Additional Powers and Duties of the Trustee

5.1   Subject to the provisions of Section 4.1, the Trustee shall have the following additional powers and authority with respect to all property constituting a part of the Trust Fund:

a. To sell, exchange, or transfer any such property at public or private sale for case or on credit and grant options for the purpose or exchange thereof, including call options for property held in the Trust Fund and put options for the purchase of property.

b. To participate in any plan of reorganization, consolidation, merger, combination, liquidation, or other similar plan relating to any such property, and to consent to or oppose any such plan or any action thereunder, or any contract, lease, mortgage, purchase, sale or other action by any corporation or other entity.

c. To deposit any such property with any protective, reorganization or similar committee; to delegate discretionary power to any such committee; and to pay part of the expenses and compensation of any such committee and any assessments levied with respect to any property so deposited.

d. To exercise any conversion privilege or subscription right available in connection with any such property; to oppose or to consent to the reorganization, consolidation, merger, or readjustment of the finances of any corporation, company or association, or to the sale, mortgage, pledge or lease of the property of any corporation, company, or association any of the securities of which may at any time be held in the Trust Fund and to do any act with reference thereto, including the exercise of options, the making of agreements or subscriptions, which may be deemed necessary or advisable in connection therewith, and to hold and retain any securities or other property which it may so acquire.

e. To commence or defend suits or legal proceedings and to represent the Trust in all suits or legal proceedings; to settle, compromise or submit to arbitration, any claims, debts or damages; due or owing to or from the Trust.

f. To exercise, personally or by general or limited power of attorney, any right, including the right to vote, appurtenant to any securities or other such property.

g. To borrow money from any lender in such amounts and upon such terms and conditions as shall be deemed advisable or proper to carry out the purposes of the Trust and to pledge any securities or other property for the repayment of any such loan.

h. To engage any legal counsel, including counsel to the Trustee, any enrolled actuary, or any other suitable agents, to consult with such counsel, enrolled actuary, or agents with respect to the construction of this Trust Agreement, the duties of the Trustee hereunder, the transactions contemplated by this Trust Agreement or any act which the Trustee proposes to take or omit, to rely upon the advice of such counsel, enrolled actuary or agents, and to pay its reasonable fees, expenses, and compensation.

i. To register any securities held by it in its own name or in the name of any custodian of such property or of its nominee, including the nominee of any system for the central handling of securities, with or without the addition of words indicating that such securities are held in a fiduciary capacity, to deposit or arrange for the deposit of any such securities with such a system and to hold any securities in bearer form.

j. To make, execute, and deliver, as Trustee, any and all deeds, leases, notes, bonds, guarantees, mortgages, conveyances, contracts, waivers, releases, or other instruments in writing necessary or proper for the accomplishment of any of the foregoing powers.

k. To transfer assets of the Trust Fund to a Successor trustee as provided in Section 12.4.

l. To exercise, generally, any of the powers which an individual owner might exercise in connection with property either real, personal, or mixed held by the Trust Fund, and to do all other actions that the Trustee may deem necessary or proper to carry out any of the powers set forth in this Section 5 or otherwise in the best interests of the Trust Fund or as may be authorized by the laws of the State of _____ .

Section 6. Payments by the Trustee

6.1   The establishment of the Trust and the payment of delivery to the Trustee of money or other property acceptable to the Trustee shall not vest in the President or the designated beneficiary any right, title, or interest in and to any assets of the Trust, except as otherwise set forth in this Section 6.

6.2   The Trustee shall make payment of Plan benefits to the President or to the designated beneficiary from the assets held in their respective Accounts (as defined in Section 6 hereof), in accordance with the terms and conditions, set forth in the Plan.

6.3   If the President's account is not sufficient to make one or more payments of benefits due under the Plan to him/her or to the designated beneficiary in accordance with the terms of the Plan, the Foundation shall make the balance of each such payment as it falls due.

6.4   Notwithstanding anything contained in this Trust Agreement to the contrary, if at any time the Trust finally is determined by the Internal Revenue Service (IRS) not to be a "grantor trust" with the result that the income of the Trust Fund is not treated as income of the Foundation pursuant to Sub-part E of Subchapter J of the code, or if a tax is finally determined by the IRS or is determined by counsel to the Trustee to be payable by the President or by the designated beneficiaries, in respect of any vested interest in the Trust Fund prior to payment of such interest to the President or the beneficiaries as the case may be, then the Trust shall immediately terminate and the full, fair market value of the assets in the Trust Fund shall be returned to the Foundation. The Foundation shall fully reimburse the President, or the designated beneficiary, as the case may be, for any tax liability either have incurred pursuant to the operation of this Section. For purposes of this Section, a final determination of the IRS shall be a decision rendered by the IRS, which is no longer subject to administrative appeal within the IRS.

6.   Notwithstanding any provision herein to the contrary, with respect to the President or the designated beneficiary, if the President has

continued in office through the year ending_____, *19*___, then the Trustee shall distribute to the President the entire sum in the trust in one lump sum.

6.6   In the event of the President's death before the expiration of the Trust Agreement, all funds in the trust on the date of death shall vest in the President's designated beneficiary, together with the payment of a pro-rated annual payment to the date of death for the year in which the death occurs. Thereafter, the entire sum in the trust shall be distributed in one lump sum to the designated beneficiary.

6.7   The Trustee shall, concurrently with the distribution of any sums from the President's Account, advise the executive office of the Foundation of the amount so paid to the President or to the designated beneficiary hereunder.

6.8   Notwithstanding anything in this Trust Agreement to the contrary, the Foundation shall remain primarily liable under the Plan to pay benefits. However, the Foundation's liability under the Plan shall be reduced or offset to the extent and by the value of any benefit payments under the Plan made from the Trust.

6.9   The Trustee shall deduct from each payment distributed under this Trust Agreement any Federal, State, or local withholding or other taxes or charges which the Trustee may be required to deduct under applicable laws.

Section 7. Funding the Trust

7.1   Amounts held for the benefit of the President (or designated beneficiary) in the Trust shall be maintained in an account (the "Account") which shall be held, administered, and accounted for separately. Records shall be maintained so that the amount held in said Account shall be identifiable at all times. The Account shall consist of, and be increased by, contributions made by the Foundation which are designated by the Foundation as the property of such Account and shall be decreased by any distributions made therefrom. The Foundation shall make contributions to such Account from time to time in accordance with the funding method provided in a separate agreement between the Foundation and the President, dated _____, *19*___, as will permit the Trust to make payment of benefits provided by the Plan. In addition, the Trustee shall allocate and credit the New Income of the Trust to the Account of the President on the last day of each calendar year ("Allocation Date"), based on the Account balance of the President on such date.

Section 8.   Trustee Responsibility Regarding Payment to the President and Beneficiaries When Foundation Is Insolvent

8.1   It is the intent of the parties hereto that the Trust assets are and shall remain at all times subject to the claims of the general creditors of the Foundation. Accordingly, the Foundation shall not create a security interest in the Trust assets in favor of the President or any creditor. If the Trustee receives the notice provided for in Section 8.2 hereof, or otherwise receives actual notice that the Foundation is insolvent or bankrupt as defined in Section 8.2, the Trustee will make no further distributions from the Trust to the President, or to the designated beneficiary of the Plan, but will deliver the entire amount of the Trust assets only as a court of competent jurisdiction, or duly appointed receiver or other person authorized to act by such a court, may direct to make the Trust assets available to satisfy the claims of the Foundation general creditors. The Trustee shall resume distributions from the Trust to the President, or to the designated beneficiaries, of the Plan under the terms hereof, upon no less than thirty (30) days' advance notice to the Foundation, if it determines that the Foundation was not, or is no longer, bankrupt or insolvent. Unless the Trustee has actual knowledge of the Foundation's bankruptcy or insolvency, the Trustee shall have no duty to inquire whether the Foundation is bankrupt or insolvent.

8.2   The Foundation, through its executive officer, shall advise the trustee promptly in writing of the Foundation's bankruptcy or insolvency.

8.3   If the Trustee discontinues payments of benefits under the Plan from the Trust pursuant to Section 8.1 of this Trust Agreement and subsequently resumes such payments, the first payment to the President, or to the designated beneficiary, following such discontinuance shall include the aggregate amount of all payments which would have been made to the President, or to the designated beneficiary, in accordance with the Plan during the period of such discontinuance, less the aggregate amount of benefits under the Plan made to the President, or the designated beneficiary, by the Foundation during any such period of discontinuance.

Section 9. Third Parties

9.1   A third party dealing with the Trustee shall not be required to make inquiry as to the authority of the Trustee to take any action nor be under any obligation to see to the proper application by the trustee of the sale of any property sold by the Trustee or to inquire into the propriety of any act of the Trustee.

Section 10. Taxes, Expenses, and Compensation

10.1   The Foundation shall from time to time pay taxes of any and all kinds whatsoever which at any time are lawfully levied or assessed upon or become payable in respect of the Trust Fund, the income or any property forming a part thereof, or any security transaction pertaining thereto. To the extent that any taxes lawfully levied or assessed upon the Trust Fund are not paid by the Foundation, the Trustee shall pay such taxes out of the Trust Fund. The Trustee shall withhold Federal, State and local taxes from any payments made to the President, or to the designated beneficiary in accordance with the provisions of applicable law. The Trustee shall contest the validity in any manner deemed appropriate by the Foundation of its counsel, but at the Foundation's expense, and only if it has received an indemnity bond or other security satisfactory to it to pay any such expenses. In the alternative, the Foundation may itself contest the validity of any such taxes.

10.2 The Foundation shall pay the Trustee such reasonable compensation for its services as may be agreed upon in writing from time to time by the Foundation and the Trustee. The Foundation shall also pay the reasonable expenses incurred by the Trustee in the performance of its duties under this Trust Agreement, including brokerage commissions and fees of counsel engaged by the trustee. Such compensation and expenses shall be charged against and paid from the Trust Fund to the extent that the Foundation does not pay such compensation.

Section 11. Administration and Records

11.1 The Trustee shall keep or cause to be kept accurate and detailed accounts of any investments, receipts, disbursements, and other transactions hereunder and all necessary and appropriate records required to identify correctly and reflect accurately the interest of the President or the designated beneficiary, and all accounts, books, and records relating thereto shall be open to inspection and audit at all reasonable times by any person designated by the Foundation. All such accounts, books, and records shall be preserved for such period as the Trustee may determine, but the Trustee may only destroy such accounts, books and records after first notifying the Foundation in writing of its intention to do so, and transferring to the Foundation any of such accounts, books, and records requested.

11.2 Within thirty (30) days after the close of each calendar year, and within thirty (30) days after the removal or resignation of the Trustee or the termination of the Trust, the Trustee shall file with the Foundation, a written account setting forth all investments, receipts, disbursements and other transactions effected by it during the preceding calendar year to the date of such removal, resignation or termination, including a description of all investments and securities purchased and sold with the cost or net proceeds of such purchases or sales and showing all cash, securities and other property held at the end of such calendar year or other period.

11.3 The Trustee shall from time to time permit an independent public accountant selected by the Foundation (except one to whom the Trustee has reasonable objection) to have access during ordinary business hours to such records as may be necessary to audit the Trustee's accounts.

11.4 As of the last day of each calendar year, the fair market value of the assets held in the Trust fund shall be determined. Within thirty (30) days after the close of each calendar year, the Trustee shall file with the Foundation the written report of the determination of such fair market value of the assets held in the Trust fund. It shall be the responsibility of the Foundation to further notify the President, or the designated beneficiary of the Trustee's report.

11.5 Nothing contained in this Trust Agreement shall be construed as depriving the Trustee, the Foundation, or the President or the designated beneficiary of the right to have a judicial settlement of the Trustee's accounts, and upon any proceeding for a judicial settlement of the Trustee's accounts or for instructions, the only necessary parties thereto in addition to the Trustee shall be the foundation and the President or the designated beneficiary.

11.6 In the event of the removal or resignation of the Trustee, the Trustee shall deliver to the successor Trustee all records which shall be required by the successor Trustee to enable it to carry out the provisions of this Trust Agreement.

11.7 In addition to any returns required of the Trustee by law, the Trustee shall prepare and file such tax reports and other returns as the Foundation and the Trustee may from time to time agree.

Section 12.   Removal or Resignation of the Trustee Designation of Successor Trustee

12.1 At any time, the Foundation may remove the Trustee with or without cause, upon at least sixty (60) days notice in writing to the Trustee. A copy of such notice shall be sent to the Trustee.

12.2 The Trustee may resign at any time upon at least sixty (60) days' notice in writing to the Foundation.

12.3 In the event of such removal or resignation, the Trustee shall duly file with the Foundation a written account as provided in Section 11.2 of the Trust Agreement for the period since the last previous annual accounting, listing the investments of the Trust and any uninvested cash balance thereof, and setting forth all receipts, disbursements, distributions, and other transactions respecting the Trust not included in any previous account.

12.4 Within sixty (60) days after any such notice of removal or resignation of the Trustee, the Foundation shall designate a successor Trustee qualified to act hereunder. Each such successor Trustee, during each period as it shall act as such, shall have the powers and duties herein conferred upon the Trustee, and the word "Trustee" wherever used herein, except where the context otherwise requires, shall be deemed to include any successor Trustee. Upon designation of a successor Trustee and delivery to the resigned or removed Trustee of written acceptance by the successor Trustee of such designation, such resigned or removed Trustee shall promptly assign, transfer, deliver and pay over to such Trustee, in conformity with the requirements of applicable law, the funds and properties in its control or possession then constituting the Trust Fund.

Section 13. Enforcement of Trust Agreement and Legal Proceedings

13.1 The Foundation shall have the right to enforce any provision of this Trust Agreement, and the President or the designated beneficiary of the Plan shall have the right to enforce any provision of this Trust Agreement that affects their right, title, and interest, if any, in the Trust. In any action or proceedings affecting the Trust, the only necessary parties shall be the Foundation, the Trustee, and the President and the designated beneficiary of the Plan, and, except as otherwise required by applicable law, no other person shall be entitled to any notice or service of process. Any judgment entered in such an action or proceeding shall to the maximum extent permitted by applicable law be binding and conclusive on all persons having or claiming to have any interest in the Trust.

Section 14. Termination and Suspension

14.1 The Trust shall terminate when all payments which have or may become payable pursuant to the terms of the Trust have been made.

Section 15. Amendments

15.1 The Foundation may from time to time amend or modify, in whole or in part, any or all of the provisions of this Trust Agreement (except Sections 1.1., 3.1, 6, 11, 12.4, 13, 14, 15, and 17) with the written consent of the Trustee, but without the consent of the President or the designated beneficiary of the Plan, provided that any such amendment shall not adversely affect the rights of the President or the designated beneficiary hereunder, or cause the Trust to cease to constitute a grantor trust as described in Section 6.4 of this Trust Agreement.

15.2 The Foundation and the Trustee shall execute such supplements to, or amendments of, this Trust Agreement as shall be necessary to give effect to any such amendment or modification.

Section 16. Non-alienation

16.1 Except insofar as applicable law may otherwise require and subject to Sections 1.1, 3.1, and 8 of this Trust Agreement, (1) no amount payable to or in respect of the President or the designated beneficiary at any time under the Trust shall be subject in any manner to alienation by anticipation, sale, transfer, assignment, bankruptcy, pledge, attachment, charge or encumbrance of any kind, and any attempt to so alienate, sell, transfer, assign, edge, attach, charge or otherwise encumber any such amount, whether presently or thereafter payable, shall be void; and, (2) the Trust Fund shall in manner be liable for or subject to the debts or liabilities of the President of the designated beneficiary.

Section 17. Communications

17.1 Communications to the Foundation shall be addressed to the Executive Officer, *(name and address of institution)*, provided, however, that upon the Foundation's written request, such communications shall be sent to such other address as the Foundation may specify.

17.2 Communications to the Trustee shall be addressed to *(name and address of Trustee)*, provided, however, that upon the Trustee's written request, such communications shall be sent to such other address as the Trustee may specify.

17.3 No communication shall be binding upon the Trustee until it is received by the Trustee. No communication shall be binding on the Foundation until it is received by the Foundation. No communication shall be binding on the President or the designated beneficiary until it is received by them.

17.4 Any action of the Foundation pursuant to this Trust Agreement, including all orders, requests, directions, instructions, approvals, and objections of the Foundation to the Trustee, shall be in writing, signed on behalf of the Foundation by any duly authorized officer of the Foundation. Any action by the President or the designated beneficiary shall be in writing. The Trustee may rely on and will be fully protected with respect to any such action taken or omitted in reliance on, any information, order, request, direction, instruction, approval, objection, and list delivered to the Foundation, or to the extent applicable under this Trust Agreement, by the President or the designated beneficiary.

Section 18. Miscellaneous Provisions

18.1 This Trust Agreement shall be binding upon and insure to the benefit of the Foundation and the Trustee and their respective successors and assigns and the personal representatives of individuals.

18.2 The Trustee assumes no obligation or responsibility with respect to any action required by this Trust Agreement on the part of the Foundation.

18.3 The President and the designated beneficiary shall file with the Trustee such pertinent information concerning themselves, and any other person as the Trustee shall specify, and they shall have no rights nor be entitled to any benefits under the Trust unless such information is filed by or with respect to them.

18.4 Any corporation into which the Trustee may be merged or with which it may be consolidated, or any corporation resulting from any merger reorganization, or consolidation to which the Trustee may be a party, or any corporation to which all or substantially all the business of the Trustee may be transferred shall be the successor of the Trustee hereunder without the execution or filing of any instrument or the performance of any act.

18.5 Titles to the Sections of this Trust Agreement and included for convenience only and shall not control the meaning or interpretation of any provision of this Trust Agreement.

18.6 This Trust Agreement and the Trust established hereunder shall be governed by and construed, enforced, and administered in accordance with the laws of the State of _____, and the Trustee shall be liable to account only in the courts of the State of _____.

18.7 This Trust Agreement may be executed in any number of counterparts, each of which shall be deemed to be the original, although the others shall not be produced.

18.8 This Trust has been executed and delivered in the State of _____ and shall be construed and administered according to the laws of that state.

18.9 It is agreed that the President and the designated beneficiaries are direct third-party beneficiaries of this Trust Agreement and the terms hereof are enforceable by them.

IN WITNESS WHEREOF, this Trust Agreement has been duly executed by the parties hereto as of the day and year first above written.

ATTEST: _____   (Institution)

_____

Foundation

_____

Witness

_____

Trust Company

ATTEST: _____

Trustee

APPENDIX
J
. . . .

Sample Letter of Presidential Appointment (Public Institution)

Dr. John Q. Appointee
Address

Dear Dr. Appointee:

This letter shall serve as your appointment as President of (*name of institution*), on the following terms and conditions:

1. You shall take office as President on (*date*) whereupon you shall become the University's Chief Executive and Academic Officer. At that time you shall also be granted tenure as a Professor of (*area*) in the College of (*field*). (*If appropriate.*)

2. Your salary shall be paid from a combination of state funds and non-state funds. The state-funded salary shall be as prescribed by state policy from year to year. For the current fiscal year (*dates*) the President of (*institution*) receives \$_____ from state funds. Starting (*date*), we anticipate a statutory increase in the range of ___%, or to approximately \$_____. In addition, the Board is authorized to pay the President, out of non-state funds, a salary supplement. For the current fiscal year, the supplement is \$_____. We have been advised that, for (*year*), we may request an increase in the supplement of an amount equal to the percentage increase in the statutory salary. Current indications are that we

may also provide an additional supplement of $_____ . Therefore, your total salary, from state and non-state funds, for (*year*) should be in the neighborhood of $_____, subject to actions of the Spring (*year*) General Assembly, and the final approval of the Governor.

3.   You shall have the responsibilities and authority as provided for by law and by the policies of the Board.

4.   You are required, for the convenience of the University, to reside in the University President's Home. Details regarding this requirement have been supplied separately.

5.   You will be furnished an automobile for use in official business, to be paid for out of non-state funds.

6.   Your fringe benefits, such as state-funded retirement, medical, hospitalization and disability insurance, life insurance, vacation and sick leave, etc., shall be as prescribed by University policies, literature on which has been provided to you. After five years' service, you may take extended leave, with pay, for up to six months (one regular semester), or for two successive summer semesters (three months each). This privilege will arise every _____ years.

7.   You will be reimbursed for the direct, out-of-pocket costs of moving your family and household possessions from (*current residence*) to (*future residence*).

8.   You shall receive from the (*name of institution*) University Foundation a letter concerning a year-to-year plan for deferred additional compensation in recognition of your service to the University. This plan for deferred additional compensation is endorsed by the Board.

9.   Your official travel and entertainment expenses, as well as club and professional association dues, will be reimbursed according to policies of the Board.

10. While you are encouraged to engage in professional activities that increase your stature and that of the University, you must dedicate your best efforts to the Office of the President and mission of the University. Non-university professional activities, whether for additional compensation or not, may be engaged in only upon prior approval of the Board.

11. In the event of your resignation as President, you may either (1) terminate your total employment with the University, or, (2) elect

to revert to your tenured status as Professor of (*area*). (*If appropriate.*) If you revert to a faculty position, you will join the faculty on the terms stipulated in the Faculty Handbook, with academic year salary equal to 10/12 of your President's salary. It is understood that, as President, you serve at the pleasure of the Board.

12. As a condition to this appointment, and within twenty-one days hereof, you shall have a comprehensive physical examination by a physician mutually agreed upon and paid for by the University. This appointment shall become effective when we receive a comprehensive written report of this examination and concur that it indicates no health impairment that would prevent you from performing the duties of President. Thereafter, you shall annually submit to a similar examination, at the University's expense, and a comprehensive report from your physician shall be provided to the Board.

13. This appointment shall otherwise become effective when officially acted upon and approved by the Board, or its Executive Committee, and when accepted by you. The provisions herein relating to your direct and indirect annual compensation are subject to law, and the approval of the Governor.

Please indicate your acceptance of this appointment by signing and returning the attached copy of this letter.

Sincerely yours,

(*official signature*)

Chair of the Board

Accepted and agreed to this (*date*)

(*official signature*)

APPENDIX
K
·········

Sample Five-Year Employment Contract (Public or Independent Institutions)

THIS AGREEMENT, made and entered into this day of (*date*), by between the Board of (*name of institution*), (hereinafter called the "Board" or the "College/University") and (*president's name*), (hereinafter called "President"). WITNESSETH:

WHEREAS, the Board of (*name of institution*) desires to employ the President as its chief administrative and executive officer, with title of "President"; and

WHEREAS, the President desires to accept such continued employment; and

WHEREAS, the parties have agreed to the terms and conditions of such employment and desire to reduce their agreement to writing;

NOW, THEREFORE, in consideration of the promises, covenants, agreements herein set forth, and for other good and valuable consideration, receipt of which is hereby acknowledged, the parties hereto covenant and agree as follows:

1. *Terms of Employment*
The Board shall employ the President for a term of five (5) years from the date hereof as its chief administrative and executive officer, with title of "President," subject to renewal or termination, as hereinafter provided.

The President is hereby also granted the title "Professor of (*field*) with Tenure. (*If appropriate.*)

2. Duties

The President shall well and faithfully serve the College/University in such capacity as aforesaid, and shall at all times devote his or her whole time, attention, and energies to the management, superintendence, and improvement of the College/University to the utmost of his or her ability, and shall do and perform all such services, acts, and things connected therewith as the Board, by its Bylaws have delegated to him or her, and which are of a nature properly belonging to the duties of a university president.

3. Compensation

The College/University shall pay the President an annual salary of $_____ payable in equal sums at such intervals as the College/University has established for its payroll procedure. The President will be eligible for, but not guaranteed, annual increases in salary and performance-based bonuses at the discretion of the Board.

4. Additional Entitlements

In addition to the annual salary, above provided, the President shall receive, and the College/University will provide the following:

a. Hospital/Medical/Surgical Insurance

The President shall be provided the benefits of the self-insured plan as provided for all faculty of the College/University, for both the President and his or her dependents, and pay the full premium therefor.

b. Long-Term Disability Insurance

The College/University agrees to maintain two policies of Long-Term Disability Insurance upon the President, and pay the premiums thereon in full, one such policy being that currently provided for members of the faculty, and one additional policy as heretofore maintained by the President individually. During any waiting period required by the policy provided for the faculty, the College/University will pay the President's salary in full, in addition to any other benefits which may be due and payable to him or her.

c. Workmen's Compensation Insurance

The College/University will provide Workmen's Compensation Insurance for payment of any medical expense, and compensation as provided by the laws of the State of _____, if the President suffers an injury or incurs an occupational disease arising out of and in the course of his or her employment. Compensability under such law is prescribed by state statute, and not by the College/University or by this Contract.

d. *Pension Contribution*

The President shall participate in the Teachers Insurance and Annuity Association (TIAA) and all required contributions thereto shall be paid by the College/University.

Initially the College/University shall pay 12 percent of the President's annual salary into TIAA on behalf of the President, who will immediately hold sole ownership to those contributions.

e. *Vacation*

The President will be entitled to vacation, with pay, of thirty (30) calendar days per year. Vacation leave not taken will be accumulated to a maximum of 30 days and its value paid to the President at time of termination, or at a time selected by the President, at the salary rate of the President at the time at which it is paid. However, under ordinary circumstances, the Board encourages the President to take full annual leave.

f. *Sick Leave*

The policy regarding sick leave, applicable to faculty and academic administrators, will be accorded to the President.

g. *Residence and Expenses Connected Therewith*

The College/University will provide the President with housing in the residence located at (address). The President shall furnish such furniture as he or she may choose to install, and if such is inadequate to completely, furnish the residence in keeping with that of a College/University President, the Board and the President will agree upon other items of furniture as may be needed and the same will be furnished by the University. The College/University shall furnish draperies and carpeting. All utilities, phone service, yard maintenance, and maintenance of the home, both outside and inside, will be paid for by the College/University. A full-time maid will be furnished at no expense to the President for use in maintaining the home so College/University guests may be properly entertained. The President and his or her family will be required to live in this residence furnished by the College/University. The College/University will reimburse the President for any cost of any premiums which are paid for contents insurance on the President's furniture and personal belongings in the residence.

h. *Entertainment Expenses*

The College/University will provide the President with adequate budgeted funds for purposes of entertaining the guests of the College/University for carrying out the duties of the office, both on-campus and off-campus.

The College/University will arrange for the payment of these expenses in a manner which is mutually acceptable to the parties.

i.   *Automobile*

The President will be furnished with an automobile for use in carrying out the duties of the office. All expenses of this automobile, including, but not limited to, insurance, gasoline, and repairs, will be paid for by the College/University.

j.   *Other Faculty Privileges Not Enumerated Herein*

Such other privileges and benefits accorded the faculty, not enumerated herein, will likewise be accorded to the President.

k.   *Preferential Hiring Conditions for Spouse*

It is understood by the College/University that (*name of spouse*), spouse of the President, is a member of the tenured faculty at (*name of institution*) and in coming to (*name of institution*) with the President has surrendered valuable property rights. Therefore, the Board agrees that, in the event of the President's death before reaching retirement age, the College/University will offer (name of spouse) a teaching position at a salary to be negotiated at that time commensurate with his or her qualifications and the existing salary structure for the department where the position is offered. (*Note: When appropriate.*)

l.   *Sabbatical Leave*

The Board agrees as a result of five or more years of exemplary service, the President shall be eligible for a sabbatical leave under the following conditions, notwithstanding provision in the Faculty Handbook which may conflict herewith:

  i.   The President is eligible for a sabbatical leave of one-half year, to be taken at the time of his or her choosing, provided reasonable notice of intent to utilize such leave is given to the College/University by the President, considering all the attending circumstances. Such leave may be reserved by the President, as an option, to commence at a time of any agreed or involuntary termination of the President's services hereunder;

  ii.   The President shall be entitled to full salary, and all fringe benefits payable during any such sabbatical, with the exception of the use of the President's house, which will be vacated by the President (and family) within thirty (30) days following termination, but only if terminated, unless extended by the Board;

iii.   Additional sabbatical leave to that provided above, may be allowed the President, at any time by the College/University, at such time by and upon such conditions as are deemed appropriate. Such additional leave shall be granted in the sole discretion of the Board.

5.   *Termination*

a.   At least sixty (60) calendar days before the end of each year of this Agreement, the Board will conduct a performance review and evaluation of the President and shall give the President notice in writing stating the number of years it is willing to extend the Agreement, if any, beyond the years remaining in its current term established herein, and the terms upon which such extension is offered. Not later than thirty (30) calendar days following receipt of such notice, the President shall respond by stating his or her acceptance or rejection, or proposed modification of the offer extended by the College/University. If agreement upon the terms of such extension is reached, a new written agreement codifying the terms thereof shall be prepared and executed by the parties. At least every four years, an evaluation of the President shall be conducted by an external authority of national reputation.

b.   If no extension of the Agreement is made beyond the remaining years then existing, as above provided, this Contract shall terminate as of the first day of the last year of the term then existing.

c.   This Contract may also be terminated by the parties at any time during the term, as follows:

1.   Upon the occurrence of any one of the following events:

i.   Illness or disability of the President, or any cause incapacitating him or her from the attendance to duties as President for more than one (1) year.

ii.   Termination of the President by the Board for just cause. The term "just cause" is defined as acts by the President constituting or involving incompetency, neglect, or refusal to perform his or her duties, or drunkenness. No termination of employment for alleged "just cause" shall occur without first giving the President notice in writing of the cause alleged, and an opportunity to be heard.

      iii. In the event the College/University terminates the President's employment for "just cause," the President shall not be entitled to any further salary or benefits following the date of such termination, unless otherwise agreed to in writing by the Board.

2. The President may terminate this Agreement for any reason upon the giving of sixty (60) calendar days' notice, prior to the effective date of the termination. Should such notice be given, the President shall not be entitled to any further salary or benefits payable hereunder after the effective date of termination, unless otherwise agreed to in writing by the Board.

3. If the Board chooses to terminate the President for any reason other that "just cause," it will be bound to pay the President or his or her estate an amount of money equal to entire value of the salary and fringe benefits remaining on the contract.

6. *Construction of Agreement*

The laws of the State of _____ shall govern this Agreement
                        (especially for public institutions)

IN WITNESS WHEREOF, the parties have executed this Agreement the day and year first above written.

BIBLIOGRAPHY

•••••••••

Alexander, M.A., and Scott, B.M. "The AICCC Perspective of Career Management: A Strategy for Personal and Positional Power for Black Women in Higher Education Administration." Paper Presented at the Annual Conference of the National Association for Women Deans, Administrators, and Counselors, Houston, TX 1983. ERIC Document 246 378.

Alinsky, S.D. *Rules for Radicals*. New York: Random House, 1972.

Allen, R.W.; Madison, D.L.; Porter, L.W.; Renwick, P.S.; and Mayer, B.T. "Organizational Politics: Tactics and Characteristics of Its Actors." *California Management Review*, 22(1979):77-83.

American Association for Higher Education. *CQ101: A First Reader for Higher Education*. Washington, DC: American Association for Higher Education, 1993.

————. *25 Snapshots of a Movement: Profiles of Campuses Implementing CQI*. Washington, DC: American Association for Higher Education, 1994.

American Association of University Professors. "1940 Statement on Principles on Academic Freedom and Tenure with 1970 Interpretive Comments." In *Policy Documents and Reports*. Washington, DC: American Association of University Professors, 1990.

————. "Joint Statement on Government of Colleges and Universities, 1966." In *Policy Documents and Reports*. Washington, DC: American Association of University Professors, 1990.

American Council on Education. *Higher Education Facts in Brief*. Edited by Charles W. Washington. Washington, DC: American Council on Education, 1994.

Andrews, F. Emerson. *Philanthropic Giving*. New York: Russell Sage Foundation, 1950.

Argyris, C., and Cyert, R.M., eds. *Leadership in the '80s*. Cambridge: Harvard University Institute for Educational Management, 1980.

Argyris, C., and Schon, D.A. *Theory in Practice: Increasing Professional Effectiveness*. San Francisco: Jossey-Bass, 1974.

Astin, A.W. *American Freshman: National Norms*. Cooperative Institutional Research Program, University of California-Los Angeles, 1981.

Astin, A.W., and Scherrei, R.A. *Maximizing Leadership Effectiveness*. San Francisco: Jossey-Bass, 1980.

Astin, H., and Leland, C. *Women of Influence, Women of Vision. A Cross-Generational Study of Leaders and Social Change*. San Francisco: Jossey-Bass, 1991.

Baker, L.C.; DiMarco, N.; and Scott, W.E., Jr. "Effects of Supervisor's Sex and Level of Authoritarianism on Evaluation and Reinforcement of Blind and Sighted Workers." *Journal of Applied Psychology*, 60(1975):28-32.

Baldridge, J.V.; Curtis, D.V.; Ecker, G.; Riley, G.L. *Policy Making and Effective Leadership*. San Francisco: Jossey-Bass, 1978.

Banks, W.C. "The Effects of Perceived Similarity and Influencer's Personality upon the Use of Rewards and Punishments." Paper read at Eastern Psychological Association Meetings, Philadelphia, PA, 1974.

Barr, B.M. *Leadership, Psychology and Organizational Behavior*. New York: Harper, 1960.

Bartol, K.M. "Male Versus Female Leaders: The Effect of Leader Need for Dominance on Follower Satisfaction and Performance." *Academy of Management Journal*, 17(1974):225-33.

Bartol, K.M., and Butterfield, D.A. "Sex Effects in Evaluating Leaders." *Journal of Applied Psychology*, 61(1976):446-54.

Bass, Bernard M. "Individual Capability, Team Response, and Productivity." In *Human Performance and Productivity*, edited by E.A. Fleischman and M.D. Dannette. New York: Erlbaum, 1981.

———. *Leadership and Performance beyond Expectations*. New York: Macmillan, 1985.

———. *Bass and Stogdill's Handbook of Leadership: Theory, Research, and Managerial Applications*, Third Edition. New York: The Free Press, 1990.

———. "From Transactional to Transformational Leadership: Learning to Share the Vision." *Organizational Dynamics*, 18(1992):19-31.

Bem, S.L. "The Measurement of Psychological Androgyny." *Journal of Consulting and Clinical Psychology*, 42(1974):155–62.

Benezet, L.T.; Katz, J.; and Magnussen, F.W. *Style & Substance: Leadership and the College Presidency*. Washington, DC: American Council on Education, 1981.

Bennis, W. *On Becoming a Leader*. Reading, PA: Addison-Wesley, 1989a.

———. *Why Leaders Can't Lead: The Unconscious Conspiracy Continues*. San Francisco: Jossey-Bass, 1989b.

Bennis, W., and Nanus, B. *Leaders: The Strategies for Taking Change.* New York, Harper and Row, 1985.

Bensimon, E. "A Feminist Reinterpretation of Presidents' Definitions of Leadership." *Peabody Journal of Education,* 66(1989):143-56.

———. "New Presidents' Initial Actions: Transactional or Transformational Leadership." *Journal for Higher Education Management,* 8(1993):5-17.

Berkowitz, L., and Daniels, L.R. "Responsibility and Dependency." *Journal of Abnormal Sociology,* 66(1963):429-36.

Berle, A. *Power.* New York: Harcourt, Brace, and World, 1967.

Bierstadt, R. "An Analysis of Social Power." *American Sociological Review,* 15(1950):730-38.

Birch, David. *Job Creation in America.* New York: The Free Press, 1987.

———. *Entrepreneurial Hot Spots: The Best Places in America to Start and Grow a Company.* Cambridge: Cognetics, Inc., 1993.

———. *Entrepreneurial Hot Spots: The Best Places in America to Start and Grow a Company.* Cambridge: Cognetics, Inc., 1994.

Bird, C. *Social Psychology.* New York: Appleton Century, 1940.

Birnbaum, Robert. *How Colleges Work: The Cybernetics of Academic Organization.* San Francisco: Jossey-Bass, 1988.

———. *How Academic Leadership Works: Understanding Success and Failure in the College Presidency.* San Francisco: Jossey-Bass, 1992.

Blake, R.R.; Mouton, J.S.; and Williams, M.S. *The Academic Administrator Grid.* San Francisco: Jossey-Bass, 1981.

Blau, P.M., and Scott, W.R. *Formal Organizations.* San Francisco: Chandler, 1962.

Boyer, Ernest L. *Scholarship Reconsidered: Priorities of the Professorate.* Princeton: The Carnegie Foundation for the Advancement of Teaching, 1990.

Bradley, J.; Carey, P.; and Whitaker, E. "Perspectives on Leadership and Black Women Presidents." *Journal of the American Association of Women in Community and Junior Colleges: Fifteenth Anniversary Issue* (1989):20-5.

Breasted, J.H. *Ancient Records of Egypt, Vol. I.* New York: Russell and Russell, 1962.

Bremner, Robert H. *American Philanthropy.* Chicago: University of Chicago Press, 1960.

Budge, E.A. Wallis. *The Book of the Dead.* New York: Dover Publications, 1967.

Burke, P.J. "Authority Relations and Disruptive Behavior in Small Discussion Groups." *Sociometry,* 29(1966a):237-250.

———. "Authority Relations and Disruptive Behavior in the Small Group." *Dissertation Abstracts*, 26(1966b):4850.

Burke, W.W. "Leadership Behavior as a Function of the Leader, the Follower, and the Situation." *Journal of Personality and Social Psychology*, 33(1965):60-81.

Burns, J.M. *Leadership*. New York: Harper and Row, 1978.

Camp, Robert C. *Benchmarking*. Milwaukee: ASQC Quality Press, 1989.

Caplow, T. *Two against One: Coalitions in Triads*. Englewood Cliffs: Prentice-Hall, 1968.

Carbone, R.F. *Presidential Passages*. Washington, DC: American Council on Education, 1981.

———. Personal conversation, 1982.

Carp, F.M.; Vitola, B.M.; and McLanathan, F.L. "Human Relations Knowledge and Social Distance Set in Supervisors." *Journal of Applied Psychology*, 47(1963):78-80.

Carter, Stephen. *Reflections of an Affirmative Action Baby*. New York: Basic Books, 1992.

Change. "The Landscape: The Changing Faces of the American College Campus." *Change*, 25(September/October 1993):57-59.

Cheng, B. "A Profile of Selected Women Leaders: Toward a New Model of Leadership." ERIC Document ED 303 397, 1988.

Chickering, A.W. *The Modern American College*. San Francisco: Jossey-Bass, 1981.

Cicero. *On Moral Obligation*. Translated by John Higginbotham. Los Angeles: University of California Press, 1967.

Clark, B.R. "Organizational Adaptation and Precarious Values: A Case Study." *American Sociological Review*, 21(1956):327-36.

Clark, Kenneth E., and Clark, Miriam B. *Choosing to Lead*. Charlotte, NC: Iron Gate Press, 1994.

Cleveland, H. *The Knowledge Executive: Leadership in an Information Society*. New York: Dutton, 1985.

Cleven, W.A., and Fiedler, F.E. "Interpersonal Perceptions of Open-Hearth Foremen and Steel Production." *Journal of Applied Psychology*, 41(1956):312-14.

Cohen, A.R. "The Effect of Situational Structure and Individual Self-Esteem on Threat Oriented Reactions to Power." Doctoral dissertation, University of Michigan at Ann Arbor, 1953.

———. "Upward Communication in Experimentally Created Hierarchies." *Human Relations*, 11(1958):41-53.

————. "Situational Structure, Self-Esteem, and Threat-Oriented Reactions to Power." In *Studies in Social Power*, edited by D. Cartwright. Ann Arbor: University of Michigan Institute for Social Research, 1959.

Cohen, M.D., and March, J.G. *Leadership and Ambiguity*, Second Edition. New York: McGraw-Hill, 1986.

Cole, R., Jr. "A Comparison of Perceived Leadership Styles among Presidents of Selected Black Colleges in the Southwestern and Southeastern United States." Paper Presented at the Annual Meeting of the AERA, New Orleans, 1984. ERIC Document 214 532.

Collaros, P.A., and Anderson, L.R. "Effect of Perceived Expertness upon Creativity of Members of Brainstorming Groups." *Journal of Applied Psychology*, 2(1969):159-63.

Cornesky, Robert, et al. *Using Deming to Improve Quality in Colleges and Universities.* Madison, WI: Magna Publications, 1990.

Cornesky, Robert, and McCool, Samuel. *Total Quality Improvement Guide for Institutions of Higher Education.* Madison, WI: Magna Publications, 1992.

————. *The Quality Professor: Implementing TQM in the Classroom.* Madison, WI: Magna Publications, 1993.

Cowley, W.H. *Presidents, Professors, and Trustees: The Evolution of American Academic Government.* San Francisco: Jossey-Bass, 1980.

Cox, A.J. *The Making of the Achiever: How to Win Distinction in Your Company.* New York: Dodd, Mead, 1985.

Cox, C.M. *The Early Mental Traits of Three Hundred Geniuses.* Stanford: Stanford University Press, 1926.

Crowley, Joseph N. *No Equal in the World: An Interpretation of the American Presidency.* Reno, NV: University of Nevada Press, 1994.

Curti, Merle, and Nash, Roderick. *Philanthropy in the Shaping of Higher Education.* New Brunswick, NJ: Rutgers University Press, 1965.

Cussler, M. *The Woman Executive.* New York: Harcourt, Brace and World, 1958.

Cutlip, Scott M. *Fund Raising in the United States.* New Brunswick, NJ: Rutgers University Press, 1965.

Dahl, R.A. "The Concepts of Power." *Behavioral Science*, 2(1957):201-15.

Davis, William E. *Nobody Calls Me Doctor.* Boulder, CO: Pruett Publishing Company, 1972.

————. "Presidential Perspectives. That Revolving Door Is Breaking Up that Old Gang of Mine—NASLGC, Presidential Tenures in the 80's." In *The Green Sheet*, (1-4). Washington, DC: NASLGC, 1988.

Demerath, Nicholas J.; Stephens, Richard W.; and Taylor, R. Robb. *Power, Presidents, and Professors*. New York: Basic Books, 1967.

Dixit, Avinash, and Nalebuff, Barry. *Thinking Strategically: The Competitive Edge in Business, Politics, and Everyday Life*. New York: W.W. Norton, 1991.

Dodds, Harold W. *The Academic President: Educator or Caretaker*. New York: McGraw Hill, 1962.

Dornbusch, S.M., and Scott, W.R. *Evaluation and the Exercise of Authority: A Theory of Control Applied to Diverse Organizations*. San Francisco: Jossey-Bass, 1975.

Dressel, Paul L. *Administrative Leadership*. San Francisco: Jossey-Bass, 1981.

Drucker, Peter F. *The Practice of Management*. Tokyo: Tuttle, 1954.

D'Souza, Dinesh. *Illiberal Education: The Politics of Race and Sex on Campus*. New York: The Free Press, 1991.

Durant, Will. *Caesar and Christ, The Story of Civilization, Part II*. New York: Simon and Schuster, 1944.

Eagly, A.; Makjijani, M.; and Klonsky, B. "Gender and the Evaluation of Leaders: A Meta-Analysis." *Psychological Bulletin*, 3(1992):3-22.

Eble, K.E. *The Art of Administration*. San Francisco: Jossey-Bass, 1978.

Edelman, M. *The Symbolic Uses of Politics*. Urbana: University of Illinois Press, 1964.

Editorial Projects for Education, Inc. *The Impossible Job: A Special Report on What It Takes to Run a College These Days*. Washington, DC: Editorial Projects for Education, 1976.

Educational Testing Service. *Learning by Degrees: Indicators of Performance in Higher Education*. Princeton: Educational Testing Service, 1995.

Entin, David H. "A Second Look: TQM in Ten Boston-Area Colleges, One Year Later." *AAHE Bulletin*, 46(May 1994):3-7.

Epstein, L.D. *Governing the University: The Campus and the Public Interest*. San Francisco: Jossey-Bass, 1974.

Epstein, Morris. *All about Jewish Holidays and Customs*. New York: Ktav Publishing House, 1970.

Falbo, T. "Multidimensional Scaling of Power Strategies." *Journal of Personality and Social Psychology*, 35(1957):537-47.

Fiedler, F.E. "Assumed Similarity Measures and Predictors of Team Effectiveness." *Journal of Abnormal Social Psychology*, 48(1954):381-88.

———. "The Influence of Leader-Keyman Relations on Combat Crew Effectiveness." *Journal of Abnormal Social Psychology*, 51(1955):227-235

————. "The Effect of Leadership and Cultural Heterogeneity on Group Performance: A Test of the Contingency Model." *Journal of Experimental Social Psychology*, 2(1966):237-64.

————. *A Theory of Leadership Effectiveness*. New York: McGraw-Hill, 1967.

————. "Leadership Experience and Leader Performance: Another Hypothesis Shot to Hell." *Organizational Behavior and Human Performance*, 5(1970a):1-14.

————. *Personality, Motivational Systems, and Behavior of High and Low LPC Persons*. Seattle: University of Washington, Technical Report 70-12, 1970b.

Fiedler, F.E., and Meuwese, W.A.T. "Leaders' Contribution to Task Performance in Cohesive and Uncohesive Groups." *Journal of Abnormal Social Psychology*, 67(1963):83-87.

Fiedler, F.E.; Meuwese, W.A.T.; and Oonk, S. "An Exploratory Study of Group Creativity in Laboratory Tasks." *Acta Psychologica*, Amst. 18(1961):100-19.

Fiedler, F.E.; O'Brien, G.E.; and Ilgen, D.R. "The Effect of Leadership Style upon the Performance and Adjustment of Volunteer Teams Operating in Successful Foreign Environment." *Human Relations*, 22(1969):503-14.

Fisher, James L. "Of Testing, Truth and Ralph Nader." *The New York Times*, Feb. 18, 1980a.

————. ed. *Presidential Leadership in Advancement Activities: New Directions for Institutional Advancement (#8)*. San Francisco: Jossey-Bass, 1980b.

————. *Power of the Presidency*. New York: American Council on Education/MacMillan, 1984.

Fisher, James L., and Quehl, Gary H. *The President and Fund-Raising*. New York: American Council on Education, 1989.

Fisher, James L.; Tack, Martha W.; and Wheeler, Karen J. *The Effective College President*. New York: American Council on Education/MacMillan, 1988.

Foa, U.G., and Foa, E.B. *Societal Structures of the Mind*. Springfield: C.C. Thomas, 1975.

Fodor, E.M. "Disparagement by a Subordinate as an Influence on the Use of Power." *Journal of Applied Psychology*, 59(1974):652-55.

French, J.R.P.; Morrison, W.; and Levinger, G. "Coercive Power and Forces Affecting Conformity." *Journal of Abnormal Social Psychology*, 61(1960):93-101.

French, J.R.P., and Raven, B. "The Bases of Social Power." In *Studies in Social Power*, edited by D. Cartwright. Ann Arbor: University of Michigan, Institute for Social Research, 1959.

————. "The Bases of Social Power." In *Group Dynamics* (3rd ed.), edited by D. Cartwright and A. Zander. New York: Harper & Row, 1968.

French, J.R.P., and Snyder, R. "Leadership and Interpersonal Power." In *Studies in Social Power*, edited by D. Cartwright. Ann Arbor: University of Michigan, Institute for Social Research, 1959.

Friesen, L. "Focus on Research: Women and Leadership." *Contemporary Education*, 54(1983):223-30.

Gaither, Steven A. "Leader Style, and Leader Behavior: The Influence on Presidential Performance." Paper Presented at NAFEO Conference, Washington, DC, 1992.

Galbraith, John Kenneth. *The Anatomy of Power*. Boston, Houghton, Mifflin, 1983.

Gardner, John W. *The Nature of Leadership: Introductory Considerations*. Washington, DC: Independent Sector Press, 1986.

Geertz, C. "Reflections on the Symbolics of Power." In *Local Knowledge*, edited by C. Geertz. New York, Basic Books, 1983.

Ghiselli, E.E. "Intelligence and Managerial Success." *Psychological Reports*, 12(1963):898.

Gibbons, T.C. *Revisiting the Question of Born vs. Made: Toward A Theory of Development of Transformational Leaders*. Doctoral dissertation, Fielding Institute, Santa Barbara, CA, 1986.

Gilley, J.W.; Fulmer, K.A.; and Reithlingshoefer, S.J. *Searching for Academic Excellence: Twenty Colleges and Universities on the Move and Their Leaders*. New York: ACE/MacMillan, 1986.

Godfrey, E.P.; Fiedler, F.E.; and Hall, D.M. *Boards, Management and Company Success*. Danville, IL: Interstate, 1959.

Goldberg, Stephanie B. "The Quest for TQM." *ABA Journal*, 79 (November 1993): 52-58.

Goodstadt, B., and Hjelle, L.A. "Power to the Powerless." *Journal of Personality and Social Psychology*, 27(1973):190-96.

Gottheil, E., and Vielhaber, D.P. "Interaction of Leader and Squad Attributes Related to Performance of Military Squads." *Journal of Social Psychology*, 68(1966):113-27.

Graves, Jacqueline M. "Management Tools That Work." *Fortune*, 129(30 May 1994):15.

Green, Madeline F. *Leaders for New Era*. New York: Macmillan, 1988.

Greenleaf, R.K. *Servant Leadership*. New York: Paulist Press, 1977.

Hackman, M.; Furniss, A.; Hills, M.; and Peterson, T. "Perceptions of Gender-Role Characteristics and Transformational and Transactional Leadership Behaviors." *Perceptual and Motor Skills*, 75(1992):311-19.

Hall, J., and Hawker, J.R. *Power Management Inventory.* The Woodlands, Texas: Teleometrics International, 1981.

Hammarskjold, D. *Markings.* Lawrence, Mass.: Merrimack Book Service, 1965.

Harvard, P.A. "Successful Behaviors of Black Women Administrators in Higher Education: Implications for Leadership." Paper Presented at the Annual Meeting of the American Educational Research Association, San Francisco, CA 1986: ERIC Document 272 092.

Hawker, J.R., and Hall, J. *The Development and Initial Validation of Scale for Assessing Power Motivation.* The Woodlands, Texas: Teleometrics International, 1981.

Hawkins, C.H. "A Study of Factors Mediating a Relationship between Leader Rating Behavior and Group Productivity." *Dissertation Abstracts,* 23(1962):733.

Hechinger, F.M. "Leadership Arises as a College Issue." *The New York Times,* Oct. 19, 1982

Henkoff, Ronald. "Keeping Motorola on a Roll." *Fortune,* 129 (April 18, 1994):67-68, ff.

Henshel, H.B. "The President Stands Alone." *Harvard Business Review,* (September/October 1971):37-45.

Hesburgh, T.M. *The Hesburgh Papers.* Kansas City, MO: Andrews and McMeel, 1979.

————. "Presidential Leadership: The Keystone for Advancement." In *Presidential Leadership in Advancement Activities,* edited by J.L. Fisher. San Francisco: Jossey-Bass, 1980.

————. "Academic Leadership." In *Leaders in Leadership,* edited by J.M. Fisher and M.W. Tack. San Francisco: Jossey-Bass, 1988.

Hill, W. The Validation and Extension of Fiedler's Theory of Leadership Effectiveness. *Academic Management Journal,* 12(1969):33-47.

Hobbes, T. *Leviathan.* England: Penguin Books, 1968.

Hodgkinson, H.L. "Presidents and Campus Governance: A Research Profile." *Educational Record,* 51(1970):159-66.

Hodgkinson, H.L., and Meeth, L.R., eds. *Power and Authority.* San Francisco: Jossey-Bass, 1976.

Hollander, E.P. "Emergent Leadership and Social Influences." In *Leadership and Interpersonal Behavior,* edited by L. Patrullo and B.M. Bass. New York: Holt, Rinehart, and Winston, 1961.

————. *Leadership Dynamics: A Practical Guide to Effective Relationships.* New York: Free Press, 1978.

Holmes, B. "A 1976 Theory of Charismatic Leadership." In *Leadership: The Cutting Edge*, edited by J.G. Hunt and L.L. Larson. Carbondale: Southern Illinois University Press, 1977.

————. "Upward Mobility, Aspirations, and Expectations: A Woman's Perspective." *Jump High at the Sun*, (1989):14-8. ERIC Document 343 649.

House, R.J. *Power in Organizations: A Social Psychological Perspective.* Unpublished Manuscript. Toronto: University of Toronto, 1984.

Howell, J.M. *A Laboratory Study of Charismatic Leadership.* London, Ontario: School of Business Administration, 1985.

Hughes, M. "Developing Leadership Potential for Minority Women." *New Directions for Student Services*, 44(1988):63-75.

Hunt, J.G. "Fiedler's Leadership Contingency Model: An Empirical Test in Three Organizations." *Organizational Behavior and Human Performance*, 67(1967):290-308.

Hurwitz, J.I.; Zander, A.F.; and Hymovitch, B. "Some Effects of Power on the Relations among Group Members." In *Group Dynamics*, edited by D. Cartwright and A. Zander. Evanston: Row, Peterson, 1953.

Hutchins, E.B., and Fiedler, F.E. "Task-Oriented and Quasi-Therapeutic Role Functions of the Leader in a Small Military Group." *Sociometry*, 23(1960):393-406.

Hutchins, Robert M. "The Administrator: Leader or Officeholder?" In *Freedom, Education, and the Fund: Essays and Addresses, 1946-1956.* New York: Meridian Books, 1956.

International Business Machines. *The IBM-TQM Partnership with Colleges and Universities.* Washington, DC: American Association for Higher Education, 1993.

Iverson, M.A. "Personality Impression of Punitive Stimulus Persons of Differential Status." *Journal of Abnormal and Social Psychology*, 68(1964):617-26.

Jacoby, Russell. *Dogmatic Wisdom: How the Culture Wars Divert Education and Distract America.* New York: Doubleday, 1994.

Jenkins, W.D. "A Review of Leadership Studies with Particular Reference to Military Problems." *Psychological Bulletin*, 44(1947):54-79.

Jones, E.E. *Ingratiation.* New York: Appleton-Century-Crofts, 1964.

Jones, E.E.; Gergen, K.J.; Gumpert, P.; and Thibaut, J.W. "Some Conditions Affecting the Use of Ingratiation to Influence Performance Evaluation." *Journal of Personality and Social Psychology*, 1(1965):613-25.

Jones, R.E., and Jones E.E. "Optimum Conformity as an Ingratiation Tactic." *Journal Personality*, 32(1964):436-58.

Julian, J.W. "Leader and Group Behavior as Correlates of Adjustment and Performance in Negotiation Groups." *Dissertation Abstracts*, 23(1) (1964):646.

Julian, J.W.; Hollander, E.P.; and Regula, C.R. "Endorsement of the Group Spokesman as a Function of His Source of Authority, Competence and Success." *Journal of Personality and Social Psychology*, 11(1969):42-49.

Kanter, Rosabeth Moss. *The Change Masters*. New York: Simon and Schuster, 1983.

Kapalka, G., and Lachenmeyer, J. "Sex-Role Flexibility, Locus of Control, and Occupational Status." *Sex Roles*, 19(1988):417-27.

Katz, D. "Patterns of Leadership." In *Handbook of Political Psychology*, edited by J.N. Knutson. San Francisco: Jossey-Bass, 1973.

Kauffman, J.F. *At the Pleasure of the Board*. Washington, DC: American Council on Education, 1980.

Keegan, John. *The Second World War*. New York: Penguin Books, 1989.

Keller, George. *Academic Strategy: The Management Revolution in American Higher Education*. Baltimore: Johns Hopkins University Press, 1983.

Kelman, H.C., and Lawrence, L.H. "Assignment of Responsibility in the Case of Lt. Calley." *Journal of Social Issues*, 28 (1982):177-212.

Kerr, C. Personal conversation, 1980.

———. *Presidents Make a Difference: Strengthening Leadership in Colleges and Universities*. Report of the Commission on Strengthening Presidential Leadership, directed by Clark Kerr. Washington, DC: Association of Governing Boards, 1984.

Kerr, C., and Gade, Miriam. *The Many Lives of Academic Presidents: Time, Place and Character*. Washington: Association of Governing Boards, 1986.

Kipnis, D. *The Powerholders*. Chicago: The University of Chicago Press, 1976.

Kipnis, D., and Vanderveer, R. "Ingratiation and the Use of Power." *Journal of Personality and Social Psychology*, 26(1971):245-50.

Kipnis, D., and Wagner, D. "Character Structure and Response to Leadership." *Journal of Experimental Research in Personality*, 1(1967):16-24.

Knutson, J.N., ed. *Handbook of Political Psychology*. San Francisco: Jossey-Bass, 1973.

Koch, James V. "The State of the University." Norfolk, VA: Old Dominion University, August 25, 1994.

Koch, James V., and Cebula, Richard J. "In Search of Excellent Management." *Journal of Management Studies*, 31(September 1994):681-99.

Korda, M. *Power: How to Get it, How to Use It*. New York: Ballantine, 1976.

Korman, A.K. "The Prediction of Managerial Performance: A Review." *Personnel Psychology*, 21(1958):295-322.

Kotter, J.P. *The General Managers*. New York: Free Press, 1982.

————. *Power and Influence*. New York: Free Press, 1985.

————. *The Leadership Factor: What It Takes to Attract, Develop, Retain, and Motivate the Best Managerial Talent*. New York: Free Press, 1988.

Lackey, Charles W., Jr., and Pugh, Susan L. "TQM and the 'Flower Child' Manager." *Change*, 26(March/April 1994):6-7.

LaMont, Douglas. *Winning Worldwide: Strategies for Dominating Global Markets*. Homewood, IL: Business One Irwin, 1991.

Lawler, E.E., *Pay and Organizational Effectiveness*. New York: McGraw-Hill, 1971.

Lehman, H.C. *Age and Achievement*. Princeton: Princeton University Press, 1953.

Lenner J.H. "The Justice Motive: 'Equity' and Parity among Children." *Journal of Personality and Social Psychology*, 29(1974):539-45.

Lipman-Blumen, J. "Connective Leadership: Female Leadership Styles in the 21st Century Workplace." *Sociological Perspectives*, 35(1992):183-203.

Luchins, A.S., and Luchins, E.H. "On Conformity with Judgments of a Majority or an Authority." *Journal of Social Psychology*, 53(1961):303-16.

MacEoin, G. "Notre Dame's Father Hesburgh." *Change*, 8(1976):45-51.

Machiavelli, N. *The Prince*. New York: Mentor Books, [1532] 1952.

Main, Jeremy. *Quality Wars: The Triumphs and Defeats of American Business*. New York: The Free Press, 1994.

Mandeville, Bernard. *The Fable of the Bees*. Edited by P. Harth. Baltimore: Penguin Books, [1714] 1970.

Mann, R.D. "A Review of the Relationships between Personality and Performance in Small Groups." *Psychological Bulletin*, 56(1959):241-70.

March, James G. *How We Talk and How We Act: Administrative Theory and Administrative Life*. The Seventh David D. Henry Lecture, University of Illinois, 1980.

Martin, Homer. Personal conversation with James L. Fisher, 1982.

Marts, A. *Man's Concern for His Fellow Man*. Geneva, NY: W.F. Humphrey Press, 1961.

Matthews, D.R. *The Social Background of Political Decision-Makers*. New York: Random House, 1954.

Mausner, B. "Studies in Social Interaction III: Effect of Variation in One Partner's Prestige on the Interaction of Observer Pairs." *Journal of Applied Psychology*, 37(1953):391-93.

May, R. *Power and Innocence*. New York: Norton, 1972.

Mayhew, L.B., and Glenn, J.R., Jr. "College and University Presidents: Roles in Transition." *Liberal Education*, 61(1975):299-308.

McClelland, D.C. "The Two Faces of Power." *Journal of International Affairs*, 24(1969):141-54.

———. "The Two Faces of Power." *Journal of International Affairs*, (1970): 29-47

———. *Power: The Inner Experience*. New York: Irvington, 1975.

McClelland, D.C., and Burnham, D.H. "Power Is the Great Motivator." *Harvard Business Review*, 54(1976):100-10.

Mechanic, D. "Sources of Power of Lower Participants in Complex Organizations." *Administrative Science Quarterly*, 7(1962):349-364.

Merton, R.K., and Kitt, A.S. "Contributions to the Theory of Reference Group Behavior." In *The American Soldier*, edited by R.K. Merton and P.R. Lazarfeld. Glencoe: Free Press. 1950.

Milgram, S. "Some Conditions of Obedience and Disobedience to Authority." *Human Relations*, 18(1965):57-76.

Miller, R.I. *An Assessment of College Performance*. San Francisco: Jossey-Bass, 1979.

Mills, T. M. "Power Relations in Three-Person Groups." *American Sociological Review*, 18(1953):351-57.

Morrison, A., and Von Glinow, M. "Women and Minorities in Management." *American Psychologist*, 45(1990):200-08.

Mortimer, K.P., and McConnell, T.R. *Sharing Authority Effectively*. San Francisco: Jossey-Bass, 1978.

Mott, P.E. "Power, Authority and Influence." In *The Structure of Community Power*, edited by M. Aiken and P.E. Mott. New York: Random House, 1970.

Moyer, K.E. "The Physiology of Aggression and the Implications for Aggression Control." In *The Control of Aggression and Violence*, edited by J.L. Singer. New York: Academic Press, 1971.

Murdoch, P. "Development of Contractual Norms in a Dyad." *Journal of Personality and Social Psychology*, 6(1967):206-11.

Nanus, Burt. *Visionary Leadership*. San Francisco: Jossey-Bass, 1992.

Nason, John W. *Presidential Assessment*. Washington, DC: Association of Governing Boards, 1984.

National Commission on Strengthening Presidential Leadership, Clark Kerr, Director. *Presidents Make a Difference: Strengthening Leadership in Colleges and Universities.* Washington, DC: Association of Governing Boards of Universities and Colleges, 1984.

Neustadt, R.E. *Presidential Power.* New York: John Wiley and Sons, 1960.

Newcomer, M. *The Big Business Executive: The Factors That Made Him, 1900-1950.* New York: Columbia University Press, 1955.

Nicklin, Julie L. "The Hum of Corporate Buzzwords." *The Chronicle of Higher Education,* 41 (January 27, 1995): A33-34.

Nisbet, R.A. *The Social Bond.* New York: Alfred A. Knopf, 1970.

Noble, K. "The Dilemma of the Gifted Woman." *Psychology of Women Quarterly,* 11 (1987):367-78.

Offerman, L., and Beil, C. "Achievement Styles of Women Leaders and Their Peers." *Psychology of Women Quarterly,* 16 (1992):37-56.

Onnen, M.K. *The Relationship of Clergy Leadership Characteristics to Growing or Declining Churches.* Doctoral Dissertation, University of Louisville, 1987.

Parks, D.J. "Create a Vision, Build a Consensus, Be an Effective Leader." *The Clearing House,* 60 (1986):88-90.

Patchen, M. "The Locus and Basis of Influence on Organizational Decision." *Organizational Behavior and Human Performance,* 11 (1974): 195-221.

Payton, Robert L. *Philanthropy.* New York: American Council on Education, 1988.

Peay, M. "The Effects of Social Power and Pre-Existing Attitudes on Public and Private Responses to an Induced Attitude." *Human Relations,* 29 (1976):1115-29.

Peddiwell, J.A. *The Sabertooth Curriculum.* New York: McGraw-Hill, 1959.

Pelz, D.C. "Leadership within a Hierarchical Organization." *Journal of Social Issues,* 7 (1951):49-55.

Pepitone, A. "Attributions of Causality, Social Attitudes, and Cognitive Matching Processes." In *Person Perception and Interpersonal Behavior,* edited by R. Tagiuri and L. Petrullo. Stanford, CA: Stanford University Press, 1958.

Peters, T.J. "Symbols, Patterns, and Settings: An Optimistic Case for Getting Things Done." *Organizational Dynamics,* 7 (1978):3-23.

Peters, Thomas J., and Austin, Nancy. *A Passion for Excellence: The Leadership Difference.* New York: Warner Books, 1985.

Peters, Thomas J., and Waterman, Robert H., Jr. *In Search of Excellence.* New York: Warner Books, 1982.

Pettigrew, A.M. "Information Control as a Power Resource." *Sociology*, 6(1972):187-204.

Pfeffer, J. *Power in Organizations*. Marshfield: Pittman Publishing, Inc., 1981.

Posner, B., and Kouzes, J. "Psychometric Properties of the Leadership Practices Inventory—Updated." *Educational and Psychological Measurement*, 53(1993):191-99.

Poundstone, William. *Prisoner's Dilemma: John Von Neumann, Game Theory, and the Puzzle of the Bomb*. New York: Doubleday, 1992.

Powell, R.M. *Race, Religion, and the Promotion of the American Executive*. Columbus: Ohio State University, College of Administrative Science, 1969.

Pray, F.C. "The President as 'Reasonable Adventurer.'" *AGB Reports*, (May/June 1979):45-48.

———. *Handbook on Educational Fund Raising*. San Francisco: Jossey-Bass, 1981.

Pruitt, G.A. *A Blueprint for Leadership: The American College Presidency*. Doctoral dissertation, Union Graduate School, 1974.

Raven, B.H. "The Comparative Analysis of Power and Influence." In *Perspectives on Social Power*, edited by J.T. Tedeschi. Chicago: Aldine, 1974.

Raven, B.H., and French, J.R.P. "An Experimental Investigation of Legitimate and Coercive Power." *American Psychologist*, 12(1957):393.

Raven, B.H., and Kruglanski, A.W. "Conflict and Power." In *The Structure of Conflict*, edited by P. Swingle. New York: Academic Press, 1970.

Richman, B.M., and Farmer, R.N. *Leadership, Goals, and Power in Higher Education: A Contingency and Open-System Approach to Effective Management*. San Francisco: Jossey-Bass, 1974.

Riesman, D. "Beyond the '60s." *Wilson Quarterly*, 2(1978):59-71.

Riesman, D., and McLaughlin, J. "A Primer on the Use of Consultants in Presidential Recruitment." *Change*, 16(6) 1984: 12–23.

———. Personal conversation, 1980.

Rosenzweig, Robert. Personal conversation, 1992.

Rosovky, H. *The University: An Owner's Manual*. New York: W.W. Norton, 1990.

Rowland, Wesley. *Handbook of Institutional Advancement*. San Francisco: Jossey-Bass, 1986.

Rubin, I.M., and Goldman, M. "An Open System Model of Leadership Performance." *Organizational Behavior and Human Performance*, 3(1968):143-56.

Russell, B. *Power*. London: Allen and Unwin, 1938.

Schell, D.W. "Effect of Machiavellian Orientation and Intraorganization Power on Resource Allocation in Reorganization Coalitions: An Experimental Approach." Doctoral dissertation, Indiana University Graduate School of Business, 1970.

Schlesinger, Arthur M., Jr. *The Age of Roosevelt, Vol 2: The Coming of the New Deal.* Boston: Houghton Mifflin, 1959.

Schroder, H.M.; Streuferet, S.; and Welden, D.C. *The Effect of Structural Abstractness in Interpersonal Stimuli on the Leadership Role* (Technical Paper No. 3). Princeton, NJ: Office of Naval Research, Princeton University, 1964.

Scientific American. "The Big Business Executive: 1964." 1965.

Scott, E.L. *Leadership and Perceptions of Organization.* Columbus: Ohio State University Bureau of Business Research, 1956.

Scott, P. "Some Thoughts on Black Women's Leadership Training." Working Paper for the Women's Educational Equity Act Program, Washington, DC, 1982. ERIC Document 254 597.

Seeman, M. *Social Status and Leadership—The Case of the School Executive.* Columbus: Ohio State University, Educational Research Monograph No. 35, 1960.

Seltzer, J., and Bass, B.M. "Leadership Is More Than Initiation and Consideration." Paper presented at the American Psychological Association Conference, New York, 1987.

Shaw, E.P. "The Social Distance Factor and Management." *Personnel Administration,* 28(1965):29-31.

Shepherd, C., and Weschler, I.R. "The Relationship between Three Interpersonal Variables and Communication Effectiveness: A Pilot Study." *Sociometry,* 18(1955):103-10.

Sherif, M., and Sherif, C.W. *Groups in Harmony and Tension.* New York: Harper, 1953.

Sherif, M.; White, B.J.; and Harvey, O.J. "Status in Experimentally Produced Groups." *American Journal of Sociology,* 60(1955):370-79.

Shirley, Robert C. "Strategic Planning: An Overview." In *Successful Strategic Planning Case Studies.* New Directions for Higher Education Series, Number 64, edited by Douglas Steeples. San Francisco: Jossey-Bass, 1988.

Shriver, B. "The Behavioral Effects of Changes in Ascribed Leadership Status in Small Groups." Doctoral dissertation, University of Rochester, 1952.

Simic, Curtis R. "The Role of the Board, the President, and the Chief Development Officer," Paper presented at the Association of Governing Boards Conference, San Francisco, CA, 1984.

Siu, R.G.H. *The Craft of Power.* New York: John Wiley and Sons, 1979.

Slusher, E.A.; Rose, G.L.; and Roering, K.J. "Commitment of Future Interaction and Relative Power under Conditions of Interdependence." *Journal of Conflict Resolution*, 22(1978):282-98.

Smith, Adam. *An Inquiry Into the Nature and Causes of the Wealth of Nations*, edited by E. Cannan. London: Everyman's Library, [1776] 1917.

Smith, B.J. *An Initial Test of a Theory of Charismatic Leadership Based on the Responses of Subordinates*. Doctoral dissertation, University of Toronto, 1982.

Smith, Lee. "The New Wave of Illegitimacy." *Fortune*, 129 (April 18, 1994):81-82, ff.

Smith, Page. *Killing the Spirit: Higher Education in America*. New York: Viking Press, 1990.

Smith, P.B. *Groups within Organizations*. New York: Harper and Row, 1973.

Standard and Poors. *Register of Corporations, Directors, and Executives*. New York: Standard and Poors, 1967.

Statham, A. "The Gender Model Revisited: Differences in the Management Styles of Men and Women." *Sex Roles*, 16(1987):409-29.

Steers, R.M. *Introduction to Organizational Behavior*. Santa Monica, CA: Goodyear, 1981.

Stogdill, R.M. "Personal Factors Associated with Leadership: A Survey of the Literature." *Journal of Psychology*, 25(1948):35-71.

————. *Handbook of Leadership*. New York: Macmillan, 1974.

Stoke, H.W. *The American College President*. New York: Harper and Brothers, 1959.

Stotland, E. "Peer Groups and Reaction to Power Figures." In *Studies in Social Power*, edited by D. Cartwright. Ann Arbor: University of Michigan, Institute for Social Research, 1959.

Student, K.R. "Supervisory Influence and Work-Group Performance." *Journal of Applied Psychology*, 52(1968):188-94.

Swingle, P. "Exploitative Behavior in Non-Zero-Sum Games." *Journal of Personality and Social Psychology*, 16(1970a):121-32.

————. ed. *The Structure of Conflict*. New York: Academic Press, 1970b.

Sykes, Charles J. *Prof Scam: Professors and the Demise of Higher Education*. Washington: Regnery Gateway, 1988.

Tead, O. *The Art of Leadership*. New York: McGraw-Hill, 1935.

Tedeschi, J.T.; Lindskold, S.; Horai, J.; and Gahagan, J.P. "Social Power and the Credibility of Promises." *Journal of Personality and Social Psychology*, 13(1969):253-61.

Tedeschi, J.T.; Schlenker, B.R.; and Bonoma, T.B. "Cognitive Disonance: Private Ratiocination or Private Spectacle." *American Psychologist*, 26(1972):685-95.

————. *Conflict, Power and Games*. Chicago: Aldine, 1973.

Thiagarajan, K.M., and Deep, S.D. "A Study of Supervisor-Subordinate Influence and Satisfaction in Four Cultures." *Journal of Social Psychology*, 82(1970):173-80.

Thibaut, J.W., and Gruder, C.L. "Formation of Contractual Agreements between Parties of Unequal Power." *Journal of Personality and Social Psychology*, 11(1969):59-65.

Thurow, Lester. *Head to Head: The Coming Economic Battle among Japan, Europe, and America*. New York: Warner Books, 1993.

Thwing, Charles F. *The College President*. New York: Macmillan, 1926.

Torrance, E.P. *Some Consequences of Power Differences on Decisions in B-26 Crews*. San Antonio: USAF Personnel and Training Research Center, Research Bulletin 54-128, 1954.

————. "Some Consequences of Power Differences in Permanent and Temporary Three-Man Groups." In *Small Groups*, edited by P. Hane, E.F. Borgatta, and R.F. Baers. New York: Knopf, 1955.

————. "The Influence of Experienced Members of Small Groups on the Behavior of the Inexperienced." *Journal of Social Psychology*, 49(1959):249-57.

————. "A Theory of Leadership and Interpersonal Behavior." In *Leadership and Interpersonal Behavior*, edited by L. Petrullo and B. Bass. New York: Holt, Rinehart and Winston, 1961.

Torrance, E.P., and Aliotti, N.C. "Accuracy, Task Effectiveness, and Emergence of a Social-Emotional Resolver as a Function of One- and Two-Expert Groups." *Journal of Psychology*, 61(1965):161-70.

Torrance, E.P., and Mason, R. "The Indigenous Leader in Changing Attitudes and Behavior." *International Journal of Sociometry*, 1(1956):23-28.

Townsend, R. "Townsend's Third Degree in Leadership." *Across the Board*, 22(1985):48-52.

Tuchman, Barbara. *Stilwell and the American Experience in China, 1911-1945*. New York: Macmillan, 1971.

Uhlir, A. "Leadership and Gender." *Academe*, 75(1989):28-32.

U.S. Department of Education. *Mini-Digest of Education Statistics 1994*. Washington, DC: U.S. Department of Education, 1994.

Vaughn, G.B. *Leadership in Transition: The Community College Presidency*. New York: American Council on Education/Macmillan, 1989.

Veysey, L.R. *The Emergence of the American University*. Chicago: University of Chicago Press, 1965.

Waldman, D.A.; Bass, B.M.; and Einstein, W.O. "Effort, Performance and Transformational Leadership in Industrial and Military Settings." Working Paper 84-78. Binghamton: School of Management, State University of New York, 1986.

Walker, D.E. *The Effective Administrator*. San Francisco: Jossey-Bass, 1979.

Waters, H., Jr. "Minority Leadership Problems." *Journal of Education for Business*, 68(1992):15-20.

Weber, M. *The Theory of Social and Economic Organization*. Translated by M. Henderson and T. Parsons. New York: Oxford University Press, 1947.

Wells, Herman. *Being Lucky: Reminiscences and Reflections*. Bloomington, IN: Indiana University Press, 1980.

Wenrich, J.W. "Can the President Be All Things to All People?" *Community and Junior College Journal*, 51(1985):36-40.

Whetton, D.A. "Effective Administrators: Good Management on the College Campus." *Change*, 16(1984):38-43.

Whetton, D.A., and Cameron, K.S. "Administrative Effectiveness in Higher Education." *Review of Higher Education*, 9(1985):35-49.

Worth, M.J. *Educational Fund Raising: Principles and Practice*. Phoenix: American Council on Education/Oryx Press, 1993.

Yokichi, N. *Leadership Styles of Japanese Business Executives and Managers: Transformational and Transactional*. Doctoral dissertation, United States International University, San Diego, CA, 1989.

Zander, A. "The Effects of Prestige on the Behavior of Group Members: An Audience Demonstration." *American Management Association, Personnel Service*, No. 155, 1953.

Zander, A., and Cohen, A.R. "Attributed Social Power and Group Acceptance: A Classroom Experimental Demonstration." *Journal of Abnormal Social Psychology*, 51(1955):490-92.

Zander, A., and Curtis, T. "Effects of Social Power on Aspiration Setting and Striving." *Journal of Abnormal Social Psychology*, 64(1962):63-74.

INDEX

• • • • • • • •

by Linda Webster

Page numbers followed by "n" refer to footnotes.